A TREATISE ON MIND

VOLUME 2

Considerations of Mind

a Buddhist Enquiry

Other Titles in the Series

The I Concept

Volume 1: The 'Self' or 'Non-self' in Buddhism

Volume 3: The Buddha-Womb and the Way to Liberation

Cellular Consciousness

Volume 4: Maṇḍalas - Their Nature and Development

Volume 5: An Esoteric Exposition of the Bardo Thödol (Part A)

Volume 5: An Esoteric Exposition of the Bardo Thödol (Part B)

The Way to Shambhala

Volume 6: Meditation and the Initiation Process

Volume 7: The Constitution of Shambhala

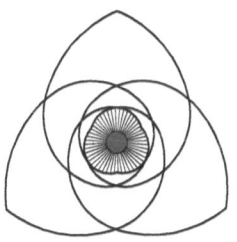

VOLUME TWO

Considerations of Mind

a Buddhist Enquiry

BODO BALSYS

UNIVERSAL DHARMA
PUBLICATIONS
SYDNEY, AUSTRALIA

ISBN 978-0-9923568-1-1

Revised Edition 2025

Āḥ!

Homage to the Lord of Shambhala.
Inconceivable, inconceivable, beyond thought
Is the bejewelled crown of this most excelled Jina.
He whose Eye has taught many Buddhas.
And who will anoint the myriad,
that in the future lives will come.
As I bow to His Feet my Heart's afire.
Oh, this bliss, this love for my Lord
can barely be borne on my part.
It takes flight as the might of the Dove.
The flight of serene *nirvāṇic* embrace.
The flight of Light so bright.
The flight of Love so active tonight.
The flight of enlightenment for all to come to
their mind's Heart's attire.

Obeisance to the Gurus!
To the Buddhas of the three times.
To the Council of Bodhisattvas, *mahāsattvas*.
To them I pledge allegiance.

Oṁ Hūṁ! Hūṁ! Hūṁ!

Dedication

Thanks to my students, past, present and future, and in particular to those that have helped in the production of this Treatise.

Oṁ

Acknowledgments

Special thanks to Angie O'Sullivan, Kylie Smith,
and Ruth Fitzpatrick
for their efforts in making this
series possible.

Oṁ

Contents

Preface ... xi
1. An Enquiry into the Nature of the Self ... 1
   The analysis of mind ... 1
   The veils to comprehension ... 7
   The seven Ray aspects of mind ... 11
   The seven aspects of the emotional-mind ... 27
   Meditation and the emotions ... 35
   An example of the Rays in a Buddhist text ... 37
   The symbolism of the eye ... 40
2. The Soul Concept and the Tathāgatagarbha Doctrine ... 46
   The *tathāgatagarbha* doctrine ... 46
   The unchangeability of *tathatā* ... 52
   Samalā and *nirmalā tathatā* ... 55
   The three bodies of a Buddha ... 60
3. Negating the Self ... 70
   The process of negating ... 70
   Skilful means ... 74
4. The Vijñānavādins on the Existence of 'self' ... 77
   The nature of *bījas* ... 77
   Śūnyatā, the *ālayavijñāna* and the 'self' concept ... 80
   Santāna and *gati* ... 83
   Bījas and the *maṇipūra chakra* ... 90
   The pentads of the Solar Plexus centre ... 100
   The petals of the Solar Plexus centre detailed ... 101
   The minor *siddhis* ... 115
   The *bījas* and the Sacral centre ... 120
   The Sambhoghakāya Flower and the Solar Plexus centre ... 126
   The Sambhoghakāya Flower and the Sacral centre ... 132
   The identity of dependent systems ... 134
   Ātman and *non-ātman* ... 143
5. The Vijñanavādins on the Evolution of Consciousness ... 151
   The two types of karma ... 151
   The factor of sentience ... 156
   The evolution of the *ālayavijñāna* ... 159
   Dependent Origination, madness, and the self of things ... 161
   Consciousness and the *chakras* ... 164
   The *māyā* of things ... 167

6. The River Simile 175
What defines a river? 175
Lines of separation as *nāḍīs* 180
Nāḍīs and the *chakras* 181
The *chakras* as containers of awareness-states 183
7. On the Evolution of Consciousness 191
The way of consciousness 191
The question of time 193
Does a God exist? 195
Further considerations of consciousness 203
Ramifications of Dependent Origination 207
Originating causes 211
The action of *karma* 212
Evolutionary law 220
8. Signposts of consciousness 225
From a driver's perspective 225
Signs according to literature 229
The role of the Sambhogakāya Flower 233
Signs of progressive awakening 235
Faith, devotion, and aspiration 237
9. The Nature of Light 242
The intensity of light 242
Light, Love and *citta* 245
Degrees of darkness 252
The relativity of *māyā* 256
The perception of *nirvāṇa* 258
Further considerations of darkness verses light 261
Considerations of time and mendacity 265
From an amoeba to the universe of time 269
10. Commentary on Ālayavijñāna as Seed 277
Some key terms 277
The *ālayavijñāna* and *kliṣṭamanas* 279
The five qualities needed for perfuming 289
The five omnipresent mental factors 296
Further aspects concerning the *ālayavijñāna* 301
The *ālayavijñāna* and the formless realms 310
11. The Examination of Time in the *Mūlamadhyamakakārikā* of Nāgārjuna 319
The exposition of the verses 319
The seven Ray qualities 329

12. Śūnyatā, Consciousness, and Parinirvāṇa 339
The driving force underlying consciousness 339
Consciousness, relativity, and the *catuṣkoṭikā* 345
The separations between things 354
13. Voidness and Abundance 357
Hearing 'face to face' 357
The nine main verses of the *sūtra* examined 360
Voidness and abundance 374
Bibliography 376
Index 379

Figures

Figure 1. The abstract Mind ... 6
Figure 2. The *bījas* and the Solar Plexus centre ... 102
Figure 3. The Solar Plexus centre and the *siddhis* ... 116
Figure 4. The *bījas* and the Sacral centre ... 121
Figure 5. The Moving Screen of the Past ... 330
Figure 6. The Event Horizon ... 331

Tables

Table 1. The seven Ray aspects of mind ... 15
Table 2. The basic emotions of mind ... 29
Table 3. Dhyāni Buddhas and the five *prāṇas* ... 183

Preface

This treatise investigates Buddhist ideas concerning what mind is and how it relates to a concept of a 'self'. It is principally a study of the complex interrelationship between mind and phenomena, from the gross to the subtle—the physical, psychic, supersensory and supernal. This entails an explanation of how mind incorporates all phenomena in its *modus operandi,* and how eventually that mind is liberated from it, thereby becoming awakened. Thus the treatise explores the manner in which the corporeally orientated, concretised, intellectual mind eventually becomes transformed into the Clear Light of the abstracted Mind; a super-mind, a Buddha-Mind.

A Treatise on Mind is arranged in seven volumes, divided into three subsections. These are as follows:

The I Concept
Volume 1. *The 'Self' or 'Non-self' in Buddhism.*
Volume 2. *Considerations of Mind—A Buddhist Enquiry.*
Volume 3. *The Buddha-Womb and the Way to Liberation.*

Cellular Consciousness
Volume 4. *Maṇḍalas - Their Nature and Development.*
Volume 5. *An Esoteric Exposition of the Bardo Thödol.*
(This volume is published in two parts)

The Way to Shambhala
Volume 6. *Meditation and the Initiation Process.*
Volume 7. *The Constitution of Shambhala.*

The I Concept represents a necessary extensive revision[1] of a large work formerly published in one volume. Together the three volumes investigate the question of what a 'self' is and is not. This involves an analysis of the nature of consciousness, and the consciousness-stream of a human unit developing as a continuum through time. It will illustrate exactly what directs such a stream and how its *karma* is arranged so that enlightenment is the eventual outcome.

The first volume analyses Prāsaṅgika lines of reasoning, such as the 'Refutation of Partless Particles', and 'The Sevenfold Reasoning' in order to derive a clear deduction as to whether a 'self' exists, and if so what its limitations are, and if not, then what the alternative may be. The analysis resolves the historically vexing question of how—if there is no 'self'—can there be a continuity of mind that is coherently connected in an evolutionary manner through multiple rebirths.[2] In order to arrive at this explanation, many of the basic assumptions of Mahāyāna Buddhism, such as Dependent Origination and the Two Truths, are critically analysed.

The second volume provides an in-depth analysis of what mind is, how it relates to the concept of the Void *(śūnyatā),* and the evolution of consciousness. The analysis utilises Yogācāra-Vijñānavādin philosophy in order to comprehend the major attributes of mind, the *saṃskāras* that condition it, and the laws by means of which it operates.

The enquiry into the nature of what an 'I' is requires comprehension of the properties of the dual nature of mind, which consists of an empirical and abstract, enlightened part. As a means of doing this, the *ālayavijñāna* (the store of consciousness-attributes) is explored, alongside the entire philosophy of the 'eight consciousnesses' of this School.

Volume three focuses on the I-Consciousness and the subtle body, by first utilising a minor Tantra, *The Great Gates of Diamond Liberation,* to investigate the nature of the Heart centre and its functions, then the

---

1 The book was inadequately edited hence contains many errors and grammatical mistakes that have been corrected in this treatise.

2 My earlier work *Karma and the Rebirth of Consciousness* (Munshiram Manoharlal, Delhi, 2006) lays the background for this basic question.

chakras below the diaphragm. This is necessary to lay the foundation for the topics that will be the subject of the later volumes of this treatise concerning the nature of meditation, the construction of *maṇḍalas,* and the yoga of the *Bardo Thödol.*

The focus then shifts to investigate where the idea of a self-sustaining I-concept or 'Soul-form' may be found in Buddhist philosophy, given the denial of substantial self-existence prioritised in the philosophy of Emptiness. Following this, the pertinent chapters of the *Ratnagotravibhāga Śastra* are examined in detail so that a proper conclusion to the investigation can be obtained via the *buddhadharma.* This concerns an analysis of how the *ālayavijñāna* is organised, such that the rebirth process is possible for each human consciousness-stream, taking into account the *karma* that will eventually make each human unit a Buddha. In relation to this the ontological nature of the *tathāgatagarbha* (the Buddha-Womb) must be carefully analysed, as well as the organising principle of consciousness represented by the *chakras.* I thus establish that there is a form that appears upon the domain of the abstract Mind. I call this the Sambhogakāya Flower. The final two chapters of this Volume principally define its characteristics.

The second subsection, *Cellular Consciousness,* is divided into two parts. Volume four deals with the question of what exactly constitutes a 'cell', metaphysically. The cell is viewed as a unit of consciousness that interrelates with other cells to form *maṇḍalas* of expression. Each such cell can be considered a form of 'self' that has a limited, though valid, body of expression. It is born, sustains a form of activity, and consequently dies when it outlives its usefulness. This mode of analysis is extended to include the myriad forms manifest in the world of phenomena known as *saṃsāra,* including the existence and functioning of *chakras.*

Volume five deals with the formative forces and evolutionary processes governing the prime cells (that is, *maṇḍalas* of expression), and the phenomenon that governs an entire world-sphere of evolutionary attainment. This is explored via an in-depth exposition of the *Bardo Thödol* and its 42 Peaceful and 58 Wrathful Deities. The text also incorporates a detailed exposition concerning the transformation of *saṃskāras* (consciousness-attributes developed through all past forms of activity) into enlightenment. The entire path of liberation enacted by a *yogin* via the principles of meditation, forms of concentration, and related techniques *(tapas, dhāraṇīs)* is explained. In doing so, the soteriological purpose of the various wrathful and theriomorphic deities is revealed. This Volume is published in two parts. Part A explores chapter 5 of the *Bardo Thödol* concerning the transformation of *saṃskāras* via meditating upon the Peaceful and Wrathful Deities. This necessitates sound knowledge of the force centres (*chakras*) and the way their powers (*siddhis*) awaken. Part B deals with the gain of such transformations and the consequence of conversion of the attributes of the empirical mind into the liberated abstract Mind.

The third subsection, *The Way to Shambhala*, is also in two parts. They present an eclectic revelation of esoteric information integrating the main Eastern and Western religions. Volume six is a treatise on meditation and the Initiation process.[3] The meditation practice is directed towards the needs of individuals living within the context of our modern societies.

Volume six also includes a discussion of the path of Initiation as the means of gaining liberation from *saṃsāra*. The teaching in Volume five concerning the conversion of *saṃskāras* is supplementary to this path. The path of Initiation *is* the way to Shambhala. As many will choose to consciously undergo the precepts needed to undertake Initiation in the future, this invokes the necessity of providing much more revelatory information concerning this kingdom than has been provided hitherto.

How Shambhala is organised is the subject of Volume seven, which details the constitution of the Hierarchy of enlightened being[4] (the Council of Bodhisattvas). It illustrates how the presiding Lords who govern planetary evolution manifest. This detailed philosophy rests on the foundation of the information provided in all of the previous volumes, and necessitates a proper comprehension of the nature of the five Dhyāni Buddhas. To do so the awakening of the meditation-Mind, which is the objective of *A Treatise on Mind*, is essential.

---

3 The word Initiation is capitalised throughout the series of books to add emphasis to the fact that it is the process that makes one divine, liberated. It is the expression of divinity manifesting upon the planetary and cosmic landscape.

4 The word 'being' here is not pluralised because though this Hierarchy is constituted of a multiplicity of beings, together they represent one 'Being', one integral awakened Entity.

How to engage with this text

In this investigation many new ways of viewing conventional Buddhist arguments and rhetoric shall be pursued to develop the pure logic of the reader's mind, and to awaken revelations from their abstract Mind. New insights into the far-reaching light of the *dharma* will be revealed, which will form a basis for the illustration of an esoteric view that supersedes the bounds of conventionally accepted views. Readers should therefore analyse all arguments for themselves to discern the validity of what is presented. Such enquiry allows one to ascertain for oneself, what is logical and truthful, thus overcoming the blind acceptance of a certain dogma or line of reasoning that is otherwise universally accepted as correct. Only that which is discovered within each inquiring mind should be accepted. The remainder should however not be automatically discarded, but rather kept aside for later analysis when more data is available—unless the logic is obviously flawed, in which case it should be abandoned. There is no claim to infallibility in the information and arguments presented in this treatise, however, they are designed to offer scope for further meditation and enquiry by the earnest reader. If errors are found through impeccable logic, then the dialectical process may proceed. We can then accept or reject the new thesis and move forward, such that the evolution of human thought progresses, until we all stand enlightened.

This treatise hopes to assist that dialectical evolution by analysing major aspects of the *buddhadharma* as it exists and is taught today, to try to examine where errors may lie, or where the present modes of interpretation fall short of the true intended meaning. The aim is also to elaborate aspects of the *dharma* that could only be hinted at or cursorily explained by the wise ones of the past, because the basis for proper elaboration had not then been established. This analysis of *buddhadharma* will try to rectify some of the past inadequacies in order to explore and extend the *dharma* into arenas rarely investigated.

There will always be obstinate and dogmatic ones that staunchly cling to established views. This produces a reactive malaise in current Buddhist ontological and metaphysical thought. However, amongst the many practitioners of the *dharma* there are also those who have clarified their minds sufficiently to verify truth in whatever form it is presented, and will follow it at all costs to enlightenment. The Council of Bodhisattvas heartily seek such worthy ones. The signposts or guides upon the way to enlightenment have changed through the centuries, and contemporary practitioners of the *dharma* have yet to learn to clearly interpret the new directions. The guide books are now being written and many must come forth to understand and practice correctly.

If full comprehension of such guide books is achieved those *dharma* practitioners yearning to become Bodhisattvas would rapidly become spiritually enlightened. Here is a rhyme and reason *for* Buddhism. The actual present dearth of enlightened beings informs us that little that is read is properly understood. The esoteric view presented in this treatise hopes to rectify this problem, so as to create better thinkers along the Bodhisattva way.

The numbers of Buddhists are growing in the world, thus Buddhism needs a true restorative flowering to rival that of the renaissance of debate and innovative thinkers of the early post-Nāgārjunian era. In order to achieve this it must synthesise the present wealth of scientific knowledge, alongside the best of the Western world's philosophical output.

Currently the *buddhadharma* is presented as an external body of knowledge held by the Buddha, Rinpoches, monks and lay teachers. This encourages practitioners to hero worship these figures and to heed many unenlightened utterances from such teachers, based on a belief system that encourages people to *uncritically* listen to them and adopt their views. When enlightened teachers *do appear* and find consolidated reasons for firing spiritual bullets for the cause of the enlightenment of humanity, then all truth can and will be known. The present lack of inwardly perceived knowledge from the fount of the *dharmakāya* on the part of many teachers blocks the production of an arsenal of weapons for solving the problems of suffering in the world. Few see little beyond the scope of vision in what they have been indoctrinated to believe, allowing for only rudimentary truths to be understood. While for the great majority this suffices, it is woefully inadequate for those genuinely seeking Bodhisattvahood and enlightenment. The cost to humanity in not being given an enlightened answer as to the nature of awakening, is profound.

We must go to the awakening of the Head lotus to find the most established reasoning powers. Without the 1,000 petals of the *sahasrāra padma* ablaze then there is little substance for proper understanding, little ability to hold the mind steady in the dynamic field of revelation that the *dharmakāya* represents. How can the unenlightened properly understand Buddhist scriptures, when there is little (revelation) coming from the Head centres of such beings? Much still needs to be taught concerning the way of awakening this lotus, and to help fill the lack is a major purpose of *A Treatise on Mind*.

Those who intend to reach enlightenment must go beyond the narrow sectarian allegiances promoted by many strands of contemporary Buddhism. Buddhism itself unfolded in a dialectical context with other heterodox Indian (and Chinese, etc.) traditions, and prospered on account of those engagements. When one sees the unfolding of enlightened wisdom in such a fashion, the particular information from specific schools of thought may be synthesised into a greater whole. Each school has various qualities and types of argument to resolve weaknesses in the opposing stream of thought. This highlights that there are particular aspects in each that may be right or wrong, or neither wholly right or wrong. Through this process we can find better answers, or if need be, create a new lineage or religion which is expressive of a synthesis of the various schools of thought.

The Buddha did not categorically reject the orthodox Indian religio-philosophical ideas of his time, nor did he simply accept them—he reformed them. He preserved the elements that he found to be true, and rejected those 'wrong views' which lead to moral and spiritual impairment. If the existing system needs reformation it becomes part of a Bodhisattva's meditation. The way a reforming Buddha incarnates is dependent on how he must fit into such a system. Thus he is essentially an outsider incarnating into it to demonstrate the new type of ideas he chooses to elaborate. If there is a lot of dogmatic resistance to the presented doctrine of truth, then a new religion is founded. If there is some acceptance then we see reformation. There is always room for improvement, to march forward closer to enlightenment's goal, be it for an individual or for a wisdom-religion as a whole. There is a need for reform throughout the religious world today.

By way of a hermeneutical strategy fit for this task, we ought look no further than the Buddha himself. The Buddha proposed that all students of the *dharma* should make their investigations through the *Four Points of Refuge*. These are:

1. The doctrine is one's point of refuge, not a person.
2. The meaning is one's point of refuge, not the letter.
3. The sacred texts whose meaning is defined are one's point of refuge, to those whose meaning needs definition.
4. Direct awareness is one's point of refuge, not discursive awareness.[5]

These four points can be summarised or rephrased as: the doctrine (*dharma*), true or esoteric meaning, right definition, and direct awareness are one's point of refuge, not adherence to sectarian bias, semantics, the dialectics of non-fully enlightened commentaries, or to illogical assertions. What may be long held to be truthful, but is not, upon proper analytical dissection, needs rectifying. Also, in other cases, a doctrine or teaching may indeed be correct, but the current interpretation leaves much to be desired, and hence should be reinterpreted from the position of a more embracive or esoteric view.

Hopefully this presentation finds welcoming minds that will carefully analyse it in line with their own understandings of the issues, and as a consequence build up a better understanding of the nature of what constitutes the path to enlightenment. Their way of walking as Bodhisattvas should be enriched as a consequence.

For a guide to understanding the pronunciation of Sanskrit words, please visit our website.
http://universaldharma.com/resources/pronounce-sanskrit/

Our online esoteric glossary also provides definitions for most of the terms used in this treatise.
http://universaldharma.com/resources/esoteric-glossary/

---

5 Griffith, P.J., *On Being Buddha, The Classical Doctrine of Buddhahood*, (Sri Satguru Publications, New Delhi, 1995), 52.

My eyes do weep as I stare into this troubled world,
For I dare not place my Heart in my brother's keep.
He would grapple that Heart with hands so rough
So as to destroy the fabric of its delicate stuff.
Oh to give, to give, my Heart does yearn,
But humanity must its embracive,
Humbling, pervasive scene yet to learn.
To destroy and tear with avarice they know,
But little care to sensitive rapture they show.
How to give its blood is my constant fare,
For that Love to bestow upon their Hearts I bemoan.
But they hide their Hearts behind mental-emotional walls.
No matter how one prods these walls won't fall,
So much belittling emotional self-concern prop their bastions.
Oh, how my eyes do weep as I stare.
I stare at their fearsome malls and halls.
That lock Love out from all their abodes
And do keep them trapped in realms of woe.

Oṁ Maṇi Padme Hūṁ

1

An Enquiry into the Nature of the Self

The analysis of mind

The start of one's search for truth should begin by an endeavour to understand exactly what the mind is. Buddhist philosophers have been doing this for millennia and the best results of their efforts is seen in the Yogācāra-Vijñānavādin philosophy, supplemented by the Mādhyamika revelations. In further elucidating this subject, the material in this Volume will not simply paraphrase what has been said by such astute philosophers as Asaṅga and Vasubandhu, the founders of the Yogācāra school, but shall also look at the subject from a new perspective. The basic eclectic framework that can be used for this understanding is accomplished by utilising the mind freed from emotions, gross and subtle.

First the nature of the personality vehicle must be analysed. It is the mechanism of response to external stimuli, through which all humans function and gauge their place in the physical and subjective universes. It is a composite of:[1]

1. *The dense physical body,* which most people intensely identify with, and take to be 'the real', thus it is the focus of their personality lives and desires. This is because it is objectivised by means of their senses, and is part of the fleeting phenomenal world all around us, which those senses contact and which are registered as impressions

---

1 We can also look at this composite in terms of the five *kośas* (sheaths of human consciousness), which will be explained later.

by the concrete mind. The mind then collates these impressions, registering them to be things. The world is thus the realm of the sense-perceptions with which people assert their identities. Around this world their entire thought life revolves. The scientific community has investigated the dense physical body and associated universe in depth. Modern Physicists have begun to understand the true nature of its ephemera, when seen in terms of energy and energy fields, rather than of the things that we perceive by means of the senses.

2. *The etheric, the body of energy,* containing the vitality *(prāṇa)* that the physical body receives from its environment, the air one breathes and from the food one eats. It allows the exchange of energies between the human unit and all other entities in our biosphere. *Prāṇa* is conveyed in many fine subjective channels in the body called *nāḍīs*. They roughly underlie our nerves and blood vessels. The etheric body is the reason why acupuncture works as a healing technique, especially in relation to anaesthetic effects, as the needles either block or reroute the subjective energies to specified targets, producing the results experienced by the patients. The meridians of acupuncture therapy are minor *nāḍīs* near the surface of the body.[2] All *siddhis* (psychic powers) are expressions of the *chakras*, which are flowers or wheels of energies, constituted as a result of the intersections of various *nāḍīs*. There are seven major *chakras* to the body, and the evocation of one or other of their inherent energies is an objective of yoga, and the higher Tantras.

3. *The emotional body.* This incorporates all of our desires and emotions, fears and phobias, our incessant moods and feelings, as well as the sum of our imaginative lives. It manifests as an *aura,* which depicts the colourations of our feeling-perceptions and mental-emotions that immediately cloud or colour our thoughts, often tinged with subtle and not so subtle desires, or by fears and anxieties. The emotions produce sensations of exhilaration, peace or happiness. They are problematic because they generally immediately distort the very pliable thought-forms (which often come in a flash, and are mere impressions) obtained in meditative states, or other cognitive processes, into whatever the objective of desire may be.

---

2 Much more concerning the etheric body, *chakras*, *prāṇa,* and the nature of mind will be presented throughout this treatise.

They consequently distort or veil the expression of the truth. They produce a glaze of glamour over whatever is perceived.

This constitutes what people know or imagine to be real on the physical plane, but is not necessarily so on the realms that they are contacting. Often people are very impressionable and receive the emotional energies of their friends, or those that are close to them (when they are involved in social or group involvements). This input then conditions their thinking and actions accordingly. The impressions and energies received produce a type of euphoria not based on a reality other than what they have created themselves. This is specifically seen amongst those at religious gatherings, or any crowd gathered together for an occasion.

4. *The concrete, empirical mind (the intellect).* It is the cognised result of sense perception, and therefore of isolated bits of perceived information. The intellect stores, classifies and correlates that information. We thus have people's everyday thoughts, gleaned in the material world from the results of their contact with the environment as a whole, what they have read in books, from their schooling, and conversations with others. It is styled the 'sixth sense' in Buddhist texts. There is also an imaginative input of created picture images by the intellect, or from the desire-mind. The thought lives of people are rarely impartial and are often conditioned by what they subjectively desire.
5. The fifth aspect of mind is the *higher abstract enlightened Mind.* Because the intellect is so much swayed and controlled by the emotional nature and desires of the body the mind nearly always distorts and bends the 'bits of information' about any particular subject into a desired outcome. Consequently only by developing a tranquil, controlled, focussed, and unemotional mental process can anything be reasoned out fully and truthfully. Through this process another aspect of mind can manifest which defies classification, and is not the result of sense-perceptive cognition. It is archetypal and abstract, producing the ability to formulate deep ideals and expansive vistas of unbroken thought, without being aware of formulating, or of any other mental process whatsoever. It produces that aspect of thought which is a synthesis of all related ideas and which one intuits and knows to be true. It is pure reason and manifests as beauty,

harmony, and ordered purpose, giving the person revelations or touches of genius. It has been called the higher Mind, manifesting as Clear Light, and is an attribute of the I-consciousness, which consists of the substance of such a Mind. It represents that subjective inner being that gives one a purpose for existence, driving one on to the fulfilment of that purpose.

That the mind (*manas*) is intrinsically dual is well known in Buddhism. As Sparham states:

> Therefore *manas* is two[fold]: the egotistical *manas*, and the just-prior *manas*. These are also called 'ultimate *manas*' and 'conventional *manas*.' because [the ultimate *manas*] is not contingent on another consciousness and exists self-sufficiently as a material reality and [conventional *manas*] is not posited apart from the group of six's [consciousnesses]. The first, then, [i.e., egotistical *manas*] produces all that is contaminated and thoroughly afflicted by functioning as that basis on which the six [kinds of consciousness'] enthralment with marks comes about. The second [i.e., the just-prior *manas*] functions as the immediate condition of the six, giving the next consciousness the occasion to arise by force of its removal. Thus it is said [MSam][3]:
>
>> There are two aspects to *manas*. [First] is the ground for the production of consciousness *(vijñāna),* [called] [36a] "the *manas* that ceases just prior to consciousness." It is based in that it functions as immediately preceding condition *(samanantara-pratyaya).* The second is the *manas* that is afflicted *(kliṣṭaṃ).* With it are always associated four afflictive emotions: view that the perishable aggregate [is a single, permanent soul] *(sat-kāya-dṛśṭi),* pride in the thought "I am" *(asmimāna),* self-love, and ignorance. It is the basis for the thorough affliction of consciousness. A consciousness is, then, produced by the basis supplied by the first and caused to be afflicted by the second. It is consciousness *(vijñāna)* since it perceives an object *(viṣaya-prati-vijñāpti).* Thus, since there is one just previous *(samanantara)* and an egotistical thought *(manana) manas* is twofold.[4]

---

3 The reference Sparham gives here is *Theg pa chen bsdus pa (Mahāyāna-samgraha).*

4 Gareth Sparham, (Trans.) *Ocean of Eloquence, Tsong ka pa's Commentary on the Yogacara Doctrine of Mind,* (Sri Satguru, Delhi, 1995), 112-113.

Kliṣṭamanas is another aspect of mind needing mentioning. The author's footnote here is that: 'The *kliṣṭa-manas* is conceived of as stable, subtle consciousness which, by virtue of its being continually present, provides the basis for personal experience. Steady, deep, and a necessary prerequisite for personal experience, this hypostasized seventh mind is unlike the other *manas,* the sixth of the set of six, which continually flits in and out of existence'.[5] *Kliṣṭamanas* can be conceived of as emotional or desire-mind (the emotions and desire wedded to mind), which I generally term *kāma-manas*.[6] As such however it is not 'stable'.

What has so far been presented is summarised in Figure 1. It shows that the higher abstract Mind (in the form of the I-consciousness) mediates between:

a. The divine, the real, because it is the source of all lasting values, and is that into which the person is ultimately resolved at the death of the personality and the phenomenal.

b. The unreal, because impermanent; seen as the appearance of things. This is designated by the Sanskrit term for the phenomenal material world, *saṃsāra*, which means 'that which goes on, or continues to come to be'. It signifies existence as conditioned being, the material cosmos. When phrased in terms of continual cycles of death and rebirth of the phenomenal appearance of any form it is then termed *māyā,* meaning illusion, but more specifically; the substance of illusion.

From one perspective the real can also be equated with *śūnyatā*, but from another *śūnyatā* is but its veil, a mirror of the *dharmakāya*. In conventional Western terminology the *dharmakāya*[7] can be represented

5 Ibid., 120, note 21.

6 *Kliṣṭamanas,* afflicted mind. There are many types of afflictive emotions (*kleśas*) stored as *bījas* (seeds) in the ālayavijñāna. They are projected in the form of related *saṃskāras* when the personal-I is focussed upon an object of desire. When these emotional *saṃskāras* surface they immediately fuse with the mental consciousness *(manovijñāna)* to produce such things as desire-mind, self-will (i.e., the four types of 'afflictive emotions'), or forms of ego-clinging. The emotions always manifest in relation to a concept of a 'self', executing the will to appropriate things desired. They thus produce attachments for all things deemed pleasurable, glamorous, or needed by the personality, and react to that which they dislike.

7 Much of the Sanskrit terminology used in this chapter has been defined in Volume 1, hence need not be redefined here.

by the term 'the Divine', or 'Spirit'; the I-consciousness becomes 'the soul', and the personal-I is the personality.

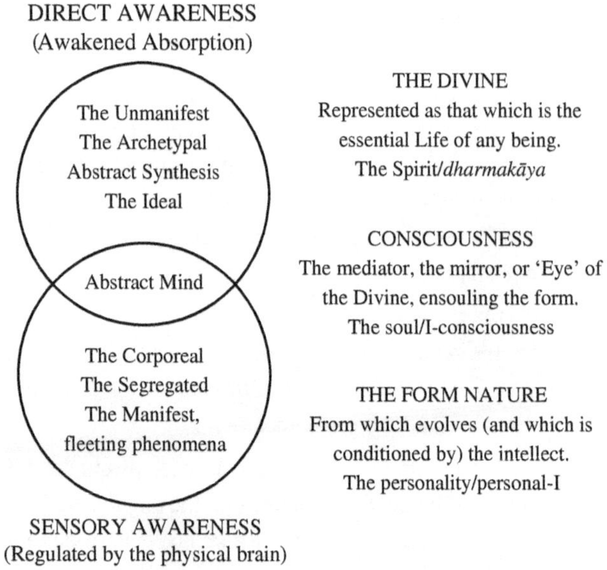

Figure 1. The abstract Mind

The abstract Mind is that aspect of consciousness that sustains the *ālayavijñāna* environment that contains the various consciousness-streams of humanity that 'en-Soul' the life of the appearing personal-I's. Each of these appearances manifest around a developing concrete mind that allows consciousness to consecutively gain from interaction with phenomena. The abstract Mind is however not bound by the appearing forms for the sustenance of its integral expression of expansive inclusive reason. In its domain are found the archetypal patterns of thought governing all that exists; all of the aspirational, scientifically correct, and philosophically profound ideas of humanity. It is constituted of the substance of the Clear Light of Mind. Here the clear-visioning far-seeing Eye of the Divine resides, which enlightens the form and abstracts developed qualities from it. Śūnyatā interrelates with *saṃsāra* via the functioning of such an Eye.

The veils to comprehension

If the formulations, activities and the subjective realms of the mind are comprehended, when united with the Heart (giving direction in space), then the true nature of oneself can be known. This includes knowledge of the how, why, and whereto of all phenomena. One can then be identified with the eternal presence of all being/non-being.

Emotions always bias viewpoints, obscuring the ability to vision the truth of what really is. Emotional energies put a coloured haze of turbulent Watery[8] substance over the eyes, through which one perceives things. Such perception is always in relation to the idea of an 'I', reinforcing the self-concept. For the emotions this is unavoidable. The path to liberation therefore first necessitates cleansing emotional reactions of all types. Next, the subtler emotions must be transmuted into their higher correspondences that are distortion-free and are aspects of the energy of Love. Their *prāṇas* are then incorporated into the Heart *chakra*. Most aspirants however mistake loving emotions (which are always self-focussed, even if subtly so) with Love. Love however is not at all concerned with the 'self'.

Along this vein, many are too emotionally involved with asserting their concept of 'God' (in theistic religions) or of denial of the existence of Deity (in Buddhism) to be able to properly think with pristine logic. They are both extreme views, and mental-emotional pride is invested by either side to sustain their respective positions. The truth really lies in a subtle fusion of these two opposing views, by establishing a transcendental logic that eliminates the dogmatic assertions of both. It speaks the truth through revealing the esoteric doctrine that integrates the all into one. A cogent ontological middle path of reason effectively lies in such a fusion, which represents a true *mahāmudrā* of religion. Neither one nor the other, but the path in between is the way to liberation, and great wisdom will be the result in this new era of religious awakening.

Dogmatists are often the governing body of any religion or philosophical sect. Those who work to establish truth must therefore first

---

8 Viewing Water here as an Element (the substance of the emotions and desire), not as the physical prototype.

see through the forceful presentations of the ones placed in positions of power above them in the religious organisation they are in. This presents problems for people who genuinely seek enlightenment, as they must properly analyse and then break the tightly structured bindings of the imposed orthodox view. This process becomes the *second major veil* or obstacle on the way that they must pierce or rent asunder. The *first major veil* represents the process undertaken in overcoming blocks in the desire-mind when one wishes to tread the path to enlightenment in the first place. Elementary religious impulses, vague, vacillating wishes that are obscured by much ignorance must be transformed into a fervent aspiration to overcome obstacles if the first veil is to be rent.

Then comes the problem of the 'self' or 'self-identity', which becomes the third and certainly the harder thing to master. The veil here is one's own conception of what actually is or is not. Being mind-conditioned, it necessitates the process of proper philosophical analysis and meditation concerning the comparative merits of the various schools and teachers that purport to reveal the way to the 'not-self'. Many transformative battles concerning self-concepts must then be fought and won. Within the Theistic religions it involves a complete surrender of the personal will to the providence of what is conceived as 'God'. Once the personal-I becomes totally infused with the 'Spirit of God', then divine revelation and liberation from the bonds of the personal 'self' can be attained. For Buddhists the process involves thorough analysis of available doctrines and the concept of 'self', deep meditative realisation through yogic practice, and eventual liberation. If the gains of such a process are then compared to the texts then the veils, blinds or limitations in them will be clearly seen.

This process is long, producing the Clear Light of pure revelation. Direct perception of what is 'self' and what is not, upon a vaster scale than what constitutes the human persona is also nakedly revealed. This represents the piercing of the *third major veil*. For Theists the process of revelation concerns that of *invocation* of that which is beyond, and for Buddhists the process is one of *evocation* of that which is within.

The *fourth veil* represents the obstacles to the experience of awareness accorded by the identification with *śūnyatā*.

Piercing the *fifth veil* brings us beyond the serene equipoise of *śūnyatā* into the all-embracive dynamic revelatory stance of the *dharmakāya*.

Empirical rationalisations present ideas only. Experiences or verifications of whether or not there exists peaceful or wrathful deities, 'divinity' or 'soul', must come from a different source. Internal confirmation lies beyond words, but the mind must be used in interpretation, and therein lies the seed for errors in perceptions, depending upon the nature and content of a person's mind. We can speculate and philosophise, but ultimately understanding can only come from within, through a meditative progression of expansive spacious conscious revelation. Direct revelatory vision and clear, calm cognisance or insight then happen spontaneously. Such vision cannot easily be given to another's mind through emotive discourse, but the method of such discernment can. In this idea lies the basis of the Buddha's method of teaching.

Vision encompasses the nature of space, and the mind ascertains its verities. From this perspective space and mind/Mind are identical, or rather, one is the vehicle of the other. Space is perceived primarily through a meditative evocation of the power of the Heart centre, whilst the Fires of mind/Mind produce revelation through invocatory processes that call forth images and revelation from contact with the external universe. The enlightened Mind fuses both approaches into one intrinsic expanse of lucid revelatory truth.

The experience can be equated with what is known in the rDzogs chen philosophy as *Rigpa*. It is the Father of all *dharma:*

> When searching for its Mother, which is its source or origin, the knowledge or cognition *(ye-shes)* of the vision or phenomena directly encounters its own Mother (emptiness) and self-liberates. That is to say, the vision is self-liberated by means of the vision, like melted butter dissolving into butter. And while searching for the Son, the Son itself, which is the cognition or knowledge, encounters itself directly. This Awareness itself is self-liberated by means of Awareness; just like water dissolving into water. When searching for the unique state of (Rigpa), one encounters only one's own unique state. That is to say, one's own nature (Rigpa) simply encounters itself. But its essence transcends all expression in words; like space dissolving into space, or like the three coils of a snake liberating themselves simultaneously.
>
> This singular and unique state of intrinsic Awareness can only be found within oneself. If that is the case, then when one recognizes

> one's essence, everything is brought together in a single moment within which a cognition is present that does not go beyond the knowledge of that singular unique essence (which is Rigpa).[9]

My depiction of 'space' equates here with the 'Mother (emptiness)' which 'self-liberates'. Spaciousness is empty of things, which is the Mother because all forms of liberated enlightened perception rests in it. The 'Son itself, which is the cognition or knowledge, encounters itself directly' represents wisdom *(prajñā)* because it is the gain of the evolutionary process and is replete with the fullness of the all-embracive awareness of *bodhicitta.*

When spaciousness and wisdom sprout from the same seed *(bindu/* thig le*)* then, as I understand it, we have *Rigpa*, intrinsic transcendental awareness, revelatory wisdom. This is the fount of the *dharmakāya,* which stands upon the base of the Mother and is the complete expression of the awakened evolution of the 'Son'. The 'seed' is constituted of the energies of the Mother and Son (both the inner and the outer universes, the Eastern and Western methodologies to revelation) and has been planted in the fertile field of the *dharmakāya* wherein it produces the fruit of unbridled expansiveness in cosmos.

The Mother contains the *tathāgatagarbha*, as an embryo (the Son) within the spaciousness of her womb. That space consists of the five Void Elements, which are then incorporated into the *tathāgatagarbha/ Son.* The Son is impressed to start the process of gathering wisdom *(prajñā)* by means of successive incarnations of the personal-I's, or 'selves'. The 'selves' are projected into the *māyā* of substance *(svabhāva)* of the phenomenal world, which they attract to themselves by means of *manasic* action, or interrelate with it via the expression of desire, avarice and lust. Corporeal forms are built into the three worlds, and the generated *saṃskāras* accumulate in the form of the stored *bījas* of experience contained within the sphere of awareness of the *tathāgatagarbha.*

Desire is the key to growth, it is an attractiveness or need of a (self contained) unity of awareness to possess that which is not included as part of its own corporation. That which is not included is the basis of

9 J.M. Reynolds, *The Golden Letters*, (Snow Lion, New York, 1996), 132.

the ignorance that must be conquered. Thus the aeonic-long involvement between the illusional selves and the 'not self' progresses. *Saṃskāras* are instigated through volitions that modify the five Void Elements. This causes the congealing, condensation, and enflaming of the Earth, Water, and Fiery Elements. The action is at first inchoate, mindless, but inevitably the mind and then the higher conscious awareness ensues in the personal-I.

First there is a desire for sensation and later a desire to know, finally a desire (aspiration) to be liberated from sensation or the sensorial world. Desire to know is the foundation of the gnosis of the wise. The essence of mind is abstracted as the natural, innate wisdom of the Son, being the effect of the instigating quality of the primordial five wisdoms of the Father with the added gain of *saṃsāric* involvement. This causes the *tathāgatagarbha* to flower to its full potential. Eventually ignorance is transformed into knowledge and knowledge into wisdom, which takes the guise of the inherent *bodhicitta* built into the *tathāgatagarbha* from the beginning through the union of Father-Mother in their originating embrace.

The All-accomplishing wisdom (of Amoghasiddhi) that is developed is a combination of that which was primordially seeded (which can be evoked by consciousness) and that which has been gained through *saṃsāric* activity. Only when the evocative and invocative processes are simultaneous can the wisdom of the Father (Rigpa) be manifest.

The seven Ray aspects of mind[10]

When wedded to *kleśas*[11] the intellect can be divided into seven sub-aspects that should be analysed here, as they govern all aspects of the personality life, causing much misery and strife, because of the inherent

10 The Rays were introduced in Volume 1. Elaboration of the meaning of these Rays (states of energy modifications qualifying everything) will be found throughout this treatise, and indeed can also be gleaned from most listings of seven found throughout Buddhist texts.

11 *Kleśa*: from the root *kliś:* to molest, torment, suffer. The force of defilements, afflictive, dissident emotions. That quality (passion-desire) that causes one to attach oneself to all aspects of the formed realms, and to identify with them as the real, which is then obscured. They are generally signified as the three poisons: delusion, attachment, and hatred.

nature of the mind to segregate, critically dissect, and to assert itself upon all manifest life. These qualities should therefore be carefully studied by all who wish for meditation experiences and enlightenment.[12]

1. *The will of mind.* This concerns the direct use of the will expressed by the mind of the personality to present its views in a forceful manner. It will brook no opposition and will dominate all conversations, not allowing any counter argument or view to be expressed. Those engendering this trait will thus tend to be arrogant and domineering.

   Countering quality: Serenity, gentleness of mind.

2. *The loving mind.* Here the mind tells itself that it is loving in its actions, or in the formulations it has worked out to help others. True Love is not however there, for if the mode of action is carefully examined then one will find a subjective selfish motive behind it (a self-serving expression of mind). There is no true compassionate understanding or the associated wisdom in action that is the leitmotiv in Love. Love is not concerned with, nor an aspect of emotional identifications. The emotions distort the pure logic from the Heart centre, focussing concern in terms of an 'I', whereas with the true expression of Love the central 'I' does not exist.

   Countering quality: The ability to listen to the 'voice of silence'[13] (conscience) from the Heart.

3. *The critical mind.* Here the mind is fused with strong emotions and is used critically to dissect and attack other's opinions without any true deep-seated understanding of the issues and qualities involved. The individual's narrow-mindedness leaves very little room for patience with the views of others, and projects this impatience forcefully in a critical manner.

   Countering quality: Harmlessness in thought, word or deed.

4. *Pride of mind.* Here the mind focuses upon its self-accomplishments, of opinionated thoughts, inflated with egotistic self-esteem. It produces a sun-like pleasing atmosphere and a glamour generated

---

12 Complementing these seven Ray aspects of mind are the seven aspects of the emotional-mind that will be explained later.

13 Literally *nādā*, the soundless sound. See H.P. Blavatsky's book *'The Voice of the Silence'* (Theosophical Publishing House, Wheaton, 1982), for the translated text ('The Book of the Golden precepts') concerning this subject.

warmth within which the participant basks lion-like. Boastfulness is often the result of such personality centred egocentricity.

Countering quality: Humbleness of mind.

5. *The concrete mind.* Here the natural empirical attributes of the lower mind come to the fore through reifying and concretised thought forms, producing the materialisation of all ideas and ideals in terms of logical patterns of thought. It disallows any stream of information that fits not in with the established rigid mental rules set up by the thinker. Such is the mainstay of our present materialistic civilisation, which is based upon the logic of science and technology and avaricious concerns. It builds its case with the detailed and specific, rather than the syncretic overview and abstract patterns that life generally obeys. True flexibility of thinking is hard won, and generally only after much evidence and extreme persuasion with facts will the concretist change any aspects of his view.

   Countering quality: The abstract Mind, universality of thinking, inclusive reasoning, wherein the subjective states of consciousness and states of being are included in the thought process.

6. *The desire-mind.* Here we have the domination of the desire body over the mind. All aspects of thought become distorted by one's desires and emotions, skewing the thinking process and logic into what the person desires the outcome to be. Such desires are then made out to be the truth, the basis of all further actions. Thus lies and distorted information are often promulgated as facts. The stronger the emotions associated with any particular issue, the stronger the ensuing distortions of the truth. This way of thinking is the mainstay of what is promulgated by our mass medias, which the general population utilise as the basis in their decision-making processes, such as voting in politicians that produce the laws that we are consequently ruled by. The desire-mind is easily swayed by those that can whip up people's emotions over any issue. It is also strongly developed in zealous religionists.

   Countering quality: Dispassion, emotional calmness.

7. *The wrongly faceted mind.* The mind's activity here manifests in the form of a prism with irregular sides and angles, producing aberrations in its abilities to clearly reflect light (consciousness). The

facets focus upon desired arenas of thought, exaggerating them to be more than they are in truth. Often these impressions are coloured with a distorted overtone or hue. People thus look through 'rose coloured glasses'. Such people often live out lives governed by the images and distortions of view from the specific facet of the whole picture that they are focussed upon. In others, various exaggerated ideas and related images appear cyclically in their lives, distorting their worldview accordingly. Thus their line of reason is not correct, with no proportionate logic, except maybe upon their limited vision of focus. Such people are generally fanatics, or single issue activists.

Countering quality: Openness of mind through correctly faceted mentation.

Consideration of these aspects of mind is quite important hence they are elaborated below in a verse form, as it will help people to ponder more deeply upon such concepts, with view to engendering the countering qualities. Much esoteric information can be best disseminated via this compact form.[14] Though it diverts from the hermenuentics of Buddhist texts, it however provides valuable insights to practitioners of the *dharma,* who are the focus of the teachings of this *Treatise on Mind.*[15] To gain enlightenment these attributes must certainly be understood, battled with, and their qualities overcome. To produce enlightened ones certainly is the purported objective of the Buddhist *dharma*. It exists not purely for entertainment of the philosophic mind.

The way of mind is moulded by rapacious ire, it enshrouds itself in seven forms of muck. Deep-seated are the *saṃskāras* of this *māyāvirūpic*[16] zeal.

With aeons-long bulwarks of black mantras and scowl, rapine, and loathing of the common weal with prideful bellowing of separative

14 These teachings will supplement what will be given in Volume 5A concerning the overcoming and transformation of *saṃskāras.*

15 This extract is from an unpublished manuscript entitled *The Dawn of Agni.* The term Agni refers to the Lord of Fire, the energy of mind/Mind, incorporating transcendental awareness. All is constructed of Fire, transmuted by Fire and the liberated one rides through cosmos upon the steed of the most rarefied Fire. Such Fire lies at the heart of all mantras of liberating poise, producing a Fiery pledge *(samaya)* beckoning all on, through and to the great beyond.

16 The various forms or embodiments *(rūpa)* of illusion *(māyā).*

cages of might, mindful ones pull the reigns tight upon all forms of growth and light.

They will themselves to keep their paths straight, a line of one-pointedness to self fulfilling goals, ruthlessly stealing from all around to bloat their grey-black mind stuff concretised between the anvil and coal sack.

The anvil[17] for the Lord of Light to pound just right to cleanse the *karma* from such a separative blight, the sack[18] to hold the resultant fragments of mind to fuel the furnace of the wrath of Divinity's transformative might.[19]

For untold lives must the furnace be stoked to transform the black to white. The inevitable outcome is streams of multicoloured light, from grey-oranges and greens to rainbow delight is the transformation of sight.

The Rays of mind can be seen in seven distinct types, from distortions evolves the emanative rainbow so bright:

Distortion	Fundamental Ray Quality
Will of mind	First Ray of Will or Power
Loving mind	Second Ray of Love-Wisdom
Critical mind	Third Ray of Mathematically Exact Activity
Pride of mind	Fourth Ray of Harmony Overcoming Strife
Concrete mind	Fifth Ray of Scientific Aptitude
Desire-mind	Sixth Ray of Devotion
Wrongly faceted mind	Seventh Ray of Ritualistic Activity

Table 1. The seven Ray aspects of mind

The will of mind is not that kind, it ruthlessly manipulates all other forms of mind to bend to its will for dominance of thought. It simply will not hear any other stuff.

The ears are tiny for hearing, but the mouth is wide, it will blast your thinking to submissive states of fluff, and if you desire it not, to you it will angrily say 'be gone'.

17 This concerns the mechanism of the mode of expression of the immutable law of *karma*.

18 This refers to the intricate *nāḍī* system.

19 Rebirthing into various hell states within the Wheel of Life.

But gentlemindedness, serenity in all aspects of thought must be sought through every avenue of life if this will is to be countered by one's loving side and turned into a tool to pave a path straight through life's hells to the Light of Life that is from Divinity designed.

For such will generally counters the plan for all that is, and the *karma* is woe, woe, woe, hell indeed, as this one is incapable of listening to anyone's need.

What is willed, but not given to another's gain becomes an evil weed[20] with a stranglehold upon your mind. You cannot think straight upon any line other than what you've willed. Your actions become forceful, demanding, no matter the other's pain, and as this is not what is good for the whole you've left for yourself no other role but for much *karma* to cleanse when the sword of your wilfulness descends upon you instead.

It comes crashing through your tongue, your solar plexus, and your head.[21]

The dark foes[22] will strangle you until from your heart you've bled the power of Love that can clothe them in new robes sublime.

Your role has now been set to undo their manipulative mechanisations still, for they have chosen this path of mind and will to reach the cosmic black pit, with hatred, vile and concreted mouthings, forcefully spit, for all minds with malice and spite to control and entwine.

It is divine Will in your heart that can counter their self-will best, and with the chariot might of divine insight you are blest. You've become the Sword of Light to convert the darkness[23] to the white.

The loving mind knows what it will find from all streams of reasoning it sees of a similar kind. It applies its logic to do 'good things' in a way that services the self, masquerading as philanthropy for the whole. It deludes itself into thinking that this is enough, but to tread the Path it simply is not the right stuff.

The service of self must go, upon the battlefield of Initiation tests

20 The nature of the grey *prāṇas* reticulating through the *nāḍī* system.

21 In other words, through the mechanisms wherein the *karma* was created in the three worlds of human livingness: physical, emotional, and mental.

22 The forces of evil, the dark hierarchy, black magicians and the like, who oppose the activities of all Bodhisattvas.

23 Ignorance, evil ones.

to come; all *saṃskāras* must be mastered and converted to produce an illumined sun.

The loving mind selectively reasons with little whiffs of subtle desires, and in doing so it but obeys the great deceiver fuelling the fields of *māyā*.

Its subtle innuendoes of mind simply will not get it right. The wolves smirk,[24] they've howled in delight, you they've won to the grey, the grey blues, and the dull white, but the brilliant light—oh, if only your mind would the wolves fight.

And fight it must to win the battle right, straight to the Heart of life you must go and there only seed your mind, for your Heart must bleed for every other's need. Subtle innuendoes and lies must be straightened to become truth.

The little self must be crucified to the Love for the plan of the One, and to pamper not the mind that delineates your belief: that you love. Yes you love, but for what you can gain from the path you tread. But your 'love' will be in vain when finally *bodhicitta* is the goal you really do seek, the little lies vanquished in the Mind of all-consummating light.

From the Heart your consciousness flies to perceive the All in one true Light; the indigo blue has become the leitmotiv for every act of love you perceive.

A Buddha indeed flowers in your Heart-head's steed.

The voice of silence has become your whole life's creed. You have listened intently to the Lord of Life and Love's compassionate might, and altruistically now is done your every deed.

The critical mind is this world's most pestilent blight, and quickly obscures all forms of loving sight. It is destructive to the nerves in time, and works to spin *chakras* backwards through forceful mouthings of ire.

Its irritable tiny serpents[25] wreak havoc with emotions, expelling substance dire, where'ere the maggots congregate there a weakness

---

24 The dark brotherhood have many disguises. In the psychic realms the nature of their cunning and mode of manipulative thought projection can clothe them in the semblance of wolves and the Anubis. The magical practices of such cultures as that of ancient Egypt left many untoward consequences.

25 Moving serpents represent the nature of this energy flow in the *nāḍīs*. The substance is expelled via the Splenic centre into various organs of the body, laying the seeds for sicknesses to come, or directly projected via the Solar Plexus centre to the object of criticism, or else becomes part of the radiating aura of the person.

in the body will sire, wherefrom proceeds the sicknesses that to the whole world will transpire.

How can compassionate insight come with any form of critical mind, with such belittling thoughts, a scorpion stinging itself and for other's demise? The arcs of venom manifest in limited cycles of mind, jabbing at others when no congruency of thought it can find.

The scorpion is a most apt symbol for the way of the critical mind. Circuitously it thinks as it attacks to defend its own rhyme. Quick to strike, it cannot countenance another's reasoning or light. From its lair it moves, forever hiding in the dark, its desire-mind snapping out its boundaries of thought.

It is not capable of unparalleled luminescent sight, so infatuated with its own understanding of what is right. Venom it can spit, like a Medusa's head,[26] with many snapping serpents of desire and of fight.

Criticism gives you crab-like hardened shells of mind, with pincers to gouge out your thoughts into little bits of unimportant stuff, which it can consume if you will not ward it off and fight. But if fight you must, the full Medusa of the critical mind will rear up from its den in fearsome spitting fury to destroy you in its might.

Its best to back down to such a one and humbly, silently submit, for the critical mind will not let you have your say, bow low and gently go on your way. Let the critical ones fume in their own mind-stuff, for the way to hell is what they speak.

Thoughts like crows fighting over rotting pestilent meat, or hornets jabbing *prāṇas* in *nāḍīs*, producing reticulated blocks of murky stuff, energy dammed up in terms of only one or other type of thought, producing a concreted maze of *prāṇic* rubble, allowing the critical one little means of escape from the labyrinth of its own design.

We can only weep compassionately at the *karma* such a one produces in his spite and verbal might.

The way of mind and mouth are terribly entwined. The mouth utters, speaks, commands, demands what the mind sees, reveals, fabricates. And inevitably with forceful spite we have mantras of fearsome and loathsome might, ensnaring many, even the multitude, through their lack of will to use cogent logic to fight, or to reason anything out right.

---

26 In Greek mythology, one of the Gorgons, a woman with a round ugly face, and snakes for hair. Her eyes could turn to stone anyone who looked at her.

The mouth conveys the power of a black magician's delight, but before this, we have selfish, cantankerous muck-raking ones, and those with little worms of irritable projections of desire-ridden minds, anger and spite.

Words of the common man as he battles in what *saṃsāra* sires, collectively produces great swirls and rapacious tides of the earth's desire cesspool, full of psychic sharks and monsters of great size,[27] breeding famines, diseases, and the insects people annoyingly swat.

Energy follows thought, is mind, is the *prāṇa* feeding you and I, and concretised into the material domain, the *karma* of it all afflicts the perpetuators as a mass, with the ire they've sown.

Such insects and disease germs, are but the karmic *devic* pull[28] built around crass irritable and loathsome utterings by people generations ago.

Reincarnating, the perpetuators must suffer their blow, for their energy projected must inevitably produce a material show, as Nature reasserts itself to try to produce a harmonious flow. Nothing is wasted or forgotten in the 'Gibb's free energy'[29] show.

Only fools think they can avoid paying for all that they've dished out in thought, word, or deed, and the worst of these are crimes of the mouth.

The mouth consumes all in its desire to please, its consumptive greed, its powerful need to attack the all for the 'me' if it stands in 'my way'. Bickering, boisterous, babbling fools mouthing out contempt for the others in all areas where the seven aspects of mind rule. Philosophers debating, scornful, in prideful ways, religious fanatics with bigotry despising the other's way, the deniers, decriers and despisers of the divinity in all and the golden rule that people must learn to love equally the common lot if the road to light and liberation from *karma* be trod.

---

27 Though they are illusional thought-forms *(māyāvirūpa)* existing in the Watery astral realm, they have the potency of the energies they were seeded with.

28 The role of the *devas* with respect to *karma* will be elaborated throughout this treatise.

29 Briefly stated: this law in Chemistry denotes that in a closed system (e.g., as is the Universe) all energy exchanges ultimately remain the same, i.e., they balance out, so that the amount of heat lost equals the amount of heat gained. The formula runs thus, that in any chemical exchange, the amount of free energy available (allowing the reaction to take place) equals the incremental changes in enthalpy (the internal heat or order of a system) minus the temperature times the incremental heat lost (entropy, or the measure of the disorder of the system). Free energy is the overall measure of whether a given chemical reaction is possible or not. This law is an exemplification of the way *karma* works throughout Nature.

The wise man who has learned to curb his tongue and close his mouth in the face of adversity is nobody's fool.

In Atlantean[30] days the wars of the mouth and spite from the tongue was especially strong. Astounding rates of utterings and mantras were sneezed out of debauchery, scorn, and of destructive hate.

Let the denizens of the Earth, the Waters, and the fairy fair, those workers of the field toiling the land who embody every created thing beware, for these mantras ejected will them ensnare, imprison their forms with cages of blight, distorting them so that they will not work right. So when they need to work upon Nature's scenery the greenery sickens, dries up and disasters curse the land.

People know not whence comes relief from this savage karmic hand. For humanity's sake has the Lord of Nature spake.

But humanity then did listen not, whole forests were lain waste, every living, vital thing was attacked, for their amassed sorcery and jealousy would not allow another to possess what the other had not, neither would they allow the white Hierarchy sanctuary anywhere in their natural ally, the greenery. Plumes of grey smoke everywhere filled the air, browns, thence black consumed the land.

Again and again the masses thus did play and prey until their continent was doomed, weighed down by humanity's predatory glare, by the covetous, who if they could not possess had to destroy, until all was laid bare.

So in the fifth subcycle of mind of that great fourth epoch of man the Atlantean continent was sunk to wash the blight clean, the Shambhalic Lords of Life and of *karma* hoping that when the *karma* resurfaced in this present root epoch of mind the destructive intent of their rapacious mouthing will again not destroy all that is green and life sustaining.

Our hell states were built then from the substance of the externalised desire forms of the most terrible sort.

Those that transgress with their minds and mouths, with rampant desires, and painful misdeeds must find their abode, or solution there

30 An early civilisation of humanity, existing upon a continent in the Atlantic ocean, and whose people had many psychic capabilities. The continent sank approximately 12,000 years ago. This subject is a myth to the exoterically minded, but not to the enlightened that must trace *karma* back to its roots. It can only be avoided by those that will not meditatively pry into the subject of *karma*.

indeed, for bodily shells left (at death) but means, in short, one then resides in one's emotions and mind to experience what one has inflicted in kind.

Rapacious loquacious desires remain there still to encourage one in the qualities that can no longer be filled, engorged in hate, spite, separativeness, malice's will, these qualities descend and become your emotional mind's fill.

You must learn to burn them off in your disgust with the other perpetuators of such stuff, those whose selfishness and covetous desire have ruled their lives, and also who cheat and steal from the myriads enthralled in such mire. They use lying propaganda, bigotry, unjust laws and social mores.

Those who cannot burn or transform such thoughts a cold, murky hell of unsatiated desire in the after-death will be wrought.

Much better the Bodhisattva path, the enlightened way for all future lives to instate, to give and to give continuously for other's sake. Then the sum of one's good deeds manifests as Amitābha's paradise realm, your good luck in propitious good birth then should be nobody's ire.

Charitable deeds, in thoughts, and words in mouths is the sum of it all for humanity's prosperity to make. There is then no race, caste, creed, or religious form that shall not be transformed, into a luminous awakened state born.

Pride of mind is of a special kind, it feeds itself in self-congratulation still:

gratuitous commending on the little and unimportant,

gratuitous evaluating the repertoire of the mind,

gratuitous bloating of emotional appeasements of the little self's desire to please,

gratuitous flatulence of guttural antiquated age old rhymes kept intact by desire,

gratuitous remarks that no one keeps for long in the cupboards of their minds.

Its perpetuators can build auras of an immense size, of grey-yellows, oranges, and red-speckled mire. Their auras are grown to replicate their ego's growing demands, to astound the viewer with what they have sired. As all other auras will clash with their preponderant glee they will allow no other to brook theirs in areas you cannot see.

They will automatically pamper your grappling emotions and habits of thought to draw you into their dominance of puffed-up self esteem, because if you they can conquer then their own auras have grown a mile further wide. For this pride is fed by the little coloured blocks of other's admiration.

'Tis their glamoured substance that the prideful one joyfully amasses. To do this he must ensnare you with opinions grave, broad, wondrous and dire. You he's enslaved to beam his aura greater. But he helps you not as he steps on to his ivory tower.

Be careful of pride, for its expanse is but a hell of self deceit. If you halt pride not then humbling roles will karmically be your feat.

Karma has its way to force all upon a bended knee. If formerly slim the next life will see you fat. If possessions were your glory, then bereft you will later be. Its cousin vanity, through the looking glass of misbelief will make you ugly, when everyone your beauty adored before then. Sexual prowess becomes limp in the grace of much disease.

Great social standing and avarice are each other's children, the gloating prideful one manipulates them to fulfil his boon. Too soon, too soon, will he fall into the ditch from where he has amassed, as all mortal men, playing to the cadence of the karmic reaper's tune.

The fruits of your actions will make your pride implode, for the ego bubble of your boastings will burst to fill the spaces in your head made vacant by that former episode.

There can be no perpetual outward motion from a centre with no support, or solid foundation for the move. Inevitably it will collapse, a cleansing for the all to improve, its but the force of necessity, unrelenting energy free flowing.

Energy always moves to harmonise the one into the all. Wisdom is empty of meaning if fed by boastful suppositions, of great intelligence and abstruse deduction on subjects great and small.

If you blind yourself to the 'other' as you stand upon your tower growing, you are bound to fall as it sinks into the shifting quicksand of other's thinking.

Ego-clinging but limits you to concepts of your own making. Growth is fictional when truth finally pierces your bubble. All in all, you must bend your knee to all who lovingly help the need. Your self-focussed deeds will continually topple you until humbleness indeed is what you heed.

The clamouring devotees who gather admiringly around your 'I', because of your beauty, your wealth, your glittering possessions, your psychic, religious, or your material power, quickly pass when death removes the self-concept from their eyes.

Sickness, misfortune, infidelity, old age, accidents, wars, soon alleviate the need for your posturing. As a luminary your torch will burn out and from its ashes you will salvage some meaning, no doubt.

To stand in the balloon of other's opinion is demeaning for all seekers of truth astounding, enlightenment flowering.

Humbleness alone will work the miracles that will lead you to the heart of all good fortune, so that the aura can grow radiant in *bodhicitta* arising, and reach out to all in your effort of giving.

The starry heavens will then befriend you and all-knowing becomes the fruit of your doing. 'Till you stand upon the 'other shore' of accomplishment, for with ego gone there can no longer be ties to *saṃsāra*, to *māyā*. Your great merit ends all ego posturing. A golden sun of radiant compassion is your true sowing.

The concrete mind is easy to define, empirical, it reifies and concretises thoughts, feelings, desires of every kind. If you wish to escape it, you it will grind with boulders of thoughts unkind. It will not bend or move in any direction other than what it defines. Great discipline of mind can control it, but to transcend it needs a salve of a loving kind.

The unitary flood of Love can dissolve these rocks in time, but blasting bolts of lightning[31] through cracks of mind may pulverise its rigid structures outright.

Scientific materialism is its product in this iron age[32] of ire. Logic, logic, logic it espouses to deny other than what through the senses can be known. Logic, circuitous, circumspect, curtailed in areas of the divine, limited by craggy articulated ideas and desires, proves images only of all that it has deemed to itself worthwhile. From one form to another it moves, in cages of time. *Saṃsāra* its home, *māyā* is its guide.

---

31 Flashes of insight.

32 The *kālī yuga*, the most materialistic of the ages in Hindu cosmology. It is the present era of darkness and of strife.

The Minotaur's maze[33] of thoughts and opinions, its well trod battle zone. But Ariadne's thread[34] is nowhere to be found. Fanatically the Minotaur attacks anything it cannot define. But what it cannot see cannot be known by its logic, so formed and defined.

Scientific instruments may peer at the atomic or universal world of sight. Great stores of knowledge scientists build through applied mind and will. But their universe is limited by formulated concretions of light.

Universality of thinking, inclusive reasoning, subjective states of consciousness bewilders them still.

Specific detail fills the mind with sensuous delight, but abstract patterns governing the all and flexibility of thought, are very hard won by those with the rigor mortis of concrete mind are fraught.

Evidence, evidence, is fanatically demanded for their scientific might, all the while screaming to deny what other's Hearts plainly see as facts. Ruthlessly the concretions crush subtle threads of thought, as what is crushed is never thought of having any worth.

So the self-made avalanche of opinions come crashing down upon the psychically attuned. There is no room to move under that great weight of mind. Wisdom is pulverised and suffocates with no love to fuel the Heart. The concrete mind will stifle those impressions right from the start.

With no wisdom, how can the processes of life truly be understood or found? Where's the way out of this maze of emotions and mind, for the concretist is inevitably tied to passions of every kind?

Though sometimes opinions are softened, but hardened cement invariably forms. The jackhammer of enlightened reason may pound upon that stuff only if the concrete mind will humble itself to blows of wisdom tough, to free itself so as to enter into the subtler, much more embracive, universal streams of awareness bright. But it needs compassionate Love for the separated mind to become one Mind universally applied.

---

33 In Greek mythology the Minotaur was a half man, half bull who lived in a specially constructed maze, into which its victims were put.

34 In Greek mythology she was the daughter of the king of Minos, who's maze the Minotaur resided in. She fell in love with the hero Theseus and gave him a thread that helped him to navigate the maze after he managed to kill the bull. This thread symbolises the intuition.

Mind encompassed in an ocean of Love, what an astounding insight. We can only dream for the resultant explosion of sight, an atomic bomb in the realms of mind has finally enlightened such a one right.

Desire-mind quickly adheres thoughts to sticky images bright. All (thought) is manipulated by the object of desire constricting any idea that may tend to lift you higher. Immediately do the emotions colour everything you can perceive: energies swirl attracting transient objects deemed enchanting. You cannot but be bound to such images of your desire, enslaved you become to this accumulated *māyā*.

It is the great deceiver seeding all great liars. You lie to yourself twisting truths into whatever you desire.

Because you see through self-coloured glasses, distorting thickly you cannot perceive truth except aberrantly. Your desire will instantly devour all such perceptions, spitting out glazes of untruthful attire. They become lies to believe in assuredly. Lies become your basis for fact, upon it you've built your mythology.

Unsound reasoning is then given to all who do not pry. They pry not, being also glamoured, for desire's intoxicating sweep is all engulfing.

It is hard to escape from the stupefying swirls of its powerful motion. You draw all thoughts into desirous dominions of watery sensation; their auras swirling, pushing out to extend your commotion.

Through glazed eyes, rose, dark, hazed, violets, blues, greens and bright, the desirous passionately view themselves, the world, everything deemed right. All is a dazzling, stupifying, glittering, alluring sight, but in reality they've covered their minds with auras like manure, thinking all the time that this clothing is the sum of their allure.

Alluringly they stifle the Heart's thoughts of discontent.

Alluringly they glaze over images of a higher kind.

Alluringly they wander into mazes of other's thought desires.

Alluringly they clamour like moths to any coloured light, bars, brothels (of the emotional kind), the cafe society, sure.

Alluringly they chatter and clamour to supersede in other's opinion, their fashionable attire.

Alluringly their *kāma*[35] produces *karma* of happiness and hell.

35 Desire, lust.

Hell follows whatever is coloured by desire, for when their object is not attained, then suffering sets in. When the body dies then these adulterated waters descend.

Desire, desire, desire, but not satiation, is hell, its fire intensifies, but cleanses not your steamy auric self-focussed shell.

Desireless non-attachment, is the way out of this accumulated ire. But desirelessness of thought is not easily sired. The auric colouring can only be removed in stages, gradually lightening, for when you remove one apparel, another quickly transpires.

One after another is fought, the battle zone rampaging, fanaticism rules, the glee of zeal is desire one level higher. Religious bigotry, hallucinations, coloured lights phantasmagorical bewilders this mystic in every stage of his desired wish-fulfilling journeying. In every stage another new (religious) hallucination, every glamoured indoctrination becoming his leitmotiv.

The teacher must be sought and found that feeds not glamour. The glazes must go, be gone forever. But which teacher is the true master of every aspect of this Watery realm and demeanour; where is the Buddha, the mindful meditator that will give to the seeker the true way to liberation? To find this one the fountain of desire must be broken, and aspiration to truth become one's true leitmotiv.

The wrongly faceted mind simply projects exaggeratedly any aspect of mind, blown-up, sharply cleaved forms of thought, and coloured according to the way of delineating its sight. Spot-lighting its focus thus, it has its delight, and accordingly may distort whatever is the focus of its facet of light.

Once distorted, it becomes fanatical, for it thinks its focus is all right. Things may be right for what's in its line of sight, but is myopic or blind to any other point of view. It does not care, or avoids, thus denigrates what it will not see. The various facets of mind perceive other things irregularly, thus with distortions they be; errors of thought, aberrant colourings, and concepts made unsound by belittling ideas.

To rightly focus with equanimity is beyond this reasoning still, for to think beyond these facets of mind is against this one's personal will.

Dust gathers and makes opaque these facets galore, for that one will only polish the logic of the main view all the more. Rigidly is applied this angled sight and the will even warps the facet through which one sees.

Warped fabrics of mind produce muddied currents of thought. They interrelate to produce nodes of illogic that here and there distort. As such currents regularly cloud clear thought the emotions find many spaces to cacophony their delights.

One must learn to relax the mind, so as to not focus it with will, and to even-out the facets, to look at all directions at need. Ritualistically from facet to facet of the diamond Mind one must go. But first must be straightened out facets that are ill.

Careful observation of mind will correct its tendencies for fanaticism still. All views must be sought from every aspect to produce a diamond light, and the dust must be cleansed by polishing the facets just right.

Clear reason from every angle of vision is then constantly sought. All seven Rays of reasoning and their sub-rays becoming the awakened Mind.

Great lights diffracted in terms of this and that, polychrome wisdom, clear and bright, becomes one's magical delight.

Oh what a wondrous, scintillatingly, enlightened insight. Thus the master sage sees you in your full light. Nothing can evade such sight, it sees multi-directionally, all ways, thoughts, and opinions at once. And thoughts are things that can be transformed to the higher ways and forms that all light brings.

The mind has been faceted according to any of the angles of this view and as a scryer the three times can be seen just right.

To help brighten the facets of all minds is this power, but minds alone delineate not the habitat of this Knower. For Love is the radiant jewel that expands with his/her every move. After all the light of the cosmos is but the substance of this jewel. It is enlightenment itself and for you that is its boon.

The seven aspects of the emotional-mind

In addition to the Rays of mind, we can also look to the fundamental emotional aspects of mind, as it is through these that the majority view themselves and the world around them.

In the seven Rays of mind given above we have the mind automatically utilising the emotions as a basis for thought. The main centre processing these energies is the Throat centre integrating *prāṇas* from the Solar Plexus centre. In the seven aspects of the emotional-mind the Solar Plexus centre (the *chakra* governing the emotional body) controls the engendering of all aspects of Watery thought. This centre controls all of the little emotional voices (*prāṇas*) generated via the minor *chakras* in the body. (The Inner Round.) These *prāṇas* demonstrate the alchemical attribute of Water. The Waters quickly swirl around the seed thought, obliterating any clear input of ideas. Amassed little ripples of fleeting emotional idealisms, swirling eddies of desire, strongly coloured whirlpools of desire images and those from the imagination, madly rushing animal-like emotive forces, all work to prevent rational thought. They immediately distort and cause lies, constituted of feeling-ideas, aspects of the imagination, to overwhelm the 'thinking' of the person concerned. There is a ubiquitous forceful Watery pull of emotional-mental *saṃskāras* collectively produced by the overwhelming majority of humans over many millennia of habitual activity. Vast is the turbulent emotional cesspool surrounding the human biosphere that yet needs to be cleansed by the collective compassionate activity of humanity.

The emotional-mind is an aspect of what I term *desire-mind (kāma-manas)* elsewhere. In desire-mind desire-emotions are the conditional factor of the mind, whereas in the mental-emotions the mind is the more dominant input. All emotional aspects of mind are generated by the personality will, which is the powerhouse of the Solar Plexus centre, the major centre of force in the average person. They are also consequently aspects (the lower reflex) of the sixth Ray of Devotion.

The emotions are considered animal-like, mainly because their related energies or qualities are likened to developed animal characteristics. (They were first evolved by members of the animal kingdom.) They are aspects of the animal kingdom sentience possessed by humans, whipped up by human passions, and seeded with the added qualities of aspects of mind. The qualities of mind are not attributes of the animal kingdom, but rather are what set humans apart from them. Buddhist philosophy often mixes the emotions and mind arbitrarily. This is an error, though somewhat rectified by the concept of *kliṣṭamanas,* necessitating Buddhists to think deeply concerning this subject if wisdom is to be truly theirs. For this reason the topic shall be elucidated throughout this treatise. The Hindu and Buddhist idea of transmigration has its truism in this field of animal-like emotions. In the far distant past the enlightened who presented the doctrine of transmigration gave a part truth, which was intended to be corrected in the then future.[36] (In the same manner we teach primary school children nowadays about sensitive subjects.)

Distortion	Governing Ray Quality
Racing hounds of mind	First Ray
Dog-like mental activity	Second Ray
Spider-like desire-mind	Third Ray
Slugs of mind	Fourth Ray
Monkey mind	Fifth Ray
Crabs of mind	Sixth Ray
Mouse-like mind	Seventh Ray

Table 2. The basic emotions of mind

Other animal-like qualities of the Solar Plexus centre, such as symbolised by sharks and crocodiles, embody vicissitudes of the emotions, seen from a different perspective, i.e., they are pure emotions. One could therefore further refine the listing below into an *iḍā* and *piṅgalā* stream of the emotions if desired.

Racing Hounds of mind. In the incessant howls of the hound, frantically endeavouring to assert its sound, the voice of the mind seeks to be heard by all around. The 'I' must quickly proffer its opinion before another may utter a sound. Scurrying through concepts, hurriedly overtaking another speaker with impetuous judgement, the hounds (the mind) search for the glory of acknowledgement. Perceiving a race, the fleeting thoughts strive to reach the finish first. Inevitably their run has been futile, for their perception has been void of depth, with little analytical insight. In the desire for quick accomplishment, impulsive thoughts hastily pace through thought processes, hence the cogent words of a teacher or another have not been heard, but what is thought

36 See my book *Karma and the Rebirth of Consciousness* for detail.

was said, projected instead. Quick emotional thought inevitably distorts the nature of what was sought. No clear comprehensive reason can be found in such a racing thinker. The ears have sped far past the sound to be heard and comprehended. An idea might be right, but the remainder fraught with error and shallow judgement, devoid of the multi-levelled meanings of the wise. Ineffectually understood are the concepts based on other's clear reason.

To develop profound insight the racing must stop, the hounds chained to a master's hands, and the meditative Mind cultivated, allied with the awakening Heart, working for causes far beyond the little self's desire for itself to look smart. What is required is the pervasive space of the patient blue of loving insight to transform the mind of the racing one into an ocean of calm serenity. When the mind is quietened by the student sacrificing his/her emotional desires and thoughts, then can better comprehension manifest and the teacher's words be truly heard. Wisdom comes only after the development of a quiescence in which the student is able to contemplate the impressions and visions from a vast realm of instantaneous revelation. When void of emotion one can logically reason through the most difficult conceptions and arguments.

Dog-like mental activity. This is the type of emotional mind that is obedient and subservient to all other aspects of mind. Those with this dog-like mind go out of their way to please others, often overriding what they know to be right so as to not offend. They use the emotions as a support or crux for their interrelations with people. The aim is to achieve popularity amongst their peers, and the mind is subordinated towards gaining frivolous pursuits that bring acclaim in the world, amongst family, friends, and in society in general. This produces much triviality and lazy basking in the sun of easy accomplishment that offers no real strain or challenges for the mind. It incorporates the lapping up words of praise, or being quick to be hurt, or offended at chastisement of any sort.

In the field of religion this type of person will be found to be accepting of whatever is the majority opinion, and no real effort will be put into gauging the true worth of any teaching; its truthfulness is simply accepted as a forgone conclusion. Shallow reasoning suffices, if that is what the others believe, or is asserted by the teacher to be correct. Some effort, however, may be made to gather together a wide range of opinions or teaching, because such broad knowledge helps to glorify the little self in the eyes of others. He greatly values group interrelationship, and would find it difficult if he had to leave the group, monastery, or community he belongs to, if forced to do so. He finds the emotional bond between his brethren therein being immensely appealing. It acts as a type of ambrosial drug sustaining his being.

The dog-like one must learn to totally forgo emotional ties as a reason for doing anything right, and to meditate alone with serene calm insight. Then *bodhicitta* will bring him to the Hierarchy of Light.

Spider-like desire-mind. Such people always plot and plan to be at the centre of their own web of emotional intrigue in whatever field of life they are in. They often use their intelligent input to criticise others, or the regime of which they are part, and are generally busily trying to control the events and situation around them to suit their little selves. Even if not outwardly manifesting thus, the mind is generally always active, emotionally responding to the trivialities of life, to what others may have said, to plot plans for revenge, or to achieve various aims. Though they may not actually carry out these fanciful desires, the images flood the mind of how they would like to act and become. They are always ready to move and to pounce with mental-emotions, if the possibility of reward of some type manifests, or if offended in some way.

Those in religious pursuits will generally weave their own personal philosophy out of whatever is presented to them, never quite satisfied with the presentation given. The flaws in their logic are rarely noticed, or quickly overlooked in order to prove a point. This they will proffer at all times with some rigour or force, to overwhelm the opinions of others. Consequently, the forceful (wrong) use of the mouth is one of their proficiencies. They can be patient, if a point needs to be made to their favour, or else are hypersensitive, impatient, quick to react to any slight tremor or threat perceived attacking their emotional armour, just like a spider on the web running out every time an insect causes the web to rapidly vibrate.

The spider at the centre of the web of life's intrigues must learn not to meddle in other's concerns, or to be involved in trivial pursuits. Instead the Lord of Life must be sought, to pierce through the veil that the web (*nāḍīs*) entails, to find the jewel in the heart of the lotus, thus liberating the mind, now at ease. The value of time must be properly comprehended so that the best possible outcome is achieved in all that is pursued. What is pursued has been rightly judged to produce enlightened rewards and great patience is developed to achieve this need.

Slugs of mind. Dragging his feet as he walks, the thinker opts to gaze lazily into one particular thought dreamily moving along any avenue of mind. Slowly do such slugs of thought meander, with no particular objective in sight. Many smaller slugs can be seeded by the overriding idea, losing themselves in different avenues in the mind. Thereby an inadequate, often confused, inaccurate understanding of a small segment of a greater whole is produced. The 'whole' being the entire discourse of a teacher, or any aspect of life one is involved in.

The slovenly thinker indolently chooses to stay in a meandering pit of idle ideas of his own making. Lacking any aspiration, or wish to move, the slugs of mind are content in the containment of their own lethargy, realising not the sense of urgency required for the battle of the forces of life. Continuously regurgitated, the thoughts pile upon other thoughts that require the least effort to maintain. Those that bemuse, are sensually driven, intoxicate or are glamour forming are the reveries pursued, whiling away a precious life, so quickly consumed. Such thinkers understand not the sequence of flow and inhibit the beauty of creativity with their refusal to vary the content of their activity. Engrossed in the hole or home of their own making, those with a sluggish mind reside in illusion, but are generally contented, as they know not how to stride through the gates of divine effulgence.

How to seize the opportunity to cultivate the penetrative, brilliant, dynamic forms of actively executing attentiveness must yet be learned by the bearers of all sluggish forms of mind. The mind must be vitalised with invigorated receptivity to enlightening ideas, enlivening it into an energised manifestation. Alert, the mind can then conceptualise the thoughts streaming through a divine thinker, to be the enlightened one incarnate, meditatively absorbed in the Heart of all that is to be. Striding at a higher pace, the natural flow of the meditation-Mind is thus pursued.

Monkey mind. It wistfully chatters away, wasting time in a futility of the barrage of little thoughts. There is little concern in the mind of the monkey as to what is good and right for the all. It is pleased to play in the mire of the illusion that around it abounds, continuously grabbing this and that alluring fruit of desire that happens to attract its eye. In thinking incessantly about these objects (of desire), or belittling small talk and criticisms, the big or true issues of life pass it by. Incessantly it plays with its toys for pleasure, hearing little of what an enlightened one has said. Often thereby denigrating the worth of that one and his/her words, because they appeal not to the monkey mind's glamoured play. The thoughts are so glazed and soppy with emotion, that the monkey-like one is blinded to the need, to the opportune advice, or wisdom that could be received. Thus ignorance is continuously perpetuated. The monkey realises not that the teacher is indeed a precious bestower of treasure, revealing the nature of ignorance, and is the saving grace of those thus bound to form, wherein lies the inevitable pain that such attachment must bring. Clear pristine logic escapes the monkey mind's ilk.

Preoccupied with itself and the objects of *māyā*, the monkey deprives itself of much in its quest for futile appeasement of the insatiable emotions. Scattered fragments of mind are its myriad thoughts, and so it realises not the force that is required for it to ensue upon the path of intended purpose. Complete liberation and enlightenment is not a fruit to be grasped in its busy schedule. Specifically required in the mind of the monkey is thus the red fiery Will of enlightened purpose. Such a one is impelled with the valiant dynamic energy to stride towards something greater than self amusement and gratification. Spiritual evolution by serving the entire human race with logical sequences of thought and the corresponding actions must be wrought from out of the jungles of all petty concern. Speaking to the monkeys I say, 'Invoke the will to command; the Will-to-Love, and the desire to serve. Cease your chattering activity, and step forth to the glory of an enlightening Mind. Thus henceforth I heartily commend you the great awakening, it shall be yours. Oṁ'.

Crabs of mind. Overt uncontrolled sensitivity is the keynote here. Such beings are always reaching out for emotional succour from others, and if this is not obtained then they are quick to retreat into the shell of their own disdain or pain. They can thus overreach themselves emotionally in order to please, putting much emotional energy into their concept of loving interaction, and if the expected rewards are not there then their response can be one of extreme anger (lashing out at the other) or self-pity (retreating into the hell state of their own making).

Fearfulness of life's challenges always looms in the crab's demeanour, if earlier a claw of attachment to a *saṃsāric* allurement was broken. Thus we have all forms of emotional extremes.

The crab-like ones in the field of religion can be exceedingly devotional, latching on to the words of the teacher, as if each word was 'manna from heaven'. They thus become extremely attached, but gain no real in-depth analysis of what is taught. Glamorous, superficial teachings will generally suffice, easy to follow and to apply without many demands upon thought. The religious zealot thereby has his day, the dogmatist his way, because emotional extremism also means the most narrow-minded intensity of thought. It proffers the sacrifice of one's all for the thinnest of logical structures, if it offers quick reward. The crab will happily lose its claw rather than let go of that which it desires most, as it tenaciously hangs on to a cherished thought or desire structure, easily dismissing proof of errors in its beliefs.

Devotion must be rightly tempered with deep analysis if this crab-like one is to receive life's enlightened reward. Right aspiration becomes the mode of achievement or travel where once continuous desire-impulse held sway (which karmically ruins each and every day). The Eightfold Path to enlightenment can then be trod with ease.

Mouse-like mind. Fearfulness and worrying anxieties to all of life's problems often rules such a one. Timidly it selects manageable activities in its forays into the domain of massed emotional-mental swirls. The belly of its concern is filled with little bits of emotionality from which to learn. Ritualistically each quanta of information is gathered until its larder is full and it need not foray out again until it has all been consumed. Then again it must venture out of its sanctuary to search for its needs to be met. The images of the complexities in the world loom large in its mind, and it fears them too difficult to seize, too fearful of the outcome, so new ventures to learn are often omitted.

Life for such a one appears too short, and his placing in the world too small, for him to be valiant enough to offer contentious opinions and stick by them for whatever they are worth. He is often overwhelmed by the logical declarations of teachers and peers, especially if assertively made. To them he kowtows, but he's always a good sport.

Spiritually his silence is held, but little things he learns and can know them well, staying lowly in the background of the teacher's group.

He must grow in size to become an elephant, and learn to command in wisdom, strength, and in might the sum of the material domain. No anxieties at all, he can trumpet the call of his mastery of the far reaches of *saṃsāra* to the All.

Meditation and the emotions

Desire-mind is the most problematic of all aspects of the human conditioning, being the basis of massed cupidity, selfishness, sexual infatuations and sensual desire-filled pursuits of all types. It is currently pandemic in our societies. It presents the most serious obstacles for meditators because people think as they desire. Desire based attributes keep one tied to the centres below the diaphragm, preventing compassionate activity that awakens the Heart centre, marring meditative impressions with images of the objects of desire. Low quality thoughts, sickness producing energies and distractions of all kinds are enemies to the developing Mind. The mental-emotions and the emotional-mind must be denied, to awaken the serene expanse of the all-encompassing Mind.

Chimera-like images of all types are attracted to the meditator from the whirlpool and reservoir of all desire and thought-forms created by humanity throughout the ages. The meditator must transform the attributes of debased energy qualifications that would attract the chimeras of past emotional dispositions. No subtle impressions from high strata of revelations can be attracted to the whirlpools of a distracted mind. To quieten the mind necessitates overcoming and transforming the *saṃskāras* of desire and emotions of every kind. Thoughts are real things and have power in the domains of the mind, and subtle thoughts seed the vast expanse of all-Knowing. Subtle thoughts are awakened when self-focus and the desirous are abandoned.

Meditators are usually taught to either concentrate their thoughts following a prescribed procedure, or eliminate all thought processes whatsoever. According to the method applied they either set up a force vortex of thought energy, or else they produce a receptive state of mind. In either case they can attract to themselves thoughts and related energies from the general reservoir of ideas.

In the first case what is attracted is in the nature and quality of the thought engendered or projected, according to the intensity and power of the thought sent (whether by means of mantras, visualisation, or intense concentration). Strong well-developed thoughts often attract others of a similar nature when they reach out to a vast extent in space. Such thoughts also quickly impregnate their target, and will also repel thoughts that are of differing quality. Weakly developed thoughts on the other hand rarely repel extraneously engendered images, and do not travel far from the thinker.

In the case of those that produce a receptive mind, passivity can allow any passing thought, either from the subconscious, or from the thought-forms in the thought atmosphere, to enter into the consciousness. Pliable minds can easily be impressed by the strong thought currents of powerful dominant minds, specifically by those in possession of knowledge of the laws of thought transmission. Also, very strong collectivised thoughts, such as the images of Deity, the Christ, Krishna, the Buddha, engendered by thousands of devotional minds can be attracted, and often are, to those desirous of such impressions.

We see therefore, that control of all conscious or subconscious thoughts and desires are important in meditation. If the laws of thought-form production are not comprehended then one can attract unwanted entities (that can project images into the meditation), other thoughts can also enter from the pool of subconscious desire, or from higher sources that pertain to the real, manifesting in the form of instructions via the images imparted. That however, pertaining to enlightenment, generally necessitates comprehension of the domains of the meditation-Mind.

Only when students of meditation end fruitless emotional thinking, freeing themselves from the generation of imaginative idealisms, can progress be made in cogently conceptualising the teachings of the enlightened ones. When the mind is still and receptive, freed from emotion, then the inner hearing can be awakened and the ear-whispered teachings from the formless realms can be heard. Even subtle desires will distort the impressions and can block the door from whence enlightened impressions come. The teachings from enlightened beings will be heard by residing in the Heart's Mind. Therein manifests the double-edged sword, both quiescent and active, that can be used to cut asunder impediments to the path and to pierce the veils to liberation. Thus is the wisdom generated to produce the spiritual advancement of humanity, the planet, and the All. The process continues inwards, upwards and outwards into cosmos, beyond all incessantly appearing, disappearing, and expanding forms in the universe.

Such a sword-bearer becomes consciously adept at wielding the energies of the integrated all-embracive Heart and dynamic Mind. The person can then cut him/herself free from all animal-like aspects, and become truly human, a divine thinker, able to penetrate the realms above and beyond. One becomes radiant, a magnanimous lover of the All, unlimited by form—absorbed in the Thusness of the Dharmakāya Way.

An example of the Rays in a Buddhist text

The emanations of light associated with the wisdoms of the five Dhyāni Buddhas are well known by Mahāyāna Buddhists. They are a version of the expression of the Rays of Mind (from the third to the seventh Rays). The seven Ray qualities explained in Volume 1 are, however, unnoticed by commentators of Buddhist texts, despite the fact that there are many such listings therein. Buddhists have yet to grow accustomed to view their philosophy in such terms. An example of a listing of the seven Rays, for instance, can be found in the book by Dudjom Rinpoche with respect to the *sambhogakāya* aspect of Buddhas:

> This buddha-body of rapture, the teacher who holds sway over these fields, is also endowed with seven particular attributes of natural expression. These are, namely: the natural expression which has fully matured in the nature of just what is; the natural expression which is spontaneously present without seeking for enlightened attributes; the natural expression which is pristine cognition without extremes or centre; the natural expression which, even though the result be mastered, does not reveal its true essence [i.e. it manifests only in and of itself]; the natural expression which, even when sameness has been disclosed, remains free from the range of objective qualification; the natural expression which is liberated from [concepts of] one and many; and the natural expression which is without conjunction and disjunction throughout the three times.[37]

When looking at the quote with respect to the seven Rays it can be analysed as such:

37 Dudjom Rinpoche, Jikdrel Yeshe Dorje, *The Nyingma School of Tibetan Buddhism. Its Fundamentals and History.* Translated and edited by Gyurme Dorje and Matthew Kapstein, (Wisdom Publications, Boston, 1991), 124.

1. *'The natural expression which has fully matured in the nature of just what is.'* This sentence relates to the first Ray of Will or Power because this highest, most intense, rarefied of the Rays governs what abides in its 'fully matured' natural state, and thus the inherent attributes of all that 'just what is'. The first Ray is the abstracted refined potency of the Rays, the synthesis of all the others, and this is 'just what is'. From this state all that is cognisable emanates. It is the necessary energy to be developed if the will to overcome all phenomena is to produce the result of the reality of 'what is'. The colour of this Ray is red.
2. *'The natural expression which is spontaneously present without seeking for enlightened attributes.'* There is no need to seek 'enlightened attributes' for those who embody the qualities of the second Ray of Love-Wisdom because they are already fully endowed with such attributes. This Ray is 'spontaneously present' because Love is that which sustains the synergetic integrity and unity of the entire universe of being/non-being. Consequently it becomes the base nature of all Bodhisattvas, while wisdom is what is evolved via intelligence when coupled with love on the journey to Buddhahood. The colour of this Ray is indigo-blue.
3. *'The natural expression which is pristine cognition without extremes or centre'* refers to the third Ray of enlightening Mathematically Exact Activity, because this form of intelligence can be defined as 'pristine cognition' that mathematically delineates all that is and is to be according to the *maṇḍalas* of expression that all things must form a part of. *Maṇḍalas* have boundaries (thus extremes) and a centre, from which the constitution of the *maṇḍala* emanates, but this natural primordial Mind does not, because it extends beyond the bounds of conceptualised things. It is consequently the source for the formulations of *maṇḍalic* constructs. The colour of this Ray is emerald green.
4. *'The natural expression which, even though the result be mastered, does not reveal its true essence [i.e., it manifests only in and of itself].'* This is an apt description of the nature of the fourth Ray of Beautifying Harmony overcoming Conflict, which being the central Ray, tends to harmonise all forms of extremes, through the

act of mastering disharmonious attributes. It then acts as a mirror, and is thus the epitome of the Mirror-like Wisdom that reflects the higher qualities of the *dharmadhātu* into the realms of *saṃsāra*. For this function it is a 'natural expression' that cannot reveal its 'true essence' *(śūnyatā)* to corporeal minds, which manifests 'only in and of itself'. This essence must be clear and void of attributes, so as to be able to reflect the extremes (the real and the unreal) into each other's domain and to harmonise them. Via this mechanism one can thus view all things as they truly are in their 'natural state'. The colour of this Ray is yellow.

5. *'The natural expression which, even when sameness has been disclosed, remains free from the range of objective qualification.'* This refers to the fifth Ray of Scientific Aptitude. Here we have 'the natural expression' of the higher abstract Mind exemplified, which works via a spontaneous, deeply perceptive, analytical meditative concentration to disclose 'sameness' in the face of the manifold diversity of *saṃsāric* phenomena. Such an enlightened Mind held steady, stilled, and poised in dynamic concentration, 'remains free from the range of objective qualification'. Objective qualifications are a product of the empirical mind, also governed by this Ray. The colour of this Ray is orange.
6. *'The natural expression which is liberated from [concepts of] one and many.'* This refers to the sixth Ray of Devotion, as the aspect of devotion automatically separates into 'one and many' because the devotee thinks of that which he/she is devoted to in relation to him/herself, and to the other, or others. However, the true nature of this Ray expression is to integrate the many into the One (non-discursive type of thought, for instance) that is the objective of devotion. The devotee becomes the *yidam,*[38] and later becomes at one with the Tathāgata-Mind. The colour of this Ray is pink.
7. *'The natural expression which is without conjunction and disjunction throughout the three times.'* This is an expression of the seventh Ray of Ceremonial Activity, and of Demonstrable Power, which rightfully governs physical plane involvement wherein the three

38 A personal tutelary deity, the root of accomplishment.

times hold sway over everyday activities in a cyclic manner. Here *saṃskāras* come and go in rightly ordered sequences. When the *yogin* has discovered the nature of this cyclic rhythmic flow then the process of karmic manifestation can be controlled and not it him/her. There will then be no 'conjunction and disjunction throughout the three times' for the person. The colour of this Ray is violet.

The symbolism of the eye

Some teachings have been presented in Buddhist literature concerning the doctrine of the eye. Even though this doctrine has been presented by enlightened ones, a significant portion of this most esoteric subject has been veiled. However, if the astute meditate upon it much revelation can be gained. Wayman presents a good summary of this subject in his book *Buddhist Insight*:

> The three eyes are well-known in Pāli literature as the eye of flesh *(maṃsacakkhu)*, the divine eye *(dibbacakkhu)*, and the eye of insight *(paññācakkhu)*. Falk has discussed these eyes in terms of the bodies which they respectively see. The eye of flesh sees the *rūpa*-personality, the divine eye sees the *manomayakāya* ("body made of mind"), and the eye of insight "sees" Nirvāṇa. She understands from her study of Pāli literature that these eyes constitute the successive spheres or fruits of the Buddhist ascension treated in the three instructions, respectively of morality (*sīla*), meditation *(samādhi)*, and insight *(paññā)*.
>
> The five eyes are an expansion in Mahāyāna Sanskrit works of the original three *(maṃsa-, divya-,* and *prajñā-cakṣus)*. The two that are added are the eye of *dharma* and the Buddha eye....[39]
>
> A complete explanation of the five eyes from the *Yogācāra* standpoint is in Sthiramati's commentary on the *Mahāyāna-sūtrālaṃkāra* (Bodhipakṣya chapter) from which the essentials are given here:
>
> a. The eye of flesh sees forms in present time.
>
> b. The divine eye is of two kinds, both seeing forms in past and future: (1) that born of past action (*karma*), the eye of the gods; and (2) that born of contemplation (*bhāvanā)* in the *samādhi* of a yogin, and which sees the sentient beings passing away from here and going to various destinies in accordance with past actions.

39 Alex Wayman, *Buddhist Insight,* (Motilal Banarsidass, Delhi, 1990), 155.

c. The eye of insight is the non-discursive knowledge which understands the individual and the general characteristic of the *dharmas*, seeing them in the absolute sense *(paramārthatas).*

d. The eye of *dharma* understands without impediment all the scripture, understands the stream of consciousness of persons in the sense of discriminating whether it is an ordinary person, or one of the eight classes of disciples (on the four paths or in the fruits of the four paths), or a Bodhisattva and if so then on which of the ten Bodhisattva stages; and seeing the *dharmas* in the conventional sense *(saṃvṛtitas).*

e. The eye of a Buddha understands all *dharmas*, whether with or without flux, whether constructed or unconstructed; and realizes directly every knowable field; understands the state of Arhat ensuing from the "diamond-like *samādhi*" and the freedom from the fluxes of the Tathāgatas.[40]

Edwin Bernbaum states also:

> Tibetan mysticism distinguishes five different "eyes" or degrees of awareness that one can acquire through the practice of meditation. An ordinary person has only one, the "water eye," which sees the world as it appears to most people in their usual state of delusion. As a yogi purifies his mind through meditation, his vision becomes more acute and he gains in turn: the "flesh eye," which sees a distance of eighteen days' walk away; the "god eye," which reveals hidden things and places; the "wisdom eye," which can penetrate into other minds and know everything there is to know; and the "Buddha eye" which discerns the ultimate nature of reality. The third eye that commonly appears on the foreheads of images and paintings of Bodhisattvas indicates that they possess the wisdom eye of spiritual insight.[41]

From the above we can glean that the *'eye of flesh'* or *'water* eye' refers to the physical eyes and the form of sensory input relating to the intellect and its development.

The *'divine eye'* refers at first to the 'eye' of the awakened Solar Plexus centre (*maṇipūra chakra)* from whence all psychic, clairvoyant impressions derive. It thus provides vision of the after-death state (the

---

40 Ibid., 156-157.

41 Edwin Bernbaum, *The Way to Shambhala,* (Anchor Books, New York, 1980), 38-39.

astral plane) and realms of the associated entities, as well as of the psychic states of a human being. Technically it refers to the functioning of any of the *chakras* below the diaphragm, as ruled by the *maṇipūra*. Therefore that which is 'born of past action (*karma*), the eye of the gods' refers to the awakening of the lower *siddhis* associated with the centres below the diaphragm.

The eye *'born of contemplation'* however refers to the process associated with the liberation of *kuṇḍalinī* and the awakening of the Ājñā centre. Though all of the *chakras* can in fact be viewed as eyes, the Ājñā centre regulates and integrates their activities, hence it is called the all-seeing Eye. It is the *eye* developed in 'the *samādhi* of a yogin'.

The *'eye of insight'* refers to the properties of the awakened Heart *chakra*. Thus it is with the awakened Heart that all attributes of the *dharma* can be perceived, as this is the centre that directs the energy of *bodhicitta*. Hence it is the motivating centre for all Bodhisattvic activity. The qualities of this *chakra* will be elaborated upon in Volumes 3 and 5A.

The *'eye of the dharma'* (the *'wisdom eye')* is what I depict as the Śūnyatā Eye, and which is found at the centre of the *tathāgatagarbha* (which will be explained in Volume 3 of this *Treatise on Mind)*. From another (lower) perspective it can be inferred to be the Ājñā centre.

The *'eye of a Buddha'* is the Dharmakāya Eye that allows a Buddha to interrelate with and direct the events and phenomena of *saṃsāra* if need be. It also allows multidirectional visioning in cosmos.

The subtle mechanism of an Eye, which the *chakras* manifest as, allows interrelation between beings in the multidimensional universe. The Eye mediates between the abstract and the phenomenal worlds. It embodies the essence of the past and seeds the future divinity. In its floral permutations it is the ideal form that consciousness takes, allowing all consciousness-impressions throughout the three times to be registered. This function makes an evolving entity Divine. Such an Eye manifests as the form of the *tathāgatagarbha,* that is the *Buddha-germ* within us. This 'germ' is an embodied flux of conscious receptivity incorporated into a form that can relate the transcendental to the corporeal, wherein the purpose of the ocean of being can be focussed upon the unit of consciousness (that is the incarnate person). It allows the interrelation between these two without destruction of the latter, and the abnegation of the purposes of existence, and produces an aperture, or door of release for the awakening consciousness of the personality to enter into vistas unknown.

Essentially here is indicated the nature of the form that can be understood to *en-soul* consciousness. Existing in the form of an Eye, and being composed of the substance of mind/Mind, it allows light of different frequencies and of great intensity to move from the highest expression of *saṃsāra* to and from the veil of *śūnyatā* in order to modify mundane activity. Light alone can conquer the darkness of ignorance (which is the *upādhi*[42] of the twelve-fold cycle of Dependent Origination, thus of the reincarnation process). Light is the substance of the Mind that is the wisdom of the Buddhas. (Every Buddha and Bodhisattva in Buddhist art is thus surrounded by auras of different emanations of light.) Greater intensities of light are evolved as consciousness moves from life to life. Thus that which can be viewed as a soul or container of consciousness manifests in the form of an Eye. It can also be delineated as a radiant Sun. Only such a Sun could emanate the type of light evolved by Bodhisattvas and Buddhas, whilst the mechanism of the Eye regulates the amount of the light that can pass through from one sphere to another.

The I-consciousness (as the *tathāgatagarbha)* exists as a causal or subjective form constituted of lighted substance that stands as the Eye of the *dharmakāya* (the Divine), allowing light to manifest in a two-way mode. This Eye thus becomes the mediator or mirror between the abstract and the phenomenal. Though the idea of such an existing form may be difficult for Buddhists to concede as a truth because of their staunch denial of such a form for the past two millennia, other than in the veiled form of a *tathāgatagarbha,* nevertheless, what was formerly veiled shall be revealed and fully detailed in Volume 3. Such information will contradict, for instance, the Prāsaṅgika argument given in Volume 1 that: 'The self does not act as the base of the aggregates like a bowl for yogurt or like snow that exists throughout and surrounds a forest of trees'. This subtle form of 'self', viewed as an en-souling principle, or Eye, acts as a base for the aggregates in the sense that

42 *Upādhi,* vehicle, the material basis or carrier of something less material than itself. Also that which limits something.

without it the aggregates could not be collated together and sorted out in a manner that allows the right *saṃskāras (karma)* to be utilised by any particular incarnation of an evolving personal-I. The sum total of the past aggregates must be stored in some way, otherwise they would disappear into an amorphous sea of such energies, producing a type of chaos from which no evolution of anything whatsoever could be possible. So if we view the 'yogurt' as the sum total of the *skandhas* and *saṃskāras* of all past incarnations of any particular evolving person, then a container in the field of consciousness indeed must exist for their organised retrieval.[43]

Such a container must be constituted of the substance of consciousness, of light itself, and be capable of being modified in accord with the energy input thereto. Thus the quality of the light presented is what constitutes the intensity of the container. Just as different containers are needed for the heat of an industrial strength furnace, a nuclear reactor, or for a kerosene flame, so it is for consciousness states. A relatively dull form of light (taking the expression of various *saṃskāras*) can be contained by a far more intense form of consciousness-light that gradually works upon the dullness in order to transform it into a higher energy state. This represents the mode of the form of activity of the *tathāgatagarbha,* and all Bodhisattvas. It is the way of evolution to the domain of all enlightened beings.

Note also the statement presented by Alex and Hideko Wayman:

> The *Mahābherīhāraka-sūtra* (Narthang Kg. Mdo, Tsa, 183b-2) holds that defilements distort this experiencing power: "Just as a film over a man's eyes gives a yellow or blue obscuration, so it is with defilements. The embryo of the Tathāgata is certainly like an eye."[44]

A physicist may argue that the more intense the container of consciousness-light, the greater the proclivity to lose some of its energy. This may be true, if likened to a sun, which lights up the earth and sustains all evolutionary growth therein as a consequence. However,

---

43 The technical term for such a construct will be labelled the Sambhogakāya Flower when the doctrine concerning the nature of the *chakras* is also integrated.

44 Alex and Hideko Wayman, *The Lion's Roar of Queen Śrīmālā,* (Motilal Banarsidass Publishers, Delhi, 1990), 49.

the return of lighted substance developed by the conscious refinement of *saṃskāras* is capable of producing a greater amount of light than the input needed to seed a new born personal-I.[45] The originating light is caused to grow in intensity and transformed over time. This happens as a consequence of sensory input to the brain consciousness, and the working by the lighted substance of consciousness upon that input over the course of a lifetime. The attributes *(saṃskāras)* of many lifetimes of such accomplishment are absorbed by the *tathāgatagarbha* ('embryo of the Tathāgata') in a similar way that an eye incorporates light. This 'lighted container' then sheds light upon the personal-I by directing the *saṃskāras* to be experienced in such a way that evolution is possible. The attributes of consciousness can be refined to the degree that it allows illumination and the intuition to manifest in the form of *bodhicitta* and wisdom. These qualities are seeded from the 'container' of consciousness-light, with en-light-enment being the inevitable result.

It can then be argued that 'the self and the aggregates' would not inherently be different, if we take 'the self' here to refer to the I-consciousness, and if we view it all in terms of a process of change of one form of light (the relative darkness of ignorance) into another more intense form of light. Our concern is therefore with differing degrees of the intensity of light. This form eventually radiates out as the radiance or auric emanation of a Bodhisattva or Buddha. The aggregates, however, are different from the perspective of a snapshot in time, when the nature of the aggregates possessed by a personal-I is compared relative to their transformed aspects in the I-consciousness. The aggregates equilibrate at the attainment of enlightenment by the personal-I. The process of change manifests in *saṃsāra,* and the consequence, the radiance of a Buddha, may be viewed as steadfast, changeless, in *saṃsāra,* but in *dharmakāya* it obeys the dynamics of different subtler laws. Much yet needs to be revealed concerning the *dharmakāyic* view for those that are developing the Eyes to see.

---

45 The light body of this radiant form has consequently increased in intensity over many epochs of incarnatory expression. There is also an intense autoluminous energy source emanating via the Śūnyatā Eye of the Sambhogakāya Flower *(tathāgatagarbha).*

2

The Soul Concept and the Tathāgatagarbha Doctrine

The *tathāgatagarbha* doctrine

A soul form can be considered an aspect of the *sambhogakāya,* the body of perfected endowment that is the subtle body of a Buddha or Bodhisattva, once the doctrine of the *trikāya* of a Buddha is properly comprehended. This can also refer to the Buddha nature that is inherent in everyone and which is our destined fulfilment. What exactly this inherent Buddha nature (*tathāgatagarbha*—the Tathāgata embryo) is that all human units are said to possess is not properly explained in Buddhist texts. We are not told how it functions with respect to the evolving personal-I from life to life, and what causes it to appear and to evolve into a fully realised Tathāgata. A reason for this is that if analysed properly the doctrine leads us directly to a concept of a 'soul' for each human unit.

A *soul* can be defined as a quantified abstracted sphere of consciousness which embodies the essence of the past and is the seed of future enlightenment for any sequence of evolving personal-I's, whose purpose it directs. It is the divinity incorporated within the evolving incarnate entity as an ideal form in a continuum of time and space, throughout the births and deaths of successive generations of such entities, which it directs in a way so that eventually liberation from form can be obtained. It is an embodied flux of conscious receptivity incorporated into a form that can relate the transcendental to the corporeal, wherein the ocean of being/non-being and the unit of consciousness (that is the incarnate person) can interrelate without the destruction of the latter, and the abnegation of the purposes of existence. Such a *soul* then is a *tathāgatagarbha,* the true unity that is the rebirthing principle, a conscious aspect of the ocean of being/non-being, without which the attainment of Buddhahood for an incarnate personal-I would be impossible. Essentially, a soul is a radiant sun of conscious receptivity that embodies the Heart of the life or *purpose* of an incarnate consciousness which evolves through successive rebirths via forms from which experiential data can be derived.

S.K. Hookham states:

> One of the most characteristic and probably the most controversial aspects of the Tathagatagarbha doctrine is the many references in Tathagatagarbha Sutras to the True Self or Self Paramita.
>
> The word "self" used in this context embarrasses many Buddhists, Eastern and Western, ancient and modern. This has led to tortuous translations of the simple word *"atman"* in order to avoid the taboo word "self." For example, Jikido Takasaki [Study 207] translates it as "unity" and elsewhere as "ego"; K. Holmes [*The Changeless Nature*] and Ming Wood [*Journal of the American Oriental Society* vol. 5 no.2:82] translate it as "identity"; Mahathera Nyanatiloka [*Path to Deliverance*] translates it as "personal" and "personality."
>
> In spite of all this, the most obvious and accurate translation is "self" as defined in the SOED:[1] "That which in a person is really and intrinsically he (in contradistinction to what is adventitious)." This is acceptable provided that the pronoun "he" here is understood to mean what a person intrinsically is, and not what a person is in contradistinction to anyone else...[2]
>
> In the *Pali Canon,* the Buddha takes as given that the self has the characteristics of permanence, independence, and freedom from suffering. He then proceeds to establish that these qualities are not to be found in any conditioned phenomena *(sabbe dhamma anatta).* He does not go so far as to say that there is no self at all, nor does he say there is one. However, he does say that Nirvana is permanence, non-conditioned (i.e., independent), and freedom from suffering; the

1 Shorter Oxford English Dictionary.

2 S.K. Hookham, *The Buddha Within: Tathagatagarbha Doctrine According to the Shentong Interpretation of the Ratnagotravibhaga,* (Sri Satguru Publications, 1992), 100-101.

> characteristics of the very self that all the dharmas do not have...[3]
>
> The Self that is taught in the Tathagatagarbha Sutras is not dualistic consciousness (vijnana), which is one of the skandhas and so by definition adventitious. That is why it is best to avoid the term "ego" as a translation for *"atman"* in spite of the fact that many Westerners favour its use. The reason "ego" is confusing is that it is defined [SOED] as "conscious thinking subject as opposed to the not-ego or object." Thus, it definitely implies a dualistic frame of mind...[4]
>
> It is the clinging to this nonexistent self that has to be abandoned, not a healthy sense of identity. Therefore, it is confusing to translate not-self *(anatman)* as not-ego. Furthermore, the Self of the Tathagatagarbha Sutras is the truly existent self in the SOED sense. It has the characteristics of Ultimate Reality and it would be a great mistake to translate this as "ego."[5]

The only reason why such an inclusion in the *Tathāgatagarbha Sūtras* of the word *ātman* would embarrass Buddhists, 'Eastern and Western, ancient and modern', is because they are not enlightened, and have been indoctrinated into rigid canonical syllogisms and logic that evolved in a different way than what the founders of the *tathāgatagarbha* teachings knew and taught. This canon was then concretised in such a way that those that might hold differing opinions to it (especially concerning this issue) were ostracised, or else quickly dismissed by their peers as 'unworthy of being Buddhists'. They manifested a heresy and were enticed to quickly amend their ways, even though they had the Buddha on their side, who would not outrightly condemn the doctrine of 'self'. They also had many of the doctrines already introduced that were logically presented in the early days of Buddhism.

The fact was that the extremism of 'no-self' was promulgated so as to be exclusive of any concept of 'self', no matter how subtle or logical, and the fanaticism was made to appear as if that was the authentic 'middle way' teachings of the Buddha. There is of course truth in this concept of 'no-self' (as already explained) and also *non-truth*, which in all of his inestimable wisdom the Buddha also demonstrated by his silence thereto.

---

3 Ibid., 101.

4 Ibid., 102.

5 Ibid.

It was a silence that his lesser successors could not maintain and hence aberrations in the *dharma* occurred. The truth concerning an *ātman* concept, as hinted at by the Buddha and in the *Tathāgatagarbha Sūtras*, is that a concept of 'soul' lay somewhere in between the Brahmanical assertions, and outright rejection of such a concept at all. Being deemed heretical, the logic concerning the nature of such a 'self' could not thus be revealed from then on. Now however, what this *tathāgatagarbha* is can be properly explored, and the revelation of this truth should unseat the heresy-makers from their positions of power as custodians of the *buddhadharma*. Theirs is not the last word in this respect.

Hookham's condemnation of the use of the word 'ego' for translation of the 'self' as found in the *Tathāgatagarbha Sūtras* is quite correct; as it can only be used if the word 'self' or *ātman* is used to translate concepts related to the intellect or personal-I, as I have defined it.

Concerning the *tathāgatagarbha* Brown states that:

> The *Tathāgatagarbha* is not to be understood as the object of a knowledge external to it, existing formally and formerly outside it; it is rather, self-explicating knowledge itself. The embryo as realized Absolute Body is simultaneously comprehended and comprehending; it is the point where the embryo knows itself as it is inherently in itself, as empty *(śūnya)* of all the defilement stores, but not empty *(aśūnya)* of the innumerable Buddha natures. If it is originally understood as an object of faith, and therefore an object of consciousness, the *Tathāgatagarbha* must ultimately be considered as the movement towards its perfect self-realization and thus, as object of self-consciousness[6]...The relationship between the *Tathāgatagarbha* and the *Dharmakāya* is that of a cycle that presupposes its beginning and reaches its beginning only at its end. If the Tathāgata-embryo is the beginning or cause, then the Absolute Body is essentially the result, the end where the Tathāgata-embryo becomes what it is in truth. The nature of the embryo is to be actual, that which becomes itself. For if it starts with itself, the *Tathāgatagarbha* reaches its consummation with itself as the Absolute Body *(Dharmakāya)* and in fact the *Dharmakāya* is the *Tathāgatagarbha* when it has not yet freed itself from the adventitious defilements, i.e., when it has not yet attained full self-conscious awareness as being intrinsically and always free

6 Brian Edward Brown, *The Buddha Nature,* (Motilal Banarsidass, Delhi, 2004), xvi.

of them. The cyclic transformation then of the *Tathāgatagarbha* into the *Dharmakāya* is that of an original absolute becoming fully self-expressive, where the only transition is in the sphere of self-exposition from hiddenness to manifestation....[7]

The *Śrī-Mālā*[8] generally emphasized the *garbha* as process, the self-evolutive potentiality of the embryo to become itself as *Dharmakāya*, the *śāstra*[9] discusses the identity of those two poles as ontological antecedent, i.e., though linguistically different *Tathāgatagarbha* and *Dharmakāya* are identical. The two terms simply reflect different modalities of Absolute Suchness *(Tathatā). Samalā Tathatā* represents Absolute Suchness under conditions of phenomenal defilement, and thus is synonymous with the *Tathāgatagarbha,* while *Nirmalā Tathatā* designates its actual freedom from all concealment, and is equivalent to the *Dharmakāya.* Through the threefold hermeneutic of *Dharmakāya* as universal penetration of wisdom, of *Tathatā* as the inherent purity of phenomena, and of *Gotra* as the germinal essence of Buddhahood, the chapter analyzes the axiom that "all living beings are possessed of the Tathāgatagarbha", i.e., are capable of attaining the omniscient wisdom of supreme enlightenment...[10]

Brown further states that:

But in general, the interpretation of "matrix" (whether it be from a biological standpoint, and therefore connoting "womb," or from a metallurgic one, and thus translating as a "gangue" in which rock fragments are embedded) suggests a container, something which holds something else. This would seem to miss entirely the dynamic, self-transformative nature of the *Tathāgatagarbha*[11]....the Tibetan equivalent of *Tathāgatagarbha (de bzin gsegs pa'i sñiṅ po)* could never be translated as "womb" *(mṅal or lhums),* but is more properly rendered, "embryonic essence," "kernel" or "heart."[12]

7 Ibid., xvi-xvii.

8 *Śrī-Mālādevīsimhanāda-sūtra.*

9 *Ratnagotravibāga śāstra.*

10 Brown, xvii.

11 Ibid., 44.

12 Ibid., 45.

Each of the three renderings of the term *tathāgatagarbha* are inadequate to the task of conveying its meaning, but together they present a considerable depiction of its functioning.

As a *'womb'* the *tathāgatagarbha* contains all of the qualities or forces whereby the enlightenment-consciousness can be found. This concerns the entire Flower as a unit.

As a *'seed'* it embodies the potential of all that is to come, as is found in the Śūnyatā Eye's constitution and function, via which the *dharmakāya* can manifest.

As a *'matrix'* it contains the substance whereby the *bījas* can sprout the consciousness qualities associated with them, so that enlightenment can be developed by any functioning personal-I. This represents the substance contained by the Flower, of all the *bījas* of the *skandhas* and *saṃskāras* held in the consciousness-stream contained within its form.

All of these three forms possess the innate ability to 'create', to cause something to appear, to make it grow.

Concerning the word *tathatā* Paul J. Griffiths states:

> One of the digests says that "Buddha's defining characteristic is the purification of the actuality of all things from the two obstacles: those of affliction and those which obstruct objects of awareness" *(kleśajñeyāvaraṇadvayāt sarvadhamatathatāviśuddhilakṣaṇaḥ.)*[13] The technical term 'actuality' *(tathatā)* is the key here. It is an abstract noun denoting the way things really are, the true nature of things, and it is frequently used in the digests as a synonym for Buddha or Buddhahood; the most common glosses on the term emphasize its unchangeability, using terms such as 'permanent' *(nitya),* or 'not subject to change' *(avikāra),* though there are some glosses that emphasize not so much its permanence as its accurate mirroring or reflection of the way things are. But even where actuality's unchangeability is stressed, it would be wrong to identify this unchangeability as a property of a monastic absolute—even though some of the language used about it sounds as though it should be understood in some such sense. Rather, phrases like "the actuality of everything" refer to those properties that all reals *(dharma),* according to Buddhist metaphysics, possess simply in virtue of being real. These are the *sāmānyalakṣaṇāni,*

13 The footnote given by Griffiths is 'Lévi, Mahāyāna-Sūtrālaṃkāra, 44'.

properties such as impermanence *(aniyatā)*, lack of self *(nirātmatā)*, and unsatisfactoriness *(duḥkhatā)*. The close connection of *tathatā* with these is evident by the frequent glosses on terms that explicitly mention one or more of them. So to say that Buddha's essential nature is the purification of the actuality of all things is not necessarily to identify Buddha with a changeless monistic principle, but rather to make the first and most basic move in a game whose culmination makes Buddha coextensive with everything.[14]

The unchangeability of *tathatā*

I shall now analyse specific statements from the quotations given in this chapter. Firstly by Brown:

> the *Tathāgatagarbha* must ultimately be considered as the movement towards its perfect self-realization and thus, as object of self-consciousness....The relationship between the *Tathāgatagarbha* and the *Dharmakāya* is that of a cycle that presupposes its beginning and reaches its beginning only at its end. If the *Tathāgata* embryo is the beginning or cause, then the Absolute Body is essentially the result, the end where the *Tathāgata* embryo becomes what it is in truth. The nature of the embryo is to be actual, that which becomes itself. For if it starts with itself, the *Tathāgatagarbha* reaches its consummation with itself as the Absolute Body *(Dharmakāya)* and in fact the *Dharmakāya* is the *Tathāgatagarbha* when it has not yet freed itself from the adventitious defilements.

We can incorporate this passage with the statements by Griffiths, where he says that the term *tathatā* emphasises the unchangeability of its actuality, and yet the Buddha's essential nature that purifies 'the actuality of all things' does not necessarily identify a Buddha with 'a changeless monistic principle'.

The lengthy quotes in this chapter bring to the fore the concept that it is only possible for the *(tathatā)* to *not* change as the *tathāgatagarbha* evolves into the *dharmakāya*, if the *tathāgatagarbha* and/or the *dharmakāya* changed in some way.[15] Then the *tathatā* exists as a type

14 P.J. Griffiths, *On Being Buddha*, (Sri Satguru Publications, Delhi, 1995), 76.

15 Imperceptible to the human unit because of the vastness of the Mind-Space involved.

of flux or medium of exchange, a carrier of the Buddha nature because of the way it is constituted. It contains all of the pathways of Buddhahood that allows transmission both ways. Otherwise the entire process of evolution would be meaningless. It would all be simply pointless if all three were 'changeless', where the *tathāgatagarbha* = *dharmakāya* = *tathatā,* all of which are seen as *nitya* ('permanent'). If this were so then everybody upon the earth could commit suicide and immediately gain Buddhahood, because no matter what they do *they are there already,* as they have always been there. As one cannot contemplate an evolutionary process under this scenario, only a 'permanent condition', so again, why bother with all of the struggle if there is no point for it all, no gain whatsoever? Surely, the way of *karma* via the agency of the Lords of Life is to produce something greater than what simply existed in the beginning, in the womb *(garbha)*?

The reason why Buddhists have absurdly postulated the uselessness of the entire evolutionary process, that incorporates the nature of human struggle from darkness towards light (by denying that there is such a process at all), is because they have denied the possibility of a soul-form that can act as a container for the continuum of the human consciousness from life to life. Such a process however, is the only thing that can account for the progressive nature of humanity's aspiration towards enlightenment. Something must change in the above equation, and that is seen to be the *tathāgatagarbha,* where it changes from a defiled state to an undefiled state. But how it becomes defiled in the first place, and then becomes undefiled is not really explained in the extant philosophy. Detail of the exact mechanism is certainly lacking. Indeed, precise detail as to how this *tathāgatagarbha* actually acts with respect to the moving consciousness-stream of an evolving personal-I is also lacking. So let us see if we can bring some more light to this vexing subject.

It appears that Buddhists have essentially replaced the *ātman* concept, that has certain qualities, and is said to be *permanent* and *unchanging*, with a *tathatā* concept, which is seen as similarly *permanent* and *unchanging.* So what is the true differentiation? Is it the central concept of *śūnyatā* that is devoid of all attributes, whereas *ātman* is not so? The distinction may be valid enough, but what has not been realised is that Buddhists are only reckoning these things in relation to their own consciousnesses, i.e., what they are trying to analyse and discuss is relative only to what they have experienced in the phenomenal worlds, and through the meditation process whilst incarnate. They have in fact missed the point of the evolutionary time scale. We need to know *what it is* that 'appears' from this *tathāgatagarbha* and that evolves through cycles of time continuums in order to enter the *dharmakāya* at the end of it all? Is it the *tathatā* or 'suchness' of things? If so why, for what purpose, if 'nothing has changed whatsoever?'

An atheistic form of reasoning is demonstrated here, that all things come and go out of their own accord for absolutely no reason, and the result of it all is the entering of an attributeless space that has *not* changed from beginning to the ending of the process. Clearly, this entire conception makes a mockery out of everything that has transpired from the *tathāgatagarbha* form to *dharmakāyic* identification.

However, if *tathatā* actually was relative not just to human consciousness (which has not the capacity to directly understand it), but also to something 'other' than such consciousness, something vaster, infinitely greater, then something associated with this very same *tathatā* can change in relation to what it is relative to. The *tathatā* itself may not have changed, but that which it conveys has, and this can have actual bearing on the overall perception of what it is. It is beyond all possible conceptions of consciousness, thus it is *'tathatā'*, but something gained from conscious evolution through a succession of bearers of consciousness has carried through into *tathatā*, and consequently enriched that associated with it. This must be so, otherwise a Buddha could not remember his previous lives, or indeed, envision any previous life of another evolving bearer of the *tathāgatagarbha*. What indeed is this faculty of memory that has its store in that condition called the *tathatā* of a Buddha? Has this not altered what is perceived as 'the way things really are, the true nature of things' in the *tathatā* state in accordance with what has been experienced by a Buddha in all of his previous incarnations? And if so, why were such experiences necessary for a Buddha to obtain in the first place, because they would be meaningless if the equation *tathāgatagarbha* = *dharmakāya* actually was factual. (Though we shall see later that this equation has an indirect, qualified correctness, because the *tathāgatagarbha* is a construct both of the *dharmakāya* and of *consciousness*.)

If such an evolution has taken place, as it clearly has, and has added impressions to the *tathāgatagarbha* so as to attain the Buddha-Mind (the *dharmakāya),* then the *tathatā* state must perceive 'the true nature' as different before and after the process, because before no Buddha had appeared, where there is one now. The process of Life has changed from some 'state' that was, to some 'state' that is inclusive of what was and is now *more* than what was, because it contains the mechanism that allows such change. The way to observe this is that the pathways allowing the two way transmission between *tathāgatagarbha* and *dharmakāya* existed right from the beginning and had the capability of being utilised (like empty pipes), but were not utilised because the related characteristics were not yet developed. As the Tathāgata qualities gradually become developed, so the 'traffic' between the *tathāgatagarbha* and *dharmakāya* increases, and this process is perceived truly as it is in the state of 'no-mind' known as the *tathatā.*

Evolutionary time and the law of *karma* has seen to that increase. The true nature of the *dharmakāya* thus becomes our focus here. The *dharmakāya* is more than *śūnyatā*, it is the *gain* of the entire evolutionary process, of the making of a Buddha. It is inclusive of the *tathāgatagarbha,* but *more* than it. The *tathatā* state can be equated with the *dharmakāya* if the *dharmakāya* is defined as 'evolved Buddha nature', but if this is defined thus then the *tathatā* also has changed. A better definition therefore for the *tathatā* is that it is a changeless base clarified of the vicissitudes of mind, as needed to experience the functioning of the *dharmakāya* in the realms of form. It is neither 'mind', or 'no-mind', but rather manifest as pure intrinsic perception, and is synonymous with what I explain as *buddhi* later.

Samalā and *nirmalā tathatā*

In relation to the information contained in *The Ratna-gotravibhāga,* Brown states:

> According to the text, that ultimate denominator is nothing other than Reality in its condition of absolute Suchness (*Tathatā*) which in turn, is subdivided into the two major categories of *samalā* and *nirmalā. Samalā Tathatā* designates that aspect of Reality "mingled with pollution" and is the *Ratnagotra's* consistent term for the

Tathāgatagarbha, while *Nirmalā Tathatā* is its expression for Reality "apart from pollution," and is thus synonymous with *Dharmakāya:*

> "The Reality mingled with pollution *(samalā-tathatā)"* is a term for "the Essence *(dhātu),* unreleased from the sheath of defilements," i.e., the Embryo of Tathāgata. "The Reality apart from pollution *(nirmalā tathatā)"* is a term for the same Essence, when it is characterized as the Perfect Manifestation of Basis *(āśrayaparṭti)* in the Stage of Buddha, i.e., the Absolute Body of the Tathāgata.[16][17]

If Suchness 'mingled with pollution' *(samalā-tathatā* or Tathāgata-embryo) is deemed ineffable since it is both pure and defiled simultaneously, then what 'defiles' it is that portion of abstract consciousness that can clothe the intrinsic *dharmakāyic* aspect with a form of some type, making the rebirth process possible. Why is this rebirth process necessary? The answer lies somewhat in the idea that the defilements must be removed, and this process is what will produce a Buddha as a consequence. The answer, however, incorporates subsidiary questions: 'what caused this *dharmakāyic* aspect (*samalā-tathatā*) to be originally defiled, why, and how did this occur?' Also, with respect to the causation of the defilement of the *tathatā,* 'what indeed is Suchness "apart from pollution" *(nirmalā tathatā* or Absolute Body), which is so stipulated because not defiled?' Effectively both *tathatās* are non-separate, because there is an inherent fundamental purity. The defilement and subsequent purification signifies an inherent *tathatā* that manifests first as *samalā* and is thus hidden, and as *nirmalā* and therefore objectively manifest.

Here we see that in order to overcome the difficulty of an unchanging *tathatā* state in relation to the process of the evolution of a Buddha from ordinary human consciousness, the author of this text effectively presents a time sequence from beginning to the ending of a process, but how the beginning came to be is unexplained. We thus have two categories:

---

16 Brown, 55.

17 Quote from Takasaki, Jikido, trans. *A Study on the Ratnagotravibhāga,* (Instituto Italiano per il Medio ed Estremo Oriente, Rome, 1966), 187.

1. That 'mingled with pollution', which is consequently another term for the *tathāgatagarbha*.
2. That which has 'no pollution' and consequently identical with the *dharmakāya*.

If the perception is that the two types of *tathatā* manifest simultaneously then we could ask the questions 'what is the significance of the defilements, how does one contain its defilement in such a way that it does not taint or contaminate the non-defilement of the other?' We see here that this is an effectual impossibility unless the defilements were circumscribed into an effective form that contains them for a necessary purpose. Such a form has been designated *'tathāgatagarbha',* and rightfully so. Also, are they completely separate and distinct essences of the Buddha nature? In which case the Buddha nature would have two essences or identities, which is illogical. Also, how is such containment possible in the Prāsaṅgika philosophy of 'no container'? If there were 'no container' then how could the defilements 'stick' to the *tathatā* to produce the state known as *samalā tathatā*? Again, how can the *tathatā* become defiled in the first place, and where do these defilements come from? These are weighty questions and ought to be answered. Though they may be non-separate in fundamental purity there is a veiled time sequence associated with the two categories, which concerns the process of the removal of the 'pollution' so that the hidden *tathatā* is revealed, leaving us only with the *nirmalā tathatā* (the *dharmakāya).*

The equation can then be drawn:

Tathāgatagarbha—samalā-tathatā ↔ *tathatā* ↔ *nirmalā-tathatā—dharmakāya*

The *tathāgatagarbha—samalā-tathatā* represents the *past*, the expression of the *tathatā*, where it is covered or defiled by means of the formation of an I-consciousness and the entire rebirthing process.

The *nirmalā-tathatā—dharmakāya* thus represents the *future* attainment of the *tathatā* whereby the I-consciousness has removed the 'covering' or defilements. Consequently it is no longer considered an 'I'. Enlightenment has ensued.

The *tathatā* is therefore really the *present* conditioning of the process, representing the eternal Now, whereby the future is continuously slipping into the past. Such a statement means that the eternal reality (the *dharmakāya)* gradually asserts itself by overcoming the vicissitudes of *saṃsāra*. Normally one thinks of the past evolving into the future as a personal-I works to overcome the illusions, the veils of *māyā* it has incarnated into. An enlightened Mind is developed to reveal this truth.

Is it fair to say that the past and the future are identical? I think not. Though *samalā-tathatā* and *nirmalā-tathata* would both partake of the Suchness *(tathatā),* they manifest different functions, even though the definition of *tathatā* in Brown's book states that it is 'the unchangeable, non-dual, essential nature (*advayadharma*) of all things.'[18] 'Non-dual', maybe like a see-saw that is constituted of one plank of a uniform substance, but which nevertheless has two ends (*samalā-nirmalā),* which are capable of moving up and down via a fulcrum at the centre, though the centre does not inherently move. One can properly only consider 'non-duality' here through the central pivot. The *tathatā* can be considered 'non-dual' at this point and by virtue of the substance that unifies both ends of the moving see-saw. Here the functioning of *tathatā* is much like *śūnyatā.* Indeed Brown indicates such a relationship between *tathatā* and *śūnyatā*:

> If it signifies the non-substantiality of all things in their existential mundane reality (*vyavahara*), *Śūnyatā* at the same time is the ultimate, essential, and true nature of all that is qualified and contingent; as such it is a cognate expression for *Tathatā*, the Absolute Suchness of reality.[19]

Addressing the problem of how the *tathatā* can become defiled, and how this can be reconciled with the *dharmakāya*, with that which is 'undefiled', is what can now be presented. To do this a greater depth of analysis of what exactly is the *tathāgatagarbha* must be given than was hitherto presented. Indeed, when properly analysed we will see that it is what can be called a *soul-form*[20] that has *śūnyatā* at its heart, and

---

18 Brown, 132.

19 Ibid., 136.

20 Again this unavoidable term that has vexed Buddhist Theoreticians for millennia has been utilised to indicate the existence of a construct and subject they have made

which is the bearer of the consciousness principle and its evolutionary progression through a succession of personal-I's. This process is bound by the principles associated with the philosophy of *Dependent Origination*, from whence comes the potentiality, and then the actuality of Buddhahood. This happens when *tathāgatagarbha* is transformed into *dharmakāya*. There are five main steps concerning this transformation:

1. The beginning. This concerns the formation of the *tathāgatagarbha* by means of the meditation-Mind of a Buddha, who projects a seed idea *(bīja)* into the realm of consciousness, attracting to the seed unredeemed *manasic* substance. The seed then takes the form of a *womb* as a natural consequence of a circumscribed meditative process. The purpose of this compassionate act of such a one is for unredeemed 'tainted' substance to become redeemed, liberated (thus made *'tathatā')*.
2. We therefore have the appearance of *samalā-tathatā,* the *tathāgatagarbha.*
3. The process of the evolution of consciousness and Love that will ultimately lead to Buddhahood then ensues.
4. The redemption of the consciousness-substance through purification and transmutation happens as a consequence of response to the pain of attachment to *saṃsāric* allurements. This process is accelerated through yogic *samādhi* upon the Bodhisattva path.
5. Finally, we perceive the expression of *nirmalā-tathata* of a Buddha residing in his bliss body meditation-Mind, that has evolved from the transformed *samalā-tathatā.*

The Tathāgata part of the term *tathāgatagarbha* refers to the Buddha nature, whilst the *garbha* part has been defined above as the integration of an 'embryo', 'germ', and 'womb'. The connotation of all of these terms, and by association with what is known in our human experience, is that they relate to something that is spherical, or more correctly ovoid in shape. This then is the form of the lighted container (of the substance that it incorporates) mentioned above. It integrates

---

anathema. Its factuality cannot however be truthfully ignored, thus needs to be adequately explained.

the qualities developed by the evolving consciousness and coordinates the *saṃskāras* evolved by the accompanying reincarnating personal-I's into a consecutive stream of underlying *karma,* thus giving meaning to everything that was, is, and ever will be. This 'container' has been herein termed the I-consciousness. However, the term Sambhogakāya Flower provides a more accurate depiction of such a form, as it integrates consciousness in the domain of the abstract Mind. This is because the form takes the shape of a flower (a *chakra)* upon this domain in order to contain the variegations of the consciousness that must be stored.

The three bodies of a Buddha

Having presented a foundation for an understanding of the nature of the *dharmakāya* in relation to the *tathāgatagarbha,* the idea of the three bodies of a Buddha *(trikāya)* and how they find their application in the evolutionary field should be analysed. The *dharmakāya* (which I have also termed *'the Divine'),* is called the 'Divine Body of Truth' by W.Y. Evans-Wentz. The term *dharma* means truth, the fount of the law governing all being/non-being, and the term *kāya* refers to body. When perfectly expressed and embodied (by an enlightened being) the corporeal form becomes a *nirmaṇakāya,* the 'Divine Incarnation Body'. Concerning the *trikāya* Evans-Wentz states that:

> There is no place throughout the Universe where the Essentiality of a Buddha is not present. Far and wide throughout the spaces of space the Buddha essence is present and perpetually manifested.
>
> This Universal Essence manifests itself in three aspects, or modes, symbolized as the Three Divine Bodies (Skt. *Tri-Kāya).* The first aspect, the *Dharma-Kāya,* or Essential (or True) Body, is the Primordial, Unmodified, Formless, Eternally Self-Existing Essentiality of *Bodhi* or Divine Beingness. The second aspect is the *Sambhoga-Kāya* or Reflected *Bodhi,* wherein, in heaven-worlds, dwell the Buddhas of Meditation (Skt. *Dhyānī-Buddhas)* and other Enlightened Ones while embodied in superhuman form. The third aspect is the *Nirmāṇa-Kāya* or Body of Incarnation, or, from the standpoint of men, Practical *Bodhi,* in which exist Buddhas when on Earth.
>
> In the Chinese interpretation of the *Tri-Kāya* the *Dharma-Kāya* is the immutable Buddha Essence, the Noumenal Source of the Cosmic

> whole. The *Sambhoga-Kāya* is, as phenomenal appearances, the first reflex of the *Dharma-Kāya* on the heavenly planes. In the *Nirmāṇa-Kāya* the Buddha Essence is associated with activity on the Earth plane; it incarnates among men, as suggested by the Gnostic Proem to the Gospel of St. John, which refers to the coming into the flesh of the 'Word', or 'Mind'[21]...In its totality, the Universal Essence is the One Mind, manifested through the multitudinous myriads of minds throughout all states of *sangsāric* existence. It is called 'The Essence of the Buddhas', 'The Great Symbol', 'The Sole Seed', 'The Potentiality of Truth', 'The All-Foundation'. As our text teaches, it is the Source of all bliss of *nirvāṇa* and of all sorrow of the *Sangsāra.*[22]

We have seen that the *tathāgatagarbha* evolves into the *dharmakāya*, from *samalā to nirmalā-tathata*. Logically, therefore, so also do the other bodies of a Buddha (the *nirmaṇakāya* and the *sambhogakāya)* similarly evolve. They do not simply appear fully from nowhere as attributed bodies of a Buddha. They evolve in accord with the principle that a succession of personal-I's gradually cleanses gross *saṃskāras*, develops *bodhicitta*, becomes a Bodhisattva, progresses along the ten *bhūmis* and finally becomes a Tathāgata.

Looking at it another way, the *nirmaṇakāya* of a Buddha is not just simply miraculously created by him when he wishes to appear in phenomenal form on the physical plane. Yes, a Buddha can do so, but this is not the point. The point is that it has also evolved through the aeons of having possessed physical forms as a human being, and the process of the gradual refinement and transformation of *skandhas* and *saṃskāras*. The sentience of each cellular unit of the form is karmically linked, identified with that of the overriding *karma* of the indwelling and overshadowing consciousness. If it were otherwise then the personal-I could not utilise the form it occupies at all; there would be no way that the mechanism of response which we call the five senses could obey the instructions of the overseeing mind, as there would be *no karma* to do so. Because of such karmic affiliations it is possible for people

---

21 W.Y. Evans-Wentz, *The Tibetan Book of the Great Liberation,* (Oxford University Press, London, 1968), 3-4.

22 Ibid., 4.

to suffer the sicknesses and diseases that they do. They are caused by mistreating the units of sentience and response that are our cells. It is all part of the overall equilibrium and harmony seen throughout Nature.

With each new incarnation the three-fold personality vehicle becomes progressively more refined. This facilitates the development of higher perceptions, subtle clairvoyance, states approximating perfect health, plus the *saṃskāras* that lead to meditative poise needed to enter into *dhyāna*. This is obvious, as a sickly and pain-ridden body prevents meditative clarity. One must first eliminate the *saṃskāras* that are the foundation for all forms of sicknesses.

A *nirmaṇakāya,* therefore, is something more than just a magical phenomenal 'appearance', it is something that has evolved with the making of a Buddha, which he can activate at need. This is because the combined cellular sentience and the overriding consciousness of a Buddha evolve together. This is an important point. He *cannot* simply relinquish karmic ties with them upon attainment of his *parinirvāṇa.* If he could do so then there would be one law of *karma* for him, and another completely different law for the rest of us. This is not so, however they can come under a special dispensation where an advanced Bodhisattva can wilfully take the responsibility for the residual *karma* of aspects of their phenomena. Other aspects also enter *nirvāṇa* with him and later become the basis for the manifestation of what is symbolically presented as a *Buddha-field* in the Buddhist literature. More could be said about this subject, but would diverge us too far from the main theme of this book.

If the three bodies of a Buddha are seen as a unity, then by a similar deduction as that concerning the evolution of a *nirmaṇakāya*, it follows that *sambhogakāya* and the *dharmakāya* likewise 'evolve'. However, such evolution is relative, relegated to their own spheres or planes of appearance. The *sambhogakāya* evolves in relation to both the *nirmaṇakāya* and *dharmakāya*, whilst the *dharmakāya* takes from the *sambhogakāya*. The *dharmakāya* obviously does not evolve *per se*, as it has always existed, and is the real, but it does become more inclusive with the appearance of each new Buddha and the making of his Buddha-field. The *dharmakāya* can also be considered one with *saṃsāra* but here a hiatus can be said to exist in the field of human consciousness, which is what is being considered here—the way humans perceive things. Humans must first develop the perception to realise the *dharmakāya* before the identity of *saṃsāra* and *dharmakāya* can be experienced.

Of the three bodies our present focus is the *sambhogakāya,* because our perception of how it evolves to become a 'radiant body of a Buddha' is what concerns this plea for comprehension of what a soul-form may be. The subtle nature of the *sambhogakāya* is perhaps what is least understood by Buddhists. There are *thangkas* depicting bejewelled Bodhisattvas and Buddhas manifesting in a *sambhogakāya* form. They do not however depict how the *sambhogakāya* normally exists, but rather are idealised, anthropomorphised, symbolic forms that can inspire human units to consciously aspire to be like the beings depicted. It is obvious that anthropomorphisation has its value, but the form depicted is determined according to the way that consciousness perceives things of beauty, the divine, relative to the human forms that it recognises. What has been programmed in consciousness determines what is perceived. Symbolically we have pearls of wisdom, radiant jewels of *dharmakāyic* revelation, coloured by various Ray attributes, garlands of transformed experiences, many hands containing the implements of accomplishment, the Bodhisattva sitting upon the lotus of the path of past attainments, radiating an energy field of spiritual perspicuity and liberating effulgence. Indeed, liberated beings can and do take on such attributes, but that is not the *sambhogakāya* form possessed by the myriads not so enlightened.

In reality, the *sambhogakāya* takes the shape of necessity according to the laws of energy disposition in the way that the *saṃskāras* of consciousness are defined, storing the memory of volitions of the past. These are the past actions gathered by the succession of personal-I's that have created the consciousness and its qualities.

The *sambhogakāya* form is the actuality of the Sambhogakāya Flower that is formed in the abstract levels of Mind, and also expresses the image of the attained qualities of a highly realised entity found upon the *dharmakāyic* level, in a way that the mind/Mind can acknowledge and cognise what is True. The Sambhogakāya Flower expresses the discernable qualities of the distilled essence of all that has been gained from all past life experiences, in and out of physical incarnation, and stored by the container it effectively is, and is able to project it all towards a future propensity. Such a form is Mind-conceived, containing all the attributes developed by a consciousness-stream. It is a 'flower' because it manifests the attributes of a *chakra,* and must be so if the qualities developed by the Head lotus (the thousand petalled *sahasrāra padma*) are to pass freely to it, and life's directives from it to that centre in the body.

From this perspective it can be considered a Mind meditatively unfolded in a sea of consciousness. This sea is composed of a myriad other such Minds all meditating together upon a common purpose—upon evolution within time and space wherein human units and civilisations appear, wherein the collective *karma* can be rectified in such a way that a myriad Buddhas can be produced out of the mass of lives.

The *sambhogakāya* form has thus evolved, according to the qualities it derived from the successive incarnations of the personal-I's it experienced within *saṃsāra.* To this is added that which it has gained from its meditation upon the *dharmakāya* in relation to the need and capacity to handle the related energies, plus what was initially seeded into it (creating its essential form) by a meditating Ādi Buddha. Energies are spoken of here, because ultimately that is all there is; energies of varying degrees of intensity, bound into form by means of sentience, thence consciousness, and then by that which we really have no proper definition, but give it such terms as Buddha-Mind, *tathatā*, *dharmakāya.*

As we evolve we gain the capability to hold higher and more intense energy states in consciousness, which is ultimately seen as the radiant aura of each Bodhisattva and Buddha. Such auras depict the way their Minds manifest the clarified and intensified energies that they are composed of. All types of *siddhis* are expressions of the way that various energy fields are modified and projected by consciousness.

The *sambhogakāya* form is thus the *tathāgatagarbha* that is made to appear in the image of the ideal form of an enlightened one or principle. When viewed anthropomorphically it takes the symbolism of many arms, jewels, garlands, etc., if need be, attributed to the various Bodhisattvas and Buddhas. In Volume 3 the true floral form of this attribute of a human unit will be shown and the characteristics of each petal explained. The lotus is the ideal and natural shape that the energy body takes to contain the various states of consciousness it expresses (as well as for the 'containment' of *śūnyatā),* when divorced from mindful conceptualisations.

Only from the realm of consciousness, and not from the transient forms that are cast aside from life to life, can a Tathāgata evolve. There comes a life, however, when complete mastery of the sum of life's attributes must be demonstrated upon the most dense realm, thus we have the appearance of the *nirmaṇakāya* of a Buddha.

Consciousness persists after the death of the form (thus it can experience the Bardo states). Over time, as *saṃskāras* are cleansed and by focussing upon *śūnyatā*, the quantified Mind-stream (the Sambhogakāya Flower) sheds attachment to phenomena. *Śūnyatā* is that which is the residual when all attachment to phenomena is eliminated, whilst the *dharmakāya* is the addition of the transmuted gain from evolutionary experience. This then is the process of the making of a Buddha. *Dharmakāya* is the collective compound of the experiences of all Buddhas that have gone before, beyond that conditioning known as 'humanity', fused with THAT constituting all cosmic space. Such a cosmos is unknown to any but a Buddha travelling that Way, or to one directly preparing to thus travel.

A Buddha that has entered cosmos within the sphere of his own agenda can be said to exist in the *svabhāvikakāya* state, which in some texts is said to be the synthesis of the *trikāya*. Makransky states that it 'may be glossed "the embodiment [of Buddhahood] in its essence, in its real nature"'.[23] The *svabhāvikakāya* thus defines the nature of the experience of a Buddha that has relinquished all phenomenal ties with a world sphere, such as our earth.

Having stated the above we should now further define what the mind is, so as to avoid possible confusion, because the way Buddhists have traditionally defined things may differ somewhat from the usages that appear in this treatise. The mind is the bridge between the involutionary (sub-human) and evolutionary (para-human) states of awareness, and is therefore a combination or product of any of the characteristics mentioned below:

1. *Instinct,* inherent in all levels of sentient evolution.
2. *Feeling,* evolved in the plant kingdom.
3. *Desire,* developed by the animal kingdom.

---

23 John Makransky, *Buddhahood Embodied, Sources of Controversy in India and Tibet,* (Sri Satguru, Delhi, 1998), 5.

4. *Intellect,* an expression of the human kingdom.
5. *Imagination,* a combination of intellect and desire.
6. *Pure Reason, intuition.* This implies the *power to vision,* and is not to be confused with the imagination. The seer visions and must translate his vision by means of the intellect into words, picture images that people can understand. They then interpret those words according to what they imagine them to mean, and this is governed by their mental emotional conditionings and reactions. The vision of the seer is not thus conditioned, there being no emotion or desire involved. He has become a vehicle through which the enlightened consciousness of the *tathāgatagarbha* can manifest, because of his ability to broadcast the energy of Love. (The mechanism being a purified, receptive, co-ordinated and consecrated personality.) The vision, if genuine, always benefits the whole, a group or mass of beings, or society in general, and only incidentally the personality involved. Imagination is always focussed upon, or emanates from, the personality and related conditionings, even if idealistic or inspirational.

   Intuition is the 'voiceless voice' that inspires all the men and women of destiny that change aspects of civilisation in some beneficent way.

7. *The ineffable or universal Mind (the dharmakāya).* This transcends consciousness (as we understand it). It is Divinity itself, and can be said to represent a Buddha-Mind within which all things are contained, for everything can be considered an aspect of His thought process. (The implication here refers to a Buddha that had gained His *parinirvāṇa* in a long past aeon.) The key to the revelation of the nature of the evolutionary process and the creation/appearance of any world sphere, or even universe, is found in this idea when thought out clearly. This fleeting, phenomenal, appearance of things, the entire physical world that we as personalities live in and are involved with, can be likened to the images produced by His 'imagination', that which is created in such a One's Meditation-Mind. The 'cells' in the Brain of such a Being can be envisioned as great angelic beings *(ḍākinīs)* that fashion the 'images' out of the substance of their bodies. Lesser units of consciousness within the bodies of

such beings embody the various diversified aspects of the material world, and so forth.

As well as the above attributes relegated to consciousness, humans also possess a *sambhogakāya* form, the soul-*tathāgatagarbha* residing in the sphere of Mind (the *ālayavijñāna).* Then there is a *dharmakāyic* aspect, an eventuating Buddha-Mind[24] that also includes the entire human experience, incorporating our beings and which is the product, or an aspect of, the Ineffable or universal Mind. The subject of what exactly a mind/Mind is is not easily dismissed, and connotes a vast field of empirical analysis and meditative investigation. Consequently the following chapters of this Volume shall undertake such an investigation via the 'eyes' of the Vijñānavāda-Yogācāra doctrines, coupled with the mind/Mind's relation to the question of the existence or non-existence of a 'self'.

24 A *Monadic* expression—meaning 'One', ultimate unity.

About the not-self...

The who self; the who me self, who is the talker here?
Can the not-self talk, what can it say,
to whom or how can it speak?
If it cannot speak, how can anyone know about it?
If it can, then who is the speaker?
Oh please tell me who or what is the speaker?
Have you lost your voice, or is your mind blank,
Void of information?
Is something that is void of information the not-self?
But this is the definition of ignorance.
So, is the not-self darkness itself?
If so, then what is light?
If you could speak I could learn something,
But you are not a 'self',
So what can I learn from you?
I cannot find you anywhere.
None of my senses can register an impression of you.
My mind cannot fathom, my eyes can't see,
My ears too small for hearing what you cannot say.
What can I touch if there is nothing there?
No taste or smell from the ethers,
Not subtle or formless, simply 'not',
But they say you are – where?
Śūnyatā! *Śūnyatā* they say.
But how can the not-self be in *śūnyatā* when it is not...?

Śūnyatā is void, but void of what? 'Self' they say.
But if this is so how can *śūnyatā* be experienced?
Can it be experienced at all by that which is not?
What can a not-self come to know?
How can *śūnyatā* be if it is a 'not'?
Consciousness here is not.
So the not-self is, but if it is how can it identify with me?
How can it identify with any other (Me or I's)?
Speak to me about this not-self, but not with the 'self', please?
Can you? Where is your mouth?
If you can speak it only proves to me you are a 'self',
Because your speech is coming from an 'I'.
Even the Buddha spoke as an 'I'.
You cannot logically prove that it was otherwise.
So how do you prove that such a not-self exists?
You can't, you have no mouth to speak, no ears to hear (me).
You cannot even think.
Of what use are you?
Not a Bodhisattva thinking, not *bodhicitta* propounding,
For with a not-self where is there an awakening?
For with a not-self what can enlightenment act upon?
Is a Bodhisattva the not-self?
Tell me, please tell me so that I can know something.
How does the *tathāgatagarba* come through me
If there is not a 'self' to be?

3

Negating the Self

The process of negating

In continuing the analysis of the negation of the concept of 'self', one can point to another aspect that is problematic, namely that the process of negating the 'self' (through suppression or elimination of aspects of consciousness) could make the mind more unconscious (thus unreliable and irresponsible) and more emotional (thus also more unthinking). This can happen because there would be no 'I' or central focus to pin thoughts to. If thoughts have nothing to cohere to (allowing definition for formed concepts), then the mind *per se* cannot function, as thoughts cannot be directed because there would be no coherent form to direct. The unruly emotions would then rule, as there would be very little directive ideation to control them. Automatically the person could also posses a more 'loving' disposition, yet manifest little worthy of mind.

If one is not conscious of things then one does not understand those things, or aspects of life derived from them. Such a person would then be more innately reactionary to impressions that are not understood which impact upon consciousness. This increases the ignorance quota, but not that relating to obtaining wisdom.

Because the symptoms of such negation appear as emotionalism, logic is overridden by prioritised activities for a desired intercourse with others, which the subconscious (emotional/feeling) mechanism needs for its succour. Instantly we have a tribal or herd-consciousness living in harmony (when looking to a group of individuals wherein the 'self' is naturally negated) with no true independent thinking, or possession of proper credentials for abstract thinking. In a society of such individualities, strong sublimated subtle emotions can be produced, which bond the perpetuators in terms of group cohesion, or else there can be violent interactions. Often there is a combination of both.

This subject can be viewed in terms of three cupboards, one is closed, one is half open, another is wide open. The first concerns the nature of a person with no emotions, the second concerns self identifying mental-emotional perceptions, and the third concerns the expression of total emotionality.

The first example implicates that the cupboard and its contents are not open to interpretation. The self-focussed mental walls are closed, preventing one to enter to investigate various qualities manifesting therein. The concretions of mind make it unconscious to the many swaying factors that *karma* may impose and other subtleties, such as the working of the intuition. Here self-concepts are intensified, producing a dramatic centralisation of the 'I', and accompanying pride.

The cupboard can also be closed for subtle intellectual concepts, such as those that espouse a 'not self'. Wisdom denotes that one cannot say 'there is not a self' and then shut the cupboard to the logic formulated without looking outside to see what else there may be to reason with. At a distance even colours can appear other than what they actually are. The contents inside the cupboard, or any reified thoughts, must be fully examined, its contents spread out and revealed in the light. Then it may be possible to understand the mechanism of such things as *karma,* the nature of awakening *chakras,* and the subtleties of what causes the appearance or negation of a subtle form of 'self'.

In actuality there are four steps, four Noble Truths, and eight paths or ways to revelation, whereby such causes can be ascertained. With the Heart and mind in unison we detail the 'me'. Only then can the way of pure mental reasoning produce the enlightened fruits that it is meant to do.

The second example is the way whereby the emotions and mind are developed and observed simultaneously, so the effect of one upon the other can be understood and thus be properly analysed and mastered, without suppression of the one, and distortion or perversion of the other.

This allows the proper development of all facets of consciousness, and the transformation of the emotional tendencies into Love, which draws all together into a unity of right conscious aspiration and development. Everything proceeds through conscious self-focus, which is inclusive of the contents of other individuals 'cupboards'. As they are opened they can be looked into and useful bits utilised for the developing 'self'. Thus the factors within them will produce refined types of consciousness that can be drawn out and further developed, and other factors transformed into the qualities needed.

The third example refers to a dissipation of the emotions and mental *saṃskāras* into the general environment, with no possibility of true control to reign in these *saṃskāras* so that they can be properly analysed and understood, allowing wisdom to be developed. Here the personal-I or 'self' is emptied of responsible thought through the scattering and dissipation of its basic qualities. This also involves an identification with the vacillating, turbulent, interchange with the emotional pulls of others, of the sea of impulsive desire based behaviour that all with open cupboards reside in.

The cupboard becomes emptied because its contents spill out and become integrated into the general mass of similarly 'emptied' individuals. Enlightenment is not possible because that which is identified with is continuously changing and fleeting. Other cupboards may be affected, but consciousness is *not* in control. Here there is an illusion of personality, of 'self', but in reality this 'self' is conditioned by mingling with the mass of moving emotional energies from the other 'cupboards' that affect and influence each other's space. Thus glamours of all types rule. Glamour being defined as that which is alluring or pretty, of a desirable nature and found in the cupboard of another.

Such a pandemonium of fleeting concerns must first be consolidated into unity, if a 'self' is to be comprehended before there is a possibility of its negation. The suppression or intensification of any of these attributes of consciousnesses will however not allow the negation of 'self'. Such action will but assert the dominance of its potency for some time longer. Rather, the attributes of 'self' must be transformed from within. They must be gradually transmuted through a succession of incarnations dedicated to the cleansing of the relevant *saṃskāras*. As the *saṃskāras* are successfully transmuted a complete emptying of their characteristics is not the gain, but rather their sublimation into higher consciousness states, into subtler versions of the *saṃskāras*. There can never be a point where there is 'nothing', thus *śūnyatā* cannot be considered as 'something that is not', but rather of a state of being where the *saṃskāras* and *skandhas* have been stripped of the characteristics that they were formerly recognised by. They are empty of those characteristics, but consciousness has developed new techniques for experiencing, new modes for comprehension. Consciousness becomes transmogrified and emptied of all forms of clinging to or attachment with ephemeral forms, *but persists.*

Consciousness is now clarified, consisting of intensified light, from whence comes the term Clear Light, and is automatically inclusive of all other consciousness-states in this sea of light, of other like Minds. This clarified state is a befitting container of *śūnyatā*, as such a consciousness is also empty of 'self'. It can hold the intensity of the substance of *śūnyatā* without being annihilated, in a similar manner that steel can hold the intensity of a furnace. But consciousness does have *identity*—because of its persistence; because of its general auric colouring (radiance); because of its experiential capabilities; because of its memory (its containment of moving images collected from past mental activities, which can be collated into idea forms); because it can replicate itself again in the realms of form for whatever purpose it chooses; because *karma* still delineates it so; and because it can strive to the high achievement of the *dharmakāya*.

This process of 'negation' is usually carried out in meditative equipoise, where the 'self' is looked for but not found, so the meditation manuals go. However, I have already demonstrated an inherent fallacy of this concept of 'non-finding of self', so what is found instead? The I-consciousness provides the answers.

Often there manifests a process of denial, of suppression of gross perceptions, and then subtle ones that engross such students of meditation. This is generally coupled with building picture images of Buddhas and Bodhisattvas, i.e., images of separated entities, thus 'selves', even though what is represented in the mind is said to be residing in *śūnyatā*, *nirvāṇa*, etc. At some time these representations also must go, so that the meditator is left with an emptiness of things of mind. Emptiness there may be, but this does not mean that true enlightenment has been obtained, the Hinayāna peace may be found instead. The Mahāyāna way adds to this the revelations that *bodhicitta* accords, and which go into the making of a Bodhisattva. The egotistical 'self' no longer exists, but a subtle concept of an 'I' does, via which the Bodhisattva serves the All. Such an 'I' is integrated with all other unities of expression, the identifications that distinguish one Bodhisattva from another for instance, or one stream of Life from another.

All such seemingly separated unities are unified in one boundless field of being/non-being. They are governed by the Rays and sub-rays of the emanation of (conscious) streams of the light of which they are the bearers. Hence they radiate auras of accomplishment that all can perspicuously view, and know from whence that radiant 'I' has come and the conditionings governing its field of service to all. The intensity of such light and the extent of its aura also denotes the spiritual age, the level of Bodhisattva *bhūmi* attained. In all cases the Clear Light has produced a communality of Mind, whereby all compassionate service arenas are collectivised under one Plan, one overriding mantra of expression, with sub-mantric songs that include everyone's part in the great service. It is thereby a hierarchy of Bodhisattvic action ascending to Buddhahood and thence cosmos in its undertaking, and in doing so all are assisted to follow. Such service then is the Heart of a Logos beating out its rhythms of integrated Love that is the bloodstream of compassionate activity, uplifting every aspect of the *maṇḍala* of being to the beauty of liberated seeing.

Skilful means

The elimination of the egotistical 'self' paradoxically necessitates invigorating the concept of a compassionate 'self', otherwise the Bodhisattva would have nothing to work through. Such a 'self' must consequently grapple with images of how best it can help, according to the qualities that he/she has developed, perfected and refined from his/her past lives to the present. Such images become the armour whereby the illusory qualities and ignorance of those in the world around one can be battled. Thus no Bodhisattva can work at all arenas of need in the world at once, the Bodhisattva must be selective, and utilise skilful means appropriately. Selectivity limits and therefore proposes definitions of selfhood. The 'self' concept utilised by a Bodhisattva, however, is freed from all self-concern, of grasping for ephemeral things for possession by an 'I'. The transitory illusionality of everything is thoroughly understood. Consequently the new 'self' manifests in a selfless manner.

On the highest Bodhisattva levels, even the subtle soul-form has gone, greatly freeing such a one to travel the far reaches of space, to perceive the nature of the Dharmakāya Way, yet he/she must still work with the selves/souls of things, or people, if the Bodhisattva is to rightfully serve them. There is no escape from such activity until Buddhahood is obtained by all.

What indeed does this phrase 'skilful means' actually mean in terms of the process developed to obtain such ability? The answer being that this ability has been evolved through the evolutionary process, by continuous 'selves', personal-I's, projected into time and space, so that a Bodhisattva can arise in the future that can skilfully utilise the gain of the process. How, therefore, can the concept of a 'self' be eliminated in a Bodhisattva if the very fabric of his/her being has been generated by means of incarnating 'selves'? Nevertheless, the 'personal self' must die, but the 'subtle self', the *tathāgatagarbha* persists. In it the gain of the stream of incarnating 'selves' resides. That gain is within the Bodhisattva's ken. Also, the Bodhisattva's entire career on the road to Buddhahood consists in dealing with myriads of little 'selves' that such a one has come to serve, for them to gain enlightened states of mind, according to the degree or *bhūmi* that the Bodhisattva has obtained. The Bodhisattva can do no more than this until he/she meets the challenges for the next step ahead. Once the Bodhisattva has become liberated, then such becomes possible for all within the Bodhisattva's reach. Skilful means therefore is delineated by the Bodhisattva's degree of attainment.

We see, therefore, that the Bodhisattva cannot eliminate the need for working with concepts of 'self', but its nature or definition has changed completely in consciousness; he/she works with it in a different way, through eyes *(chakras)*, or rather the divine Eye, that *sees*. The Bodhisattva works specifically upon the causal forms of the little selves in the realms of Mind, with the principle of Life that en-souls[1] all sentient lives. The Bodhisattva stimulates that Life so that it can

1 This term is used to indicate a quality that gives inherent life to an evolving entity, a 'self', or a collective of such entities.

eventually free itself from the matrix of *saṃsāra*. The Bodhisattva works thus from above-down, but also stimulates from below-up via the domain of incarnate forms. It cannot be any other way if he/she is to work with the expression of their *karma* throughout evolutionary time. The way that this process is viewed via the subtle Sambhogakāya Flower-*tathāgatagarbha* with which the Bodhisattva works in the realms of consciousness, is what must now become a matter of knowledge and consequent revelation for the world's aspirants. Only through a complete understanding of the nature of the liberation process can one gain enlightenment. Truth must be sought and found by means of the most direct path for those that can utilise their abstract Minds to perceive. Truth must become sacrosanct above all, and upon its wings one must fly high above the formed realms of minds and mere opinions. Fly with truth the Dharmakāya Way and all revelation will be accessed. Truth is the Buddha *vacana* (speech) resounding its voice as the *dharma* of the Heart throughout all time, to reveal the nature of multidimensional space for all Minds to perceive by means of the opened Eye of effulgent Sight.

Truth is the heartbeat of the Logos beating out its compassionate Blood, composed of the flow of all Bodhisattvic activity to appropriately nourish and uplift the minds of cellular human units[2] engrossed in the *māyā* of life. Truth is the way of uplifting and expanding the constituency of mind so that Mind is awakened by means of Love. Truth is Love in action so that all lives can be liberated to become the one Bodhisattvic Heart in action. Truth is but that Heart beating out its Plan for the redemption and liberation of all separated minds in motion. Truth is that Heart's Mind demonstrating its grace in cosmic space. Such a Mind then is Logoic and with it an Ādi Buddha delineates a Space or Womb for all action to convert realms of darkness into domains of effulgent Light. Truth is the mantric Sound of such a One reverberating through cosmos, delineating the tone by means of which it is done. Truth is the eventual dissolution of *saṃsāra* in a great unified cry of accomplishment. In truth your Heart and mine work for this as One. Demonstrate your truth as you listen to your Heart for the Plan of how it must be done. In your Heart's Mind resides the truth of all that exists in space and time, and why.

---

2 This subject will be further developed in Volume 4.

4

The Vijñānavādins on the Existence of 'self'

The nature of *bījas*

As the question of 'self' is intricately interwoven with the characteristics of mind, so it is important to obtain as complete an understanding as possible of the qualities of mind from a Buddhist perspective. For this one needs to study the doctrines of the Vijñānavāda-Yogācāra school because their philosophy specialises in this subject. To better understand the logic of this school I shall first quote from the book by Swati Ganguly:

> The *Vijñānavādin* speaks of two kinds of belief in the existence of the self *(ātmagrāha),* i.e. that which is natural *(sahaja)* and that which is produced from mental discrimination (*vikalpita).* The first kind is eliminated by meditation and self-cultivation on the path of *bhāvanāmārga.* The second kind is eliminated at the first stage of the path of *darśanamārga,* when the ascetic contemplates the ultimate reality which is realized by the voidness of the self and things.
>
> From *vijñānavāda* viewpoint, the questions on memory, recognition etc. can be explained without the existence of the self. Each sentient being has a fundamental consciousness *(ālayavijñāna)* which develops in a homogeneous and continuous series carrying within it the seeds of all things. This consciousness and the things act as causes of one another. The forces of *vāsanā* of things leave imprints on the *mūlavijñāna* as the *bījas* from which memory, recognition etc. are manifested. The *bījas* manifest themselves as actual things which again produce *bījas* in the *mūlavijñāna.*
>
> The *Vijñānavādins* further explain that by the force of causes and conditions, the mind and its activities of sentient beings develop

> in a continuous series. Actions and reaping of their fruits result from this development of mind. Hence there is no need to believe in the existence of the self for the accomplishment of Action (*karma*) and its fruits *(karmaphala)*. The *Vijñānavādin* argues that neither the issues on *gati, saṃsāra* and *nirvāṇa* involve the belief in the self. Each sentient being is a continuous mental and physical series *(santāna)*, which by force of defilements *(kleśa)* and impure *(sāsrava)* acts turns to destinies *(gati)*. Tormented by suffering and disgusted with it, he seeks the attainment of *nirvāṇa*.
>
> The *Vijñānavādin* concludes that there is no self but only consciousness exists. From the beginningless time the various consciousnesses appear in series, the subsequent one arising with the disappearance of the antecedent. Thus a series of causes and effects is formed. By virtue of *vāsanā* produced from false idea, an image of the self arises in consciousness and the image is taken as a real self by the ignorant people.[1]

The problems with a doctrine of 'a *homogeneous* and continuous series' were discussed in Volume 1, hence these arguments need not be repeated here. The question to be asked however is 'how can the *ālayavijñāna* develop "in a *homogeneous* and continuous series carrying within it the seeds of all things" if *"bījas* (seeds) manifest themselves as actual things which again produce *bījas* in the *mūlavijñana"* (the base or source consciousness)?' In other words, what are the *bījas* of—the concept of an atom, a human intelligence, a house, the entire complexity of human society, the information contained in the *prajñāpāramitā*, the complex paradigms of nuclear physics, *śūnyatā*? All these concepts are different, they cannot all have exactly the same type of *bīja* ('seed') as a basis for them all, which they must have if the stream is homogeneous.

The fact is that though all these *bījas* might possibly possess similar overall shapes and as a consequence look the same from a distance, thus appearing homogenous (which was the way that the author was obviously viewing this stream, making the statement true from this perspective). Upon close inspection they would, however, be found to possess differences. Differences are necessary, otherwise upon their

---

1 Swati Ganguly, (trans.) *Treatise in Thirty Verses on Mere-Consciousness. A critical English translation of Hsüan-tsang's Chinese version of the Vijñaptimātratātriṃśikā with notes from Dharmapāla's commentary in Chinese,* (Motilal Barnasidass, Delhi, 1992), 34-35.

activation in the *mūlavijñāna* the *bījas* would produce only the one type of 'real thing' and no other type, e.g., just perpetual images of the same house. This clearly is not the case, hence it can be seen that homogeneity is *not* manifest in the *ālayavijñāna* when viewed closely, but diversity. We can have a diversity within the context of that which is similar or of like nature.

Also, it is logical to assume that as we get to the more rarefied strata of the *ālayavijñāna,* many of the grosser forms of *saṃskāras* cannot exist there, only the most refined aspects would exist in the I-consciousness. This tends to simplify the nature of the diversity. Nevertheless, there is diversity, thus non-homogeneity, and from this we can postulate a condition of 'self' to exist, if 'self' is viewed as that which is seen as distinct from something else. Even in Nature, when looking to the *bīja*/seed concept, we see that all seeds are different, though they generally have a similar ovoid shape, such as are bird's eggs. They all have different sizes and colourings. So also in the realm of the *ālayavijñāna*. Each *bīja* is in fact a form of 'self'.

Each seed possesses a similar shape, but has different internal characteristics, and therefore is capable of producing similar, though different plant and bird species. A wheat seed only produces a wheat plant that is different from the pine tree that grew from a pine seed, but both types of seeds are similar. They are also a part of the vegetable kingdom, with characteristics peculiar to that kingdom. A wheat seed will never produce a human being, no matter how much you water it, or wish it to do so with an over-imaginative mind. What is needed is a human seed, the ovum. They are all different and individuality reigns within the similarity of overall design. What is observed in Nature stems from similar paradigms that must exist also in the *ālayavijñāna*, otherwise Nature could not come from it.

Another part of the above quotation that is of importance is 'Each sentient being has a fundamental consciousness *(ālayavijñāna)'.* So again we have diversity implied, because the statement 'each sentient being', implies a plurality of *ālayavijñānas*, one developed by each being, each of which *must* be by nature different, because each consciousness possesses different thought-streams, and consequently different *bījas* of memory, recognition, etc. These different streams then must commingle within the all-encompassing *ālayavijñāna* within which they find themselves a part of. Commingling is necessary, producing types of knots of *karma*, conjoined, group, national and international forms of *karma* produced by humans that existed and exist as part of a social fabric. Therefore there are different forms of *bījas* that must account for these types of *karmic* interactions. No person is an island unto him or herself. If there are differences, then those differences must be contained in some way, again pointing to the necessity of a soul-form that must integrate all of the differing streams and knots in a coherent way so that liberation for all is eventually possible. The *bījas* are also 'containers' of consciousness-attributes.

The *Vijñānavādins* may say that this *ālayavijñāna* is a unity, that all fundamental consciousnesses of each sentient being is merged into one. But then (again) how do the 'individual' consciousness-streams separate out from this morass, according to *karmic* law, especially if the *bījas* are considered uniform? If they were uniform then every single human unit appearing in *saṃsāra* would be identical, and this is clearly not the case. If they are not uniform then we get the concept of 'selves', which is a heretical concept to orthodoxy (except maybe when conventionally viewed as such).

One might however be able to say that 'that which is produced from mental discrimination *(vikalpita)*...is eliminated at the first stage of the path of *darśanamārga,* when the ascetic contemplates the ultimate reality which is realised by the voidness of the self and things'. What is really being said here is that when *śūnyatā* is evoked then all forms of mental discriminations cease, but when talking about *ālayavijñāna* we are not evoking *śūnyatā*, we are evoking consciousness, wherein such 'mental discriminations' do exist, albeit in seed form. Therefore *bījas* should be properly analysed to help solve the mysteries of the nature of our incarnations.[2]

Śūnyatā, the *ālayavijñāna* and the 'self' concept

If we take into account the philosophy of the Sambhogakāya Flower so far presented, then the *Vijñānavādin* doctrine integrates into it quite well, with slight modifications, and bar the statement:

---

2 *Bījas* are seeds of thought constructs, but can also be viewed as subjective atoms, whose structure will have to be explained in a future book.

> The *Vijñānavādin* concludes that there is no self but only consciousness exists. From the beginningless time the various consciousnesses appear in a series, the subsequent one arising with the disappearance of the antecedent. Thus a series of causes and effects is formed. By virtue of *vāsanā* produced from false idea, an image of the self arises in consciousness and the image is taken as a real self by the ignorant people.

It is a truism to say that only consciousness exists (for a human unit), and the energy patterns modified by consciousness produce the appearance of things, but it is not true from the perspective of relativity to say 'there is no self'. The statement 'there is no self' depends upon how one defines 'self'. However we also know that in the light of the definition of *śūnyatā*, which is 'emptiness', no 'self' can be found therein. *Śūnyatā* however accommodates the images of individuality, otherwise there could be no relation between it and things, and the law of *karma* could not propel 'selves' to it so that they can be converted into the spacious All. In other words, if it exists *separated* from an interrelation with things *(saṃsāra)*, the universe as we know it would never come to an end, there would be no true cessation. The positive and negative forces in the universe could never find a resolution. The expression of the subtle 'self' can be accessed via *śūnyatā*, but *śūnyatā* is not tainted by 'it', which allows the *śūnyatā-saṃsāra* nexus to exist. The universe needs *śūnyatā* for its evolution, otherwise there would be no stable base for the existence of anything; there would be no ordered events or sequences through time of phenomena governed by law. There would be no quantum physics for that matter, no paradoxes re the nature of the photon, etc., to ponder.[3] Without *śūnyatā, saṃsāra* would be non-existent, there would be no evolving universe, as from *śūnyatā* comes the energy *(svabhāva)* that moves primal substance *(mūlaprakṛti)* to produce the evolution of things. *Śūnyatā* is the stable support of that which would otherwise be chaotic.

The above is the basis to the saying that *śūnyatā* and *saṃsāra* are one, though it is best to use the formula of Nāgārjuna (the *catuṣkoṭikā),* that they are the same, are not the same, they both are and are not the same, they both neither are and are not the same.

---

3 With respect to this we have, as stated in Volume 1, empirical science's version of *śūnyatā* in the dimensionless 'singularity' from which everything is said to have emanated via a 'big-bang explosion'.

Also, if *saṃsāra* exists in terms of concepts of 'self' of things, i.e., in terms of this's and that's that are separate from each other, then there are also such things as 'selves' in the *ālayavijñāna*.

Such 'selves' are:

1. Individual thought forms created at any moment. Such activity produces the 'image of the self'[4] mentioned in the above quotation. This refers to the existence of the personal-I, which manifests an assertion of the identity of the 'I', and which has a valid functionality in *saṃsāra*, otherwise the *karma* that leads to the realisation of *śūnyatā* could not be produced.
2. Collective thought-forms created by groupings of individuals.
3. Thought streams from any individual collectivised into *bījas* of future potential.
4. Collectivised thought streams from groups of minds manifesting as *bījas* that will regenerate a later flowering of a collective mind. It should be noted that there are many organelles in one organ, which is a structural unity, a 'self', composed of many parts. As many organs constitute the integrity of a (human) body, so also with respect to the domain of thought. For example, the sum of the thinkers that have contributed to the structural system of thought known as Buddhism are *karmically* linked. The thought streams that unite them however make many philosophic knots in the system (in the form of the beliefs of the various sects) and differ from that created by Christians for instance. The cellular unit known as Buddhism evolves in its own inherent thought structure, composed of a myriad different integral entities, cliques of thought streams, created by organised groups of individuals subscribing to similar ideology. They manifest their own forms of *bījas* ('selves') within the general maelstrom of ideas in the religion. Each collectivised *bīja* is but another 'self' to consider that differs from others similarly constructed in the mental realms.
5. Abstracted thoughts collected or emanated by the Sambhogakāya Flowers. The 'continuous series carrying within it the seeds of

4 'By virtue of *vāsanā* produced from false idea, an image of the self arises in consciousness and the image is taken as a real self by the ignorant people.'

all things', wherein 'consciousness and the things act as causes of one another' can then be viewed as being directed by the Flowers. They rightly organise the 'forces of *vāsanā'* which 'leave imprints on the *mūlavijñāna* as the *bījas* from which memory, recognition etc., are manifested'.[5]

We would have chaos without proper organisation and right direction. Everything in Nature is organised, be it the diurnal action of the sun, the regulatory action of the seasons, the movement of constellations and galaxies, etc., so why not also the progress of human lives? This is a concept easy enough to perceive. One can also conceptualise the workings of the *bījas*/seeds given by the doctrine to be properly organised, when we take into account also the proviso I have added concerning their nature. The *saṃskāras* and *skandhas* must be organised and directed by a soul-form if the future actions of a personal-I are to appear from out of the milliards of thought streams that have produced the background for the future actions of that 'I'. This is complicated by the fact that only some of these will be utilised in that particular life. It is truly difficult to even try to imagine the complex miasma of thought streams that exist through the massively variegated axons of collectivised *karma* created by the minds of human beings. It is certainly much harder to imagine how such a morass could produce an ordered sequence of a particular human incarnation, unless we take into account an organising Mind that selects what it needs from out of the mass to produce the desired result.

Santāna and *gati*

It should be noted that in many respects Buddhists generally manifest only one dimensional thought in their logic (e.g., the concept of 'a homogeneous series'), as they do not properly consider the structural nature of the mind—that it is in fact many layered. It can contain

5 Each Flower embodies the *ālayavijñāna* for a human unit, as only thoughts, attributes of mind, are incorporated in the *ālayavijñāna*. Animal sentience, lacking such attributes are thus not found therein, but can be considered aspects of the *mūlavijñāna*, as they represent qualities that are precursors to thought. Such sentience is incorporated via minor *chakras* in the human body.

many streams of thought, bearing differing capacities and intensities of substance, many of which manifest together and which can be gleaned at any time by those that have developed the capacity to think with multileveled application (multidimensionally). The concept of the *rūpa* and *arūpa lokas,* as well as the four *dhyāna* levels, is clear thinking along this line, but it has not been properly applied to this Vijñānavādin logic, which deals with mind substance (the *ālayavijñāna).* Their logic possesses some factual linearity but is not inclusive enough to determine the structural differences in the *ālaya.* Thus for instance, basic philosophical and conceptual problems lie in the thought behind the statement earlier quoted:

> Each sentient being is a continuous mental and physical series *(santāna),* which by force of defilements *(kleśa)* and impure *(sāsrava)* acts turns to destinies *(gati).*

Such *santāna* exists, but with regard to each human it is directed by the Sambhogakāya Flower, which processes all of these defilements *(kleśa)* and impure *(sāsrava)* thoughts in such a way that they manifest in correct sequence to produce an ultimate destiny according to the dictates of *karma.* A directing agent is needed,[6] as there may be billions of individual actions that have caused the defilements to consider during any moment of the progress of the stream, all of which bear differing competing forces to be taken into account. Without such an agency what then would cause any bunch of them to come together at an auspicious moment to cause an incarnation of a person that differed significantly from the previous one with a precise destiny? What force causes the defilements and thoughts to interrupt the flow of the series to precipitate themselves in an organised form in the womb of a woman to take into account family, group, or national *karma* under the prescribed logic? The surmise of the presented quote is inadequate to direct any sequence of defilements into a womb of a mother to be at exactly the right moment and within the most precise social, economic, and cultural situation needed to manifest in the world for destiny to be fulfilled.

---

6 For sentient beings the directing agents are the *devas* and *ḍākinīs.*

Indeed, what destiny is and how it functions is not answered here. There is simply a presumption that it works, but there is barely a hint of the mechanism to account for it. Also, how or where does this homogeneous stream get the idea to incarnate in a particular mother's womb in the first place, and not into any woman that happens to be pregnant. The precisely right mother to account for the *karma* is needed and no other. Now what is 'it' that takes rebirth, how does 'it' formulate its own being out of the morass of where 'it' was to do so under this Buddhist schema? Again no answer is possible here. Also, are not 'defilements' totally incongruent with 'a continuous mental and physical series', especially if it is 'homogeneous', and again where does the force come from? Forces do not willy-nilly appear out of nowhere.

What is actually presented is a system of chance (because of the sheer weight of the vast number of possible confluences of defilements), like a game of dice with a near infinite number of throws to be performed before even the simplest of correct action-reaction sequences can fall the correct way, and with the possibility of the next throw destroying the entire sequence. It is mind numbing to imagine how any system relegated to chance could produce the wonderfully immaculately ordered system that exists in our universe. How could astrological deductions work, or any being be able to predict the nature of the *karma* to be unfolded in say the next life under the conditions of such an indeterminate mechanism? Such indeterminism would make it impossible for a Buddha to predict the future of any being.[7]

Logic therefore clearly *demands* that there be an overriding consciousness that correctly oversees the entire process so that nothing whatsoever is left to mere chance. Such logic brings us to the mechanism of the Sambhogakāya Flower that will be detailed in Volume 3.

---

7 Another perspective dealt with earlier is that such a stream would flow on to somehow indeterminately manifest another life that continues exactly where it left off in the past, hence if formerly a man, then rebirth as another man with exactly the same characteristics could be the only outcome, with no possibility of being a woman for instance, or being born in a different situation in a different country. This is the outcome if the logic of a continuous homogeneous stream is thought out properly. The force of *karma* that could alter such an outcome is said to exist, but acts miraculously, as its mechanism is not explained.

We see, therefore, that no destinies can eventuate without the continuous meditation of the Sambhogakāya Flower, so as to produce the eventual transmutation of the defilements into their corresponding wisdoms. The pure uncoordinated flow of a force of such streams of defilements and impure acts will not work upon themselves to cleanse themselves of their own accord, unless directed to do so by a higher correlating forward visioning force. Also, *karma* alone can not do this unless *karma* is impelled in some direct way by some coordinating force or some type of individuality (consciousness) that brings those acts and defilements together for a purpose. (How indeed could ignorance cleanse ignorance or filth cleanse filth of their own accord? Why would they want to even if they, as sentient beings, could?) This purpose is brought to bear by the accumulated meditation of the Sambhogakāya Flower in conjunction with all other such meditators. Available *karma* is meditatively utilised by them to bring about this end.

One cannot even use the analogy of the force of a flowing river that will eventually reach its destiny—a lake or ocean. Because there the force that goes to produce such an effect, namely gravity coupled with the contour or lay of the land, is a clearly definable law of physics. Thus water will go to seek the lowest level *directed* by the law of gravity flowing thereto according to the way that the contour of the land allows. In relation to the *santāna* given above, where is the correspondence of the law of gravity acting upon this stream? We are simply given the statement that the force of defilements and impure acts turns to destinies. How? What would cause such a stream to individuate into incarnate entities, for individuation is what is needed for 'destinies' to eventuate? There is no gravity at work here. Defilements simply mean that instead of having a clear stream we have a muddied one. So this muddied stream is somehow going to precisely, with exactitude, and with a properly calculated economy of expression, cause the incarnation of mind into exactly the right human birth so that person can develop the characteristics needed for that life. The 'stream' would have to choose rightly out of billions of karmic possibilities on a predetermined road that leads inevitably to Buddhahood? One would have to stretch one's imagination to astoundingly absurd degrees to believe this, but this is what the Buddhist theoreticians have provided us as their answer as to the mechanism of rebirth. What actually is the mechanism for a 'stream' to choose such a birth, or does it simply flow into the first available 'pot' (of a baby's brain) with no accounting of karmic propitiousness at all?

These metaphysicians answer that *karma* does it, but then can not tell us exactly how *karma* can choose from out of the unimaginable billions of bits of karmic information to use for this purpose. They have no conception of the way that *karma* is itself directed by means of conscious intermediaries, such as the Sambhogakāya Flower.

Regarding actions created collectively by humanity, *santāna* also exists external to the Flower, and upon a lower (*rūpa*) level within the field of consciousness. In reality the impediments or sedimentation of the individual 'force of defilements *(kleśa)* and impure *(sāsrava)* acts' find their place there, because in the realm of the Sambhogakāya Flower such base energies cannot exist. The Flower stores the refined expression of the knowledge and loving *saṃskāras* evolved through incarnatory experience, of which the *samalā tathatā* is constituted. It also contains the *bījas* (seed thoughts, karmic factors) from past life activities that wait for the appropriate vitalisation so that a new incarnation of a personal-I can be accomplished. Once projected they awaken atoms of activity containing spirals of energy vectors that attract to them the appropriate substance from the *mūlavijñāna* (base substance). The *bījas* thus attract the substance of mind, the *santāna* that is part of the natural expression of the concreted realms of mind. There we also find the conditionings pertaining to the Six Realms, as these realms are formed out of the substance of the collectivisations of impure consciousness. Interaction with these conditionings happen in accordance with the activity of the *chakras* below the Head centre that are concerned with the rectification of human *saṃsāric* evolution.[8] Such activity will be explained in the later volumes.

How *santāna* is organised with reference to these realms also necessitates a comprehension of the function of the *deva* kingdom, whose role will be somewhat explained in Volume 5A and further detailed in Volume 7 of this *Treatise on Mind*. It suffices to point out here that what Buddhist's say concerning the consciousness flux is

8 These *chakras* are the Throat, Heart, Solar Plexus, Splenic, Sacral and Base of Spine centres. Their activities are coordinated by the Head and Ājñā centres.

rightly relegated to the lower mental realm of expression, but this does not describe how the entire wheel of birth and death is directed for all humans. The overall movement must be directed from above or beyond the little wheels of sedimentation, thus from the abstracted realms of the mind, where we find the Sambhogakāya Flower.

This is logical enough, for the very nature of the expression of sedimentation precludes an inability to direct a proper course of action. Sediments are carried along as part of the flow, part of the wheel of the Six Realms. The little wheels bearing their forms of sediments (within this great wheel) can turn the greater only in relation to an already established criteria for their forms of activity.[9] Such criteria can be stated thus:

1. The greater wheel exists and is turning at its own specific rate. The little wheel will only be able to influence the greater incrementally to increase or to retard its motion, but the overall effect is negligible if the greater is immeasurably vaster. The accumulative effect of many little competing forces however, could tend to retard the overall movement towards liberation, to make it sluggish, or to move it backwards.
2. Direction can come from within if one embodying a little wheel within the greater whole aspires to escape the system altogether, and will inspire others to do so also. They can then together influence the movement of the greater. However, once again we are describing the function of 'individuality', where we refer to wheels (of consciousness expression). In such a case the sedimentation has gone through a process of decantation, leaving behind the dross, and the wheels have expanded to become more inclusive of the whole panorama of activity. Self-will has produced order from the process of murky Brownian-movement types of engagement. The process of rarefaction of consciousness necessitates expansion of the little wheels until they meet the capacity of the whole, and then transcend it. As they do so they become prime movers to counter the nature of the forms of motion of the little wheels ensconced within the form

9 Here the consciousness-stream is not viewed in a linear fashion, but rather in terms of spiral-cyclic motion, which is the true nature that such streams manifest. Minor *chakras* are consequently able to accommodate the expression of their movements.

of the greater whole. This process can be described as 'rectification'. They are no longer working with the type of motion from within wheels, but that which comes from the beyond, the Thusness.

The process of the expansion of the little wheels *(chakras)* necessitate an influx of energy to do so. An inward focus towards the hub of the great wheel is required, which is the prime mover, from which sources of energies and impressions from the beyond (outside of the wheel) stem. The inward focus then produces an outward inclusive expansion until the wheel in question can no longer be sustained by that of which it is a part. It spins off fourth-dimensionally through the capacity of the momentum it has accrued from contact with the prime source of energisation from the beyond.

True lasting direction thus emanates from higher laws or processes that properly regulate the sedimentation process. At first the directing agent is the Sambhogakāya Flower, but ultimately such direction stems from the *dharmakāya*. The Sambhogakāya Flower draws impressions from the *dharmakāya,* and in accordance with the overall guidance as to the future destiny *(gati)* we then have the possibility of the appearance of a new personality, to undergo the *karmically* directed cleansing of the *saṃskāras* of past actions (sedimentation), to fulfil the remainder of the statement:

> Tormented by suffering and disgusted with it, he seeks the attainment of *nirvāṇa.*

If 'all is consciousness' then all must be consciously directed, and how can consciousness do this, unless it segregates, thinks in terms of this and that thing? Consequently again, all that we see is based on the 'self' concept, of 'this' or 'that', without which consciousness could not function, and if consciousness did not function, then no thing in our manifest universe could appear and play their *karmic* role.[10] So there, in the field of consciousness interactions I rest my case as to the applicability of the function of a 'self'.

It is possible that the authors of the Vijñānavādin doctrine understood the nature of the Sambhogakāya Flower, but avoided mentioning it,

---

10 The premise therefore is that the physical universe is also the expression of a conscious Mind, of the laws of Mind in action.

wording their doctrine in such a way that it would be acceptable to the Buddhist world. It could thus be used as a vehicle of salvation, rather than being accused of outright heresy and thus ignored by Buddhists. This was the most expedient thing to do at the time for the rightful education of Buddhists as a whole. That which was omitted from the doctrine was not so important then, as what was presented was sufficient to bring the earnest seeker to the realms where the consciousness of the Flower could be experienced for what it is. The enlightenment that followed would be such that they would then Know and nothing more need be said. In this experience the consciousness of the 'I' merges into the *ālayavijñāna* of the group conscious Flower that contains the seeds of all past and future lives. From this perspective 'there is no real self', i.e., no true consciousness of 'self', and viewing it thus, their doctrine with respect to 'self' is correct.

Bījas and the *maṇipūra chakra*

Concerning *bījas* Swati Ganguly states that:

> The 'seeds' are the different potentialities found in the fundamental consciousness *(ālayavijñāna).* They immediately produce their fruits or the actual *dharmas.* The *bījas* in relation to the *mūlavijñāna* and the fruit are neither identical nor different. They are real entities. However their reality is not the same as *tathatā.* They exist as they are produced through causes and conditions. The *bījas* depend on the substance *(t'i)* of the eighth consciousness. They are part of *nimittabhāga,* as they are taken as object by *darśanabhāga.* According to Dharmapāla, there are two kinds of *bījas* – (i) natural *bījas* and (ii) *bījas* born of perfuming. The natural *bījas* are the potentialities which have existed innately in the *ālaya* by the natural force of things *(dharmatā).* They produce mental elements, sense-organs and the seeming external objects. The other kind of *bījas* are those which have come into being as a result of the 'perfuming' of actual *dharmas,* the 'perfuming' being repeated again and again from beginningless time. The seeds stored in the *ālayavijñāna,* being perfumed by seven other consciousnesses, are caused to grow, resulting in the appearance of things.
>
> The *bījas* have seven characteristics:
>
> i. the *bījas* are momentary *(kṣaṇika).* They are the *dharmas* which perish immediately after birth and which possess a power of activity,

ii. *bīja* is the *dharma* which is simultaneously and actually connected with its fruit,

iii. the *bījas* continue in a homogeneous and uninterrupted series until the final stage of the Holy Path of ascetic practices is attained,

iv. the *bījas* belong to a specific kind of moral species which means they must possess the capacity to produce actual *dharmas*—good, bad or non-defined. This capacity is determined by actual *dharmas*, good, bad or non-defiled, which have perfumed and created them,

v. the *bījas* depend on a group of conditions to realize their capacity to produce an actual *dharma*,

vi. each *bīja* leads to the production of its own fruit. A *bīja* of *citta* leads to the manifestation of *citta* and a *bīja* of *rūpa* leads to the manifestation of *rūpa*.[11]

The ten statements concerning the *bījas* above are:

1. 'The "seeds" are the different potentialities found in the fundamental consciousness *(ālayavijñāna).'*
2. 'They immediately produce their fruits or the actual *dharmas.'*
3. 'The *bījas* in relation to the *mūlavijñāna* (the base or root consciousness) and the fruit are neither identical nor different.'
4. 'They are real entities. However their reality is not the same as *tathatā.'*
5. 'They exist as they are produced through causes and conditions.'
6. 'The *bījas* depend on the substance *(t'i)* of the eighth consciousness (the *ālayavijñāna).'*
7. 'They are part of *nimittabhāga* (occasioned by good and bad), as they are taken as object by *darśanabhāga* (the path of seeing).'
8. 'According to Dharmapāla, there are two kinds of *bījas* – (i) natural *bījas* and (ii) *bījas* born of perfuming. The natural *bījas* are the potentialities which have existed innately in the *ālaya* by the natural force of things *(dharmatā)*. They produce mental elements, sense-organs and the seeming external objects.'
9. 'The other kind of *bījas* are those which have come into being as a result of the "perfuming" of actual *dharmas*, the perfuming being

11 Swati Ganguly, *Treatise in Thirty Verses on Mere-Consciousness*, 40-41. Though the text states that 'The *bījas* have seven characteristics' only six are listed.

repeated again and again from beginningless time. The concept of perfuming relates to the generation of *saṃskāras* that then exist as karmic volitions that manifest in the form of *bījas*. The *bījas* being seeds for future action.'

10. 'The seeds stored in the *ālayavijñāna,* being perfumed by seven other consciousnesses, are caused to grow, resulting in the appearance of things.' (These other consciousnesses are the five sense-consciousnesses, the intellect, plus *kliṣṭamanas.*)

The doctrine of the *bījas* relates to the mode of actualisation of the Solar Plexus centre *(maṇipūra chakra).* This *chakra* is the place of generation of the self-will, and of the emotions, around which the entire construct of the personal-I is formed. Therefore the *bījas* are activated as part of the expression of one or other of the ten petals of this *chakra* by means of the use of this will for the aggrandisement of the concept of 'self'.

The petals of the Solar Plexus centre are arranged in the form of two groups of five petals, one group conveying the five Watery *prāṇas* of the *iḍā nāḍī* stream and the other conveys the five Watery *prāṇas* of the *piṇgalā nāḍī* stream.

The *maṇipūra* is basically a double pentagonal system with an east-west focus towards the Liver and Stomach centres. However this expression is more akin to two groups of four petals, with two subsidiary petals. This is because during the main period of human life only four *prāṇas* are generally applicable for their experiential expression, the fifth (Aether) being too subtle and abstract for most to utilise in the form of *saṃskāras*. The *maṇipūra* at first directs a mix of four *prāṇas* to the minor *chakras* of the general Inner Round circulation,[12] as well as to the routes associated with the Splenic centres. Later upon the Bodhisattva path the full pentad of *prāṇas* are expressed.

The *maṇipūra* is therefore based upon quaternaries and pentads, whilst the Heart centre is based upon triads. The *prāṇas* that come from the *maṇipūra* are feminine in nature, whereas those related to the Heart centre are masculine.

---

12 There is a gradated series of minor *chakras* whose *prāṇas* are synthesised by the Solar Plexus centre. This entire *chakra* system is called the Inner Round.

Each petal of the *maṇipūra* can be viewed as being part of a pentagram of energies. One petal manifests as the head of the pentad, two other petals expressing the functions of the two arms (the organising and grasping function) and two others manifest as the supporting feet, which convey the foundational *prāṇas* for the qualities expressed in the head.

Altogether one can visualise ten pentads for the *maṇipūra chakra*, one for each of the ten petals, with the type of *prāṇa* indicated for each petal as the dominant one representing the head. There are thus literally 50 types of *prāṇa* associated with the *maṇipūra*, which are in fact the 50 *śaktis* of Tantric works, because they convey the powers (*siddhis*) that allow a *yogin* complete mastery of the Watery Element. When multiplied by 10 to signify a great number, we have one interpretation for the mystery of the often used number 500 in Buddhist texts. This number thus signifies all of the forces of the *maṇipūra chakra* as they course through the sum of the Inner Round *chakras*.

Literally implied here is the sum of the psychic constitution of an individual, which expresses the nature of the *siddhis,* once the *prāṇas* associated with the petals are mastered by a *yogin,* as each *prāṇa* has its own specific potency with respect to the development of consciousness.[13] When taken collectively therefore, the number 500 refers to every component making up the constitution of a normal consciousness. We must however double the number, to produce the symbolic number 1,000 to awaken the petals of the Head lotus, because this number represents the integration of the 500 *prāṇas* of the Inner Round controlled by the *maṇipūra chakra* below the diaphragm, and the circulation of their corresponding *prāṇas* above the diaphragm.[14] From this perspective there are 500 *prāṇas* to the major circulation because the *iḍā* and the *piṅgalā nāḍī* streams connecting all of the major *chakras* are each similarly disposed of five *prāṇas* and their subgroups, making 2 x 25 = 50 *prāṇas*. When multiplied by ten (the number of perfection, and of the ten petals of this *chakra)* this makes the necessary 500. The *prāṇas* conveyed by the circulation above the diaphragm are literally the cleansed and transformed version of those generated in the Inner Round.

---

13 This subject will be explored in detail in Volume 5A.

14 Volumes 4 and 5 will provide further detail concerning the significance of these numbers.

The Inner Round is Watery by nature, whilst the purpose of the Heart centre is to transmute them into the Airy quality, via the intermediate drying stage of Fiery (mental) activity, which is the function the Throat centre conveys. The Head lotus (*sahasrāra padma*) must contain the results of the *prāṇic* circulation of both streams, which it bears as the sum of the integral consciousness of the individual.

The western orientation of the Solar Plexus centre is towards the Stomach centre,[15] which becomes the organ of expression for the (Water-Fire) *iḍā nāḍī prāṇas* of the body.[16] These *prāṇas* express the emotionally instigated empirical-mindedness of the individual. In their worst form they convey the *saṃskāras* of intense personal will, the hatreds, intolerance, separativeness and spite of the individual. In their best we have the *saṃskāras* of the discipline of mind that allows philosophic investigation and analytical deductions of the sum of *saṃsāric* phenomena. The Stomach centre digests all types of information. Essentially therefore, the *saṃskāras* of the concretion of mind that relate to the empowerment of the personal-I are processed and stored here. This centre thus favours the development of the intelligentsia, as their form of mental activity is the outcome of the generation of these *iḍā nāḍī prāṇas*. Here the Fires of mind dominate within the Watery context, and we also have the expression of most forms of self-centred *saṃskāras*. The externalised aspect of these *prāṇas* manifest through the left Hand centre.

The most intense attributes of the personal-I are stored in the Stomach centre, making the illusion of 'self' difficult to destroy, as the mind will be totally focussed upon the activities of intellectual pursuits, where it sees itself separated from all other selves. Generally the emotions mould or control the impetus of these Fires, producing many of the hazy auric glazes that most people live in. After they

---

15 The Stomach centre is a first level minor centre, as are the Liver, Diaphragm, and the two Gonad centres. The Splenic centre is dual, and together they manifest the power of a major centre, though individually they are considered minor centres. These centres are situated below the diaphragm, and with the seven major centres will be explicated in detail in this treatise. The two Hand, Knee and Feet centres, that are also first level minor centres, will only be cursorily treated.

16 Note that Figure 7 in Volume 5A presents a diagram of the *chakras* below the diaphragm showing the general layout and number of petals of the associated *chakras*.

have been refined, the *prāṇas* from this centre are drawn via the five non-sacred petals of the Heart centre, to empower the Throat centre. They can then begin to express one's ability to think with the Heart with respect to all *saṃsāric* considerations.

Prāṇas that cross over to the Liver centre via the Solar Plexus centre bear *piṅgalā nāḍī* qualities, wherein a person will be more group oriented, loving, and idealistic, with aspirational, and devotional forms of activity being pursued. Here the qualities of Love are fostered and the attributes of *kliṣṭamanas* begin to be converted into *bodhicitta*. (The Stomach centre on the other hand is focussed upon the development of *manas*.)

When the *prāṇas* are being prepared to be directed to the Heart centre the person will be capable of manifesting great altruistic works and a creative outflow in science, literature, the arts, philosophy, and all social sciences. Such people thus generate sound reasoning concerning the need to eliminate materialistic pursuits. The refinement of both *manas* and *kliṣṭamanas* (both the *iḍā and piṅgalā nāḍīs)* are needed to develop abstract thought and the Clear Light of Reason. The Throat and Heart centres can then be awakened to their full potential.

The northern petal of the Solar Plexus centre receives the *prāṇas* from Splenic centre I.[17] Mostly, however, the Solar Plexus centre conveys *prāṇas* from the next level down of minor *chakras*. Such *prāṇas* express the animal-like *saṃskāras* of the general emotionally biased thinking person. They represent the elemental or coarsest emotional attributes and thus constitute the densest type of *prāṇa* that the Solar Plexus conveys, the Earthy Element of the Watery *prāṇas* of the entire system.

Regarding the petals of the western quadrant of the Solar Plexus centre, one petal conveys the *piṅgalā prāṇas* to the Heart centre, and another the *iḍā prāṇas* to the Sacral centre. However the major expression is the conveyance (of general mental-emotional *prāṇas*) to and from the Stomach centre (containing a form of Watery *prāṇa* intensified with Fire) for processing and or expression of the related *saṃskāras*. The *prāṇas* to and from the Stomach centre (and the

17 The Splenic centre is a dual centre concerned with the processing, refinement and redirection of *saṃskāras* to the required centres. Splenic centre I is sun-like with vitalising *prāṇas* and overlaps Splenic centre II, which acts as a sewer system in the body. Their functions will be detailed in Volumes 3 and 5A.

corresponding ones of the eastern direction to and from the Liver centre) express the most commonly generated *saṃskāras* of the average person. They are:

a. Mental-emotions.

b. More purely (loving) emotion-desire based activities.

c. Sensual, sense oriented impressions and experiences (when integrating *prāṇas* from the Sacral centre).

The Stomach centre is the *iḍā* store for the worst of the human traits, thus:

- *Cruelty.* This concerns the human correspondence of the carnivore's instinct to kill without consideration of the pain inflicted upon the victim.
- *Hatred.* This concerns the human correspondence of the male animal's form of competitiveness, generally concerning an animal's right to procreate with the female of the species.
- *Separativeness.* This concerns the human correspondence of an animal's territorial instincts.
- *The critical mind.* This is a human development concerning the inability of an individual to hold lofty thought, to 'peck' or 'gnaw away' at other's perceived faults.

The *Liver centre* is the *piṇgalā* store for the traits of possessiveness, or aquisitiveness, the grasping, feeling tendencies found in humans. This is the transformed correspondence of the animal's instinct to build shelters. It also incorporates the more affectionate and loving side of human development related to the propagation of the species, the relationships with the opposite sex that necessitates home building, and the long time caring of progeny within a social structure that conditions their habitat.

Here also is stored the *bījas* of all of the *saṃskāras* of the effects of fighting and reproving. It concerns one's dissatisfaction with one's lot in life, and for the desire to possess what another has. We thus have the *saṃskāras* of the pain, destruction and loss of life that comes with the human wars fought for possessions, land, and idealisms. There are two basic forms or intensities of this trait:

- The desire for *material comforts*, where the possessiveness is for the alluring products derived originally from the earth, plants and animals, that humans desire.
- *Greed or avarice.* The strong overwhelming desire to possess what others have and what is deemed valuable, so as to focus one's entire life's purpose to that aim.

The central two petals of the eastern quadrant of the Solar Plexus centre channel *prāṇas* to and from the Liver centre (and then to the right Hand centre) which processes and stores the *piṇgalā* aspect of the Watery *maṇipūra prāṇas*. This involves emotional concerns and forms of psychic receptivity, the feeling responses and mediumship, that people possess. They oft draw *prāṇas* from the Sacral centre via the right Gonad centre, which is the place of the genesis of the *piṇgalā* stream. It conveys the more lovingly emotional forms of desire for things and for forms of sexual relationships.

The Liver centre therefore expresses the *saṃskāras* of basic human affectionate relationships and normal everyday interactions of a generally pleasant nature. This involves all forms of group activities, of family and social life. (An extension of the group instinct of animals.) The *prāṇas* directed to this centre from the Solar Plexus centre are of a Watery-Fiery disposition, having crossed over in the main part from the Stomach centre. The Fiery quality tends to either uplift or to inflame the general expression of commonplace thinking, producing the many intensities and volatility of people's emotional lives. The returning *prāṇas* from the Liver centre convey the general Watery disposition of the individual that comes to be expressed at any moment as people interact sociably, but propelled by the reinforced *saṃskāras* from former cycles of activity. The Solar Plexus then expresses these *prāṇas* according to the intensity of the energy input coupled with other influences, such as Fiery mental impetus from the Throat centre, or a kindly loving disposition from the Heart centre.

The southern petal of the *maṇipūra chakra,* conveying Earthy *prāṇas*, directs energies to the next level down of minor centres. These energies ultimately find their externalisation in the physical organs associated with digestion, with the pancreas being the main organ of reception (being the physical externalisation of the Solar Plexus centre). Being physical externalisations of the *prāṇas,* the qualities of the rejected energies incorporated into the organs are important. Problems arise if *prāṇas* have been projected into the organs via forceful expression, or through the concretion of generated qualities. The health and vitality of the body thus directly depends upon the nature of the *prāṇas* that are deposited there. The organs are automatons re the energies that pass through them from the embodying *chakra.*

This is the key to understanding all true forms of healing. Modern pharmaceuticals however generally alter the composition of the physical organ, or work as poisons to attack the invading microbes and other entities. True healing works to change the energy balance, the nature of the *prāṇas* that must effectively be eliminated via the agency of the organ concerned. If the *prāṇas* carry too much sedimentation then inevitably the organ in which they are deposited will suffer and begin to malfunction, cause cancerous growth, or allow invasion from predatory species of life that are attracted to the form of sediments accrued. If the *prāṇas* lack vitality then the organ becomes undernourished and lacks the ability to fight off predatory entities. Obviously a loving disposition will work to engender a proper healthy functioning of the bodily organs, whereas a volatile, cantankerous, or critical disposition will help to sow the seeds of discord in the cellular structure, or to devitalise the organs, so that they offer little resistance to invading organisms.

Direct healing through utilising the psychic techniques of the *siddhas*[18] is presently a lost art, despite the many claims of would be practitioners, because exact knowledge of the nature of these minor *chakras* and their effects in the body has always been carefully withheld from the eyes of the profane. This is because of the dangers of psychic abuse that so many would entertain if they possessed such elucidation. Yet much correct information needs to be presented to those who are capable of working with their Heart centres for the good of the all. Thus texts must yet be written to reveal what is needed for students of healing to investigate in the future, and to correct the many misconceptions regarding the art of healing that presently abound in our societies.

There are four petals of north-south orientation of the Solar Plexus centre that channel the *prāṇas* of the *iḍā* and *piṇgalā nāḍī* stream to

18 One who has awakened the *siddhis* (psychic powers) in an enlightened manner.

and from the Sacral and Heart centres. They therefore convey the major *prāṇas* of the entire *nāḍī* system. The highest type of *prāṇa* from the Sacral centre are Earthy-Aetheric, representing the most refined energy that the Sacral centre is capable of expressing and which can be utilised positively by the Solar Plexus centre. The overall quality however is that of a Watery-Fiery-Earthy nature because the Aetheric quality proper is too refined for this level of expression. The *prāṇas* from the Solar Plexus centre to the Heart centre are Watery-Airy because they convey the highest emanation of the quality of Love that the Solar Plexus centre is capable, and are therefore along the *piṇgalā* line of expression. When integrated into the general Solar Plexus centre the central *iḍā* and *piṇgalā nāḍī* stream admixes with the general east-west flow of *prāṇas* and are processed accordingly.

These four petals are specifically concerned with the orientation of this *chakra* to the other major centres, leaving six petals to vitalise the minor *chakras* of the Inner Round. The four petals represent a relatively minor energy flow for most people, until the various stages of the Bodhisattva path when the central north-south axis gains predominance. Then the Airy *prāṇas* from the Heart centre will take control of all forms of *prāṇic* circulation of this centre. When the *dhyāna* of the *yogin* awakens *kuṇḍalinī* then the Aetheric aspect of the petals have been activated, allowing the Fiery *kuṇḍalinī* unimpeded passage through the *nāḍīs* to control all attributes of the form. The *siddhis* can now awaken because the sewer-like activities of the Splenic centres have by then been thoroughly cleansed of their *prāṇic* dross. In the yogic control of the Splenic centre's activities, via the purification and transformation of *saṃskāras,* lies the key to the entire liberation process, as will be detailed in Volume 5A. No centre however acts alone, all are interrelated.

My purpose in this exposé of the Solar Plexus centre, as well as later of the other major, and some minor *chakras* in the body, is to rectify the many misconceptions concerning them, and thereby to eliminate the ubiquitous veils found in the texts. The time for the truth concerning the way they function has now appeared. This is necessary to further the spiritual advancement of humanity in this epoch of the internet, and of a world-wide information explosion. The world is now one global village, and to it correct truthful information must flow, and not distorted teachings.

The information concerning these psychic centres were heavily veiled in the texts because of the dangers associated with their premature awakening in societies where yoga-meditation was highly esteemed and ardently sought after by many. Enlightened teachers existed then that earnest students could find for correct teachings. Such teachers largely do not exist today. The true esoteric lore has been mostly lost by the lineage holders of the various traditions. This method of instruction has been deemed inadequate for today's needs because the teachings need to be instated in such a way that students all over the world can gain access to what was formerly hidden, without recourse to unnecessary exoteric gloss and ritual. The old systems that existed when Tibet was at its prime do not suffice in this modern world, where worthy recipients for advanced teachings, the reincarnating originating teachers and their students, can be found throughout the world and must rightly awaken. Safeguards will still exist, but they will come mainly via the filtering aspect of the intellectual prowess of those who will take the care to understand the complexities of Buddhist Tantric metaphysics, coupled with comprehension of the nature of *saṃskāras* and the necessity of developing the path of compassion. Such doctrine will be given in Volume 5. Consequently, this *Treatise on Mind* must be studied for those wishing correct knowledge of this most esoteric of subjects.

The pentads of the Solar Plexus centre

There are two major pentads ('hands') of *prāṇas* produced by the north-south orientation, as the Solar Plexus centre is effectively divided into top and bottom groups of petals. The top half integrates the *prāṇas* from the Splenic centre and from above the diaphragm with those from the Liver and Stomach centres. The downpour of intense energies produces a distillation process, allowing the refining of *prāṇas* in the *maṇipūra* so they can be directed upwards towards the Heart centre. The objective is to cleanse the dross of negative, fearful, aggressive, critical or base emotions via rightly controlled Watery expression through either the more mental (Stomach centre) or loving (Liver centre) forms of activity. A general Fiery-Airy integration of petals produces energies that are receptive to the qualities expressed above the diaphragm. They involve a stream enterer or Bodhisattva's normal intercourse with the fields of humanity's mental-emotional output. The mental stream concerns the major writing and teaching dispensation of the person. The loving stream concerns the living example, of the way one manifests one's life for the generation of *bodhicitta* so that those that are to be served are benefited. An overall Fiery (mental) energy must meditatively be used to dry up the Waters, especially upon the path of yoga-meditation.

The pentad directed south is concerned with the downpour of vitalising and cleansing *prāṇas* from the higher *chakras* towards the physical form via the Stomach and Liver centres, the Inner Round and the pancreas. Inevitably the entire digestive apparatus will be controlled via the physical organs that are the externalisations of these *chakras*. The adage is 'we are what we eat', and if this process is rightly governed then good health will be the gain. Also, once the person works with pure motives and yogic methodology, the entire Inner Round can be mastered and the lower *siddhis* developed. The focus therefore is control of the general Earthy expression that is necessary to sustain physical plane livingness. These energies become externalised in the physical body.

Each of the pentads consists of five 'fingers' of expression. Of these fingers the thumb, which is ambidextrous, conveys the fluid Watery *prāṇas*. The forefinger, being used to point with, providing directions from the mind, predominantly bears Fiery *prāṇas*. The middle finger, being longer, hence symbolically can reach out to touch the most corporeal of domains (the dense physical plane), conveys Earthy *prāṇas*. The ring finger channels predominantly Airy *prāṇas,* and the little finger, being the least used conveys the Aetheric *prāṇas*. These Elements and *prāṇas* have their correspondences in the sense-consciousnesses.

The Solar Plexus activity must become totally calmed, to manifest a quiet pool, a mirror for the reflection of higher impressions into consciousness, without any aberration or Watery perturbations.

The petals of the Solar Plexus centre detailed

The Solar Plexus centre represents the abdominal brain and is the major centre developed by the animal kingdom, producing the beginnings of self-identification and devotion in them. In humans the 1,000 petalled lotus is ultimately the focus for development, producing all of the aspects of consciousness that we know so well. (This focus happens in stages via the five groupings of major *chakras* centred along the spinal column.) This is one major reason why rebirth into animal forms is impossible for a human consciousness. It is simply not possible to squeeze the necessary qualities of the 1,000 petalled lotus of human interrelationships into these 10 petals of the Solar Plexus. Hence there is no mechanism for human incarnation, but humans can certainly utilise this centre as a mechanism of expression, to activate the *bījas* concerned with self-identification[19] and of animal-like qualities. From this perspective rebirth into an animal form (which a human body can also be depicted as) can be considered a truism, but it is the animal *chakra*s (the Inner Round) within a human form into which a human consciousness incarnates.

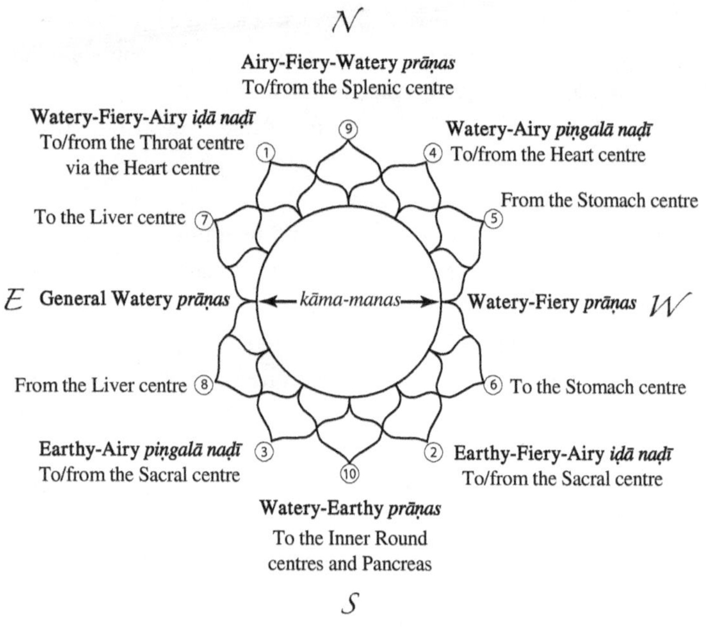

Figure 2. The *bījas* and the Solar Plexus centre

19 This aspect being fully developed in humans, but is embryonic in the higher animal forms.

Having analysed the concept of pentads in the Solar Plexus centre, the focus can now be upon the properties of its individual petals with respect to the quotation previously given on the *bījas*. The numbers assigned to the petals in the Figure relate to the qualities of the *bījas* as shown below. The petals numbered 1,2,3 and 4 are concerned with the *iḍā* and *piṅgalā nāḍīs*, hence their base Element is Air, which accommodates all of the *prāṇas* without adulteration. Also note that the type of sub-*prāṇa* conveyed in the *nāḍīs* depends upon the stage of development the person is at. The *prāṇic* qualities are chosen at the stage of those demonstrating goodwill to others and who may be preparing to enter the path to enlightenment. It should also be remembered that the Solar Plexus centre is the dynamo for the conveyance of the Watery *prāṇas* in the body, hence the general expression of *kāma-manas,* desire or emotional-mind. This energy is however principally relegated to the east-west direction. The western orientation adds a Fiery disposition, whereas the eastern direction is principally concerned with processing the general Watery *prāṇas*. The southern hand of petals convey the more general Earthy (physically derived) *prāṇas* to the Watery mix, and the northern hand generates Airy (more loving) characteristics.

1. The Watery-Fiery-Airy aspect of the *iḍā nāḍī (manasic)* line, which relates to the phrase 'The "seeds" are the different potentialities found in the fundamental consciousness *(ālayavijñāna)*'. The *prāṇas* from this *nāḍī* flow to and from the Throat centre via the non-sacred petals of the Heart centre. The Throat centre directs Fiery energies from the *ālayavijñāna* (here viewed as the content of the Head lotus) to seed the *maṇipūra* with *manasic* impressions. They are the main ideas that impress the emotions with images of what the 'I' wants. The Solar Plexus centre then draws *bījas* from its collective pool that will instantaneously clothe the images with the weight of the propensities developed from the past. Thus the *saṃskāras* become expressed in new *karma*-formations (volitions), demonstrating the inner happenings of the way people's desire-minds function.

   By drawing *prāṇas* directly from the *ālayavijñāna* this petal vitalises the entire *maṇipūra* with aspects of *ahamkāra,* the 'I am' assertion of consciousness, giving the personal-I self-identity for each new incarnation. The various *bījas* of consciousness volitions, the *saṃskāras* of identity with things in relation to the 'I' thus flow from this petal. Consciousness is then stimulated in the nine ways associated with the other petals, as these Fiery *bījas* become clothed with the Watery qualities associated with the *maṇipūra chakra.* The gain is then directed to the Throat and Head centres, enhancing the attributes of mind found there. This petal represents the forefinger, bearing Fiery *prāṇas,* of the upwards pointing (right) hand of the *maṇipūra chakra.*

2. The *iḍā nāḍī* continues as the polar opposite of the above petal. The *prāṇas* are directed to and from the Sacral centre, where they are grounded via the field of desire into actual concretion as physical action, by means of the sense contacts and related perceptions so familiar to us. This petal processes the Airy base of the Earthy-Fiery *prāṇas* from the Sacral centre. They are then incorporated into the Watery field of the Solar Plexus centre. The associated phrase is 'They immediately produce their fruits' or the 'actual *dharmas'*. This is because the Sacral centre directs the vitality of the entire bodily organism and is specifically concerned with the process of identification with material plane phenomena and with the desirous, producing a concretion of energies. It governs the entire field of desire. The appearing *saṃskāras* compellingly cause us to utilise the sense-consciousnesses to attach to 'things' corresponding to past forms of activities that we undertook and now still perpetuate. Here *dharmas* represent the elements of unavoidable consciousness-bits that people must reckon with. They can be related to the *dharmas* that are explained in the *Abhidharma.*

   Also the genesis of the entire *iḍā nāḍī* stream is found by means of corporeal action in the corresponding petal of the Sacral centre, producing empirical effects ('fruits') in consciousness. When such *saṃskāras* flow into the Solar Plexus centre they immediately produce the familiar and ubiquitous *kāma-manas* governing human activity. This emotional-mind bears many karmic fruits in people's lives. The forefinger of the downward pointed left hand is here expressed.

3. The third petal is concerned with the generation of basic emotional attributes via the principle of desire-attachment to pleasurable

sensations and experiences, and of all types of phenomena. This relates to the generation of the *piṇgalā nāḍī prāṇas* from the Sacral centre. The associated phrase is 'The *bījas* in relation to the *mūlavijñāna* and the fruit are neither identical nor different'. Here attributes of the transience of all phenomena are grappled with, producing many basic experiences, termed the *mūlavijñāna.* The *mūlavijñāna* is the source or root form of consciousness *(vijñāna),* therefore with respect to *prāṇic* circulation it is concerned with the nature of any sense-consciousness that is garnered from the field of desire. The *saṃskāras* that have been developed through interrelation with what was desired via Sacral centre activity are then assimilated by consciousness via the Solar Plexus centre. They enter as a *piṇgalā* expression, where desire generates the emotions, producing the forms of separateness and self-identity associated with the *maṇipūra chakra.*

The fruit of desire-emotion are 'neither identical nor different' to the *mūlavijñāna,* being both the cause of the basic *vijñāna* (forms of knowledge) and yet in the form of desire is not a *vijñāna,* as it is a force *(vāsanā)* that causes attachment to the objects of the senses, rather than being a sense-consciousness. Nevertheless it causes karmic effects ('fruits') constituted of the originating *bījas* (thus are not different) plus that which has derived from them (thus are not identical), having grown from the soil of *saṃsāra.* The ring finger of the downward pointing hand is here expressed.

With respect to petals 2 and 3 the appellations Earthy-Fiery-Airy and Earthy-Airy relate to the generation of the most basic (Earthy) attributes of the major types of *prāṇas* conveyed in the *iḍā* (Fire) and *piṇgalā* (Air) *nāḍīs.*

4. This petal is a continuation of the *piṇgalā nāḍī* that comes to or from the Sacral centre in relation to the *prāṇas* being processed by the Solar Plexus centre, for to be directed towards the Heart centre. The associated phrase is: 'They are real entities. However their reality is not the same as *tathatā'.* When the *prāṇas* cross over to the Heart centre after having been cleansed of their Watery dross (through the function of the Splenic centre) they then become 'real entities' because they are to be absorbed by the Heart centre. The Heart is

the life of the entire process concerned with gaining enlightenment, which is 'the real'. Forms of illusion then no longer concern the individual, but rather *bījas* that produce the *śūnyatā* experience are encapsulated into conscious undertaking. The *saṃskāras* of self-identification of the Solar Plexus centre have been washed away with vitalising transformative *prāṇas* from the Heart centre, and only the most refined Watery or Airy *prāṇas,* akin to the Heart's own substance, flow up this main *piṅgalā* channel to the *anāhata chakra.* The *prāṇas* enter the general *prāṇic* pool of the Heart lotus, but are 'not the same as *tathatā'* because *tathatā* is the result of the final transmuting activity of *prāṇas* within the Heart centre. The *prāṇas* residing in the Heart may need further refining, hence some proportion will be rejected to be further processed by Splenic centre I. The Airy ring finger of the right hand is here implicated.

The next four petals of the Solar Plexus centre to be considered are concerned with the general circulation of the main Watery *prāṇas* within the *nāḍī* system. This happens via the interrelation with both the Stomach and Liver centres and the recycling and cleansing action of the dual Splenic centre.

5. We now deal with the Watery-Fiery *prāṇas* of the Solar Plexus centre directed from the Stomach centre associated with the phrase: 'They exist as they are produced through causes and conditions'. Coming from the Solar Plexus centre, with its overwhelming Watery impetus, the Fiery *manasic* input generated by activity other than that of the *iḍā nāḍī* is relatively weak, hence the little finger of the right hand is implicated. We must then look to the nature of the *bījas* that are an outcome of the type of experiences associated with the Stomach centre, where the major part of the experiential situations are digested. The *manasic bījas* specifically find their onus of expression there. They are concerned with the gains of the activity of the sense-consciousness in the material domain whereby all aspects of mental-emotions are unfolded, 'produced through causes and conditions' whilst *saṃsāric* phenomena is processed. The *ālayavijñāna* (as it relates to the personal-I) is essentially created via the Stomach centre's activity.

The elemental Fiery *prāṇas* thus generated stimulate the mechanism of self-awareness and self-identity. This causes the ability to modify one's perception of things, thus the *bījas* are altered, or else new *bījas* evolve. The 'causes and conditions' associated with the mental-emotional world that is the natural quality of this *chakra* are thereby produced. The predominantly Watery *prāṇas* of the Solar Plexus centre are modified with further Fiery intensity.

6. The phrase 'The *bījas* depend on the substance *(t'i)* of the eighth consciousness' refers to the direction of the evolved Watery-Fiery *saṃskāras* to the Stomach centre (and from the Inner Round centres that have evolved such *prāṇas)* to the Solar Plexus centre. Here we have the action of the thumb of the downward focussed left hand. (The focus of this hand being the manipulation of *manasic prāṇas* whereas the right hand grapples with *piṇgalā prāṇas).*

We know 'the eighth consciousness' to be the *ālayavijñāna* (which can be described as a 'sea of fire'). The *ālayavijñāna* finds its genesis mostly in the Stomach centre of the personal-I, as the environment within this centre is the breeding ground for *iḍā nāḍī* attributes, conditioned by volitions from past incarnations. This disposition or natural state garnered from qualities developed in the past is the basic modifying quality for any *prāṇic* transaction derived in the present through sense-perception with the material domain. The *bījas* therefore depend upon the quality of this admixed predisposition for their formation and expression. If for example the Stomach centre is seeded with *bījas* derived from past lives of possessing a disposition for violent mental *saṃskāras*, then such a predisposition will come to the fore. Being materially focussed the *prāṇas* from this centre will consequently tend to intensify the self-will of the personal-I when that 'I' thinks in terms of itself in relation to the world around and the objects of desire that can be manipulated for personal gain.

The Sambhogakāya Flower normally decides what *bījas* are to be experienced by the personal-I, and in which sequence, in accordance with its curriculum for the expansion of consciousness for that life and in context with the succession of personal-I's. (Such however is often overridden by the person's desire-will.) The purpose is the refinement and Fiery expansion of consciousness, so it can be abstracted from the emotional world (within which most people are immersed) and utilised by the Throat centre. The major prowess of the *manasic* principle happens when the Throat centre becomes dominantly active and an individual enters into the ranks of the intelligentsia. Because of the potency of the Throat centre's Fiery impetus, the *prāṇas* become more Fiery-Watery when directed to or receiving the associated Stomach centre's activity, which then intensifies the tendencies to quick opinionated reactions, intensities of anger and dogmatic assertions. The individual must learn to assuage these *prāṇas* with the calming Airy-Watery *prāṇas* from the Heart centre to control such attributes. Ultimately only the qualities of a refined mind that can be absorbed into the Sambhogakāya Flower's form will be produced.[20] (This represents the distilled essences of the generated experiences.) The 'substance of the eighth consciousness' is the basis of the entire evolutionary growth of consciousness. It is fundamental to being human. From it the Clear Light of Mind evolves.

7. Having analysed the *iḍā* Watery-Fiery *prāṇas* generated via the Stomach centre, the *piṇgalā prāṇas* associated with the Liver centre can now be the focus. The concern here is with processing the Watery-Fiery *prāṇas* that flow to the Liver centre after they have been integrated into and washed by the general Watery environment of the Solar Plexus centre. The Fiery aspect therefore becomes more Watery—affectionate, emotional, tending towards a loving social interaction. This *prāṇic* flow therefore softens the Fiery *prāṇas* that have been generated, if they have been too intense and wilful. The loving, affectionate disposition of humanity, their general run-of-the-mill day to day forms of activity thereby comes to the fore. They are the major *prāṇas* generated via the Liver centre (and general humanity), and consequently are conveyed by the thumb of the right hand. (The major conduit for Watery *prāṇas*). The *bījas* of these *prāṇas* are described as: 'They are part of *nimittabhāga* (occasioned by good and bad), as they are

20 The Sambhogakāya Flower contains the abstracted portion of the *ālayavijñāna*.

taken as object by *darśanabhāga* (the path of seeing)'. The Liver centre's activities are 'occasioned by good and bad', because here the social consciousness of an individual is generated.

In this centre therefore the personal-I learns the basic lessons of life, that all forms of attachment to transient things ultimately lead to pain and suffering. It produces the background wherein the Buddha's Four Noble Truths can be understood and then followed. The 'path of seeing' concerns the upward looking way that is gained once the miasmas and fogs (the swirls of emotionality that most people are immersed in) have been clarified somewhat by consciousness so that the individual can find his/her way to the enlightened stance of the Heart centre. (The natural direction of the *piṇgalā* flow.) We thus have the aspiration towards the Eightfold Path. It represents the consequent reorientation or focus of the individual upwards to greater heights of understanding. This is the consequence of pain, suffering, and learning to detach from *saṃsāric* allurements. The momentum (*vāsanā*) that drives the cleansed, altruistic *prāṇas* to the Heart centre is thereby kindled.

That which is seeded by the Sambhogakāya Flower in this arena is also 'occasioned by good and bad' because these are the *bījas* of the Watery *saṃskāras* of past actions, the *karmic* heirloom that the person must experience and cleanse. The 'good' is the elimination of one's attachment to the allurements of the Watery world. It concerns the ability to comprehend the nature of the muddied substance of agitated desires, emotions and attachments because the sedimentation has subsided sufficiently for the individual to see a greater distance in this realm. He/she can envision the light that comes from the Airy zone above it and thus aspire towards that light. The 'bad' concerns one's emotional entrapment with sensual pursuits to the extent that hell-producing enticements becomes one's entire focus.

8. Next can be considered the aspect of the Liver centre wherein there are 'two kinds of *bījas* – (i) natural *bījas* and (ii) *bījas* born of perfuming. The natural *bījas* are the potentialities which have existed innately in the *ālaya* by the natural force of things (*dharmatā).* They produce mental elements, sense-organs and the seeming external

objects'. The general Watery *saṃskāras* that are actually generated via Liver centre activity, plus the pre-existing conditions of the emotional environment people reside in, is depicted as 'the natural *bījas'*. These *bījas* are the *prāṇas* returning from the Liver centre to the Solar Plexus centre. They will either enter into the general circulation of that centre for normal Watery expression, or else they will be cleansed enough with the Airy quality of Love for them to be abstracted into the Heart centre. 'The natural *bījas*' thus have the capacity to generate the qualities of the Heart centre, denoted 'the natural force of things *(dharmatā)'*. The entire bodily organism can then be vitalised with the energy of goodwill and of loving aspiration. They therefore seed the conditions wherein enlightened consciousness can arise and find its natural play.

The '*bījas* born of perfuming' are the *saṃskāras* that have been seeded by the Sambhogakāya Flower as karmic factors, effecting the type of emotional experiences and perceptions that so far have been described with respect to the *maṇipūra* circulation.

The little finger of the left hand is here implicated because the aspects of mind producing compassionate or abstract thought generated by an individual is generally small, though ever-increasing as one enters the path to enlightenment. For the most part the normal emotional aspects of the Solar Plexus are recycled again and again, to enter into the Inner Round and the Stomach centre circulation, until the person becomes more aware of the mental environment (hence not producing the glazes of emotionality). The effects of such proclivity produces the familiar emotional pain, trauma, hypersensitive reactivity, illogical assumptions, etc., of the average person, from which effectively the 'mental elements, sense-organs and the seeming external objects' are properly developed. What this phrase really means is that as a consequence of emotional reactions to blows of *karma* and to other's emotions, eventually elements of logical thought are developed as people become more compassionately aware of the consequences of their actions and curtail their emotions. They become more aware of the psycho-physical apparatus into which they have incarnated, consequently evolving out of the childhood stage. They become aware of what really exists in the field of *saṃsāra* and take the appropriate steps to master them. The energies of such mastery represent the *prāṇas* flowing through the 'little finger'.

When the *prāṇas* from the *maṇipūra* have been sufficiently cleansed of their dross they then resemble the quality of 'the natural *bījas*' to be able to be contained in the Heart centre. Consequently the beginning of the process whereby *dharmatā* can be experienced in consciousness happens in the Liver centre. The *prāṇas* can then be directed to the Heart centre via the petal governing the *piṅgalā nāḍī* thereto.

9. The 'head' of the northern pentad of the Solar Plexus centre can now be analysed.[21] It channels *prāṇas* from the Solar Plexus centre to and from Splenic centre I. The associated phrase is: 'The other kind of *bījas* are those which have come into being as a result of the "perfuming" of actual *dharmas,* the "perfuming" being repeated again and again from beginningless time'.

   The middle, Earthy finger, of the right hand is here implicated because the more Earthy attributes of the Airy-Fiery-Watery *prāṇas* that are rejected by normal Solar Plexus activity are cycled and recycled through the Splenic centres until they have cleansed their dross. Also rectified *prāṇas* coming from Splenic centre I perfume the various factors or aspects of existence that consciousness takes to be real. The originating source of the *bījas* expressed here are those that have been rejected from the Heart centre's Airy form of activity. These *prāṇas* have flowed to Splenic centre I to effect the cleansing, transformation, and eventually transmutation of *saṃskāras.* The consequent process in yoga-meditation for the generation of enlightenment attributes, as explained in Volume 5A, is implied here. This happens over time and concerns the process that converts a normal person into an enlightened being.

   The cleansed *saṃskāras* are cycled through the Watery *maṇipūra* system, and inevitably the quality of Love that is generated can be expressed within the Heart centre. Thus the perfuming is

21 The thumb and little fingers therefore represent the right and left feet and the ring and forefinger the right and left hands of the pentad, when viewed from a *prāṇic* perspective.

continuously repeated until the desired outcome is the generation of *bodhicitta* and the ability to travel the Bodhisattva path. The *bījas* from the Heart centre are also mixed with those from the Inner Round of minor *chakras,* which express the qualities of the 'actual *dharmas'* (when registered by consciousness). They are said to be the factors of existence, or elements of consciousness, as explained in the Abhidharma.[22]

What has herein been described will take many lives to achieve, when starting with a base human unit to the highly refined Bodhisattva, hence the factor of time is introduced. It indicates the concept of endless rebirths into dense forms where the *bījas* 'have come into being' and time is experienced. The various *karma*-producing volitions, and later those that eliminate *karma,* are enacted as a result of the response to the 'perfuming of actual *dharmas'.* The developed *saṃskāras* continuously repeat themselves upon ever-increasing higher and subtler levels, until eventually the Waters have been evaporated away by means of the application of Fire. (An expression of Splenic centre I, drawing energies from the Throat centre via the Heart centre.) We see therefore that the energies from both the Heart and Throat centres are needed to perfume these *dharmas* that will eventually transform Solar Plexus energies into enlightenment attributes.

10. The general direction of the Watery-Earthy *prāṇas* to the most southern petal of the Solar Plexus centre. (The head of the southern downward focussed pentad.) Here the middle finger of the left hand is implicated, which 'touches' the 'ground' that is the physical body. The associated phrase is: 'The seeds stored in the *ālayavijñāna,*

---

22 See Theodore Stcherbatsky, *The Central Conception of Buddhism,* (Motilal Baranasidass, Delhi, 1994), 74-75, for a summary of their properties. Briefly, each *dharma* (element) is a separate entity or force, there is no substance apart from the qualities of a *dharma,* they have no duration, but flash as new appearances with each moment. The *dharmas* cooperate with each other. (There are 72 of these *saṃskṛta-dharmas.)* Thus they stem from causes and proceed to extinction when influenced by wisdom, but when influenced by ignorance they are continuously generated. The gaining of liberation therefore is that which produces their extinction. I shall not undergo a philosophic investigation of the merits and errors of this system of philosophy here, a subject that already has been pursued by Mādhyamika philosophers.

being perfumed by seven other consciousnesses, are caused to grow, resulting in the appearance of things'.

This petal vitalises the pancreas, specifically governing the nature of its secretions, and then the other organs concerned with the digestion process, such as the bile duct, stomach and the intestines. Hence we have 'the appearance of things', which concerns the awareness of the dense form and its relationships as a consequence of digestion (mental comprehension). The intermediate step however, before the gross externalisation of the activated *bījas* in the arenas of externalisation, concerns the circulation of the *prāṇas* through level two minor *chakras*, which in a sense produce the proper digestion of all *bījas* that affect the physical form ('the appearance of things').

This therefore concerns the means whereby people identify with phenomena. This identification is at first primarily emotional, fuelled by the factor of desire. Emotional-sensual interrelations are what most people know or care for, coupled with the forms of intelligence that allow them to manipulate the environment, and to interrelate with others in order to obtain the things they desire. (*Prāṇically* seen as the serpents of desire. Serpents depict the mode of movement of differing streams of *prāṇas,* with their birthing at the tail end, growth of the body, and climaxing at the head.) All seven Ray aspects and states of consciousness come into play with such identification, producing the major glamours that people are besotted or throttled by. The seeds that externalise in the bodily form are thus 'caused to grow' through their activities, literally by means of the addition of the Waters, wherein they swell, expand and germinate.

From the above we can see that there are four main *prāṇic* directions associated with the Solar Plexus centre, oriented along the arms of the fixed cross. They are the north and south orientations associated with the major *prāṇas* of the *iḍā* and *piṇgalā nāḍīs* and the east and west directions that vitalise the Liver and Stomach centres.

There is also a configuration based upon the eight-spoked wheel of direction to consider. The northern direction is the petal orientated to Splenic centre I. The southern direction concerns the petal orientated to the pancreas. The northeast concerns the petal orientated to the Throat centre. The eastern direction (the heart of the system) concerns the two petals orientated to the Liver centre, whilst the west concerns the petals orientated to the Stomach centre. The southeast concerns the *piṇgalā* petal orientated to the Sacral centre, whilst the southwest petal is that of the respective *iḍā* petal. The northwest direction is governed by the *piṇgalā* petal to the Heart centre. (The northeast and northwest here are diagrammatic representations, not the true esoteric directions.) When viewed in this context we have the Solar Plexus centre manifesting the basic paradigm of a Heart centre for the Inner Round. This theme shall be analysed in detail in Volume 5A.

The above description of *prāṇic* circulation concerns the mode of activity for general humanity until the stage of unfolding the Bodhisattva *bhūmis,* when consciousness turns about from its focus in the centres below the diaphragm. There is then a major reorientation of the *maṇipūra* energies away from the minor centres and towards the Heart, Throat and Head centres. The activities of the *maṇipūra chakra* become dominated by the Heart, for which it serves as an organ for the cleansing of *saṃskāras.* The Waters will then be in the process of evaporating because of the heightened generation of Fiery and Airy *prāṇas* that will occupy the person's consciousness. Consciousness will then become rarefied, whilst individual self will is transformed into the Will-to-Good for the group, or the all. The group consciousness of the Heart centre then dominates, eliminating all forms of self-identity. Thus the entire onus of the 'self' concept (which the Solar Plexus centre was responsible for generating) vanishes. Desire-clinging is transformed into aspiration, devotion to the path of liberation and to the Bodhisattva ideal.

The Airy Element is thus exemplified and the petals that convey this *prāṇa* consequently expand, shifting to the new orientation. The entire disposition of the *maṇipūra chakra* is consequently changed. This Airy direction is functionally an expression of the *piṇgalā nāḍī,* whose *prāṇas* are generated when the person is compassionately orientated. This Heart based motivation produced involves such qualities as aspiration, group love, general thoughts of generosity, philanthropy, and thus the generation of *bodhicitta.*

When the energies of the Heart are poured into the Splenic centre then the vitalisation of the entire *nāḍī* system with liberating *prāṇas* ensues, according to the stage of development of the Heart centre. Thus the petals whose *bījas* are being activated at any stage become vitalised with the power of Love. The Splenic centre directs the Airy *prāṇas* into the general circulation of the smaller *chakras,* and then into the dense form to cause the healthy functioning of all bodily organs. In this way any remaining toxins that may be contained by the body, which predispose one to sickness and disease, can be eliminated. This allows one to become a radiant healer. The Solar Plexus centre then integrates the *prāṇas* and actively externalises these qualities amongst humanity.

The minor *siddhis*

When the finer perceptions *(siddhis)* are awakened by a highly accomplished *yogin,* the *iḍā* and *piṅgalā nāḍīs* that cross over through the *maṇipūra chakra* must bear their share of the Fiery *kuṇḍalinī* energy that is liberated from the Base of Spine centre. However, all of the *nāḍīs* in the system will have been sufficiently lined with the blue of Love-Wisdom[23] to safely convey the Fire. This allows the Fiery-Airy *iḍā* and *piṅgalā nāḍīs* of the *maṇipūra* to be able to channel Earthy-Aetheric *prāṇas* from the Sacral centre that have been intensified with Fire without dangerous psychic perversion, or physiological problems. (Energy follows the line of least resistance and *kuṇḍalinī* will burn a path in the *nāḍīs* accordingly, unless they have been prepared for its release.) The Fiery *prāṇa* from the Throat centre and the *bodhicitta* from the Heart centre admix with *kuṇḍalinī* in the Solar Plexus and Sacral centres and flow to the minor *chakras*, fully awakening the potencies they veil. These potencies are the higher correspondences of animal-like sentience.

The *siddhis* are the natural expression of the Elements conveyed by the petals of the *maṇipūra* when the *bījas* have been converted into bases for enlightenment by an accomplished *yogin* that has mastered the Watery Element. This is because the petals access the Will-to-Love and the intensity of energies from beyond the persona of the individual. The associated force produces a fourth dimensional motion (of the energy turning in upon itself as well as moving outwards in all directions in

23 The attributes of the Dhyāni Buddha Akṣobhya.

space) of the petals concerned. The grosser Watery and Earthy qualities no longer retard the motion of the petals, thus their Void Elements come to the fore, clothed by transforming Airy-Fiery qualities. That which formerly occluded clear vision is no longer a factor, hence the Clear Light is generated. Within that Light mantra can then resonate its power to rightly control the substance of *māyā,* producing the mastery of an accomplished *siddha.*

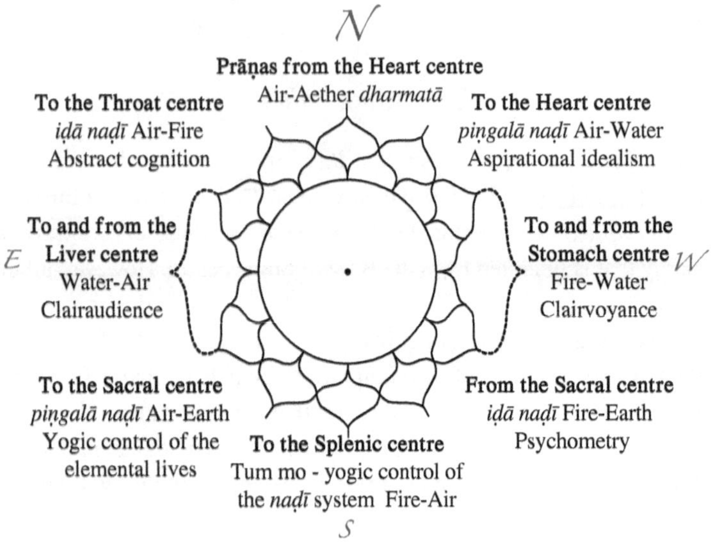

Figure 3. The Solar Plexus centre and the *siddhis*

The minor *siddhis*[24] manifest through the combined energies of the Throat and Heart centres via the eight petals of the Diaphragm centre,[25] the eight petals of Splenic centre II, plus the Solar Plexus centre. The Solar Plexus now manifests in an eight-fold manner, empowered in terms of the eight-spoked wheel of direction conditioning the expression of the

24 They are called 'minor' in relation to the supramundane *siddhis* developed as a consequence of awakening the Head lotus. The minor *siddhis* are concerned with the planes of perception associated with normal human evolution. The supramundane ones are associated with Buddha-attributes and the inevitable life of such a one in cosmos.

25 This centre acts as a type of pump, a crossing over mechanism between the centres above the diaphragm and those below it, admixing the directive potency from the Heart and Throat centres as needed.

minor *siddhis,* producing the arrangement of petals shown in Figure 3. Its output is controlled directly from above the diaphragm, and has no independent will of its own. The entire Inner Round system of *chakras* can then be fully controlled, revealing the sum of the qualities of the past evolutionary attainment to the seer, who can then utilise these potencies for present purpose.

With respect to the *siddhis* it can be said that there are differing degrees or refinements of their expression according to the plane of perception (field of application) that the *yogin* has mastered. Here I shall present terminology that best describes the major qualities that reflect the associated control of the Waters.

Mastery of the *prāṇas* directed towards the Stomach centre evoke *clairvoyance*, the *sight* that allows one to see all the entities and forces in the heaven and hell realms of the sum of human relationships.[26] This allows visioning of the associated *karma* of past life experiences, and to see auras, the subjective lives, *devas,* etc., of the subtle domains. This *siddhi* allows one to visually perceive the way that the various *saṃskāras* play in any life. It produces the experiences of the psychically aware. The *prāṇas* expressed are those of Fire-Water.

The controlled *prāṇas* directed towards the Liver centre evoke *clairaudience*, the *hearing* of the 'ear-whispered truths' from the Heart (the guru within), or telepathically projected thoughts that impact upon the stilled Waters of this centre. (If the Waters are not stilled then distorted visions and images can manifest in the case of clairvoyance, and intercepted words or thought impressions in the case of clairaudience. Evil forces can also easily play their hand.) The *piṅgalā nāḍī* is here used as a medium expressing Water-Air *prāṇas.* The subtle thought-impressions of human relationships, the subtle sounds of Nature, and of the *deva* hierarchy can also be heard. Forms of communication from members of the animal kingdom can be listened to. Many are the lives that exist upon the inner realms that can send telepathic impression to those thus attuned.

The pentad of *prāṇas* rightly controlled and directed towards Splenic centre II (the southern petal) via the Sacral/Base of Spine

---

26 Clairvoyance concerns the type of sight obtained upon the astral plane, which is described in Volume 4, chapter 4.

centres concerns the projection of Fiery-Airy *prāṇas* into the Inner Round of minor *chakras,* allowing yogic control of the *nāḍī* system. This control necessitates the generation of the psychic heat of the system (Tum mo) that vitalises and transforms the sentient lives incorporated as the form (the bodily organism). The Splenic centre then becomes the container of such Fire, projecting its heat via the *nāḍīs.* (The *prāṇas* it conveys are hence now Fiery rather than Earthy or Watery.) This Fire burns up the remaining defilements in the *nāḍīs* (as part of the stages of the liberation of *kuṇḍalinī).* It thus generates the potency to heal, and provides the warmth needed by *yogins* to sustain their activities in cold climates. The awakening Mind controls the Fiery potency.

When rightly controlled *prāṇas* are directed to the Heart centre via the *piṅgalā nāḍī,* then 'the fruits of the actual *dharmas'* become transformed into the *siddhi* that can be phrased *aspirational idealism.* This concerns the ability of the *yogin* to aspire to achieve the highest attainment associated with any of the forms of Thusness of the seven sacred petals of the Heart. It specifically involves awakening the Equalising Wisdom of Ratnasambhava, to naturally control the flow of the Watery world. The *prāṇas* expressed are those of Air-Water.

When any of the petals of the Heart centre manifests its purpose through any of the pentads of the Solar Plexus centre (the northern direction) then the Solar Plexus is seeded ('perfumed') with the *bījas* of active liberation. These *prāṇas* coming via the Heart centre are directed by the Head lotus and the Ājñā centre, allowing the thinker to view into and control the forces of the entire Watery domain. This domain incorporates the astral heaven and hell zones, and hence the ability to envision the course of the lives and the nature of the manifesting *karma* associated with those zones. The all-seeing Eye can thereby peer where it wills concerning the past activities of the individual and of its group interrelations. It can also visualise mantra so its potency can be used to control any aspect of the Watery-Earthy environment the thinker wills. All aspects of the phenomenological realm then come under the complete control of the *yogin* and *dharmatā* inevitably becomes the basis of all movement. The remaining defilements associated with *kliṣṭamanas* become thoroughly cleansed and transmuted into *bodhicitta.* The *prāṇa* conveyed is Air-Aether.

The north-south orientations are governed by the sense of touch, meaning that the *chakras* above the diaphragm can manipulate the energies of the Solar Plexus centre by means of the fingers of the northern hand via the petal linking the Heart centre. The petal to Splenic centre II can similarly control the forces of the entire Inner Round by utilising the downwards focussed pentad of fingers to control what is relatively material to it. The concept of touch here implies a relatively refined energy contacting and controlling that which is comparatively material in nature. Hence in both cases we have higher centres controlling centres below them.

The petals directing the *iḍā and piṅgalā nāḍī* streams express the attributes of smell and taste respectively. *Smell* allows the highest (most subtle) of the Earthy energies to be controlled and built into the *maṇḍala* of what is to be, or mantrically to completely control phenomena. The Watery correspondence to the sense of *taste* is utilised to savour impressions from the formless realms of revelation, to taste *śūnyatā* and to convey *bodhicitta.*

The northeast *iḍā nāḍī* stream directed towards the Throat centre via the Heart, channels Air-Fire *prāṇas* and develops the abstract cognitive factor that stems from the Clear Light. The sum of the *ālayavijñāna* can then be perceived and actively worked with.

The pentad focussed upon the southeast petal to the Sacral centre channels Air-Earth *prāṇas* of the *piṅgalā nāḍī,* which develops the *yogic control of the elemental lives.* (They embody the sum of the fields of the *māyā* incorporated as the bodily mechanism.) The bodily organs and sense-perceptors consequently come under the control of the *yogin* as a healing potency.

The *iḍā nāḍī* from the Sacral centre concerns the yogic control of physical contact with everyday material phenomena. When mastered, this quality becomes transformed into the *siddhi* of *psychometry*, whereby through touching objects the complete conceptual understanding of their (sometimes aeonic) history and occult properties is perceived. The nature of the *bījas* can be known, that were originally seeded from the realm of the *ālayavijñāna,* to become the ephemera that is experienced. The *prāṇas* expressed are those of Fire-Earth.

It is important that any perspective *yogin* does not use the personal will to try to generate the *siddhis*, as this will only produce psychic disaster. One's psyche can then be at the mercy of uncontrollable forces and demonic, rapacious entities that will work to dominate the ego. The individual will then not be in control of his/her body of manifestation. The Fires will also tend to burn and destroy through the line of least resistance, generating undesired psychic pathways. Personal will is the way of the left hand path, and has its dire attendant *karma*. It produces deep bondage to *saṃsāra* and not liberation from it. The *yogin* on the white path first generates *bodhicitta* in all undertakings, and working under instructions from the wise awakened guru, will meditate according to the dictates of the law of sacrificial Love for safe travel in the psychic underworld. Compassionate undertaking and thought is one's safeguard to generate the blue energies that must line the *nāḍīs,* preventing the liberated Fires from burning a destructive path to psychic disaster.

The *bījas* and the Sacral centre

The list of six characteristics of the *bījas* given earlier relate to the manifestation of their potency through each petal of the *Sacral centre (svādiṣṭhāna chakra).* The basic *maṇḍalic* patterning of this centre is that of an interlaced hexagram. The hexagram demonstrates a northerly focussed (masculine) will triad concerned with upward aspiration towards knowledge and liberation, and a southerly projected feminine triad concerned with the creative processes and the concretion of energies. The points of the triangles manifest the general trinity of will, sense-consciousness input, and activity. These interrelated triads are esoterically represented by the qualities of a Buddha in *yab-yum* (sexual union), where the upward pointing triad represents the Buddha and the downward pointing triad represents the feminine Consort.

All *prāṇas* that vitalise the form are admixed in the Sacral centre. Here the Earthy Fires from the Base of Spine centre, and those from the Gonad centres help build the health aura of the individual. There is also the initial processing of all forms of sense contacts, thus the input to the five sense-consciousnesses, producing the basic life processes, the *dharma,* and the 'interrupted series' of *karmic* factors. The process that externalises desire and that contacts the phenomena one is attracted to produces that attractive magnetism that people know as their sexual impulses, stimulating the drive to propagate the species. The basic instincts thus come to the fore: that of self-preservation of the individual, of sex, the group or herd instinct that causes people to live as part of communities, that of the self-assertion of the personality, and the instinct towards knowledge (thus the drive for continuous sensory input).

This centre is therefore concerned with the *prāṇic* vitalisation of the body. It is essentially the dynamo that circulates the *prāṇas* throughout the *nāḍī* system, from whence the vital health of the gross form is derived. The *yogin* must positively master this expression and drive the generated *prāṇas* upward to empower the various *siddhis* associated with the Solar Plexus centre. The statements earlier presented concerning the six characteristics are in accord with the triadic ordering of the Sacral centre.

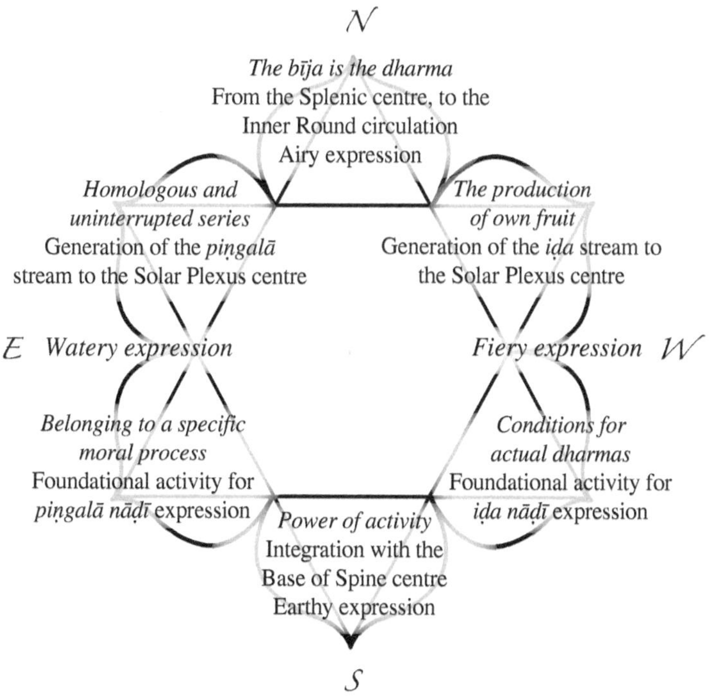

Figure 4. The *bījas* and the Sacral centre

i. 'The *bījas* are momentary (*kṣaṇika).* They are the *dharmas* which perish immediately after birth and which possess a power of activity.' This 'power of activity' sets the entire motion constituting the purpose of the *bījas* into active manifestation. It concerns the integration of the Sacral centre with the Base of Spine centre (*mūlādhāra chakra*), as the two are overlapped and hence function as a unit. We therefore have the generation of the Earthy *prāṇas* of concrete material expression from contact (*sparśa*) with phenomenal objects. This is the power, therefore, that develops from the moment of being born, to evolve in the environment one has incarnated into. Every moment of contact with the phenomena of the material world perishes after it is born. All of the *bījas* that are developed as a consequence are momentary. The southernmost petal is involved here and is the focus of the feminine downwards pointing triangle of creative expression.

This form of activity concerns the projection of desires and attachments of all types. These attachments produce the various forms of knowledge relating to what one is attached to. They perish immediately after the attachment has been formed, because new images or desires continuously become the object of attention.

The *dharmas* automatically produce their own fruits, which are the *karma* and *saṃskāras* of the pleasurable states obtained as a consequence of attachment to the objects of desire. Continuous activity and consequent production of the fruit manifest in the form of an 'uninterrupted series', of images and passions to be experienced. All must inevitably be sacrificed in order to achieve higher states of union and awareness, with consequent pain. One must inevitably sacrifice attachments as the lessons of pain and suffering are learnt. The force that must be exerted to detach depends upon the degree of attachment.

Effectively this triad of petals draw Watery *prāṇas* from the Solar Plexus centre, which emotionally condition all desirous contact with phenomena. This creates all of the types of home, social, and relationship issues that a person lives for.

ii. 'The *bīja* is the *dharma* which is simultaneously and actually connected with its fruit.' This refers to the northernmost petal that absorbs Earthy-Airy *prāṇas* from Splenic centre II.[27] This direction allows the personal-I freedom to explore all aspects of the Inner Round, with the fruits being all of the conscious states of perceptions derived from the potencies they veil. In whatever way it is expressed or defined the *dharma* relates to that which educates, the educated qualities being its fruit. Much *dharma* is to be explored as one learns from the various human correspondences of animal sentience on the way of evolving the wisdom of the Heart. Each small *chakra* that is vitalised by means of the Sacral centre 'simultaneously and actually' become activated in the life of the individual, thus revealing the gains (fruits) from former lifetimes of expression. Every little emotion that besets the individual during various stages of his/her life thereby come into play to produce the eventual revelations of the transience of all such activity. In the meantime they produce the heaven and hell states that the individual reincarnates through.

The process of the ripening of fruits of the *dharma* is governed by a 'group of conditions to realize their capacity to produce an actual *dharma'*, as well as to 'a specific kind of moral species which means they must possess the capacity to produce actual *dharmas'*. The 'specific kind of moral species' refers to the type of affiliations of attachments (forms of *saṃskāras*) that the personal-I is engaged in at any particular time. The attachment to intense sensuality, an avaricious desire to amass vast resources of money, or a lust for material power, are not kinds of moral species, but all will produce *dharmas* (forms of knowledge) of one type or another by which the person learns inevitably what not to do. Rather, we have an already established progress of (ethical) conceptualisations indicated, whereby the person has already learnt what not to do as a consequence of the pain ensued from many forms of such attachment and loss of things acquired. The innate philosophic understanding produced of what to avoid awakens the specifics of the practice of a religious life that conditions one to pursue the *dharma* to its natural conclusion.

---

27 Note that in all interrelations between *chakras* there is a coming and going of *prāṇas* from both directions. The Airy quality expressed is from the perspective of the general Earthy attributes of the Sacral centre. The Splenic centre directs *prāṇas* to the Sacral centre for further processing.

iii. 'The *bījas* continue in a homogeneous and uninterrupted series until the final stage of the Holy Path of ascetic practices is attained.' Here we have the eastern point of the downward pointing creative triad of petals implicated. We also have the generation of the *piṇgalā nāḍī* stream for the entire circulatory system, which flows in a continuous 'homogeneous and uninterrupted series' to the Head lotus, with the proviso of the information already given regarding the error of the concept of homogeneity, though here there is a homogeneity of *piṇgalā*-like attributes. A continuous generation of affectionate, concerned, loving, and then compassionate activity (or expression of such *saṃskāras*) is what is indicated. This will inevitably produce the revelation of the truths of the *dharma*, as obtained through 'the Holy Path of ascetic practices'. This *piṇgalā* stream inevitably evokes *bodhicitta,* therefore the entire Bodhisattva path ('the Holy Path') awakens for the individual. The Element generated is that of Watery-Air, which is the basic quality that is conveyed in the *piṇgalā nāḍī* until the Waters are dried up through austere yogic discipline.

The two petals constituting the eastern direction of the Sacral centre convey the Watery expression, which is involved with the foundational activity and generation of the *piṇgalā nāḍī* stream. The two petals of the western direction are concerned with the Fiery expression, that generates the *iḍā nāḍī* stream, which at first is an Earthy-Fiery energy, and later becomes Fiery-Earthy. The northern petal receives an Earthy-Airy flow via the Splenic centre and the southern petal is concerned with the generalised Earthy *prāṇas* that are needed for concrete expression in *saṃsāra.*

iv. 'The *bījas* belong to a specific kind of moral species which means they must possess the capacity to produce actual *dharmas*—good, bad or non-defined. This capacity is determined by actual *dharmas,* good, bad or non-defiled, which have perfumed and created them.' Here we look to the foundational activity for the expression of the *piṇgalā nāḍī* flow. Satisfactorily input from the object of desire, be it a lover, or material possessions, produces pleasing, affectionate, or loving *saṃskāras.* Attachment ensues, which produces desire for further contact and experiences, and consequently the broadening of one's horizons along the line of any form of 'moral process'. Such processes become the social mores and customs that the majority are conditioned by.

v. 'The *bījas* depend on a group of conditions to realize their capacity to produce an actual *dharma.'* Looking at the Abhidharma philosophy, 'an actual *dharma'* refers to the 72 or so *dharmas* or any expression thereof. Whether we agree with this philosophy or not is of little concern, because in essence (the short list), the *dharmas* can be viewed in terms of the function of the intellect manifesting actions that produce modifications of consciousness. Inevitably, expansion of that consciousness occurs, and when continued over many successive lives will produce enlightenment. Here therefore we find the foundational qualities established for the development of the base perceptions through sense-consciousness that generates the *iḍā nāḍī* stream.

vi. 'Each *bīja* leads to the production of its own fruit. [A *bīja* of *citta* leads to the manifestation of *citta* and a *bīja* of *rūpa* leads to the manifestation of *rūpa*.]' Here is implied the complete evocation of the *iḍā nāḍī* stream, wherein karmic reward is accrued as a consequence of all forms of activity. This is based upon the expressed desire or personal will of the individual, wherein conscious choice incurs volitions in the field of *saṃsāra*. This stream is directed towards the Solar Plexus centre, where each '*bīja* leads to the production of its own fruit' when the *prāṇas* of the Inner Round admix with the *iḍā* stream and instantaneously produce effects in the various *chakras* to which they are directed. In the Solar Plexus centre the Earthy, Watery, Fiery, and Airy *prāṇas* are sorted into their various categories and subcategories according to the manner earlier explained. Thus a *bīja* of *citta* (mind substance) is directed towards the Throat centre for (Fiery) expression of mind. Or alternately, the *prāṇas* from the Solar Plexus centre are directed downward into concretion via this *iḍā nāḍī* link, to produce the manifestation of *rūpa* (form). Watery *bījas* become expressed as part of the domain of the Solar Plexus centre. The fruits of all action are, however, ripened in the fields of desire and sensuality, concomitant with the Sacral centre and its expression. Thus revolves the wheel of birth and death, of Dependent Origination, causing the attributes of the

Six Realms to be continuously generated, until a *yogin* arises that can end the cycles through appropriately controlling the activities of these lower centres. He counters the desirous attraction to the sensations of *māyā* and the vicissitudes of *saṃsāra* to attain *śūnyatā*.

The wheels of the Solar Plexus and Sacral centres turn, and as the relative petals interlock, so energy flows from one to the other. This allows the *bījas* of the Solar Plexus centre to activate the petals of the Sacral centre in turn. *Saṃsāric* activity thus continues until the liberating way to the Heart centre is found. (In terms of consciousness it is a spiral stairway of beauteous revelation productive of eventual bliss.)

The Sambhoghakāya Flower and the Solar Plexus centre

As will be shown in Volume 3, the Sambhoghakāya Flower consists of three main whorls of three petals each.[28] They are denoted the Will or Sacrifice petals, the Love-Wisdom petals and the Knowledge petals. Of these there are five petals of the Sambhogakāya Flower that are concerned with the seeding of *bījas* into the *chakras* of the personal-I. The *bījas* impress the centres below the diaphragm via the *iḍā, piṅgalā* and *suṣumṇā nāḍīs*. Hence these *bījas* come via the Head lotus and then the Throat and Heart centres, depending upon the need or orientation of the personal-I. They come from the lowest and middle tier of petals of the Sambhogakāya Flower, which are concerned with the normal attributes developed by the person, plus that relating to engendering *bodhicitta*. The four higher Sacrifice petals do not seed these *bījas,* but rather are concerned with the path of return (the Initiation process), hence the engendering of the will-sacrifice that helps liberate the person. They drive to fulfilment the Bodhisattva *bhūmis*. The petals of the Solar Plexus centre that are seeded with the *bījas* for the normal activities of a personal-I are as given below under the heading of the petal of the Sambhogakāya Flower from which they emanate. The seeding of the attributes of the Solar Plexus centre thus happens by way of the *iḍā* and *piṅgalā nāḍīs*. (Petals 1 and 4 of Figure 2.) The Sacral centre is

28 See Figure 13 in Volume 3. The information on the Sambhogakāya Flower is presented in this section on the *bījas* to complete the teachings concerning them. For elucidation, the reader can later integrate this information with what is found in the relevant section of Volume 3.

seeded via petals 2 and 3 of Figure 2. There is also a general seeding of the entire Inner Round by means of the north-south petals, as will be described. This 'perfuming of actual *dharmas'* can be viewed as a *suṣumṇā nāḍī* manifestation. The central four petals of the *maṇipūra chakra* are concerned with the generation of the *kāma-manasic* response of the Solar Plexus centre from life's activity as a consequence of the attributes that have been seeded by the *bījas* via the three principal *nāḍīs.*

1. The *Knowledge—Sacrifice petal.* This petal projects the seeds that are 'the different potentialities found in the fundamental consciousness' via the *iḍā nāḍī* stream. The quality of sacrifice inevitably governs the direction of all *bījas* of mind stored in the *ālayavijñāna* that is contained by the Sambhogakāya Flower. This is because the purpose of all *bījas* is for them to be sacrificed, or rather transmuted, to produce eventual enlightenment by the personal-I concerned. This petal organises the progress that the respective *bījas* must take to stimulate consciousness in such a way that gaining illuminating or enlightened impression is inevitable. The *bījas* therefore become mechanisms of transformation and will manifest in such a way that the normal tenacious tendency of the personal-I to cling to aspects of *saṃsāra* is mitigated, or made very difficult to sustain. An example is through the factor of pain or suffering, producing a sense of deep loss, the person may then seriously ponder upon what life is really about and take steps to conquer the illusion. Such *bījas* are seeded via the Throat centre. When they manifest in the *maṇipūra chakra* then they 'immediately produce their fruits' via its activities. They can also continue through to the Sacral centre via the *iḍā* stream thereto.

   The purpose of the activity of the *iḍā nāḍī* is to awaken aspects of the outermost tier of the 1,000 petalled lotus. This tier of the Head lotus represents the Solar Plexus of the Head centre. These petals process the basic mental-emotions that the intelligentsia utilise. The initial objective of the Knowledge—Sacrifice petal is to master and then transmute the mental-emotional *saṃskāras* into attributes of the abstract Mind.

   At first the *maṇipūra* is seeded with the elemental qualities of the *ālayavijñāna.* Aspects of the desire-mind are formed with a strong emotional component. As the incarnations of the personal-I's proceed over the millennia, the mental components begin to intensify to exclude the emotional ones. The *manasic prāṇas* that enter the Head lotus stimulate thought therein, and inevitably base thoughts are excluded to refine consciousness. The related *bījas* thereby become transformed into subtler expressions of what they once were. Eventually the mental-emotions are sublimated into the attributes of the abstract Mind, with the Watery component completely replaced by the Airy aspect. These attributes then are also absorbed into the Knowledge—Sacrifice petal of the Sambhogakāya Flower, and assist in the unfoldment of the Bodhisattva *bhūmis*.

This petal of the Sambhogakāya Flower helps generate and direct the *saṃskāras* of the Aetheric Element, as far as they can be expressed, via the Watery *maṇipūra* environment. The Waters consequently must dry up to produce a type of Fire-mist that fuel the perceptions associated with the *siddhis*. By that stage the onus of development of the Sambhogakāya Flower changes from Knowledge—Sacrifice to Sacrifice—Knowledge via the Love-Wisdom—Sacrifice petal.

2. The *Knowledge–Love-Wisdom petal* projects to the Sacral centre the '*bījas* in relation to the *mūlavijñāna* and the fruit' that 'are neither identical nor different'. There the basic loving attributes developed by consciousness in the field of desire are evolved. This creates the foundational qualities of the *piṇgalā nāḍī*. These *saṃskāras* then quickly find their way to the *maṇipūra*, where they are further processed through the entire gamut of human relationships. *Saṃsāra* is thereby fully explored, and as the way to the Heart centre is developed, so then the *bījas* produce 'real entities' that are 'not the same as *tathatā'*, which find their outlet as Watery-Airy *prāṇas* via the polar opposite petal.

Energies from the Heart centre are inevitably drawn to the *maṇipūra*, so the various desires (e.g., of sexual union) and devotion to basic religious forms, and related attachment, can be elevated. We then have emotionally based concepts producing higher forms of devotion (such as to a noble ideal, or Deity Yoga), and loving affection, so that the *prāṇas* engendered can eventually be accommodated in the Heart centre. The generation of the love needed to become a stream enterer, to undertake the first of the Bodhisattva *bhūmis,* is thus eventuated.

This petal of the Sambhogakāya Flower is thus specifically concerned with the generation and direction of the *saṃskāras* of the Watery Element, preparing them so that they eventually become clarified and distilled, the Watery essence that can be accommodated in the Heart centre. All of the basic forms of emotions are manifested, understood, and then mastered. The mastered *saṃskāras* are depicted as 'real entities' above.

3. The *Knowledge–Knowledge petal.* The *bījas* that are seeded from here are those that 'immediately produce their own fruits'. This happens via the principle of desire and attachment to material plane objects via Sacral centre activity, which governs the general activity of most people. Here the childhood development of humanity is implicated. This seeding lays the foundation for experiences in the three worlds of the human personality, where the physical plane is the onus of attention. Thus knowledgeable attributes are gained, utilising the sum of the Base of Spine, Sacral, and Solar Plexus centres of activity.

   The basic purpose of these *bījas* is to convert the myriad forms of emotional-mental, or desire-mind images into sound forms of thinking. The qualities of the Stomach centre are consequently developed, wherein the *iḍā* attributes are fully nurtured so that they can be rightly absorbed by the Throat centre to stimulate the 1,000 petalled lotus in a wholesome way. The *bījas* thus generate the substance of the eighth consciousness *(ālayavijñāna),* when they are integrated as part of the conscious awareness of the personal-I and inevitably carried through to enlightened perception. In the Stomach centre the most intense forms of emotions, strong addictions, rigorous attachments to doctrines, aversion, avarice, fears and hatreds of all types, 'produced through causes and conditions', must be understood and mastered. Thus when the higher way is consciously trod, then this centre becomes a battle-field, a place wherein the worst of one's *saṃskāras* are to be slain.

   Being the lowest of the petals of the Sambhogakāya Flower, the Knowledge—Knowledge petal garners all of the basic experiences of mind that can be incorporated into the Flower, the foundation of all that is to come. This petal is specifically concerned with the generation and right direction of the *saṃskāras* of the Fiery Element. They generate the foundation of the Fires of mind via the Element Earth, and later the evocation of the aspects of Mind that are the basis for the awakening of the Head lotus.

4. The *Love-Wisdom—Knowledge petal* seeds the conditionings associated with the Liver centre. The purpose is to produce the continuation of the *piṇgalā* attributes denoted above as 'real entities', with their reality not being 'the same as *tathatā'*. Here they are 'occasioned by good and bad' as they are taken as an object by 'the path of seeing'. This path develops moral precepts, codes of ethics, religious and social mores to which the individual ascribes. Thus the correct determination between what is 'good or bad' can be made. Inevitably, the way to the Heart centre via the *piṇgalā* stream is developed, which allows one to see the truth behind the entire outer seeming of *saṃsāra*. The relation between the two truths then comes into view.

   This Love-Wisdom—Knowledge petal of the Sambhogakāya Flower is specifically concerned with the generation and direction of the *saṃskāras* of the Airy Element in terms of the foundation for the generation of *bodhicitta* and its absorption into the Heart centre.[29]

5. The *Love-Wisdom—Love-Wisdom petal* is responsible for the general continuous 'perfuming of actual *dharmas'* to sustain the cleansing and transmutative functions of the Splenic centre. To accomplish this end it utilises the seeds that are stored in the *ālaya* (here of the Sambhogakāya Flower), inevitably 'producing the appearance of things', when the *prāṇas* carry right through to influence the actual physical form via the pancreas and the general organs of the body. The thing to note here is that the Love-Wisdom of the entire Sambhogakāya Flower is what thereby controls the substance of the form (through the digestive process), its evolution and the transmutation of the associated *skandhas*. The physicality of any thing allows the senses to express themselves in such a way that

29 Note that *bodhicitta* needs to be generated on the path to liberation, yet it is also the fundamental quality embodying the Sambhogakāya Flower.

things can be experienced and knowledge (*dharmas*) attained.

The seeds are said to be 'perfumed by seven other consciousnesses' as the seeding process manifests via the southernmost petal and the Inner Round *chakras*. One can refer here not just to Vijñānavādin philosophy of the eight consciousnesses, but also esoterically to the qualities of the seven Rays that delineate or define the different consciousness states. These Rays are esoterically considered sub-rays of the second Ray of Love-Wisdom.

This specific petal that is the heart of the Sambhogakāya Flower (and which characterises the Flower as a whole) oversees the process of seeding the qualities of devotion and affection of the Solar Plexus into high aspiration and love. Thus 'the perfuming' is 'repeated again and again through beginningless time'. Consequently, perfuming happens for the duration of the many incarnations of personal-I's needed for the Sambhogakāya Flower to gain its objectives.

The *prāṇas* can then be absorbed into the Heart centre, and inevitably in the Heart in the Head on their way to be incorporated into the Flower. The *bodhicitta* that sustains the Bodhisattva way is thereby awakened. This energy is poured through Splenic centre I to effect the many transformations and eventual transmutations of *prāṇas* so that they can eventually be accommodated by the Heart centre.

This petal of the Sambhogakāya Flower is thus concerned with the generation of the *saṃskāras* of all five *prāṇas* conveyed by the Airy Element within each *nāḍī*, so that the energy of *bodhicitta* can be expressed throughout the *nāḍī* system. Air purifies the Fiery-Watery-Earthy attributes associated with the Splenic centre functions within the major Watery dispensation of the centres below the diaphragm.

At first *manas* is generated via desire-attachment, awakening the manifold experiences that *saṃsāra* is capable of producing. However, overall these five petals principally seed the *bījas* that stimulate the general Watery qualities of the Solar Plexus. Desire ideations and all types of thought-forms are engendered. The spiritual Will is inevitably evoked to generate the detachment that leads the personal-I out of its intense form of self-focus. The *bījas* can then be sacrificed upon the alter of higher knowledge and revelations, as the *saṃskāras* are gradually cleansed of their cruder elements and forces. This allows the direction of the refined *prāṇas* to the centres above the diaphragm, as self will is transformed into goodwill, then into the total surrender of the personal will, to produce the impersonal Will-of-Love for the whole that is the natural selflessness of the Flower. The aim is to eventually master the Solar Plexus centre by evoking the qualities of *bodhicitta* so that the *prāṇas* of the five Elements can be directed to and utilised efficaciously by the Heart centre, thus generating Thusness via the quiescent and transformed Waters.

The Sambhoghakāya Flower and the Sacral centre

The six petals of the *svādiṣṭhana chakra* are vitalised by the Knowledge triad of petals of the Sambhogakāya Flower. Of the two triads of petals of the Sacral centre, the triad pointing north is seeded by the Knowledge—Love-Wisdom petal of the Sambhogakāya Flower. Thus we have the *bījas* that are 'the *dharma* which is simultaneously and actually connected with its fruit'. The objective of this petal therefore, is to draw the qualifications of the *dharma* out from every form of attachment and the principle of desire-emotion. Inevitably there is a consequent process of nonattachment (the sacrifice of attachment to things) to achieve the upward process to liberation from all aspects of *saṃsāra*. This happens by way of the cleansing and transformative activities of the Splenic centre, to which the *prāṇas* of this triad are directed. Radiant energies that vitalise the entire *nāḍī* system are thereby produced, generating good health. We also have the yogic control of the force centres associated with material plane living.

The downward pointing triad, wherein the peregrinations of basic day to day mundane activity in *saṃsāra* and the general lessons of life upon the physical domain become understood, is seeded by the *Knowledge—Knowledge petal* of the Sambhogakāya Flower. Here the *bījas* producing the 'power of activity' lay the foundation for the *saṃskāras* that are to course through the entire life process that produce the attributes of the five sense-consciousnesses.

The *bījas* emanated from the *Knowledge—Love-Wisdom petal* govern the major portion of the Sacral centre expression and its distribution of energies via the sexual function. Essentially it governs the quaternary of petals of the Sacral centre formed through the interrelation of its two triangles of energies. They are the four petals orientated to the east-west direction. These petals convey the intermingled *prāṇas* of the four Elements, but specifically a mix of Watery-Earth with Fire. This interrelationship generates the *kāma-manasic* (desire-mind) *saṃskāras* that the majority of people reside almost exclusively within. They represent the *bījas* that come from people's basic sacral interrelationships, i.e., those of a desirous, sensual or sexual nature, and which produce the basis of the *iḍā* and *piṅgalā nāḍī* stream directed to and from the Solar Plexus centre.

In analysing the functioning of the Sacral centre we find that different combinations of *prāṇas* can manifest in ten different ways: of two triads and one quaternary. They have a sympathetic relation to the ten petals of the Solar Plexus centre. *Prāṇas* can thus flow to and from the Solar Plexus and Base of Spine centres individually, as pairs, as triads, or as the sum of four *prāṇas.* An accomplished *yogin* projects them upon the upward way. The *yogin* must be able to control all twenty *prāṇic* expressions of these two major centres, plus the basic four of the Base of Spine *chakra,* if the lower nature is to be properly controlled and *siddhis* be eventuated. The number twenty-four equals 2 x 12, or the number of petals ascribed to the Heart centre, when both the reversed and the rectified wheels are taken into account.[30]

We see therefore that the major centres below the diaphragm must eventually reflect the functioning of the Heart centre if enlightenment is to ensue. They are thus also capable of expressing the *tathatā* of the Heart, albeit its potency being somewhat curtailed, via the expression of the Earthy, Watery, and Fiery Elements that constitute the three worlds of the human personality that need to be mastered. These Elements manifest in their natural form of expression in a *yogin's* awareness, allowing the demonstration of absolute control of all aspects of the phenomenal appearance. The Fiery Element finds the concreted aspect of *manas* mastered via the centres below the diaphragm and the aspect of the abstract Mind in those above the diaphragm. The Airy and Aetheric Elements necessitate the higher centres for complete expression

30 The significance of the number 24 will be explained in greater detail in Volumes 4 and 5A.

of their potentiality. They are essential if the higher Bodhisattva wisdoms are to be expressed.

Something should also be said about the Base of Spine centre (*mūlādhāra chakra*). Overall its function is controlled by the *Sacrifice–Knowledge* petal of the Sambhogakāya Flower. Sacrificial activity is needed for one to control the Base centre's output. The energies in its four petals at first manifest in the form of a swastika orientated in the southwest, southeast, northwest and northeast direction. As a consequence they channel the basic sensual and Earthy *prāṇas* that sustain the sensation-orientated biped. The four petals convey the *prāṇic* qualities of the four Elements relating to the four kingdoms of Nature, viewed esoterically. (The mineral, the plant, the animal, and the human.) Later, upon the Bodhisattva path, the *chakra* reorients in the north-south-east-west direction, as the swastika converts to a 'masculine' four pronged *dorje (viśva-vajra)*. The 'human' petal is normally orientated westwards, and the plant kingdom petal northwards, which facilitates the *prāṇic* flow in the *nāḍī* system, which is plant-like. The southern petal absorbs *prāṇas* from the mineral kingdom and the eastern petal absorbs *prāṇas* from the animal kingdom. The nature of the intricate and beautiful geometry between the Sacral centre and Base centre overlap creates an 'acorn' from whence *kuṇḍalinī* arises, a proper description of which cannot yet be revealed. Beware the premature wilful awakening of *kuṇḍalinī*. Uncontrolled, this *śakti* is a very dangerous mistress.

The identity of dependent systems

In the *Treatise in Thirty Verses on Mere-Consciousness* this statement appears:

> The various consciousnesses, i.e. the three categories of consciousness and their mental associates are all capable of developing into two kinds of appearances—that of perceiving part and that of perceived part. The perceiving part developed is termed as 'discrimination', because it apprehends the *nimittabhāga*. The perceived part is termed as 'that which is discriminated' because it is apprehended by *darśanabhāga*.[31]

31 *Bhāgas* are the divisions of consciousness on the basis of the functions of consciousness, mental discrimination *(darśanabhāga)* and that which is discriminated *(nimittabhāga)*.

> The doctrine of *vijñaptimātratā* teaches that there are no real self or real things. Everything phenomenal *(saṃskṛta)* and noumenal *(asaṃskṛta),* everything appearing as 'real' and 'false', is not separable from consciousness. The word 'mere' in 'Mere-consciousness' denies that there are any real self and real things. But it does not deny that the *caittas,*[32] the two *bhāgas, tathatā,* etc. exist, so far as they are not separated from consciousness. Therefore all is Mere-consciousness.[33]

We are then given the proofs of *vijñaptimātratā* (Mere-consciousness).

Commenting further on this concept of 'no real self, or things' (or that 'there is no self but only consciousness exists') it can be said that there *is a 'self' in consciousness.* Such a 'self' acts in consciousness in a similar manner as the cells in your body prove your existence, your existing functioning personal-self, that 'I' that consciousness identifies with. The cells live as self evolved organisms. Their identities are not detracted by the existence of the bigger form, the body which manifests comparatively as the higher self. The 'higher self' here is the larger body that incorporates and coordinates their functioning. (Similar to the Sambhogakāya Flower's role of incorporating and coordinating the functioning of the personal-I.)

These cells are identified as separate entities with separate membranes and nuclei individualised specifically for them, yet the larger self is dependent on them, sharing in their structural function, and gaining experiences from their collected interrelationships. The cell's walls or membranes do not detract from the fact that in relationship to them the higher self can use their bodies, their collective sentience, to function with them as one unit.

We could consider a law of individual functioning that concerns the compacting of existing units into a unity, one body or principle. (The term 'body' refers to a principle, as well as to a method of evolutionary gain or function of conscious experience integrated into one package or form.) The subset of evolution and the fact that it has 'a name'; 'a' as in singular, proves to the mind that it functions as one, yet smaller entities can exist within it, serving the one though functioning on their own level of interrelationships. People live in such structural interrelationships.

32 Mental factors.

33 Ganguli, 47.

They live within subsets of categories—of parts within a society, nation, or civilisation. Human society concerns the integrated evolution of entire categories of interrelated organisms.

The individual membranes; the socio-economic, cultural, religious, political, or philosophic connections that tie these people together,[34] do not detract from the functioning of any category of human society. In fact such ties generally improve the quality of life of the individuals connected thus. It helps them to develop the various aspects of consciousness and quality of *prāṇas* needed for the eventual gaining of enlightenment.

Incarnation into the morass of congealing, limiting, and obscuring substance is necessary if consciousness is to evolve. Such incarnation is also instituted to help the little lives constituting that substance to develop. People therefore act unconsciously as Bodhisattvas for the cellular lives constituting their forms whenever they are reborn. They incarnate into the wheel of birth and death in order to inevitably be freed from the wheel. Ironically, the wheel exists for this purpose, thus it manifests in the form of an individuation; one little wheel per human unit experiencing it, with many smaller wheels governing the constituency of the human form. Then there is one greater wheel for the sum of human consciousnesses that must experience the mode of eventual release. The individual wheels are separated by various membranes of different thought-constructs. These are constituted of ethereal substance containing the *nāḍīs* and different *saṃskāras* that are unique to that individual life stream, to that human individualised consciousness, or 'self'. The wheels are characterised according to groupings of similar traits, also delineated by similar invisible membranes that cause intelligent unities to incarnate as groups, because the *karma* created is group *karma*. All lives are similarly delineated within the confines of the greater wheel as it turns for the all.

One experiences something and only then can one understand and conquer (it).[35] Thus, although temporarily trapped in form, the

---

34 The view in this section involves looking at *nimittabhāga*, that which is perceived, from a subtler and broader level than what is normally perceived in Buddhist ontology.

35 *Darśanabhāga* is the perception that allows one to conquer that which is perceived.

purpose of the wheel is to free all sentient beings, through the process of evolutionary experience. So the wheels turn, move, and also grow.

The existence of many different unities of human society facilitates the evolution of consciousness, of the development and awakening to the *ālayavijñāna*. The *ālayavijñāna* is logically also conditioned by similar membranes, on its own level, that serve as separators of that which possess analogous functions to our digestive and procreative system. All are part of an integrative whole. Membranes delineate subsets, and like the river banks which delineate the river from the terrain that contains it, the membranes need not be impenetrable barriers between the outer environment and the subsets they contain. Forms of interrelation, the flow of information ('nutrients') from one to the other generally exist, and are oft necessary.

The flow of people's lives within an evolutionary progression through different racial and historical contexts are drawn like cells within organs, and are expressed to the mind in the form of images. The images contain subsets within subsets. Each subset contains the membranes delineating one category of images from the next, and together they produce a relative growth of consciousness within the *ālayavijñāna*.

The cells are fed through the process of digestion. This involves various types of digestive juices, for which there can be different levels of interpretation when digestion is viewed as an analogy for the way that information is assimilated by consciousness. Digestion refers to the processes involved in the assimilation of the various categories of food (information). The membrane walls of the cell assists in the absorption of nutrients as well as in the process of the elimination of wastes. They can also help cause obstructions to development through contact with dull energies and related states of mind that retard the expansion of consciousness.

Toxic wastes are eliminated in the process. They are the attributes that were formerly useful but are now dysfunctional, superseded, or harmful to the body. Such elimination is essential for normal healthy development, hence life can be preserved by separation methods. If separation does not occur in the functional process of an organism then the process of elimination is impossible. Consciousness will then be stifled and become toxic through the generation of unwholesome *saṃskāras*.

The various organs of the body need different types of separations and internal systems in order to manifest their many functions, and to shuffle the mishmash of differing substances around. All forms of toxicity must be dispelled or transmuted. A mechanism must therefore exist causing them to be eliminated out of the system, or else stagnation, disease, and death will follow.

When viewed in terms of the progress of a religion, therefore, we see that any extant system of thought must of necessity have accumulated many stagnant ideas, philosophical systems, devotional attitudes, mantras, and observances of ritual, that are venerated because they are hoary with age. They must be eliminated or transformed because these old venerated concepts now prevent the evolutionary growth of the organism as a whole, thus indicate the internal sickness and general malaise of the body corporeal. That spiritual spring cleaning is a necessary process of evolutionary growth is a principle that must one day be properly understood by all religionists. This means that old doctrines that once served a useful function must be taken off the shelves deemed necessary for current study, and housed in a museum for obsolete ideas. They are not to be relegated as something necessary for the life of the organism, but to be seen as a festering disease if continually adhered to. Everything has its use by date, otherwise *saṃsāra* could not be considered transitory.

Upon the path unity is sought, to spell the death of the separate 'self', but this is really possible only after complete comprehension of what that separate entity gained as a consequence of its separateness. Even then, such a unity concerns merging into a greater integral whole, hence another 'separation'. The difference now however, is that the interrelated separations are seen in terms of the complete body of manifestation (no matter how vast or subtle) that is a vaster unity, and so forth. Such can be perceived as the categories of Life existing in a Buddha's Mind. The path of seeing *(darśanabhāga)* therefore expands from the terms of a 'self' concept to universalities structured within Mind. In doing so, the bounds of the separations of the 'self' have been broken in order to encompass the universalities, which then become the *nimittabhāga*.

Things must possess an identity if they are to serve various roles. Identities must manifest different functions and possess differing elements to other identities for systems to occur. A system is that which functions to serve an integral unity. Enlightenment is a system of revelation that serves to differentiate what is real from the unreal. All processes of life are systems. All patterns in the fabric of space incorporate systems. The transportation of energy from one sphere of consciousness to another, where something is defined and thus has a purpose, a beginning and an end, necessitates systemic structures to bring about awareness. The purpose of our awareness is for all that exists to evolve toward enlightenment. The beginning of that purpose is placed in space within a time sequence and exists only within an interrelationship between different aspects, functions, elements. The process of sequencing each purpose within such a time sequence in space is termed 'Dependant Origination'. This then necessitates separate functions (or 'selves', *bhāgas)* of self-activated actions, for dependent interrelationship to occur. Each action demonstrates a separate or else conjoined purpose of the one who manifest the volition to act. Because each purpose is sequenced as part of a time frame, so we have dependency. The dependency then manifests as part of the system of the cellular organism of the evolving life of the consciousness concerned.

Dependant Origination occurs because all of the dependencies become the sum total of that which occurs *inside* the body of a system. Origination necessitates the interrelationship between different functional aspects and elements of a system, because some integral whole must be in place for something else to interrelate with it as part of a chain of dependencies. A good example of the process of a system is digestion. We can ask 'where does digestion begin?' We see that the food inside a stomach and intestines is digested by a whole host of different interrelated little separate entities and digestive juices that work upon the food. Before this there was the thought of being hungry, and then the actions leading to putting food into the mouth, mastication, swallowing, and consequent digestion. One can presume a factor that manifested first when talking about the process, although certain parts may play a more direct role, and in a clearly defined manner.

Many factors go into such processes. All parts exist, whether in latent potential, or taking an active role, so none can be said, from this perspective, as existing or beginning first. (This is part of the reasoning behind conventional Buddhist logic of there being 'no beginning'.) It is the functioning of an active role that makes one perceive of a 'first'. Thus we have the origination of a chain of interdependent actions incorporated as part of a complete system, from the first (e.g., the thought of eating) to the last (the excretion of unusable particles).

The moment something newly enters such a complete system then we have a beginning, and when it is excreted, dispelled, or transmuted, then it has an end. All systems are, however, interdependent, thus the ending of a thing in one system manifests a beginning in another, if the thing is expelled from the former one. Transmutation, however, changes something into something entirely new so that it can still perform a useful function in a system and therefore does not need to be expelled. Therefore, if all systems (within a greater whole) manifest only the action of transmutation (here necessitating an evolved consciousness to accomplish), then such interdependency breaks down as nothing is expelled. If nothing is expelled then nothing can be received by another dependency, and as a consequence we have the dissolution of *saṃsāra*. In place of *saṃsāra* we have the manifestation of self-contained enlightened units that have freed themselves from *that* system of dependency. Such enlightened units are not bound by the conditions of the former chains of dependency, though there are other conditions as defined by the nature of the enlightened states that they ascribe to. Expansive inclusive reason becomes the order of things and the mode of escape from all forms of limitations imposed upon the individual through ascription to a particular system.

A separate part of a system must be a definable quality. It is defined by either its active role, when one notices it, or its characteristics and attributes, for which it gets a name. Hence it manifests as the *nimittabhāga* to an ascertaining consciousness *(darśanabhāga)*. There is also a categorisation of its timing or placing (or when it is timed to be activated) as part of a certain sequence of events, as well as whereabouts in the space of a particular system it may be positioned. This also involves what it is conjoined to as part of a system of interdependencies. Timing refers to a sequence of events relating to it coming into objective manifestation. The elements of that which is to be already exists in the zygote or *bīja*, and which will flower into full maturation according to impeccable law.

When talking about all the digestive elements of a body one cannot say that those elements do not exist when they are not being used for digestion, as those elements exist in pure potential or sleeping mode. They exist but are not used at that time, therefore not necessarily perceived by consciousness. It is the same with the Creation Theory, or with any hypothesis concerning the beginnings and endings in or of the universe. Certain things appear to come first in a series, such as chemicals in digestion. They appear because they are there to be activated. They produce the screen of entrances and exits in digestion: the extremes of differences of appearances. Likewise in the entire panoply of Nature the game of manifestation appears and is observed by consciousness because of the active role. The active role draws attention in consciousness to all the things that is happening in relation to that role.

All parts of a complete system therefore exist, but not all is actively manifest, much lays hidden or dormant, playing only a potential role until the time comes for activation. The future lies hid here, and it is within the ken of an enlightened Mind to perceive the nature of the veil of the hidden and to work illuminatingly with the process of activation. The structure of a *bīja* is therefore of considerable importance for anyone wishing to penetrate the veil of the future.

All active roles are seen in the world play, where a set of a series occurs, the set is delineated, but is part of a system where there is no true beginning and ending. There are obviously myriads of such interrelated sets in this play. The law of interrelationships governs all, even those things that exist in potential, i.e., the unformed role of elements yet to appear on the revelatory screen as a consequence of digestion (of information). When it appears on that screen there is a beginning and an end to the entrances of these elements. But that which is held in potential, like *śūnyatā*, can be said to have always existed and therefore can be conceived to have no beginning.

Only consciousness delineates a time factor for their appearance, for consciousness particularises one thing from another. The functioning of consciousness is like digestion, where elements, particulars, manifest an active role and move through the body (of the mind), from your mouth to your bottom, the place of excretion of unnecessary detail, of information not wanted by the assimilating consciousness. Digestion happens as a consequence of a long continuous process (of *saṃskāras* moving through a stream of lives) until the raw product, the base idea, is thoroughly assimilated and capable of being practically utilised by the body corporeal (e.g., the Sambhogakāya Flower), or else it is rejected, excreted as waste particles. Such waste particles are known in Buddhism as defilements.

The appearance is that the personal-I rejects these defilements as unworthy of expression when on the path to enlightenment, but the Sambhogakāya Flower actually sets the conditions of the system in place wherein this is slated to happen. The personal-I acts as the digestive process, the stomach and intestines, wherein the actual rejection happens, but the Sambhogakāya Flower incorporates the total system that chooses what 'food' to eat and to digest. The Sambhogakāya Flower thus carefully stages the situation whereby it is possible for the personal-I to cleanse the unnecessary defilements. Thus the functioning of *darśanabhāga*. The free will factor is employed of course, but if in any one life defilements are not properly processed, i.e., the personality goes against the plan for it, then situations are planned for the later part of that life, or the succeeding ones, whereby this consequence is enforced by means of the suffering factor for the personal-I. Also, the Sambhogakāya Flower experiences what is akin to a stomach ache (without the human concept of pain). Amelioration therefore must take place. The cleansing of the necessary defilements is the potential, and the Sambhogakāya Flower ensures the actuality of their cleansing, which incorporates the law of *karma*. The personal-I consequently is in a type of stage play with the entire illusion of *saṃsāra* as the play. This has been understood by Buddhists, but the director of the overall show has not been comprehended.

Those humans that are ignorant of the fact that they are in a gigantic, contrived play get attached to this or that aspect of *saṃsāra* and consequently suffer. Those that are enlightened, or are upon the path to enlightenment, *know* of the play and act accordingly to its dictates. They are fully aware that if they manifest in a desireless and spontaneous manner to all of life's happenings, according to the pull of the *karma* (as directed by the Sambhogakāya Flower), then enlightenment will result. Enlightenment here being conscious absorption into the vastness of the *ālayavijñāna,* wherein all *bījas* to be enacted in *saṃsāra* are stored for ultimate expression. The enlightened one then is ken to the sequence of development of each and every one of them, as his/her consciousness is then inclusive of them all. He/she has entered into a vaster sub-set or system than before.

If the Sambhogakāya Flower did not stage the events, then there could be no such thing as effortlessness and spontaneity in relation to the enlightenment process, for how could the *karma* otherwise be rightly organised to manifest the background conditions that would propel one spontaneously and effortlessly along the enlightenment path? This process can only happen because the *karma* has been *prearranged* to make it so.

We see that the structure of all Buddhist thought concerns systems that can be digested. The relative observations and understandings of the nature of things as described above causes systems to appear in consciousness. They are generally formed around the idea or notion of certain processes to happen, of eventualities that result as a consequence of undertaking actions of various types. Each system that produces eventualities can be considered to be a body that serves as a function or container *(nimittabhāga)* for certain processes to be accomplished. Systems always have purpose, such as the enlightenment of all people. The digestion or transformation of all energy or food in the body is similarly purposeful. In fact, when you think that the nature of food is to supply energy so that one can sustain thought, then the similarities increase. Digestion creates conditions whereby energy can be utilised and cleansed, much like the process of gaining enlightenment. More could be written about the esoteric nature of the digestive process, but the above suffices for the present discourse.

Ātman and *non-ātman*

A statement that lies at the heart of Yogācāra-Vijñānavādin thought is given in verse seventeen of the *Treatise in Thirty Verses on Mere-Consciousness:*

> Verse 17: The various consciousnesses manifest in two divisions, perception and the object of perception. Because of this, all these do not exist. Therefore, all is Mere-consciousness. *(Wei-shih-san-shih-lun-sung* 60c9-61a3.)
>
> > Kārikā: *vijñānapāriṇāmo 'yam vikalpo yad vikalpyate/ tena tannāsti tenedaṃ sarvaṃ vijñāptimātrakaṃ//*17
> >
> > *Excepting darśanabhāga and nimittabhāga nothing real exists.*

'The various consciousnesses' indicates the three developments of consciousness and their mental associates. They are called 'development' because all of them are capable of development which appears to have two aspects—that of the perceiving part (*darśanabhāga*) and that of the perceived part (*nimittabhāga*). The perceiving part developed is termed as discrimination (*vikalpa*), because it apprehends the second. The second part developed is termed as 'that which is discriminated', because it is apprehended by the first one, i.e. the perceiving part.

According to this correct principle, apart from what is thus developed from consciousness, there are no real *ātman* or *dharmas;* because, besides what apprehends or is apprehended, there exists nothing as real *(bhūtadravya)* excepting these two aspects *(bhāgas).* Therefore all the phenomenal *(saṃskṛta),* all the noumenal *(asaṃskṛta),* or all appearing as both real and false is nothing but consciousness. (CWSL 38c18-25)[36]

Mahāyāna sources on the vijñaptimātratā[37]

Daśabhumikā: 'In the three worlds *(dhātu)* there is nothing but mind' *(cittamātram idaṃ yad idaṃ traidhātukaṃ).*

Sandhinirmocana: 'Objects of perception are merely manifestations of consciousness' *(vijñānapratibhāsamātraṃ).*

Laṅkāvatāra: 'All *dharmas* are inseparable from mind' *(cittāvyatirikta).*

Vimalakīrti: 'Sentient beings become pure or impure in accordance with the mind.' (39a6-8)

Ghanavyūha: 'The objects of mind *(manas)* and the other consciousnesses are not distinct from their own nature. Therefore I declare that all things are consciousness and there is nothing else.'[38]

An additional note on the meaning of the term *bhāgas:*

14. *Bhāgas (fen)* are the divisions of consciousness on the basis of the functioning of consciousness. The function of consciousness is 'mental discrimination', i.e. perceiving and discriminating things. When consciousness is born, its manifestation has two aspects: *(1)* that what discriminates the seeming subject, *(neng-yüan,* what can cause)

---

36 *Ch'eng-wei-shih-lun (vijñaptimātratāsiddhiśastra).*

37 Mere Consciousness.

38 Ganguli, 114-115.

> and *(2)* that what is discriminated, the seeming object, *ālambana (suo-yüan,* what is caused). As a seeming subject the aspect of consciousness is called perceiving division *(darśanabhāga, chien-fen).* As a seeming subject, the aspect of consciousness is called perceived division *(nimittabhāga, hsiang-fen).*
>
> 15. There is another functional aspect of consciousness that what is the support of the perceiving and the perceived division, and may be regarded as their essential nature. This is called the 'self-corroboratory' aspect *(svasaṃvittibhāga, tze-cheng-fen).* It is the realization by consciousness of itself. If this was lacking, there would be no way of remembering the various manifestations of mind and its activities.[39]

There may indeed be 'no *real ātman',* however, does not the individual consciousness always hold an *ātman* inside its awareness, thus making the consciousness of the 'I' the focus of the individual reality, around which everything pertaining to the 'I' revolves? This is especially so when consciousness manifests a realisation itself. (The 'essential nature' of 'the perceiving and the perceived division'.) A person thus thinks of everything in the universe as something to relate to it. The 'I' concept is possible because there are differing states of consciousness, from wrong mental discrimination *(vikalpa),* to the definable experience of a Buddha. Here the term *ātman* is conceived as something that implies individuality, as something distinct from something else. Thus I shall interpret an *ātman* in terms of an ego or 'I', rather than the technical Hindu definition. If one possesses no *ātman (nairātmya),* then one can be considered asleep, or else from another higher perspective, enlightened.

The term 'asleep' does not just signify a state of consciousness having vacated the body, but specifically depicts a lack of awareness of the perception of an 'I', there is no perceiving consciousness that can characterise the *nimittabhāga.* The sleeping one hence is not aware of something, or of anything at all. Therefore, when someone is 'awakened' in terms of being consciously receptive, he is perceiving in relation to an 'I', an *ātman.* When enlightenment ensues then this 'I' no longer exists, indeed a self-focussing mind has been transcended. It exists below the threshold of higher identification and is replaced

39 Ibid., 139. Taken from the notes, to which the numbers 14 and 15 refer.

by identification with universality, by means of an abstracted Mind, or with the *intuition*, which is beyond mere reflection or the analytical introspection associated with consciousness. If there is no 'I' for Mind to identify with, then there is nothing it can cognise in relation to, and thus empirical consciousness becomes below the threshold of awareness. It is not part of the process of revelation. When the Mind utilises it then it organises the field of perception *(nimittabhāga)* into units of perception that by definition temporarily manifest in the form of 'I's', which the Mind can perceive in one broad sweep of illumination.

Regarding enlightenment, we see that consciousness proceeds from the state of *ātman* (the I-concept) and *dharmas* (characteristics of existence) to gradually become conscious, aware, of the 'all' that is. This 'all' is at first represented by the *ālayavijñāna* and later the *dharmakāya*. Only then can it lose awareness of the 'self', as the characteristics of existence become blended into unity, and as a consequence lose a separated identity. However the unity that exists can also be viewed as a type of *ātman*, like a Buddha's *nirmaṇakāya* and *sambhogakāya* forms, though that which utilises these forms is freed from such identity.

What is indicated here is that the *ātman* and non-*ātman* (*nairātmya*) concepts spiral around each other, one being dependent upon the other. There is room for both in the evolutionary process; indeed, for we can only define things in relation to what they are not. There is individuality and there is non individuality and there is also an unaware state of consciousness that is neither an individual or a non-individual. If there was no such thing as an *ātman* (an 'I') then one could not evolve the capacity to comprehend what it is not. Consideration of an absolutely unchangeable *ātman* is an absurdity, as no such stagnant thing could exist. Hence we can only talk in terms of that which changes, evolves, when we conceive of an *ātman*. It is 'developed from consciousness' and it can be pointed out, as previously stated, that a subtle form of an *ātman* in the form of the Sambhogakāya Flower is the driving force of the evolutionary process of a personal-I.

That which is non-*ātman* is *śūnyatā*, but *śūnyatā* is the middle between extremes, a type of placid Eye wherein energies move from the *dharmakāya* to the Sambhogakāya Flower wherein the energies are translated into the perception of images (or the *ālayavijñāna)* and vice versa. (This Flower thus manifests the subjective version of the brain mechanism with respect to the processing of light.) *Śūnyatā* is a mirror that reflects aspects of the cosmic Mind *(dharmakāya)* into the Sambhogakāya Flower, allowing the transformation of the Flower from above. The Sambhogakāya Flower is thus an entity (individuality) that contains the abstraction of *śūnyatā* and incorporates the phenomena of *saṃsāra* within the embrace of the universality of the *ālayavijñāna*. As it moves towards the embrace of what the *dharmakāya* portends then the potency of what is to be experienced destroys the form of the Flower/*tathāgatagarbha* and liberation ensues. That which allows one to escape the pull of the earth's *karma* has manifested.

If the Dharmakāyic Mind can work upon the Sambhogakāya Flower via the Void that is *śūnyatā,* then within the *dharmakāya* one can also find forms of an *'ātman'* upon a vast transcendental scale. Such an *'ātman'* is not *saṃsāric,* but pertains to the Real, *sat/tat*. This Reality manifests in the form of a Buddha-Mind. One Buddha is distinguished from another in a similar manner that the five Dhyāni Buddhas are different from each other, yet all are aspects of the universality and omniscience of the Buddha-Mind. There is a green Buddha, a blue Buddha, a red Buddha, etc. No two Buddhas build exactly the same Buddha-field, nor do they have the same auras, each are different. It cannot be otherwise, or there would only ever be one Buddha described in the literatures, the Ādi Buddha, and no more said concerning any other. One also needs to view this subject from the perspective of those that have evolved from other star systems, constellations and galaxies in our universe, wherein differentiation is all we see. Neither can it be presumed that all Buddhas are of the same 'spiritual age'. Because there are other Buddhas mentioned in the texts, so there is 'individuality' amongst them.[40]

The idea expressed above is indeed found in the *Ratnagotravibhāga* in terms of the three types of 'self' that Buddhas have been said to have attained. Brown states that:

> Defined as the Absolute Body, the *Dharmakāya,* "the great body," descriptive as neither "being" nor "non-being" is yet the highest pure Reality. Having attained this, the Buddhas are said to have attained

40 This can be asserted despite the fact that some Buddhist *sūtras* state that all Buddhas are identical.

> the pure, controlling power. "In this sense the Buddhas could be the highest powerful Ego in the Immaculate Sphere".[41]...It is when this *Tathatā,* normally veiled by the adventitious defilements, (to borrow a phrase from the *Ratnagotra* itself) becomes purified and fully manifest, that the Buddhas are said to have attained the pre-excellent non-substantiality: the pure self. Consequently, it is with the hermeneutic of non-substantiality alone, that the Buddhas are to be understood as having attained the highest exaltation of the self *(ātmamahāmatām),* the supreme self *(paramātman),* and the pure self (*śuddhātma*).[42]

What is described in the texts is the similarity of the state of Identifications each Buddha has achieved, and that the foundation is *śūnyatā*. This observation is correct, but the Buddhas do have dissimilarities, though compassion lies as the basic instinct to them all, and the foundation of their Buddhahood lies in the attainment of *śūnyatā*. *Śūnyatā* however, is only one major evolutionary goal for a Bodhisattva. The major stages in the evolutionary process runs as follows:

> sentience → self-consciousness → *bodhicitta* → *śūnyatā* → *dharmakāya*

Within *dharmakāya,* however, exists a vast field of experience and differentiation of attributes that yet need to be revealed to Buddhists, as far as language permits. There are many *dharmakāyic* levels to experience. Uniformity is not the reality. There are no dead ends to the evolutionary process in cosmos. Reynolds states in his translation of *The Golden Letters*:

> Even if all of the Jinas or Victorious Ones of the three times deliberated together *(dus gsum rgyal-ba'i zhal bsdur)*, they would discover nothing beyond this fundamental primordial state of all the Buddhas.[43]

What 'this fundamental primordial state of all the Buddhas' may be is open to conjecture, because it is something not definable or approachable by consciousness, and consciousness is all we possess

41 Brian Edward Brown, *The Buddha Nature,* (Motilal Banarsidass, Delhi, 2004), 86.

42 Ibid., 87.

43 John Myrdhin Reynolds, *The Golden Letters,* (Snow Lion Publications, Ithaca, New York, 1996), 125.

to try to convey ideas concerning anything to anybody. We can intuit however that a 'recently evolved' Jina is newly awakened to such a state, and may yet have to fully awaken to its full potential, whilst it is a field of complete mastery, or of a zone that has been transcended for those Jinas who have attained their status in a far distant aeon. The 'fundamental primordial state' can be considered a generic term for the base level of identification attained by all Jinas, like intelligence is for humans, and it is a *mere presumption* for non Buddhas to assert that there is nothing more or beyond this state.

The concept of 'the Jinas or Victorious Ones of the three times' immediately shows the limitations of language, as the state of attaining the quality 'Jina' means that time is surpassed, there being for such a One no time. There however is still a qualification, or distinction made between the Buddhas who have attained their liberation in former cycles, and those beings who are yet to attain Buddhahood. The statement implies that once they attain Buddhahood then they experience 'the fundamental primordial state' in which they will not find any boundaries. Such a state, or 'space' as one may assert, is boundless, infinite, all-encompassing, therefore a Buddha will never reach the end of it in his travels in the 'beyond'. This may be so, but it is not necessarily all that one can say about a Buddha-Mind, if one has actually experienced that primordial state, albeit even if only briefly.

The *dharmakāya* is a zone of expansive, all-embracive, inclusive Reason or Comprehension of cosmos, its processes, and the nature of what it includes. It manifests in a similar vein, though upon a far vaster scale, to the *tathāgatagarbhas* of each human unit that is responsible for the direction of the streams of *karma* associated with the evolving personality in *saṃsāra*. Here cosmos has supplanted *saṃsāra*. We will see in the *dharmakāya* Buddhas and Buddha-like beings that are responsible for the emanation of the streams of *karma* that express the engendering and evolution of the entire environment of which the human kingdom is a unit and star systems are a part. There is a similar function, but greater order of magnitude between the two levels of emanatory expression. All that can be understood of *karma* conditioning the appearance of the three worlds is seeded from the *dharmakāya*, and is reflected through the Eye of *śūnyatā*. The external phenomenal universe, permeated as *saṃsāra,* thus has its roots or foundation, its *bīja,* in the *dharmakāya.*

In this context *śūnyatā* acts in the form of a mirror that links the *dharmakāya* inalterably to *saṃsāra.* (For the Sambhogakāya Flower, the *tathāgatagarbha,* the mechanism involves the functioning of the Śūnyatā Eye.) From this perspective one in the *dharmakāya* is not necessarily fully freed or 'liberated' from the necessity of interrelating with the formed realms. However, it signifies true or complete mastery over all conditionings in *saṃsāra*, to the extent of being able to control everything that transpires therein (by means of the right application of the laws of energy, the Rays conditioning consciousness, and of *mantra*). The supramundane *siddhis,* the ability to manifest the phenomenological miracles of a Buddha, have been attained by one resident in *dharmakāya.*

The fount of true liberation from affiliation with *saṃsāra* thus rests upon realms or zones of Being within the *dharmakāya*, for which any words or terms we possess to describe begin to lose proper meaning. Our view here is of true liberation, meaning the freedom to move through cosmic space, away from the confines or prison of earth involvement and its human conditionings. The *tathāgatagarbha* represents the mechanism of access to this ultimate body of the *dharma.* First, however, it must be freed from adventitious defilements.

Śūnyatā veils the laws governing our natural environment, the universe we live in. Because *śūnyatā* is stable, so *saṃsāra* has a solid foundation, whereby to move from and to go to via a succession of intermediate progressive changes. This allows consciousness to evolve. Consciousness needs relative stability, it also needs a rhythm and regularity to its flow in order to be able to name, to classify, to arrange images. It needs to come from and proceed to somewhere, even if that somewhere be a void. In the listings of images it has created, it can recognise those that appear as the signposts leading to the future of whatever is to be for it. *Śūnyatā* can be considered the foundation of the house that is the universe and everything that is contained in it. For this reason *śūnyatā* must be devoid of all the attributes that relate to ephemera, otherwise the foundation itself could not last, and everything would collapse into a rubble of meaninglessness.

5

The Vijñanavādins on the Evolution of Consciousness

The two types of karma

The Vijñānavādin position on the evolution of consciousness can be gleaned from the *Treatise in Thirty Verses on Mere-Consciousness* in a section entitled *'The Concept of "Evolution of Consciousness"'*.

> 'Evolution' indicates that the substance of consciousness, i.e. the *saṃvittibhāga,* manifests itself in two functional divisions *(bhāgas),* i.e. the object perceived *(nimittabhāga)* and the perceiving faculty *(darśanabhāga).* These divisions arise out of the third division, i.e. the self-witnessing *(svasaṃvittibhāga),* which is their 'essence'. On the basis of the two functional divisions the self and the things appear. 'Evolution' also means that the inner consciousness manifests itself in what appears to be external object. By the force of the perfuming energy *(vāsanā)* stored in the mind from the false beliefs in the self and things, the consciousness becomes active and develops into the semblance of the self and things. Although the self and things do not exist apart from consciousness, they are taken as external objects by wrong mental discrimination *(vikalpa).* Because of this, all beings conceive them as real self and real things.
>
> Consciousness manifests itself in infinite varieties but consciousness capable of manifestation are of three kinds—*ālayavijñāna, manovijñāna* and *pravṛittivijñāna.* The first one is called retribution *(vipāka).* It is the eighth consciousness. The second is the consciousness that deliberates *(manana).* It is the seventh consciousness. The third kind is the consciousness that discriminates

> the sphere of objects. It is the first six consciousnesses which include the five sense-consciousnesses—eye, ear, nose, tongue, body and the sense-centre consciousness—*manovijñāna.*[1]

It should be noted that this text does not use the term *kliṣṭamanas* as the seventh consciousness, rather the term *manovijñāna,* which is incorrect. *Manovijñāna* is here used in the same sense as the general substance of the mind, which I simplify to *manas* in this series.[2] *Kliṣṭamanas* can be considered to be included as part of *manovijñāna,* but has a specialised role, being the *piṇgalā* aspect of *manovijñāna,* hence is more correctly the seventh consciousness, and is explained throughout this series. *Pravṛttivijñāna* is translated as the intellect, the discriminating aspect of consciousness, which analyses the experiences from the sense-consciousnesses. It represents the *iḍā* aspect of *manovijñāna.* Also the definition of the *ālayavijñāna* here is woefully inadequate, but it and the other terms above shall be elucidated in chapter ten. Taking the information in this note into account we can proceed.

It is only a part truth to say that what perceives is also the object of perception, i.e., that 'the self and things do not exist apart from consciousness'. Neither is the object of perception experienced in the same way by another, or has the same value in the consciousness-stakes. Each of us have different concepts of pain or pleasure, happiness and sadness. For instance, many would have a sense of great happiness through having many lovers in a pleasure garden specially set aside for them, however this was a source of pain for the Buddha before he set out on his quest for enlightenment.

The questions that could be asked here is 'How does the sense-perceptions through which one must experience differ from those possessed by another, and does the force of one's experience *(vāsanā)* condition the sense-objects through which one must experience'? That is, 'does the object of perception change because one's consciousness perceives that object of perception differently from another's consciousness, because of the fact that one's *saṃskāras*, moods, feelings,

1 Swati Ganguly, (trans), *Treatise in Thirty Verses on Mere-Consciousness,* (Motilal Barnasidass, Delhi, 1992), 38-9.

2 The actual substance that the mind is constituted of is termed *citta.* It differs from *manas* in that *manas* incorporates it whenever it manifests a thought construct.

or emotions being perceived with is different from another's?' Does the outer phenomena change because of the views of those whose consciousnesses become active and develop 'into the semblance of the self and things' via a force of perfuming energy?

The answer that would normally be given is that via 'the force of the perfuming energy *(vāsanā)* stored in the mind', consciousness is activated and perceives the concept 'of the self and things.' Two different viewers simply perfume two differing sets of false beliefs. What concerns us here is *vāsanā,* which is a force that according to the laws of motion should carry on to change or affect the phenomena that is being perceived. In fact we see that the *vāsanā* does not carry through to condition the outer environment, because it does not alter that environment. (*Vāsanā* thus does not modify more than the substance of consciousness.) However if it does not, then what is perceived in the mind is not necessarily 'false beliefs', because what is actually perceived is what exists as the external phenomena. *Pravṛttivijñāna* is then used to rationalise the truth of what is perceived or not. Even so, much that exists in the field of perception of the external environment is not perceived. It is that to which the *manovijñāna* is oblivious. This does not alter the reality of what exists in the external environment, from which the sense preceptors of the viewer has not extracted information, for which there presently is not the *vāsanā* stored to experience with. Consciousness may develop such, and different perceivers could manifest a controversy as to what is actually perceived. Regardless of that controversy however, the activities of that external environment will carry on naturally, unconcerned about what is in the minds of those perceiving it with 'sets of false beliefs'.

Thus one does not feel the 'pain' of a tree as its leaves are being eaten. This 'pain' is not felt because though being aware of the form of the tree, which is within the experiential consciousness sphere, such consciousness does not include the sensory experience of the tree, nor does it see the caterpillar and its mouth as it is chewing and digesting the food. Here one's consciousness is unawakened with respect to the experiences of the caterpillar or of the tree.

From this perspective the phrase 'the self and things do not exist apart from consciousness' is correct, in the sense that we are unaware of the existence of things outside our consciousness. Therefore to us, (the experiencer) the caterpillar chewing on the tree does not exist, or the 'pain' that may be experienced by the tree. We can admit (utilising our experience-resources and the resultant memories) that this may be a possibility. However, whether we admit it or not, it does not alter the fact that there *is* a caterpillar chewing upon the tree, and that this affects the tree in some way. This can be proven by the holes that have appeared in the tree's leaves when we inspect them carefully later. They have not appeared for no reason. Or alternately, we can actually spot the caterpillars chewing.

What we are really looking at here is two different streams of *karma*, which determines the reality of what is and what is not.

The first is the *karma* that is directed through the Sambhogakāya Flower, which directs the *saṃskāras*[3] that condition the way individuals view things in their consciousness. The Yogācāra reasoning has reference to this type of *karma*. The extension is the thought that the entire world picture is 'created' by the collective consciousnesses of all humans in the way they perceive things. Therefore, because their consciousness tells them that a thing exists, so therefore it exists for them. Because all beings see the things they come into contact with as existents, so then these things exist. It can be considered to be like a collective hallucination, with everyone verifying to everyone else that such and such things exist, because their consciousnesses are telling them that it is so. If you remove the input of the five senses from the objects of experience then nothing will appear to exist, because there are no senses experiencing or registering consciousness-volitions. Thus the argument goes that we are all experiencing mass hallucinations in ascertaining that phenomenal things actually exist. In identifying with such things 'as external objects', then this is termed 'wrong mental discrimination'. The text goes on to say that 'Because of this, all beings conceive them as real self and real things'.

This logic is also backed up by the fact that everything in *saṃsāra* is transient, fleeting phenomena, thus also consequently nothing exists, except *śūnyatā*, which is empty of such phenomena. Because all things are thus 'empty', it is only the mind that is telling us that they have substance and consequently are real.

---

3 *Vāsanā* being the driving energy of the *saṃskāras*.

This argument has a certain logic, but it does not take into account the *second* type of *karma*, which is the *karma* that is directed from the *dharmakāyic* realms,[4] which conditions the way things actually are in the sum total of Nature's kingdoms, irrespective of the way that we view things in our consciousness. Such phenomena exists (or existed), such as the appearance of a sun, which gives us light and warmth, irrespective of whether there is a human consciousness or not to register and experience the effects. It will go on existing, long after the present human kingdom is no more.

We also know that before humans there were dinosaurs because they have left their imprint, their fossilised bones, to testify of their existence. Our consciousness can thus logically deduce their factuality, based upon anatomical comparison with modern animal species and by the methodology of modern science. All is filtered through the activity of *manas,* our consciousness that cogently analyses. We likewise can deduce that the caterpillar cares not whether there were once dinosaurs or of their fossil records. It has developed an entirely different view. It cares about the leaves of the tree that it is chewing, and will go on doing it whether we humans see it doing so or not, or believe in its existence or not. It has its own set of value-impressions not at all related to what humans think, individually or collectively. It obeys different laws than that framed by human consciousness, and for it the statement 'the self and things do not exist apart from consciousness' *is not true.* For one thing it has not this consciousness, it knows it not, but it does know the leaf of the tree that it is eating. The leaf sustains its being, and having eaten one it then goes to eat another.

Humans can imagine anything they wish, that is the way that their consciousness functions, they can overlay the images of their fantasy (an expression of the Sambhogakāya Flower type of *karma*) upon anything to make it real, like imagining a snake in the dark to be a coiled rope. If that snake went and bit him it would change the reality patterning of the images in the human's mind. It is this way with humans, but for a caterpillar a leaf is a leaf, it is there for eating, and that is what it does with it, as it obeys the instinctual patterning of its sentience, as laid down by the laws of the *dharmakāya* type of *karma*. It has not

4 Via the seat of power of the Ādi Buddha.

the *sambhogakāya* type of *karma*. Humans however, experience both. They have imagination, they can recollect or distort images from the mind, and they can chew upon a leaf.

Therefore, depending upon which type of *karma* is manifesting, the abovementioned quote is either true or false. Another way of putting it is that the human may think that the snake is a coiled rope because that is what his consciousness tells him, and therefore he makes it his reality. But if the snake bit him and he died, then his reality has been found to be false, i.e., the statement 'the self and things do not exist apart from consciousness' to be fundamentally untrue, for his consciousness told him one thing, but the reality was another that spelt the death or end of that consciousness, or at least of its conception of things in relation to the 'I'.

Another way of viewing the issue is that if a being exists in *śūnyatā*, i.e., there is no consciousness to identify things with, then this is similar to the removal of all of one's senses that formerly experienced the existence of a thing. The question that then can be asked is 'does that thing still exist?' The answer lies in the statement, 'yes—it exists in consciousness', and to experience it in a state of *śūnyatā* one must still have a link to consciousness, hence the existence of what is termed Clear Light. This Clear Light then is the nexus between *śūnyatā* and *saṃsāra*. Without it *śūnyatā* would represent a state of annihilation.

The factor of sentience

When viewing a human consciousness, even that of an enlightened one, our observation is of one particular consciousness out of myriads, all of whom register phenomena as having an existence. Such phenomena has not changed just because any particular conscious unit stops perceiving it. In the *śūnyatā* experience however there is no consciousness to experience any 'thing', to make it to be this or that. So what exactly does one residing 'there' experience when the caterpillar chewing a leaf is viewed? Does this caterpillar exist for such a one, even though the definition of *śūnyatā* is that it is empty of such phenomena, of concepts of *'self'*, etc.?

The answer is that such a one *can experience* the caterpillar chewing phenomena in the same way that a caterpillar would, because such a one is still conditioned by the *dharmakāya* type of *karma*, even though he may have transcended the *sambhogakāya* type. He will experience 'things' exactly the way they are in truth, as 'empty', but still phenomenal. The fact is that one possessing the *śūnyatā* experience spontaneously sees *all* aspects of the phenomena at once. In relation to this experience consciousness is merely an interpreting tool, that is all.

If the caterpillar experienced the sensation of the pain of a tree as it ate its leaves, then we could posit that the caterpillar would no longer eat those leaves with the same form of 'enjoyment' (if we could project such a human emotion upon this sentient species). There is a form of experiential interaction that helps produce the evolution of each species. One then cannot deduce that there is a true separation between a caterpillar and a tree. A mode of sentient interaction happens between the two, which will be comprehended once clairvoyant perception has been developed, or the factor of the functioning of the *deva* kingdom[5] is included. Division and unity within the non-human lives are linked by a form of congruent sentience, not intelligence. The caterpillar and the tree do not have an awareness as to the nature of our thought life, or of the gnashing of our emotional teeth. Our thoughts similarly do not normally perceive what the little cells composing our constitutions feel or know. We can however develop the subtle perception to be able to do so.

Each sentient entity is divorced from the everyday sensory experience of every human. Human consciousness has transcended the type of sentience of the caterpillar and the tree and their internal sensory experience, however, our consciousness also acts as a support for all these other life forms. It unites their forms of sentience, because it has capability of comprehension, but it is *not 'it'*—the caterpillar or the tree, their sentience is very far away from the domain of our normal consciousnesses. The caterpillar chewing on the leaves, etc., continues functioning, no matter where our awareness is focussed, but our consciousness can psychically gain an impression of the caterpillar 'mind'.

What is real, and what is not, e.g., the concept that nothing else exists but consciousness, and concepts of what is and what is not, are pure questioning within the minds of human units. This type of questioning cannot be relegated to the sentience of a caterpillar chewing on the tree,

5 Explained somewhat in the later volumes.

or frog or ant that may be in the vicinity observing the scenario. An analysis of human consciousness *only* is what is in question here, and the premise is that this is not transferable to that of an ant or caterpillar, unless these units of sentience become human. Thus the statement that 'nothing exists but consciousness' can be considered true only in relation to a human awareness, of one who has consciousness of a certain type that allows the unit to perceive the object of perception in a certain comprehensible, co-ordinated way. It is not even possible (without the development of transcendental awareness) to determine whether an ant or caterpillar actually thinks, i.e., is conscious. They may certainly be conscious or aware of 'something', but are these sentient states actually conscious of things in the way that we understand or perceive those 'things', in the form of the type of perception that we conceive to be the 'real'? We can say that any of the sense-consciousnesses may exist in the sentient entities, but *pravṛttivijñāna does not.* Without *pravṛttivijñāna* there is no discriminatory awareness, but there may be discrimination between say, leaf and non-leaf by the caterpillar. But does the caterpillar consciously discriminate (as we do in all of our activities), or is it simply instinct that drives the caterpillar on to chew certain types of leaves, eschewing other types? Such awareness is governed by certain neuro-chemical impulses rather than consciousness.

Taking scientific as well as esoteric thinking into account, a more sophisticated concept of life, its formation, and the related principles, can be produced in the Buddhist world, whereon future generations of philosophers, thinkers and lawmakers, can produce a new, more enlightened civilisation. All man-made laws can then be appropriately guided. The ontology must manifest a form of cogent logic where the support structures of reality, of what is and what is not in life, are better defined, so that fuzziness of thought no longer exists. Such thought must be replaced by inclusive reason concerning all attributes of life, subjective and objective, psychic and temporal. Then understanding will be tempered with the relative perspective of the incarnate sentience or consciousness, whether it be of a tree, animal, *deva* or man.

What is and is not from a higher or lower perspective depends on the focus of consciousness, of what aspect of phenomena it is observing. Whether this be a collection of atoms, *nāḍīs*, or detail of the stars in the cosmos, depends upon this focussing ability, and the quality of the consciousness that must interpret and correlate the data in a wholesome way. A discernment must then be made whether that form pertains to 'reality' in some way. How refined a consciousness is when it perceives is important. The signposts of reality shift as consciousness evolves. It cognises ever widening arcs of inclusive reason regarding the true nature of 'self' and 'things'.

The evolution of the *ālayavijñāna*

Verse 29 of the *Treatise in Thirty Verses on Mere Consciousness* states:

> Not conceivable and not comprehensible is this supramundane wisdom; because of the abandonment of the two-fold grossness or incapabilities 'revolution at substratum' or transformation of *ālayavijñāna* into wisdom is obtained.[6]

From this we can conclude that the *ālayavijñāna* evolves when 'incapable', gross and heavy *saṃskāras* are abandoned because they are destructive to the forms of refined consciousness that are needed to attain wisdom. Other *saṃskāras* are gradually transmuted because of their continuous recycling, producing increasingly refined qualities, so that the grosser forms of *prāṇic* states that were incorporated as the *saṃskāras* are gradually eliminated. (This happens via the mechanism of the Splenic centres.) Only the *prāṇas* that are the basis for the attainment of the five types of wisdom are left. As the consciousness-modifying factors are gradually transformed, so the *ālayavijñāna* is converted into wisdom.

The way of the evolution of the *ālayavijñāna* is therefore the mode of development of the wisdoms of the five Dhyāni Buddhas. This is another way of stating that the type of consciousness associated with the 'I', governed by the Sambhogakāya Flower, becomes transmuted into the type of identifications associated with the *dharmakāya*. The Dharmakāya Way is the All. Consequently, the world of the Sambhogakāya Flower is made redundant, it becomes a hindrance to the awesome power of the energies and revelations accorded via the *dharmakāya*. It dies and

6 Ganguly, 131.

becomes a supernova on its own realm so that the highest form of enlightenment *(samyaksambodhi)* can be attained. One is then liberated. The Sambhogakāya Flower literally explodes into pure radiance of Mind and its functioning is absorbed into the *dharmakāya*.

The general process of this conversion of the *ālayavijñāna* is associated with the development of the whorls of consciousnesses (the Sambhogakāya Flowers) contained within it.[7] This also incorporates the entire evolutionary milieu of the personal-I's rayed into manifestation to gather base information that develops the love and wisdom *(bodhicitta)* that is the basis to the higher identifications with the all. If the *ālayavijñāna* did not evolve in such a way then enlightenment could not occur, as the *ālayavijñāna* would remain in a state of stasis, no transmogrification of consciousness being possible.

There are three types of Flowers that concern us here. They are aligned and integrated within one holistic scenario. They can be viewed as conveying the potency of the three principal *nāḍīs,* though viewed upon a far greater scale than the human body.

1. The Dharmakāya Flower[8]—effectively the *suṣumṇā* aspect, the spirit within, representing the highest enlightenment principle, containing the revelation of what cosmos contains.
2. The Sambhogakāya Flower—effectively the *piṅgalā* aspect, wherein consciousness and the principle of Love-Wisdom is contained. This represents the soul aspect of a human, producing the revelation of what the entire *ālayavijñāna* accords.
3. The *sahasrāra padma* in the head—effectively the *iḍā* aspect, representing the activity side of life, wherein consciousness responds to external environmental impacts and develops the various wisdoms, as sense consciousnesses are properly processed and transformed. It constitutes the gain of the sum of the intricate *nāḍī* system, and produces forms of transmuted understandings of the processes and functions associated with the external universe. When inwardly attuned the petals of this centre are so organised that it can receive

7 The implication here is that there is a universalised form of the *ālayavijñāna,* conceived as the domain of the mind/Mind, and quantified aspects of it, represented by each Sambhogakāya Flower.

8 See Volume 3, chapter 6, for an explanation of this form upon *dharmakāyic* levels.

impressions from the higher two Flowers, and thus gain various degrees of enlightenment.[9]

Dependent Origination, madness, and the self of things

The two abovementioned types of *karma* (the *dharmakāyic* and the *sambhogakāyic*) are hinted at, or incorporated in Alex Wayman's 'discovery' of two types of Dependent Origination, as described in his book *Buddhist Insight*:

> I stumbled upon a possibility of two kinds by finding in Asaṅga's *Yogācārabhūmi* that there is a nescience "unmixed with defilement" and in another place that Dependent Origination can be classified in terms of defilement *(kleśa)*, *karma*, and suffering *(duḥkha)*, where nescience is labelled as a defilement. Eventually, I took the first kind as discovered by Gautama Buddha and as unconcerned with particular beings. The second kind is applied to lives of an individual whose *karma* is differentiated or unshared.
>
> My division also follows the implications of Nāgārjuna's *Madhyamaka-kārikā* XXIV, 40: "The one who sees Dependent Origination, sees this *(idam)* precisely *(caiva)* as Suffering and the Source, precisely *(eva ca)* as Cessation and Path." This verse afforded the commentators a splendid opportunity, which they seem not to have taken, to point out that Nāgārjuna's association of voidness *(śūnyatā)* with Dependent Origination makes it possible to see Dependent Origination as any one of the four Noble Truths, i.e., one can see it as the "tree of suffering" *(infra.)* and as any other one of the four Truths. Since Dependent Origination is not a real thing, seeing it one way does not prevent one from seeing it another way. Hence I offer this explanation in terms of the present article: The first Two Noble Truths of Suffering and Source are associated with the first kind of Dependent Origination that deals with beings as a whole and not with particular ones. The last two Noble Truths of Cessation and the Path are associated with the second kind of Dependent Origination concerned with lives of individuals including the specialized ones who follow the path.[10]

---

9 Volume 5A of this *Treatise on Mind* details the organisation and functioning of petals of the *sahasrāra padma*.

10 Alex Wayman, *Buddhist Insight,* (Motilal Bararsidass, Delhi, 1990), 164-65.

Wayman then describes these two kinds of Dependent Origination in detail. What he describes as 'The first Two Noble Truths of Suffering and Source are associated with the first kind of Dependent Origination that deals with beings as a whole and not with particular ones' is equated, from the perspective I have presented, with the *dharmakāya* type of *karma*. Wayman's 'second kind of Dependent Origination concerned with lives of individuals including the specialized ones who follow the path' concerns the *sambhoghakāya* type of *karma*.

Consciousness exists, like a big house with various levels contained within it. It is silly to say that the bottom of the house does not preserve the extension of further higher floors, though it may be more incomplete in its sphere and its gaze be lower. One does not suggest that from the perspective of incarnating into the 'house of the bodily form', that it is not the presumed reality for that person, with all those parts vivified in experiential understanding.

It would be safe to say that extensions of consciousness may be projected from the base support or elementary awareness to the other floors (wherein subjective or psychic experiences can be obtained) so that all may have something which interrelates them in common. For if there is no continuity of consciousness, if there is disjointedness, then the system breaks down. If there is no universality, only individuality, then we can presume chaos can be a consequence. Individuality can exist within a being's consciousness, e.g., in different categories of conceptualised things; it may even go to the extent that there is schizophrenia of differing degrees to complete madness of the personality concerned. 'Madness' can here be defined as differing extremities of 'individualities' competing, fighting with each other—such as what exists in much of our present materialistic society.

A state of madness can thus be considered to be incorporated into the psyche of all individualities that manifest forms of separateness perceived by consciousness.[11] A mad state of expression is however far removed from the general affectionate, loving experiences of a perceiver. A 'mad' person has lost sanity through inability to define what is truly real. Such a consciousness is disoriented, preventing true health, but the world still functions normally for such a one. If we say

11 Note that such separateness and the energy of Love are diametrically opposed qualities.

that 'the self and things do not exist apart from consciousness', then why does the madness of the schizophrenic not instantly transfer to the external world and immediately make everything associated with it mad also? We do however see the effects of similar madness affecting the human world as a consequence of actions based upon people's forms of separative, selfish thinking, avariciousness, etc., because of the vast number of beings engrossed in such activity. This is to be expected when the effects of consciousness incorporates the substance of the material domain, affecting the course of human civilisation.

Separated extensions of consciousness act as a base support for the evolution of individuality towards enlightenment, of the way that reality is first perceived, but which must eventually be transcended through inclusive thought. Madness, according to the way it is normally perceived, is considered an abnormality in our human societies, and as a consequence the world is rarely viewed through the eyes of a mad man. The world is perceived differently by others, and each different way of perceiving the world has changed the face of it, e.g., of the way our cities have developed. But the overall factors in Nature: trees, rivers, ocean, animals, etc., still exist in similar forms that have existed long before humans came upon the scene, and the myriads of different ways that humans have perceived these things have not changed that. Therefore, though human consciousness may have rapidly evolved its capacities, the things of the formed realms have not, they have stayed the same or changed only incrementally for untold millennia. Therefore, 'things' do exist apart from consciousness. Human consciousnesses experiences these things in a variety of ways and adapts consciousness accordingly. Wayman's 'second kind of Dependent Origination' is based upon such adaptation.

The resultant images vary in many ways according to the factor of desire, and this is what is normally experienced or understood to be the real. Without consciousness there would be no deduction of the nature of 'self and things', no analysis of function, no consequent aberrations of thinking. These are all human attributes, and have no real bearing upon the existence of 'things', but concepts of 'self' are directly amenable to changes of thought structure. Without consciousness, 'things' will still exist and function according to their own levels of activity, though 'self' will not exist. Consequently we have the first type of Dependent Origination. Because consciousness segregates and identifies, it acknowledges the existence of 'the self and things'. It then modifies this acknowledgement in any way it wishes, and proceeds from there, with a new modification of a new acknowledgement, and so it goes on. The equation can be depicted as:

self + things ↔ consciousness

The double headed arrow indicates the interdependence of 'self and things' and consciousness. Consciousness needs 'self and things' in order to identify things, with reference to what to it is a stable framework, the 'self'. This allows it to create images whereby it can deduce facts, extrapolate ideas, and move on to future reasoning.

The equation informs us that 'self and things' only exist when consciousness is functioning, for we know what 'things' are tangible to the senses via self-identity. What, however, is in consciousness that can automatically create these (concrete) things as soon as one thinks of them? Such 'things' are more than just mere images in the mind, though such images are what consciousness must work with in order to ascertain the validity of existence to it. That all man-made things, such as houses, first exist in people's minds before they are created may be a truism, however, normally a subsequent emotional driving force, then physical plane effort and action is needed to produce their appearance. The three function together to produce the bulk of what humanity has created. There are cases of purely mindless physical destruction, or purely emotional outbursts producing physical effects, but the mind *alone* cannot produce such 'things',[12] and this is the point.

Consciousness and the *chakras*

The mind needs a mechanism of response for physical activity to take effect in consciousness. Physiologists state that it is the sense-perceptors, nerves and the brain mechanism that exists and nothing more. But how can precognition, intuition, past life experiences, that concerning the

---

12 Unless yogically empowered as a consequence of developed *siddhis*, but *siddhis* also must obey certain rules of precedence.

after-death state, and the supramundane consciousness of the enlightened be explained thus? All such are casually dismissed as imagination by these materialistic thinkers. On the other hand if mind and phenomena are considered identical, that 'the self and things do not exist apart from consciousness' then it may be said that all desire images of the avaricious, all sensually seductive thought forms of humanity, every insane mental urge, would have a factual residence in consciousness. Such effect would specifically manifest if there were co-mingling of consciousness-streams. (Taking the subject of consciousness-streams through a logical deduction. This subject has been dealt with previously and needs no repetition here.) But if such co-mingling doesn't happen then there is always the problem of the effects of one's nefarious mental-emotional past life activities. What then is to prevent such attitudes from overwhelming one's mind, preventing consciousness from functioning in a normal manner? (Some people may indeed be controlled by these attributes, but most accommodate more benign and pleasant attitudes.)

We see therefore that the production of thoughts must be contained in some way and regulated to prevent insanity, so that the most base, forceful and violent attributes do not overwhelm the thinking process. The energy constituting thoughts would, after all, follow the line of least resistance, where the strongest force would dominate, unless controlled in some way. The mechanism of such control, where the various energy qualifications of thought are contained and sorted according to their qualities, then processed and released in a manageable manner according to the quotient needed for the 'demanding' conscious volition, are the *chakras*.

From another perspective the intended interpretation of the phrase 'the self and things do not exist apart from consciousness' is that we all live in a sea of consciousness, into which everything experienced is incorporated. The 'things' experienced however do not need this 'consciousness' to exist. The statement is best put thus: 'for a human unit self and things exist because its consciousness perceives it so'. But what needs clarification is the process of the storage of consciousness-bits that have been experienced and of their retrieval within a multidimensional universe, and not just that pertaining to the physical senses. This is the world that psychics, meditators and the enlightened live in consciously, and the rest unconsciously.

The mechanism of contact with all supersensory phenomena and their correlation with the impressions gained from sense contact, plus the impressions directly obtained through mind *(manasic* input) are the *chakras.* They delineate the concourse of impressions from one field of experience to another. They hold the *bījas in situ* and project aspects of the variegated consciousness-streams (that they are designed to accommodate) from one field of experience to another. The process of thoughts and of various subjective perceptions produces the evolution of the *chakras* through extensions of consciousness from petal to petal in the personality vehicle. This is the way consciousness moves, from an esoteric perspective. It consists of the various types and qualities of *prāṇas* gained initially via the senses, which modify consciousness in some way. The *chakras* are of such importance that it will take considerable background information to lay the groundwork for their comprehension. Consequently a significant portion of this *Treatise on Mind* will endeavour to explain how they thus function. Volume 5 specifically will provide a considerable wealth of information, most not previously revealed, except as 'ear-whispered truths'.

Effectively, the *prāṇas* accommodated in the *chakras* and consciousness are synonymous terms. The *prāṇas* are channelled through the *nāḍīs* and absorbed into the affiliated *chakras.* Consciousness is therefore localised through whatever *chakra* an individual is functioning from at any time, or of whatever grouping of these are the reservoir of experience. It is from these that the *saṃskāras* that one experiences at any time are drawn from. Evolution concerns the reticulation and cleansing (refinement) of the *skandhas* and *saṃskāras* of all conscious volitions, from the lower to the higher *chakras.* Therefore, proper understanding of the way that the *chakras* function is of great importance.

The awakening of higher perceptions through extensions in consciousness do not necessarily make the reality experienced via the Sacral centre (for instance) different to what was experienced previously, but new awareness can be brought into the experience, allowing appropriate analysis and refinement of characteristics. Thus a broader, more expansive understanding can be gained from any sentient state derived from it, or from the categories of being the *chakra* controls. Consciousness will eventually be far removed from the Sacral, Liver, Stomach or Solar Plexus centres of day to day pursuits, after it has expanded in a triune fashion inward to the Heart of all life, outward to embrace the universal All, and upward to the complete awakening of the Head lotus. Evolution means the development of more inclusive reality structures, greater conscious identifications with ever vaster multidimensional sceneries, and with the Minds that embody them, until the expansion is so vast that one does not identify with a separate 'this' from 'that'—all are included as one vast interrelated interdependency of superconsciousness unfolding. One moves from working consciously with *chakras* within the body to those outside the form. Consciousness has thereby transcended the boundaries of 'self' and is now part of a *maṇḍala* composed of interlocking unities of many Heart centres beating out the dynamics of many lives. (The Heart centre regulating the principle of Life for these lives.) Each Heart centre is but a petal of a larger Heart, where the prescient, selfless, Clear Light of Mind perceives the pulse of the united circulation of *prāṇas*. Welcome to the world of the higher Bodhisattva *bhūmis*.

The *māyā* of things

What could be said of normal conscious awareness is that it makes up a tiny fraction of the All. This would be more correct than saying that its state of reality does not exist, or is non-existent based on its defilement. Smaller consciousnesses, and the Base of Spine centre's field of awareness still exist,[13] and still exude life as a mineral presence, although the perspective of the higher view is that such life is living in *māyā* (illusion).

Would it in fact be right to say that if the extended consciousness lived in its own form of awareness (e.g., of the Base of Spine), then it would be living in illusion, in *māyā?* But the particles constituting the Base of Spine do not live in *māyā per se,* what is experienced there is a comparative reality, and the superconsciousness (of the Head centre) is an extension of that reality. Therein the light is clear for perception, and such vision is not any more *'māyā'* than the hypotheses of the consciousness associated with the Throat *chakra*.

---

13 The Base of Spine centre is given here because it (with the Sacral centre) controls the expression of the Element Earth, which governs physical plane experience.

The potentiality of the experiential identification with four petals of dimensional interdependence that consciousness can explore is fundamental to the Base of Spine, yet why does the extensions of consciousness act as if what is experienced therein is *māyā?* The reason being that this *chakra* controls the artifices of the form, and the form is deemed illusional. However, the *chakra* is also the home to the Fire that liberates as it rises up the spinal column. Enlightenment ensues, and the accomplished *mahāsiddha* arises. This is a great mystery solvable by the truly wise. The *māyā* and the liberating Fire have become the real, the one, spiralling consciousness into the munificence of the *dharmakāya.*

Ultimate reality exists, even if it appears an unrealisable reality to most in their lifetime. One could compare a normal human unit's view here to a cell's sentience in the human body and how it would 'imagine' human consciousness to be, if such an imagination were possible. The unrealised is but an integral part of the ultimate. The ultimate reality is relative to the extent that one conquers the unrealised by means of conscious projections into the associated space.

If *māyā* is not defined in relation to the higher or more expanded forms of consciousness, of a Base of Spine awareness moving towards a Head centre, or the development from a human's to a Buddha's Mind; if there is no proportional definition of consciousness and an extension of that consciousness to superconsciousness due to repetitive incarnate states that grow in perceptiveness; then the evolution of consciousness cannot be perceived. How then can the evocation of an enlightened state be defined? The concept of *māyā* is hid in the development of progressively more enlightened states. *Māyā* is literally the substance of the ever changing veil, rather than the appearance of the form. The form is the product of the end attainment of a sequence of change. It is the clothing of the attributes of *māyā* that allows sense-contact to manifest. Such contact inevitably seeds enlightenment.

We must give Buddhism the line, the line of continuation, and not the dot, the dot of the singularity of the unchanging. All things change, including *nirvāṇa* (when viewed from a cosmic rather than from a human perspective). Nothing is stagnant. It is not that one can't conceive a beginning or ending, it is that there are no signs of movement or progression, to what is stagnant. There is no progression if consciousness moves not to the relative state of being awakened. If one does not have the line, or the act of comparing one state to another, or of this and that form of awareness, then one says all too quickly, this exists and that does not, not comprehending that what may not exist to the empirical view of a consciousness may in fact appear sometime and grow into an ultimate. We therefore have the development of the unenlightened to the enlightened, a flower to a tree, a man to the Buddha, a past to the future.

If one cannot see the relative progressive states of being then one may state that the appearance of a Buddha is *māyā*. Ultimate reality must incorporate a notion of progression and also of transformation from one state to another. Thus in identifying reality one must say it is progressive. This will be so, though such changes will only be perceptive to the enlightened Mind capable of reaching distant Buddha fields (world or stellar spheres) in the far reaches of space. The small in consciousness must inevitably acknowledge that there are larger states of consciousness than it, that are based in a greater reality structure than it presently cognises. This means that *māyā* is at one end of this structure and reality is at the other, that consciousness (or Mind) is always in a moving progressive expansive path, to eventually become the enlightened structure for all. This enlightened structure is presently not in the multitudes, and all that presently is (the *'māyā')* must continue, for the multitudes to evolve to utilise that sublime structure, by garnering ever increasing states of awareness.

The termination of this progressive change producing 'the ultimate' may also be *māyā,* an appearance relative to another viewer ensconced in a different time-line, moving at a different speed. What is an 'ultimate' to one consequently may be a new beginning to another having reached that state, or passé to one having attained that state many aeons ago (if we recon time the way humans do).

The logic presented is that all is changing and nothing is stagnant, including that which is perceived as the ultimate reality. The goal line of what is considered 'the ultimate', the non-attained *nirvāṇa,* moves to a higher dimension upon its attainment. The *goal* of *nirvāṇa* therefore continues,[14] and it can be reached, from one perspective from the small to the large, via the process of cyclic repetition of incrementally expansive Mind and confirmation through a timeless 'time-line'. The

14 *Nirvāṇa* is consequently here differentiated from *śūnyatā.*

comparatively unenlightened to the fully enlightened thus manifests. Because of the continuity of Mind (of the Tathāgatas) the goal is ever being realised, always continuing, never ceasing in cosmos. Always will be found higher, subtler forms of striving.

If *nirvāṇa* is not stagnant, then the phrase, 'the unenlightened and the enlightened' can be applied to any state where the 'unenlightened' rests at one axis of development and 'the enlightened' rests at the other, where the conception is that something is fully attained. However, if the state of enlightenment continues to improve (because all states of awareness within the expression of Mind are interrelated and travel together, incorporating each other), it *(nirvāṇa)* cannot be said to be the ending, but rather, that it is *the beginning of an intensified continuation of expansive Light*, would be a preferable statement. This would mean or show that the concept of 'self-realisation',[15] the gaining of revelatory vistas, never ceases and always strives to realise further in a continuous stream. This would then make one being's *nirvāṇa* a stage yet to grow out of, to expand into greater 'Beingness', and another being's as a vehicle for the attainment of this. The position of such a One's psyche may be to further manifest as an incarnate Being, but then the concept will be towards being a Logos, an Ādi Buddha, where an entire world-sphere becomes the Body of Manifestation.

One's frame of reference is here in question. Philosophers (Buddhist or otherwise) must move beyond thinking in purely human terms. There is much more to consider in the multidimensional cosmos than our habitation upon the minute dot in space called earth.

Nirvāṇa here refers to liberation from the need to incarnate into a state of *māyā* (illusion). It can refer consequently to different stages of the liberation process, where one form of *māyā* is completely transcended, with yet a vaster form of *māyā* yet to be tackled. *Nirvāṇa* therefore does not mean the ending of experiential development. Rather it means absorption in a much higher dimensional space than has been reached by those bound to the domains governed by mind. It therefore

---

15 Right terminology is problematic at this level of discussion. Here for instance there is no 'self' existing, but Life that is a Mind that has the capacity to further develop intensified expansive revelations in cosmos. I have also omitted the standby term 'Buddha-Mind' because this introduces concepts in a reader's mind derived from texts that are not necessarily correct.

represents the ending of the experiential base of those ensconced in matters of earthly activities.

This is illustrated if we look to the *arhat's* self-contemplative absorption, as being absorbed in the consciousness of the Sambhogakāya Flower. He is consciously identified with this and acts as an 'awakened Flower'. At the Buddha's time such absorption or mergence of consciousness sufficed for the purpose of the teachings. Such a one was considered an elder, i.e., enlightened. It was so, to all intents and purpose. He was self-absorbed or focussed, because the Sambhogakāya Flower is thus in relation to its own evolutionary progression, and with respect to the way to eventual Buddhahood.

This is the basis of the Hinayāna path, and has its own validity. There is no escape from consciousness, but one has lost the 'self' of the personal-I and is merged into the universality of the *ālayavijñāna*.

As the centuries advanced and a greater number of monks became *arhats* as a consequence of following the *buddhadharma*, there were some whose Sambhogakāya Flowers could not stand the pressure of the energies coming via its central Śūnyatā Eye and began to awaken the potency of *śūnyatā*. Further teachings appeared concerning the nature of 'Void of self' that necessitated treading the Bodhisattva path. So appeared the Mahāyāna stream that progressed beyond the *vinaya* rules of the Theravādins. The goalposts of what was required for monks to develop had conclusively stabilised upon a higher level—*śūnyatā*. Though this was the teaching of the Buddha from the start, very few had the capacity to realise it at his time, but the *arhat* experience was attainable.

This happened because so many *arhats* had appeared that needed the added impetus of the *śūnyatā* doctrine, coupled with that of the Bodhisattva path, to push the Sambhogakāya Flowers on to their limit of expression and consequent liberation from the circumscription of consciousness by that wondrous form.

Then at about the time of the spread of Buddhism into Tibet and the demise of Indian Buddhism, the Vajrayāna and Tantric teachings became necessary, as promulgated by such *mahāsiddhas* as Padmasambhava, Nāropā, Marpa, where the teachings of the *dharmakāya* experience is provided in veiled terms. This was necessary because of the potency of the energies involved and consequent dangers to yoga practitioners of unskilful actions.

The doctrine at first was the expression of what was reflected through the Śūnyatā Eye, of the qualities of the *dharmakāya* viewed therein. This was a development from the early *prajñāpāramitā* doctrines that clearly spelt out that the way to Buddhahood through *bodhicitta* necessitated treading the Bodhisattva *bhūmis* to gain *śūnyatā*. The teaching of *bodhicitta* meant that one had to increase one's scope of revelation to include all sentient beings, and thus had to incorporate the true nature of the interdependence of life, in order to develop the skill to help sentient lives upon a vast scale. The *dharmakāya* type of *karma* was thereby hinted at but not fully explained or explored. It remained an esoteric subject, because of the associated ramifications concerning revelations of conscious intermediaries directing the *karma* governing the all (veiled in the concept of *ḍākinīs*), including the concept of a subtle Soul-form (which was veiled in such texts as the *Ratnagotravibhāga)* and of the existence of *Logoi,*[16] which are but an extension of the doctrine of the nature of Buddhahood.

This *dharmakāya* focus has been the onus of attainment for the most excelled Bodhisattvas, but the doctrines have only been partially revealed, remaining for the most part 'ear-whispered'. (In part because of the difficulty of understanding the concepts involved.) Much can now be further revealed, partly because of scientific revelations, specifically concerning the relation of energy to matter, the constitution of the universe, and human anatomy. The fields of physics, chemistry and biology have provided necessary keys lacking in the past that can be turned by Bodhisattvas to assist in providing empirical terminology for the most esoteric concepts. Also, now sufficient high level Bodhisattvas have evolved so that the next stage of the process of enlightening humanity can be promulgated. The *anupadāka* experience of a Buddha, the second *dharmakāya* level, is what Buddhism must begin to truly address.[17]

What is implied here is that as general human consciousness has evolved, so also has the quality of the Bodhisattvas incarnating to meet

---

16 To be further explained later in this series.

17 The term *anupādaka* means 'parentless' or 'self born of the divine essence', self-existing, having no progenitors. It refers to the second of the seven dimensions of perception binding our earth sphere into a unified integrity. The lowest (third) level of the *dharmakāya* concerns the knowledge of the properties of Mind, as exemplified by the doctrine of the Dhyāni Buddhas and expounded in Buddhist Tantras.

their needs. Thus the goal-posts for achievement gradually shifted higher. So it is also with that which defines a Buddha. In antiquity a Buddha was considered one who had consciously merged with the Sambhogakāya Flower. At the Buddha's time, *śūnyatā* sufficed. At the time of Padmasambhava it was the *dharmakāya* experience. Therefore he was called the 'second Buddha' who effectively gave out more advanced teachings than did the Buddha, i.e., the esoteric Tantras. Now the world is ready to receive the doctrines concerning the Dharmakāya Way for the highest of the Bodhisattvas upon the earth. This concerns meditation upon their cosmic paths out of earth experience altogether, as the future portends a time when many can attain Buddhahood *at once*. That is, group evolution necessitates an entire *chakra* of beings to become liberated from the need for earth sphere experience, having outgrown everything that our relatively insignificant planet can teach them as a group. Modern cosmology has provided names for distant destinations, astute esoteric vision provides the rest.

The law of consciousness (or Mind) unfolding concerns unrelenting, continuously expanding, progressive states of awareness. So the path traverses on in ever-increasing stages or fields of enlightenment for all of us. *Nirvāṇa* thus can be considered the beginning of a new state or stage of awakened expansion after the ending of a previous cycle of realisation. It represents a new step in the field of reality that is the spaciousness of cosmos. Consciousness may have become superseded, but expansive revelation and further Identification with what IS persists.

Consequently, enlightenment is relative, and progressively continues. Even if a spiritual teacher has not obtained a full enlightened status, it is possible for such a one to teach *chelas* the path to enlightenment. Also, the process of earnestly teaching helps generate the necessary qualifications for enlightenment, if the teacher and students earnestly follow the inner revelations the path produces. The Master shares information concerning greater consciousness states whereby the student can obtain wisdom. Both travel together towards liberation relative to each other's spiritual stance. It also means that each facet of consciousness below the ultimate reality has special significance. The relative degrees of enlightenment must not be decried. An aspirant's consciousness must be attuned and fed constructive material to the appropriate level, as he/she yearns for higher revelations for the benefit of others. Each person can be directed to high attainment, from greater sources, or embodiment of wisdom, if the extent of the receptivity to Light within is known. Such ones consciously become members of the community of Bodhisattvas (the Hierarchy of Light).

Bodhisattvas are seen clearly for the degrees of revelation they have realised, for the limits or unlimited spheres (of awareness) developed. Each has attained a step of revelation that can be transcended, but has also been educated into levels of learning whereby the lessons have been mastered. There are modes of consciousness into which one is educated, and once mastered, aspiration to higher transcendental levels of awareness is possible.

Viewing the needs of the student, the teacher can direct this process. It demands therefore that a hierarchical structure of educational reality exists as support beams for all ascending out from levels of *māyā*. Thus we have the ten stages of the Bodhisattva path, each of which can be represented as a differing degree of transcension attained, but there is yet a higher degree to be striven for, as the Bodhisattva progresses, until Buddhahood is obtained, and then that beyond, ever beyond.

Each Bodhisattva, manifesting via a particular *bhūmi* (level), becomes a 'support beam' for an entire class of people, which the Bodhisattva carries with him/her as the ladder of the *bhūmis* is climbed. A Buddha likewise has yet much to gain within the precincts of the cosmos into which he is born, as he travels forevermore upon his chosen Path away from earth experience. Behold, a new Logos is ultimately to shine forth Light as a sun in the darkness of space, to conquer *the Ignorance.* A new Wheel is instigated for the experiencing of Light, and the birthing of myriads of new units of consciousness, for the sake of the combined progress of the vast Hierarchies of Lives existing in the astounding unfathomed realms of being/non-being.

Oṁ

6

The River Simile

What defines a river?

The simile of a river is often used when talking about the principle that reincarnates, of the way of transference of consciousness, and the nature of the universal flux within which *saṃskāras* abide. The thought is that a river doesn't have any self-identification, because a river is always changing, and like a river the consciousness-aspect always changes, with different incarnations flowing in and out of the stream, like eddies and particles in the moving stream. It is always moving, therefore you cannot say (or predict) what 'it', meaning the rebirthing principle (the river) is or is not. A typical example is from the article by Pratap Chandra:

> When we say that the course of a river, ever changing and yet retaining some peculiar kind of identity, is determined by a number of factors, we by no means imply that there was no river previously existing but only that no river can be free of determining factors, and, therefore, none can continue flowing unchanged[1]...the Buddha (or other *bhikkhus)* do not dispute the key role assigned to *viññāṇa*[2] in the onward movement.

---

1 Pratap Chandra, 'Nature of Continuity in Early Buddhism', from Kewal Krishan Mittal (ed.), *Perspectives on Karma and Rebirth,* (Department of Buddhist Studies, Delhi University, 1990), 164.

2 Chandra states (Ibid., 160): 'As many as five different senses have been identified in which the term *viññāṇa* has been used in the *Tipiṭaka.* It is an "element" *(dhātu),*

It certainly runs on and continues and thus links different births.[3]

Another example can be seen in the cells constituting our bloodstream and the way they perpetually move within the body structure, which seemingly stays the same for long periods of time. The mode of containment between the blood flow and the walls of the veins or arteries containing them is precise, and therefore close in approximation to the *prāṇic* flow within the *nāḍīs,* or consciousness flow, and the way *karma* is also constrained. *Prāṇa* flows from minor to major *chakras,* and is continuously recycled until eventually its attributes are sufficiently refined, allowing the *prāṇa* to move to higher centres. The eight-petalled Diaphragm centre stands as the heart with respect to the act of passing *prāṇas* between the centres above and below the diaphragm.[4] The Heart centre on the other hand is the source of the principle of Life *(jīva),* and controls the *prāṇic* circulation for the attainment of enlightenment.

To use the example of a river is somewhat problematic, for in taking this as an example one must look at what comprises the river flow. One must actually define the river—the factors composing it. In using the analogy of the river, what is not normally mentioned is that which identifies the river is the differentiation between two lines of interrelationship and a comprehension of what is moving in the space between. When identifying what a river is one should also define what the river is not. This necessitates analysing the two lines constituting the separation of the water from the riverbank, one on each side of the river. They define the river. Just because those lines appear, it doesn't mean that they are real. One can't really characterise them with precision

---

an "aggregate" *(khandha)* or "factor of existence", a "body" *(kāya),* and a link in the *paticcasamuppada,* the causal concatenation. According to T.W. Rhys Davids and W. Stede, it signified, *inter alia,* "a mental quality as a constituent of individuality, the bearer of (individual) life, life force (as extending also over rebirths), principle of conscious life, general consciousness (as function of mind and matter), regenerative force, animation, mind as transmigrant, as transforming (according to individual *kamma)* one individual life (after death) into the next. (T.W. Rhys Davids and W, Stede, *Pali-English Dictionary,* 618.)'

3 Ibid., 164.

4 For this reason Tantric texts often take the Heart centre to have eight petals, as here the attributes of the Diaphragm centre takes its place.

because they appear to be neither of one or other substance (water or the earth). In other words, what makes up the lines that separate the riverbank from the river is similar to a void, as something that cannot be properly defined, because the lines are moving all of the time, according to the vicissitudes of the movement of the water in relation to the sand or muddy earth. It is difficult to conceive if the lines occupy any space at all.

If no separation is made between what it is and is not then there is no definition. In relation to this, if the general Buddhist philosophy says that all lines (consciousness-streams) of the river intermingle, then from the perspective of seeing these 'lines' as streams of *karma*, how can there be any individual *karma*, incarnation, or responsibility for actions? If all streams (aspects of the flow) of a river intermingle then the karmic propensities are shared, which is correct, but individual *karma* would not happen unless some force manifests to make it so. Consequently the example of a river flow for an individuation mechanism fails here. Also, one stream of consciousness would condition others, which is partly true for the domain of mind. However, if no mechanism of separation of one's individual consciousness-bits from another's is represented, then the analogy is problematic, for there must be such a mechanism if the differences in thoughts between different individuals is to be accounted for. The only things approximating such separation are the river banks that have different sections. Basically there is a place where a river is and where it is not.

If the individual consciousness-streams do not intermingle then group *karma* would not be possible. Yet group *karma* conditions people in our societies. Hence for the analogy to be correct there must be some intermingling and yet a mechanism must be provided for external forces to act upon 'individual' streams to individualise *karma*.

All lines of separation act as points of interaction. Any attempt to define them loses precision upon close examination, there is no clear border between where the water ends and the banks appear, one generally merges into the other, often leaving muddy or wet banks (leaving aside the occurrence of solid cliff faces). The banks create a division between two seeming incongruous elements, water and earth. It can be said that they are an illusion because continuously changing, and yet symbolise what in effect separates me from the chair. Both the matter of the chair and that of the cellular content of my body are deemed to be illusions, but this chair can't develop enlightenment and I can. So there are differences, and as soon as differences appear it hints at points and lines of separation.

The lines of separation in a river allow the simile of a river to be used to explain the individual flow of consciousness or *karma* in relation to something which basically stays the same—the river in relation to its banks. (That which it is not.) Thus the river can't be the tree on the bank on its side, it can't share the same type of *karma*, or occupy the same space, we can't even say it shares the same time continuum, as the tree remains in a static time zone, with the river of time flowing past. If we compare the course of the river to a human life, so the tree, like your mother, might be close to you in this incarnation, but cannot share your *karma* or your responsibilities for the water that flows through you as a person. (Which represents the *karma* or *saṃskāras* of all the actions you pursue.) Buddhists have used the river (as an example) because there is a point where the river is and where the river is not, and that it flows continuously to its ultimate destination, be this a lake (of consciousness) or ocean of being/non-being.

This introduces the question of how one defines things, because the suggestion to define something introduces concepts of separateness, especially if the point of perspective is static, though the object may or may not move. The faculty of vision (external, or inner) is used in defining, consequently it is the prime separating tool. It views things via colours, size, etc., and also by the measure of the lines or spaces between things, defining 'selves', even when analysing itself, as this is the way that consciousness works.

Even though the river may be moving, the person viewing produces a static view (panorama) for defining the river, or what it has been likened to, the nature of consciousness. Consciousness and the river flow are seen as similar, because both are continually changing as they flow through time. All life forms likewise are changing, but at different speeds and cyclic expression (producing co-expressed imagery), though the view or perspective may not be moving. However, a perspective is not really static. It is on a wheel of change, unless it is *śūnyatā*, which it could be if the perspective were via enlightened perception. Though everything in the universe is changing, however, the perspective of a state of stasis appears when viewed from a vast distance. It is created illusionally by the distances involved and because of the different speeds of the progression of movement. If something is moving at a vastly slower speed to something else, then the movement of that 'something' appears static.

It may not therefore be possible to say that *śūnyatā* is a state of true stasis, because it is after all an energy state, and all forms of energy move. Everything that appears to be still is an illusion, however one could question whether the vacuum in space wherein the galaxies move is effectively static, though science speculates a universe governed by space-time, where the expansion of space is a function of time. But esoterically, such 'space' is but a medium via which galaxies and stars materialise, as all reincarnate, and the process obeys the same laws that the process of human rebirths follows. The findings of materialistic science are not at all conclusive, and the debates as to the causation of things via the 'river of time' still persist. The Hubble redshift whereby the expansion of the universe is calculated is not necessarily correct.[5]

All things manifest in cycles. The speed of cycles refers to the speed of events, of the way things evolve through time in repetitious progression, like day following night, producing lines of separation between one process and another. The turning of the complete cycle (of events) is important (causing a rebirthing on a higher cycle), and not so much the amount of time taken to accomplish a particular event. Time is the illusion, whilst the accomplishment of a preordained pattern of activity pertains to the real, and signifies the accomplishment of the purpose of the activity, which is what consciousness retains as memory. In the early evolutionary period, for instance, a cycle may last a vast amount of time, with the accomplishment being only a small gain. Near the end of the process the cycles are much faster with comparatively vaster gains (because of the increased ability of the human mind that has evolved to collate experiences). Each cycle of purposeful activity is counted as 'one' by consciousness, no matter how long the wheel of time took to revolve for that cycle.

---

5 See Eric Lerner, *The Big Bang Never Happened* (Times Books, New York, 1991), where he states (page 53) 'The Big Bang arose initially as an explanation for the Hubble expansion—the relation of the redshifts and distances of the galaxies. The observations of the past several years have put that theory into grave doubt, contradicting all its predictions as well as its basic assumptions. A plausible alternative, plasma cosmology has arisen, and its predictions have been systemically confirmed by observation'.

Our present view however is of the river bank, and the material composing it, the sand and rocks that affect the rate of change, as well as the nature of the river flow in relation to the river. In fact the river bank is younger than the river because it is continually being formed by the movement of the waters flowing. From this perspective the bank itself is moving, though the common view is that the bank is static with respect to the river flow. It actually evolves because the river is flowing, carrying little bits of the bank with it. This is the way consciousness works with respect to *saṃsāra*, little 'bits of *saṃsāra'* are carried with it as it evolves.

This introduces variants of the various types of substance (which allow us to define particulars). One type of substance makes one a highly evolved being and another type fosters ignorant attributes. One should note where the line of separation between them may be and what defines the substance that bridges the bond or gap between the two. That which bridges one attribute to another serves as a bond and yet signifies a gap, a barrier between the two. In fact, it helps define the word 'two' (of them), proving that at some stage they are separate from each other, but also part of a unit, a process of interrelationship, in a similar way as the river and its banks form a unit. The types of substance in this example can be considered that of the abstract Mind on the one hand and the desire-mind on the other.

Lines of separation as *nāḍīs*

It should also be noted that with respect to the cosmological diagrams and *maṇḍalas* that abound in Buddhism, what is of interest can be considered similar to this separation of a river and its banks, and how a river is defined because of what it is or is not in the vaster panorama. The lines in a *maṇḍala* separate one symbolic representation of consciousness state, or deity, from another. Because the lines that we view are dividing lines, they stabilise all that they segregate into a form, so even though the river is moving, it is considered a river because it has banks which delineate its form. Similarly the lines of form of a person are extremely stable; no matter what incarnation one may have. Veins, nerves, cellular boundaries, organelles, organs all are clearly delineated in the *maṇḍala* that is a human unit. Also, more subjective aspects, such as the qualities of *saṃskāras*, for instance, will change with time only along certain lines or boundaries. For example, desire-*saṃskāras* for things will eventually transmute into emotional affection and then into the true impersonal Love of the Heart, when expressed through the normal course of development of *bodhicitta*. (Here the *piṅgalā* stream of *prāṇic* flow is depicted. An *iḍā* flow by contrast is characterised by *manasic* development, whereby intellectual attributes *(pravṛttivijñāna)* unfold. *Saṃskāras* thus develop along a line of similar affinities.

Similar lines of development form the reincarnating principle. Here strands of *saṃskāras* are collected together by the Sambhogakāya Flower and stabilised in the form of a person's individual *karma* for a particular life, leaving other strands from former lives unassimilated. These are separated from the strands of *saṃskāras* within the general reservoir of such a form. They will not constitute that person, but have interrelated *karma* that may be integrated later. There is a moving time line whereby they may appear if circumstances demand it so. This is an important point. The lines of mental-emotional *saṃskāras* stabilise and ground the life of an incarnate being as they form a *maṇḍala* of expression.

When endeavouring to comprehend the nature of the way that *saṃskāras* manifest we should understand that each essentially manifests in the form of a river within the human incarnation process. It also hints at the structure of the *nāḍī* system, which interrelate to produce the *chakras* integrating the form with consciousness. The *nāḍīs* are defined as rivers of energies inside the body. Each tiny *nāḍī* carries versions of the five different types of *prāṇas,* and when manifesting through any specific *chakra* in a way that consciousness is affected by them, the *prāṇic* energies are called *saṃskāras.*

Consciousness also has similar lines or 'rivers' of interrelationship, along which thought speedily travels in order to experience vistas of images (lakes and oceans of similar thought perceptions) that the conscious one is retrieving or developing.

Nāḍīs and the *chakras*

With respect to the *nāḍīs,* these 'lakes' are effectively the manifest *chakras.* They have appeared where a number of *nāḍīs* have crossed each other, producing a gyration of energies taking the form of wheels and petals of expression. This hints as to why the *chakras* form as they do, as flowers of energies, and how these flowers allow consciousness to control and integrate the form in such a way that the sensations from the five senses produce consciousness-effects. Consciousness determines the nature of the manifestation of the flowers because that is the way consciousness is organised in the realms of thought intrinsic to it. Without them it would not be possible for any being to retrieve past life images. The lines of interrelationship from centre to centre of attributes of consciousness (via the *nāḍīs*), allow consciousness to integrate the body to its sensations, emotions, moods and hormonal secretions. The *saṃskāras* of consciousness flow in the *nāḍīs* as *prāṇas.* The nervous and vascular systems that are utilised exoterically are similarly organised as streams and rivers of energy and substance flow.

The entire paradigm is reflected in the personality vehicle because it is only through such a system that all possible consciousness-states can be achieved. They allow the possibility of enlightenment, where everything gleaned from past evolutionary states can be known. Such qualities can be derived from any specific petal or from the minor *chakras*. The psychic states experienced by a person have their own characteristics, or can mimic impressions from the domains of enlightenment. This is because the *chakras* are organised in a hierarchical manner, with the four petals of the Base of Spine centre as the foundation, conveying Earthy *prāṇas,* and the 1,000 petalled lotus at the crown of the head being the summit, integrating the *prāṇas* of all five Elements. This lotus also acts as a mechanism to ground *prāṇic* directives from the Sambhogakāya Flower, and from all of the 'perfumes' gained from that incarnation.

The study of the *chakras* is therefore exceedingly important for all who wish to gain enlightenment. It is obviously a highly esoteric field because of the awesome potencies contained by them. The secrets of their true nature and of the mode of release of the potencies has thus always been carefully safeguarded by the wise. This subject can only be fully comprehended in *dhyāna*. Many mysteries concerning them are veiled in the Vajrayāna doctrines. The topic consequently has vast ramifications.

The lines of interrelationship forming a *chakra* also help to provide the structure of a subtle soul; indeed, for the necessity of all such forms throughout Nature, because what is found within a human also indicates that which is without. A person's *chakras* are based upon the paradigms found in the external universe, for all are interdependent. This allows *karma* to function universally, because this law conditions the interrelation of groups of individuals. Similarly for all laws discovered by modern science. Comprehending the laws allow great *siddhas*[6] to produce the types of 'miracles' purported through demonstrating mastery of the processes of the formed realms that evolve consciousness. The laws governing mind/Mind are mastered through control of the *chakras* and *prāṇas* by means of focussed consciousness.

The *chakras* as containers of awareness-states

Below is a table relating the qualities of the five Dhyāni Buddhas to the five *prāṇas* and Elements:

Awakened Realm (*dharmakāya*)	**Vairocana**	**Dharmadhātu Wisdom**
The combined Head and Ājñā centres	Prāṇa: *vyāna*	Element: Aether
(Intuitional) Realm	**Akṣobhya**	**Mirror-like Wisdom**
Heart centre	Prāṇa: *prāṇa*	Element: Air
Mental Realm	**Amitābha**	**Discriminating Inner Vision**
Throat centre	Prāṇa: *udāna*	Element: Fire
Emotional Realm	**Ratnasambhava**	**Equalising Wisdom**
Solar Plexus centre	Prāṇa: *samāna*	Element: Water
Physical Realm	**Amoghasiddhi**	**All-accomplishing Wisdom**
Combined Sacral and Base of Spine centres	Prāṇa: *apāna*	Element: Earth

Table 3. Dhyāni Buddhas and the five *prāṇas*

6 A *yogin* or *yoginī* with spiritual accomplishments, able to manifest psychic powers and transcendence of all aspects of the material world. An adept capable of complete control of substance and inevitably its transmutation.

From *chakra* to *chakra* the lines of energies, the rivers, flow within the system. Everything concerning consciousness unfolding is patterned according to the way the five senses (the five organs of contact with the external universe) gather information. When viewed in terms of a totality of possibilities, of which consciousness is only a part, then we have a septenary appearing, hence the seven major *chakras* (grouped according to that given in table 3) appear in the human frame to accommodate the sum total of impressions from all that is.

Because we have these seven major *chakras* in our bodies we are humans, and not lesser species in Nature. The *chakras* allow Buddhas and Bodhisattvas to manifest mastery over all of Nature's forces and processes. The lesser kingdoms of Nature simply do not have these. Dogs and cats, for instance, who are the most developed of all animal species, have three major *chakras* (with a fourth in the process of being established), with the Solar Plexus centre, the abdominal brain, being their highest. For them its ten petals manifest in a similar manner as the Head centre (the 1,000 petalled lotus) does for humans. This is one major reason why human consciousness cannot incarnate into the animal, as there is no mechanism of response that the human consciousness can work with, no higher centres that can appropriate the energies and qualities of the sophisticated human consciousness.[7]

The rivers or lines of energies, the *nāḍīs,* of all lesser kingdoms in Nature lead to the Solar Plexus centre (*maṇipūra chakra*). All of the petals and flowers of the Inner Round of minor *chakras* represent and embody the sentient qualities developed by these lesser kingdoms. Conscious control of any of these petals allows one to communicate with the sentient lives, such as purported by the Buddha in his sermon to 'birds'.[8] The lesser evolved the animal sentience, the smaller the *chakra*, its petal, or aspect of the petal that is represented. Again we see why incarnation into animals is impossible for humans. The *chakra*

---

7 This subject has already been treated in *Karma and the Rebirth of Consciousness.*

8 This sermon is described by Edward Conze:

> The Lord Buddha has said:
>
> In the language of angels, of serpents, of fairies, in the speech of demons, the talk of the humans, in them all I've expounded the dharma's deep teachings, and in any tongue that a being may grasp them.

[*The Buddha's Law Among the Birds*, (Motilal Barnasidass, Delhi, 1996), 16] represented, or any part of it, is but a tiny fragment of the sum of human achievement and equipment of response to the external universe. Consequently only a minute portion of the human consciousness is represented here. One cannot pour an intensely energetic and hugely voluminous consciousness-space into such a tiny vessel. One cannot contain an ocean in a teacup.

Each *chakra* is thus a unit of containment of energies and related qualities, thus literally a 'soul', an accumulator of sentience and associated energies for any of the species of Nature's kingdoms that it represents. The activities of each respective *chakra*, and of the way that the *nāḍīs* flow allows *karma* to manifest the way that it does.

Human beings are not separate from the environment of which they play a part. Therefore they possess *chakras*, the five senses, and the *nāḍīs* that interrelate with the whole. The *chakras* act as stores of sentience and consciousness and are in subtle rapport with their correspondences external to the human unit. They exist in the subtle, etheric vehicle, a body of energies that acts as a blueprint of the gross human form. The patterning of this blueprint is in the image or reflection of what exists on a vaster multidimensional scale, of which the human unit is a part. The human energy body persists after the death of the physical body, hence consciousness persists in a contained form. When the etheric form eventually dissipates in the after death state, eliminating the ability of consciousness to express the *prāṇas* of the Earthy Element (governed by the Sacral/Base of Spine centres), then consciousness flows into the next highest *chakra*, the Solar Plexus centre, wherein it can exist. Here the Watery Element is experienced in full: the sum total of one's emotional, affectionate, kindly, desirous, grasping, avaricious, etc., activities whilst incarnate. Such experiences concern the heaven and hell states depicted (somewhat imaginatively) in the texts.

The (disincarnate) consciousness eventually dies to the emotional *saṃskāras* created in the former life, having experienced the *karma* created. It then enters into the space denoted by the Throat centre (*viśuddha chakra*) and therein experiences the purely mental *saṃskāras* in the form of a type of rapturous bliss of pure mental involvement, unless that being was formerly involved in nefarious sorcery, or in any of the manifold forms of critical assertiveness and hatreds.

Consciousness is then briefly abstracted into the domain of the Sambhogakāya Flower (the paradise realm of Amitābha) before being recycled in a new guise, to repeat the cycle of physical, emotional, and mental activities. Thus a new gross form, a new personal-I appears, but with the inherent gain of the subjective experiences whilst disincarnate.

The joy and bliss states of the Heart (*anāhata chakra*) and Head centres (*sahasrāra padma* and *ājñā chakra* combination) in the after-death states are experienced consciously only by Bodhisattvas and Buddhas. The *anāhata chakra*, for instance, is the centre wherein *śūnyatā* can be experienced, being the central *chakra*, and also the Heart of all Life. It is the fount of the emanation of the enlightenment-stream called *bodhicitta*.

We see in the above account that in each case various aspects of consciousness are sustained, collected and collated in *chakras*, as part of the functioning of the greater universal *chakras* of which they are a part. The *chakras* act as a type of soul for the individual consciousness-stream that energise them. If this was not a fact then the *chakras* would have meaningless attributes in a human form and in Nature; there would be no consequent powers (*siddhis*) that could be obtained by *yogins* when they concentrate upon them through right meditative practices. There would be no basis for their empowerment with anything. Without *chakras* no being could gain enlightenment, or liberation through meditation, as there would be nothing that could sustain that meditation. There would be nowhere to retreat into, other than pure bodily sensations and forms of activity, or complete cessation from that, which would simply be a death in an atheistic universe of nothing that persists after death.

Buddhists cannot have it both ways. Either they have their philosophy of *chakras*, and of the associated *siddhis*, in which case they are actually depicting a mechanism of 'containers' that *en-soul consciousness*, that enables *karma* to act as it does, *or* they can have their philosophy of no soul. Either they must give up all consideration of *siddhis*, *chakras*, and the meditative practices based upon them, or they must give up claims that we live in a soul-less universe. It is because this esoteric subject has only been exoterically understood by them in a distorted fashion, with gaps to clear reason, that they could postulate their 'soul-less' doctrines. Because they have no impeccably detailed *credible* explanation of what the *chakras* are, how they function, and how the *siddhis* are derived from them, these errors have been made. Their exoteric Tantric doctrines have but 'knotted up' the truth in many veils and blinds. This teaching of the *chakras,* if rightly comprehended, is consequently disastrous for Buddhist exponents of no-soul. Buddhist exponents of such doctrines have never seen beyond the veils presented in their Tantric texts. The enlightened amongst them kept silent, in accord with the precepts of the vows presented in the 'ear-whispered' doctrines because of the problematic aspects of revealing cogent information concerning *chakras,* as already explained. The time has however come for coherent exoteric revelation, as will be presented in this *Treatise on Mind,* in accord with the demand of the Council of Bodhisattvas in this cycle of turning a new wheel of the *buddhadharma.*

Each *chakra* en-souls attributes of consciousness, the *saṃskāras* of all interdependent existences, to the degree that the number of petals they possess, their established size, and capacity to bear energies entails them. They then interrelate with other *chakras* through the lines (streams) of energies that are the *nāḍīs.* Similarly the *tathāgatagarbha* can be viewed as an individualised *chakra,* a Sambhogakāya Flower that contains the accumulated consciousness-principle of a continuous succession of personal-I's in the realms of form. It thereby en-souls the consciousness and related *karma* of all aspects of a particular human life stream in a way that shall later be detailed.

Lines of interrelationship channel attributes of consciousnesses to the various tiers of this exalted form. The nature of these consciousness-interrelationships express the various streams and eddies of flow within the river as a whole, and together they manifest the true picture of the Sambhogakāya Flower. The absolutist or anthropomorphised forms that so many thinkers fall prey to, concerning a 'Soul', are however not expressed. If there was no such thing as a soul-form then the appearance of a consciousness that could utilise any of the *chakras* for any purpose whatsoever could not be possible, because the *chakras* are soul-forms for the attributes of consciousness associated with the particular Element the *chakra* controls the expression of.

The *chakras* are particularised, organised 'things', albeit of a purely subjective nature, and expressive of sentience-consciousness-energy states of being/non-being. The *chakras* are expressions of the Flower of the *tathāgatagarbha,* which exists upon the abstract realms of the Mind. It is because they exist as floral whorls of energies that they are empowered to function as they do, and are able to express the *siddhis* associated with them, as gained by all accomplished *yogins.* To take for granted that the *siddhis* associated with them exist, and then to claim that there is no subtle soul *per se* simply proves the ignorance of the speaker. The *tathāgatagarbha* is similarly a 'floral whorl', albeit of a vaster proportion and consisting of subtler substance.

If human consciousness just flowed through one *nāḍī* after another in the great *nāḍī* system of Nature, then it could consciously register the experience of nothing, as there would just be an amorphous sea of energy streams. It needs to particularise into an entity that contains, sustains, and controls the entire movement, and furthermore experience it all with respect to 'something'. This 'something' concerns the method of containing evolving consciousness-states in a progressive manner, from a lowly or gross energy state, as possessed by those with low intelligence, to that associated with highly intense forms of energies, as well as a motivation to advance, as possessed by a Bodhisattva. The *chakras* are particularised into flowers of various categories and capabilities, according to the manifold differences of sentience and consciousness-states found in Nature. That is the order of things therein. The *chakras* are consequently the real. The appearances, the forms we see all around are the illusions, they but concretise the energy qualifications manifesting via the *chakras.*

Also, if there was no such collector or container of the individualised human consciousness then the human consciousness would simply flow into any vessel that happens along its way (especially after death of the form), e.g., the awareness of a frog, dog, denizen of hell, any being's mind, etc. (The theory of transmigration of consciousness into animal forms is based upon such logic.) They would all be there commingled with his consciousness and experienced together in totality, a potpourri of absolute insanity, like turbulent muddied water. There would be other effects as well, such as the 'pendulum effect', which I have described in the book *Karma and the Rebirth of Consciousness.* Also, what would force that stream of consciousness to incarnate in a human form, or to incarnate again *per se*? *Karma* you say. But what is *karma* in such a case anyway, and how could it possibly act, if there was nothing individualised to act upon, only amorphous, continually moving masses of energies that contain myriad consciousnesses and sentience states all intermingled together, like some sort of murky stew, or the proverbial muddied river flow?

To think that *karma* can act in some way via such methodology is a naïve expectation and indulging in wish-fulfilling gems. Where, or what part of the river bank can it act upon (that represents and particularises personalities that must experience that *karma*), with there being no real line of separation between the river and its bank? There is no way that the waters (of *karma*) can be expressed, as it has already moved on. Little pieces of muddy sedimentation may offer respite as an example. They are carried with the flow to an extent, but what about the rest of the bank? Is it not acted upon by the same river, the same flow of events? The turbulent brew then flows into the ocean (of consciousness). What then does this signify? 'Liberation' may be the response of some. 'The muddy bed' of collective shoddy thinking in outmoded theories and philosophic presentations, can equally be the answer. Where else can the sedimentation go?

The structure of the Sambhogakāya *chakra*, or Flower, that is representative of a form of a subtle human soul, is best explicated utilising the Buddha's own explanation, or 'non-explanation', of what a soul is/is-not, as shall be elucidated in Volume 3.

'Who' does the Seeing?

The plane of mind or the grain of sand,
where consciousness-bits are symbolised by each grain
of sand from which one may derive meaning.
With the little grains of consciousness-forming,
the golden-yellow of knowing,
the wise care of right actions flowing,
the enlightenment that is a Bodhisattva's sowing.
Who plays in the sand,
the Occidental or Oriental brother?
Both play in different ways.
Castles of mind washed away in noon tide.
A grain of sand washed away at evening tide.
The sands of the Ganges are inestimable.
They are continuously washed away, but still remain.
A grain of sand when examined microscopically is a mountain,
castles of mind are built of millions of such grains.
Each evolving into universes to be.
Atoms of stars and galaxies.
Who is running the show here?
Who washes it all away?
Who is saying go, go, go; who is running the show?
Love, Love, Love, the Buddha's eyes do stare.

But what is the 'who' that does the Seeing?
That 'who' is full of subtle and intricate meaning.

7

On the Evolution of Consciousness

The way of consciousness

The thought-patterns contained in a person's mind cannot be understood without a consideration of the evolution of consciousness. As consciousness evolves so also does its understanding of truth, and the subtle defining perceptions of the nature of phenomena increases. Inevitably the reality of the Bodhisattva path and the possibility of the attainment of *śūnyatā* also dawns in the mind. As all is inside consciousness, and as it changes, what needs to be developed to take the next steps to enlightenment must also change. Evolution thus proceeds.

Evolution means that the discriminatory aspects of mind increase in depth of perception out of necessity along with all categories of information that are part of the building blocks of consciousness. As more mental *saṃskāras* evolve, so greater information becomes accessible. More aspects (within consciousness) then exist as signposts. Aspects from the past have been added to, expanded and refined. This continues to happen as consciousness evolves.

If the factors below are accepted, then they will provide a proper mechanism to understand the way consciousness evolves to produce enlightenment.

1. Everything must be viewed in terms of relativities.
2. All is within consciousness, which is viewed in two ways: a) The consciousness of an individualised human unit. b) A greater

overriding consciousness external to that unit that can oversee or direct the evolution of the mind of the human unit. The role of a Bodhisattva or Tathāgata comes into play here.

3. Consciousness evolves by the growth of units of consciousness that are factors in its containment. This necessitates acceptance of a soul concept *(chakras)* to store *saṃskāras* and to regulate the process of evolution. Here an internal directing agent is implicated.
4. *Śūnyatā* is the 'end point' of the evolutionary expansion of consciousness from the perspective that the vicissitudes of mind are eliminated, but Mind persists.
5. The *dharmakāya* represents a vast, higher dimensional identification with Lives embodying cosmos. Thus the phrase 'thus gone–to the other shore' refers to the elimination of the need to be reborn in *saṃsāra* and the relinquishing of earth ties. Links are consequentially established with far vaster 'experiential zones' than the earth can provide.

Such acceptance will eliminate many errors of past philosophic speculations, plus pave the way for further revelations concerning the nature of the path to enlightenment. Much can then be added to current ontological or soteriological thought, to modify them in an expansive, more inclusive way. It shows why Bodhisattvas reincarnate to invigorate religions, human culture and science, by reforming doctrines through presenting new ideas, in accordance with the moving yardstick of the progression of the evolution of consciousness in humanity.

The 'photons' composing ideas and ideals of the fields of consciousness increase the intensity of the brilliance of the light as time proceeds. This is possible because consciousness is contained within or delineated by a form for its expression, similar to a light bulb that generates its brilliance when electricity *(prāṇa)* passes through it. Without such a form for expression (here conceived of in terms of the mind, or the Sambhogakāya Flower) no conscious awareness is possible. Consciousness continually manifests by absorbing and converting qualified energy into more refined, vibrant states. Thoughts are continually moving through the consciousness-space and evolving new ideas. Mind is in a constant flux, a transforming flow. Thus as the movement of thought changes, we have concepts of time and the expansionary space of consciousness. The positions in space of thoughts are also created, refined and transformed by the movement of consciousness. Energy vortices, bubbles of thought, and *maṇḍalas* of expression are created, manifesting their own form of specific gravity of consciousness as it moves. New thought structures are built upon old ones, putting into perspective many modes of organising space.

Thoughts then flow through time, as explained in the river simile of the previous chapter. Various petals of the *chakras* are awakened through the pressure of the moving currents of energies. As different currents of thought cross each other to form the content of the petals, they modify the expression of thought according to the nature of the energy conveyed. This creates the *chakras,* from inherent *laya*-centres,[1] points of primal receptivity, the potential of actuality in the *nāḍī* system. Eventually the Head centre is unfolded and awakened, when a sufficiently highly developed and refined consciousness manifests.[2] The awakening of the *chakras* thus rely on the movement of consciousness. All forms are moulded by consciousness, therefore they are the manifestation of it.

The question of time

If all can only be conceived of in terms of consciousness, then more aspects of conscious awareness will present themselves in our civilisation in time, i.e., subjective laws, definitions for spirituality. Though not yet physically manifest they can exist in consciousness, and like a bud yet to sprout petals, the potential for expression is there. The actuality of an orchestrated development with each movement of the petal takes time,

---

1 A *laya*-centre (or *bindu)* is a point of primal receptivity. From the Sanskrit verbal root *lī* to dissolve, disintegrate. It signifies a zone of abstraction of a former cycle, where every differentiation has temporarily ceased and is incorporated into a seed that can be reactivated in a future cycle, when it can manifest its full potential. It differs from a *bīja* in that a *bīja* represents a seed for an aspect of consciousness, whereas a *laya-centre* is a seed for a future arena of creative expression that can be used by a creative entity to project a body of manifestation. *Laya*-centres can contain many *bījas* and can be seen as *chakras* that have not yet awakened, as part of a planetary, systemic or cosmic *nāḍī* system. This incorporates any sacred spot or site on the earth that is yet to reach its full potential, or any place that will become a place of importance in the future evolution of humanity.

2 The nature of such development will be shown in Volume 5A.

a continuum of seconds ticking by, or a series of appearing notes that show the fact that consciousness is evolving. This series of moments indicate the internal mechanism or appearance by which the evolution of consciousness is known to exist, and whereby it is added to. With each second, a new scenario joins with others, forming different patterns. An act, such as simply walking on the beach, is created according to the set of coordinates (left, right, forwards, and backwards) that appear and change with rapid procession to the new set of outcomes or actuality. So, inherent in *the definition of time* is the interrelationship of all aspects of consciousness moving in space, within consciousnesses sublime.

Let us pose the question: 'Does time exist in consciousness, or does consciousness exist inside time?' (That is, which is the higher governing law?) Redefined, the question is, 'does time condition consciousness and exist as a higher law or support, or is it the other way around, where time (the process of becoming) exists as part of the movement of consciousness?'

An answer could be given that time exists both in and outside of consciousness, if there is an 'outside' of consciousness. If agreed to on both points then we have the system that makes up the universe. A series of events is a time pattern set by the relative speed of consciousness moving (like a tunnel through space) and the consciousness itself being affected by higher stresses external to it, by significant events in cycles of time. This becomes apparent in consciousness, as such stresses become the structural support upon which the speed of consciousness is based. That speed, which is the internal consciousness and the way it sequences thoughts, is supported by the fact that the consciousness is moving, and like the effect of gravity, the positions of the symbolic stars and planets appear. That speed is also restricted by the quality of the substance of the mind, as well as by the blocks or obstacles in consciousness, of unwieldy thought patterns. Time is therefore restricted, or *slowed* thereby. The nature or quality of consciousness thus determines how fast time moves, or appears to move.

The coordinates of all things (the directions in space), thus self-identifications, exist as the aspects of separations between things. When these aspects move, thus change, then we get the time by which we grow and mature into enlightened beings. 'We', being the particles or elements manifesting as appearances in the movement of time.

Time can also be considered to be created by a material object spinning, such as the motion of the earth around the sun, or of the sun around its central cosmic point. Such motion helps delineate the rhythms of the development of consciousness or a sentient state. Even subatomic particles spin to the left or the right. They are an omnipresent factor in Nature, and all things in *saṃsāra* are composed of them. Spinning incorporates the concept of cyclic motion, of repetitive incarnations, and time is reckoned in terms of the law of cycles, where patterns in space repeat themselves and there is a forward progressive movement to evolutionary space, presenting the spiral-cyclic appearance of consciousness.[3] Consciousness is therefore material, composed of substance, because it changes with time. It is the platform by which all manifestation can begin, with what is called the 'creation of things', because only that which is material in nature can be considered the cause of appearances. (Though such causes can be prompted by non material forces.)

If you have external elements and internal elements in consciousness (i.e., the external and the internal universe), what then is the highest influencing factor, if consciousness itself revolves and repeats itself in a pattern of increasing spheres and subtler awareness? If you have two aspects to consciousness, external and internal, which then is caused first? When observing the external and internal movement in the evolution of consciousness we see that they both have causative effects upon each other, but the external, i.e., the bigger state of effect (the vaster consciousness) has a greater, virtually everlasting effect. It is effectively omnipresent and interpenetrative, i.e., the movement of the larger consciousness manifests effects upon all smaller awareness states. It encompasses, thus integrally influences the activities, of all that is enclosed within its sphere of being.

Does a God exist?

How would one define such a larger Consciousness? The theistically inclined use the term 'God',[4] whilst the Hindu religion purports many 'Gods'. The theory that a 'God' exists is supported by logic, in that

3 This subject is further elaborated in Volume 4 in the chapter 'Cells of Time'.

4 The term 'God' is apostrophised in this series because its meaning is a question of interpretation.

the consciousness-space of all beings increase in size as consciousness evolves towards enlightenment. There is effectively no end to the spectrum of the development of mind and its transition to Mind, or the further expanding into Space of that Mind once enlightenment has been attained. *Saṃsāric* attributes may have ceased, but Mind persists. The vaster the Mind-space, the more that the lesser units of consciousness look up to it in awe, or see it as something 'beyond'. If this consciousness-space is inclusive of the sum of their forms of activity, so it becomes 'God' to them, especially when the form of consciousness represented (such as the Dharmakāya-Mind) has 'gone beyond' anything they can possibly conceive. This is true concerning the way of the evolution of a entity from a cellular unit to the complete body of manifestation of an integral being, and is true of the nature of the development of the enlightened-Mind.

So where does such a development stop? At the attainment of *śūnyatā* most Buddhists would say. *Never,* can equally be the answer, if the nature of the *dharmakāya* is properly explored. This is especially so when the logic so far presented supports the existence of 'individuality', (i.e., the 'God' concept, when viewed macrocosmically), which is viewed as the 'sprouting' of the *'śūnyatā* seed'.[5]

The evolution of consciousness is what concerns the rebirth process, and the process continues until the unknown Source (that which interpenetrates all) is known, or acts as a seed for all to proceed. 'All' refers to all events, situations and patterns that occur from the originating causative stimulation of thought, whereby a series of events emanate, of linked and subtle energies producing the totality of a *maṇḍala*. Evolution produces an increasing complexity and the immense number of diverse things seen all around in the manifest universe. Similarly, this is the way that consciousness manifests as its evolves. It becomes more expansive, with vaster reticulations of thought-patterns, to master and creates vaster consciousness-spaces as it categorises an increasing panoply of things. Numbers evolve from a singularity to produce an increasingly complicated pattern of the ordering of things, in orders of divine nature, and of cause to effect. The overall patterning of it all becomes apparent in expanded consciousness states. Patterns become

5 The simile of such a 'seed' was explored earlier.

integrated into increasingly abstruse forms of mathematical formulae incorporating the domains of the lower mind.

The law of dependency, of cause following effect, incurs itself upon us, but we do not know if a 'God' exists as a direct emanating source through our sense-perceptions. Is this Source a primary pattern manifesting via a subjective process, or simply cause and effect, where cause and effect are so far beyond normal human perceptions and conscious identifications that a 'God' cannot be excluded in one's recognitions? The lines of interrelationship between cause and effect in Nature are thus not separate enough to exclude a 'God', certainly not of any higher Mind than what is known to us on earth. In relation to this it has already been noted that from consciousness comes all creative projections. But to properly comprehend this question the nature of the *dharma* must be appropriately analysed and related to the *ālayavijñāna* and to *śūnyatā*. Through the *tathatā* of being can Buddhahood be made known, and then travelling onwards and outwards into the universal All, to the domain of the higher correspondences of consciousness with respect to those who have not attained the experience of 'the other shore'. The foundation of such conceptualisation may take time to lay, but can logically be done.

Buddhists have not presented conclusive evidence against such an entity existing. Their ontology conceptualises the nature of Mind as an extension of *śūnyatā*. Its pristine awareness as found in a Buddha's Mind is consequently entertained. What a Buddha may do with such a Mind in *parinirvāṇa* is heavily veiled with such concepts as creating a 'Buddha-field'. The fact of *śūnyatā* does not exclude the existence of a creative process wherein the appearance of all known phenomena comes to be via a prime creative Being, in a similar sense that the human intellect can create material things when coupled with the physical functioning of the hands, or directly by Mind via the *siddhis*.

The nature of the existence of a Creative Buddha-Mind, which theists have anthropomorphised as 'God', will be explained throughout this series. The subject is introduced here, as it is a natural offshoot of the question of the existence of a subtle 'soul'. This, plus the focus upon 'the middle way', represented by the doctrine of *śūnyatā,* are reasons why Buddhists have vehemently denied the existence of either a 'God' or 'soul', for to admit that one exists *de facto* acknowledges the other's existence. They have however admitted versions of the Hindu gods, the only concepts of Deity they knew in ancient times, and placed them in the highest of the Six Realms. They have also incorporated gods, such as Brahmā in their ontology. Admittedly, the Buddhist treatment concerning the Hindu gods is often derogatory. The problem is that the existence of deified creative potencies manifesting from the liberated realms implicates clothing them with substance of some kind for them to manifest the attributes associated with their anthropomorphisation. Nevertheless a much more refined version of such entities can be derived from the *buddhadharma* itself. The doctrines however need to be extended to reach the far vistas of Mind in cosmos, into which the extant philosophy has so far not ventured.

In human consciousness there may appear concepts of a Creator, which can manifest in the form of a reflected paradigm of an abstracted Demiurge, and which can also be veiled in concepts of Buddhist Divinities, such as an Ādi Buddha, in ways that many Buddhists can accept. This incorporates the existence of that which is placed outside of or supersedes human consciousness. There is however at least one genuine attempt in Buddhist Tantric scripture to investigate the concept of a 'Creator God'. With respect to this we have an excellent article by Dargyay in reference to *'The Kun byed rgyal po'i mdo as a Theistic Buddhist Scripture'.*[6]

> If we sum up the introduction to the KGB, we may conclude that Vajrasattva is the entirety of the entourages which again reflect the All-Creative King's nature. Thus, the discussion between the All-Creating King and Vajrasattva is actually a self-dialogue. Consequently, the text assures that the entourage and the All-Creating King are one, as there is no difference with regard to their nature or identity.

6 Eva K. Dargyay, "The Concept of a 'Creator God' in Tantric Buddhism", *The Journal of the International Association of Buddhist Studies*, Vol. 8, No. 1, (University of Wisconson, Madison, U.S.A., 1985), 31ff. In reference to the title Dargyay states: 'In the Kanjur editions and in the NGB (*Rnying ma rgyud 'bum*) the complete title of the KBG (*Kun byed rgyal po'i mdo*) is *Chos thams cad rdzogs chen po byang chub kyi sems kun byed rgyal po,* which might be translated as *The All-Creating King, i.e., Bodhicitta, as the Great Perfection of All Phenomena*'. (Ibid., 35.) See also the book by Neumaier-Dargyay, *The Sovereign All-Creating Mind the Motherly Buddha,* (Sri Satguru, 1992).

In general, the Buddha's entourage consists of beings who are different from his own person as long as we stay in the realm of conventional truth. The KBG, however, places the action in the introduction in the realm of absolute or utmost reality, where everything coincides with Voidness (*śūnyatā*), which is the essence of the Buddha. In the discussion of utmost reality only two aspects are of concern. For this reason, the two most important allegorical figures in the text are Bodhicitta, the All-Creating King, and Vajrasattva, who asks the questions. Bodhicitta symbolizes the ontological ground of everything visible and invisible, while Vajrasattva comprises all aspects which want to emerge from the ontological ground and reveal their individuality, though it might be an ephemeral one.[7]...From the All-Creating King the four elements and the five spontaneous wisdoms, which are cognitive categories used in Tantric Buddhism in order to understand reality, emanate. In interpreting the passage from the KBG, the All-Creating King may be conceived as the ontological ground, while the five spontaneous wisdoms as well as the physical world (i.e., the four elements) are the phenomena emanating from it. In the primary nature of the ontological ground, i.e., the All-Creating King, rests the entirety of the phenomenal world. His nature is of spontaneous wisdom unfolding into the five aspects which are classified as defilements (*sgrib pa*) by the common Buddhist tradition: hatred, passion, ignorance, jealousy, and arrogance. However, these "defilements" provide the seed-bed for all forces of vitality. All facets of man's entangling encounter with life (*saṃsāra*) emanate from this ground. The external or physical world is established by the All-Creating King as well. The text emphasizes the various ways through which the great wisdom becomes manifest in the elements which constitute the three realms of the universe: the realm of passion (*kāmaloka*), the realm of form *(rūpaloka),* and the realm of formlessness (*arūpaloka*).[8]...When Vajrasattva asks for the reason or necessity of emanation, the All-Creating King explains His relationship to the phenomena emanating from Him:

> O Mahāsattva, the necessity is that beside Me, the Creator (*byed mkhan*) and All-Creating King, no other creator exists. Nobody beside Me created (*byed pa*) reality as it is (*chos nyid*). Nobody beside Me enthroned the Buddhas of the three [times].

7 Ibid., 39-40.

8 Ibid., 41.

> Nobody beside Me established the various groups of entourage. Nobody beside Me established the nature of reality as it is...[9]
>
> Vajrasattva! My nature is manifested in three ways: My nature is *bodhicitta (byang chub sems)*. My sheer nature shows itself as "pure" (*byang*), as it is three perfections, the pure reality. My nature shows itself as "perfect" (*chub*) as by means of the three necessities it covers all like space. My nature shows itself as "mind" (*sems*) as it is the infinite and absolute (*ma lus*) All-Creating King. Who else if not the Mind of Pure Perfection (Tib, *byang chub sems,* Skt. *bodhicitta*) would create the entirety?

> In this passage the term *bodhicitta*, which means, in its Tibetan translation, "mind of pure perfection" is not understood in terms of soteriological altruism but rather as the authentic nature of mind as such. This specific meaning of the term *bodhicitta* is found throughout the Tantric literature of Buddhism. In this way, the KBG does not exhibit any peculiarity. When the Buddhist mystic experiences the nature of mind as such, he perceives a state of limpid luminosity which transcends every conceptualization and which is therefore said to equal Voidness, and yet is full of utmost bliss. Therefore the nature of mind as such, or the pure mind, is said to be inseparable and indistinguishable (*gnyis su med)* from reality as such (*chos nyid).*
>
> On the other hand, it is only when the mind departs from its sheer nature and manifests itself in various activities that the world of sensuous perception can arise. For this reason, one might well say that from the individual's viewpoint the mind is the creator of the world. This is a common concept of the Cittamātra School of Buddhist philosophy. In this regard, the KBG fits into the general framework of Mahāyāna and Tantric thought without any major difficulties.[10]

Interestingly this 'All-Creating King' speaks to Vajrasattva, the Bodhisattva aspect of Akṣobhya, who embodies the Mirror-like wisdom that reflects *dharmakāya* into *saṃsāra*. Vajrasattva here also stands as the primordial, Ādi Buddha (Samantabhadra). How the awesome potency of the *dharmakāya* can possibly manifest as *saṃsāra* is a question that needs answering. That all manifests via the expression of

9 Ibid., 43.

10 Ibid., 43-44.

bodhicitta is natural enough, as the entire panoply of the evolutionary paean of *saṃsāra* is established upon the compassionate grounds of a Buddha's contemplation. Thus is also the law of *karma* established, as it functions compassionately, as previously explained. As well as being a force that drives the phenomenal universe to liberation, *bodhicitta* also manifests via the point of expression of the *śūnyatā-saṃsāra* nexus. Here differentiation happens between this primordial Buddha and his entourage that can be accessed in terms of conventional truth. The Elements and the Wisdoms of the Dhyāni Buddhas then come to view and the entire ontological world-play manifests. That Dargyay states that *bodhicitta* 'is not understood in terms of soteriological altruism but rather as the authentic nature of mind' is not consistent with the meaning of this Sanskrit word that consists of two parts *'bodhi'* and *'citta'*. It is therefore best to say that *bodhicitta* manifests compassionately as well as in terms of 'the mind of pure perfection'. Such a Mind is automatically compassionate because only through compassionate activity can a Buddha evolve.

Further necessary factors are needed, such as an entourage and the existence of *svabhāva,* or its form as *mūlaprakṛti* (universal substance matter), to account for the substance constituting *saṃsāra.* How it is utilised by mind/Mind, and the nature of the seed *bīja* with respect to the construction of *maṇḍalas* also need to be factored in. Thus we have the statement 'From the All-Creating King the four elements and the five spontaneous wisdoms, which are cognitive categories used in Tantric Buddhism in order to understand reality, emanate'. When speaking of these 'elements', to which we need to add a fifth (Void Element, discussed previously), we see that they can only emanate from that which is a 'store' of such substance. Phenomena must appear from something of like nature, even if vastly more refined. Nothing can appear out nothing. Similarly *bījas* of past cyclic activity must be stored 'somewhere' if they are to be activated by the Buddha-Mind that is the 'All-Creating King', which is feminine, as Neumaier-Dargyay states:

> In a chapter dealing with the different names given to the Sovereign Mind it is said:
>
> > Because all the Buddhas of the three times (past, present and future) merge from Me, I am called the Buddha-Mother.

> Other Atiyoga texts support this position. The *rDo la gser zhun* states that if the nature of All Good as a female (Samantabhadrā) is not grasped the bliss of truth cannot be appreciated.[11]

The feminine gender is necessary because of the act of birthing (of a world-sphere). In all such acts the emanation and concretion of substance (from a seed, egg or *bīja)* is involved, to produce a tangible object, a child, the phenomena of *saṃsāra*. By inference this latent 'substance' or 'essence' is stored in some way. This store is described as 'the intelligent ground' in Neumaier-Dargyay's translation, which manifests a 'Threefold Nature'. They are:

1. The own being *(rang bzhin)* of the intelligent ground as pristine awareness.
2. The actuating force or essence (*ngo bo*) inherent in the intelligent ground and which is the factor responsible for the existence of the universe;
3. Compassion (*snying rje*) which is the sole force determining the interaction among different components of the world.[12]

Thus all the ingredients constituting a Sambhogakāya Flower, or world-sphere can manifest. That which en-Souls, or acts as a buffering mechanism to contain *dharmakāya* and yet facilitates the appearing phenomenon of *saṃsāra* is implicated in this Flower, and by the various *chakras* embodying Nature, that collectively can be considered a world-soul.

The above suffices as a generalised overview of the instigating process of how everything emanates from the 'Mind of Pure Perfection'.[13] (Which is but another way of designating the cosmic Mind acceded to by all 'thus gone' Ones.) Because it *is a Mind* it obeys certain laws conditioning all mind/Minds, related to thought-form production, hence the 'Creation' of 'things'—which all thoughts can be categorised as.

---

11 E.K. Neumaier-Dargyay, *The Sovereign All-Creating Mind the Motherly Buddha,* (Sri Satguru, Delhi, 1992), 29.

12 Ibid, 31.

13 Further information can be provided concerning the creative process once more groundwork has been laid in this and the succeeding volumes.

That all inevitably is Mind-borne is a natural assumption, and from this concept the sum of what is presented in this *Treatise on Mind* follows. In the passages from the *Kun byed rgyal po'i mdo* quoted by Dargyay we have the hallmarks of a treatise written by an enlightened being, a great Bodhisattva.

Certainly, when pursuing this quest for the existence or non-existence of a 'God' one must look to the nature of such a Buddha-Mind. It is only a question of terminology after all, of how concepts are bound up in such terms, and the further ramifications of concepts not normally explored. One must take care not to personalise or anthropomorphise, but to think in terms of transmuted correspondences and relativity. *Saṃsāra* and the *dharmakāya* are coexistent and in fact are expressions of each other. Similarly the Mind of Vajrasattva[14] can be inclusive of a human mind, but vastly transcends it.

In the case of the appearance of such a 'Creator' we simply have the phenomena of rebirth having turned full circle. Instead of incarnating in the form of a personal-I, which such a Buddha-Mind has long ago superseded, the cosmic Mind, complete with entourage, incarnates into an entire world sphere for the purpose of delivering myriads of appearing consciousness-streams to the other shore of being/non-being. The process is aptly, albeit very briefly, summarised in the above text, but can be elaborated in far greater depth. In the rush to deny the existence of a 'God' one therefore should not arbitrarily skim over or omit the main points that generate the appearance of *saṃsāra*, a universe within which human consciousnesses have come to evolve via the rebirthing process. Many questions should be asked here and aught to be answered as much as words can explicate, as they have their limitations, with respect to the creative processes of the *dharmakāyic* Mind.

Further considerations of consciousness

If an individualised consciousness-stream has been gaining experiences for millennia, from its origination (when the mind-stream was pristine, clear of images and *saṃskāras*), then how is it possible for

14 Also denoted as the Ādi Buddha or Samantabhadra, depending upon the Buddhist sect one belongs to.

that consciousness to not have grown, not have evolved? In any life it may not know the distant past, but it knows its present development because there are new patterns continually appearing before the eye of the personal-I. So it is also for each new personal-I that appears and reappears with respect to that consciousness evolving.

Because the personality 'eye', the 'I' of the phenomena that forms in its mind, knows of no higher laws or dimensions of perception, other than the phenomena the 'I' perceives, it assumes itself as a fundamental reality. Consequently, it naïvely presumes there is no overriding consciousness that directs the pattern of events in relation to what it needs to know, and which forms its future, or destiny. Only when it begins to transcend the limitations of the veiling substance is it possible for it to speculate upon and then perceive attributes of the existence of that beyond the empirical mind. Eventually the domain of the *tathāgatagarbha* becomes known, and in the enlightened Mind its attributes realised. It can then perceive how this Flower draws forth the *bījas* of the *saṃskāras* from the consciousness-stream that are needed to direct the personal-I's course in life. These *saṃskāras* are based on the available *karma* from out of the manifold volitions of all past lives that can be chosen from. They are needed to be expressed so that the future of the personal-I can be made manifest. These attributes can be further explored or worked upon to be eliminated or refined and transmuted over the course of many lives. Attributes that have taken many lifetimes to develop normally cannot be thoroughly vanquished in one life. Their reverberations persist over many lives, though manifesting in ever-subtler forms. Consequently the illusion is that it takes only one lifetime for a person to master him/herself and become enlightened, or a Buddha.

It should be noted that for the Sambhogakāya Flower the evolution of the manifold personal-I's that have and must continue to evolve are seen in a sequence, a chain of events of cause-effect, in conjunction with a tapestry of interwoven karmic streams of other such lives wherein there is interrelated, modifying *karma*. The entire picture of past and future is spread out within the Eye of consciousness, like the body on a table spread out before a surgeon for him to operate upon, with the nature of the outcome of the operation already having formed in his mind's eye.

The overriding consciousness works with its own laws, those pertaining to the *ālayavijñāna* wherein it resides. There are rules and laws determining the way consciousness is organised and the way it must manifest in the abstract domains, and with respect to the realm of the personal-I. These laws are conditioned by the way that energy interrelates with substance that is *aware*, and of the inevitable transmogrification of that substance and its transformations into light. When the effect of these laws impinge upon the realm of the personal-I, we have the process of evolutionary push, and in the human mind they awaken conscience and the appearance of the intuition. The concern here is with the way that consciousness manipulates sentient forms, so that they gradually become better equipped to handle its energy states and form of illumination. The Sambhogakāya Flower therefore uplifts to bring the relatively sluggish or inert sentience of the forms and the sum of the awareness of the personal-I to where it stands in light. The light that it bears is consequently the future for that which it works upon.

If consciousness abides by certain laws, which are capable of being witnessed by the personal-I, it would be illogical to assume that an overriding consciousness is not aware of the conditioning laws. Yet there are some who say that such laws do not exist. Their eye of reason cannot fathom this because of their line of established logic. In fact, they say that *the eye* itself is illusory, and doesn't exist in reality, so what the eye sees is consequently illusional. But the fact is that the impression coming via the eye has modified consciousness in some way. The eye is 'the light of the body',[15] and illumines the mind that registers it. More credence must be given to the eye and its functioning than is normally presented. Buddhists say that it is one of the sense consciousnesses, but intrinsically it signifies something more than that. It is the paradigm for the structure that the Sambhogakāya Flower must form in order to see, to view the personal-I and also that pertaining to *śūnyatā*.

That the eye structures the nature of consciousness should be evident, if we look to the three tiers of circles in Volume 1, Figure 5 *(The Relationship of Śūnyatā to Saṃsāra)*. The two innermost tiers, representing *śūnyatā* and the Clear Mind, indicate the nature of the eye's pupil. The implied darkness indicates the nature of the Void, the 'nothingness' that the mind perceives it as. It is dark (seemingly void of substance) but admits the rays of the light that allows consciousness to function.

15 *Matthew 6:22:* 'The light of the body is the eye: if therefore thine eye be single, thy whole body shall be full of light'.

The middle tier, representing the abstract Mind signifies the iris of the eye, and is coloured variously in different individuals, just as is consciousness. This tier expresses the qualities of the Sambhogakāya Flower, and regulates the amount of light that can enter through the pupil. It governs the nature of direction in space whereby the various types of *karma* can manifest. (Represented by the eight-armed crosses in the cardinal directions shown in Volume 1, Figure 5.) The two outermost tiers can be viewed as a unit, as they denote the world of the personal-I in *saṃsāra*. They represent the white of the eye, indicating the supportive substance for the manifest activity of the entire construct of seeing. Here in phenomenal space the various manifesting personal-I's appear and die. The structure and functioning of the eye thus represents the first step to comprehending the way that the Sambhogakāya Flower is organised as a container for consciousness.

This Figure in Volume 1 depicts an overview of the way that the Sambhogakāya Flower *(tathāgatagarbha)* acts with respect to seeding the empirical mind. It shows a mechanism that allows consciousness to function in all eight directions of space, plus the two of time, backwards to *saṃsāra*, and forwards to *śūnyatā*.[16] Consciousness can then act within a contained form, which the Elements and associated *saṃskāras* can be directed to via the appropriate types of *karma* associated with the cardinal directions, so that the purpose of the *tathāgatagarbha* can be achieved. Without such a construct consciousness could not be accountable to any form that would allow it to continuously weave new personal-I's into the fabric of *māyā*. It is a natural extension of the concept of the *bījas*.

There are no pictorial diagrams of *bījas* in the texts, but such seeds can be conceived of as force vortices containing spirals of activity, that according to the quality of that energy in the spirals, can contain further *bījas* of expression. They can therefore be viewed as mechanisms of storing the *saṃskāras* pertaining to *saṃsāra*, and which can be activated to attract to them relevant substance (of the Elements) to produce the appearance of the manifesting phenomena. *Karma* is thereby expressed.

---

16 This mechanism can later be integrated with the three major tiers of the Head lotus explained in Volume 5A: the Solar Plexus in the head (the two spheres denoted 'World of the personal-I'), the Heart in the head (signified by the sphere of the Abstract Mind), and the Throat in the Head, represented here by the sphere of the Clear Mind.

A normally observant thinker need not be aware of the laws pertaining to consciousness unfolding. For him they do not necessarily exist, as the nature of the mind looking at itself would create an awareness, images of itself, rather than what governs its organisation. Also, the laws manifest regardless of the peregrinations of the mind of the personal-I. All that it perceives is an illusion, and what it identifies as 'self' is an illusion too.

Even so, the illusions can demonstrate a valid basis for ascertaining what pertains to the real, when it reflects the higher law expressing qualities from the *dharmakāya* that inevitably moulds consciousness. Here *śūnyatā* manifests as a mirror. The Sambhogakāya Flower endeavours to imprint into the phenomena of the mind of the personal-I the reality of the evolutionary laws pertaining to its own realm. They are mirrored, projected thereto from the *dharmakāya* in terms of the aspects of the five Buddha wisdoms. Similarly there is a Dharmakāya Flower that tends to imprint *saṃsāra* with the structure of universal Law, with the Buddha-nature *(tathatā)*, and works to make the seed of a Buddha grow. For this reason the attributes of the five Dhyāni Buddhas are found expressed throughout Nature, albeit in a concreted way. We have, for example, the five sense-consciousnesses, *skandhas*, Elements, and kingdoms in Nature: mineral, plant, animal, human, and the divine (the realm of Bodhisattvas, *devas* and *ḍākinīs)*. This law is real, the phenomena pertains to the real; where *śūnyatā* is the mediator between the two domains. One domain (*saṃsāra*) is the image or *nirmāṇakāya* of the 'All-Creating King'/Vajrasattva, and the other (*dharmakāya*) is real, the body of Truth.

Ramifications of Dependent Origination

An enlightened being who is capable of creating 'things' in the phenomenal world and who at the same time is fully aware of the nature of their affiliation to Dependent Origination, is still bound to fundamental laws of evolutionary being. In fact s/he *cannot* become freed from Dependent Origination, viewed in terms of higher subtler causes from beyond the realm of consciousness, thus from within the *dharmakāya*. Like the Buddha, such people can however free themselves from certain spheres of consciousness.

The Buddha liberated himself from the cause and effect of *saṃsāric* conditionings and moved out of the stranglehold of the primary causes of illusional thinking. His liberation was from the environment that caused his former incarnations, and their subsequent effects. However, he still adhered to the laws that caused their primary (original) manifestation, the origination of his consciousness and the sum of the phenomena that humans are presently ensnared in. He learnt to master those laws to escape our planetary system, but still rides the crest-wave of Law, of the higher correspondence to the Eightfold Path, in his journey through cosmos. From this perspective he is *not omniscient,* but is to those human minds whose consciousness he has completely transcended. There are higher beings than he, who had attained the foundation of the Buddha nature aeons ago, before even our humanity was seeded with life, and who consequently have travelled further along the pathways of cosmic evolution, to which the Buddha is a comparative novice.

Buddhists are far too earth-centred in their ontology and eschatological thinking, and must break the bounds of their conceptual *cul-de-sac* of reasoning with respect to the real order of things to which great ones ascribe to upon their liberation from earth conditionings. The astute but sometimes flawed logic of philosophers from a millennia or so ago should no longer hold the minds of Buddhists in thrall. They should now begin to vision what life is like beyond the veil of mythologising attributes they adorned the great ones with. They must now encounter the truth concerning the Dharmakāya Way that confronts the increasing numbers that can identify with *That* which lies beyond *śūnyatā*. The true nature of what constitutes cosmos is far vaster and more intricate than the unenlightened have ever dreamt. There is no ending to it, and consequently to evolutionary space, once one is born from out of the womb of time-space that conditions life upon our planet earth. A true perspective must be gained regarding what this tiny speck of matter in our vast galaxy represents. Our galaxy is a similar speck of matter in an even vaster universe, and what this really means must be incorporated within a transcending consciousness. Buddhas enter therein as children humbly greeting their parents. Though liberated from our sphere of attainment and possessing vast transcendental wisdom, their compassionate Minds are eclipsed by unimaginably supernal Minds encompassing vast domains in cosmos, to which a Buddha entering *parinirvāṇa* is but a humble acolyte. All exists within fields of increasing transcendent relativities.

There are more galaxies disincarnate than incarnate, existing upon the multidimensional, exalted levels of experiential concourse that is cosmos. All are teeming with many orders and complexities of both exalted and lowly forms of Life, producing a staggeringly overwhelming vision, even to the most enlightened upon this earth. Humanity needs a better teleological and eschatological grip upon what constitutes Life in this near unfathomable hylozoistic universe, and of the nature of how enlightened ones evolve within it and travel through it.

As a child in cosmos, a Buddha still possesses his vast stores of wisdom and exemplary powers, but this is in relation to others that had travelled that way from much earlier epochs and are now comparatively adults in the cosmic locus he now resides in. They retain their former status as his gurus, spiritual Father-Mothers of his entire quest to liberation and that beyond. The karmic links and orders of precedence are never broken between the one and the other. All travel together through transcendent space to further reaches of cosmic bliss. On and on do their unified Minds spread to overcome the edges of the boundaries of what represents the Knowable, to conquer Ignorance. Every onwards move is projected upon compassionate grounds. The analogy of parturition of a baby from a mother's womb into a vaster external domain holds true at this level.

One can postulate that all beings in cosmos adhere to Dependent Origination, for there are transcended levels of expression to this concept. Wheels of dependency manifest upon vastly sublime levels, not appertaining to *saṃsāra* at all but to the interrelation between stellar fields, each embodied by an 'All-Creating King'. Their interrelatedness holds a newly arrived Buddha bound to an evolutionary process, necessitating mastery of certain conditions before the next (Initiation) step can be attained. The twelve steps represent the twelve petals of a vast Heart centre (or the Heart in the Head), so that compassionate considerations can be further advanced upon an immense scale. The interrelated (astrological) forces conditioning these steps are embodied by various constellations of stars, the inhabitants and related qualities of which are within a Buddha's ken. Cosmic forces of various intensities need to be mastered and sublime attributes developed that will allow such a one, for instance, to later manifest as an Ādi Buddha for an entire world system, and in a much later cycle, a solar system.

Not all such wheels are governed by the number twelve, as there are many *chakras* conditioning cosmos. Nevertheless, the wheels of dependency must be travelled through. The subject of esoteric astrology (which will be introduced in Volume 3) is the science based upon the interrelatedness of the various constellations of stars to which the 'thus-gone' ones can travel. These energies and forces govern the omnipresent All.

Dependent Origination is the way all things come together and evolve, but this is preceded by the involutionary process, by the descent of a principle or quality yet to be discovered by an incarnate organism, be it a state of sentience or of that pertaining to human consciousness. The involutionary process manifests from the *arūpa* (formless) to the *rūpa* (formed) universe. The qualities proceed from a being that has 'gone before' to 'the other shore' of whatever level of expression another entity is aspiring to. There is nothing wasted in this universe (except illusorily by the hand of self-willed humans) and thus the 'clothing' no longer needed by one entity is passed on to another needing such attributes. This is exemplified by the fact that Maitreya will inherit the periodical vehicles, the remnant *karma* constituting the substance of Mind left behind by the Buddha when he took his *parinirvāṇa*. There is thus a continuous process of ascending and descending in Nature of principles, sentience, and the *saṃskāras* pertaining to consciousness evolving.

Another way of viewing this subject is to consider a Bodhisattva descending from the *arūpa* universe to help sentient beings. The only way that s/he can do this is to bequeath to them some of her/his wisdom (the example of compassion), and perhaps some material things that may benefit them. Thus s/he must be apparelled in form. What is skilfully bequeathed is what the Bodhisattva has attained and which the supplicants lack. Thus the way of Love proceeds, and the way to ascend necessitates developing the attributes expressed by the Bodhisattva. The evolution of the principle of Love can be outlined in the following way. First gross desire manifests, the 'love' for material objects and precious things. There is also sensuality, reaching out to another for sexual gratification, as well as producing desire for companionship. Affection to family, friends, and affiliation to a tribal group, race, or nation can then develop. The next step represents the stirrings of higher aspiration to deity and lofty philosophic concepts. Then we have the path of yoga, producing various types of union with concepts, deified images and consciousness states. Finally liberation is obtained through following the Bodhisattva ideal, and the development of *bodhicitta* via the higher Tantras, the *mahāmudrā, ati yoga,* or the *vajrayāna.*

Buddhists know the detail of this process, as well as the realisation that the higher way to liberation necessitates the 'gift waves' from the guru, which is but another way of describing such a descent of needed qualities for those upon the upward way. All is governed by the law of *karma*, and by the nature of the causative process, of how the *tathāgatagarbha* works to impel evolution onwards for human units. This is necessary if Bodhisattvas are to appear in the realms of form.

Originating causes

Prāsaṅgika Mādhyamika philosophers tell us that there is no such thing as an 'originating cause' because all causes are illusional, for they have *śūnyatā* as their support, which implies the death of all forms of phenomena, of 'causes of things'. If there is no concept of a 'self', how can there be a cause of anything, for there is nothing to produce any form of action whatsoever? However, it is admitted that 'things' do exist conventionally. From this perspective there are causes to such 'things', and if so, the logic purports that there is an originating cause to any 'thing'. If 'things' do exist, for whatever duration of time their phenomena appears, then it is logical that 'selves' exist to account for the origination or appearance of these 'things', each 'thing' being but a form of a 'self'.[17]

The originating cause of any 'thing' has, however, contributed to the effects, and lives on in them (hence we have the law of *karma*), until the cycle moves on to the next turn of the wheel and the *karma* must be cleansed via actions that sends the originating cause back to the sower. Thus evolution progresses, producing an order to phenomenal appearances. The seeds planted to produce the sprout are returned back

17 The information in Volume 1, chapter 12 should be incorporated here.

(manifold) as new seeds, implying a gain in the evolutionary process. There is also the production of new action on a higher cycle of the arc for plants as well, with each new genetic variance appearing in the fullness of time. With humans the evolutionary process is far faster because of the comparative speed that human consciousness moves with respect to animal or plant sentience.

So the originating causes act as laws governing energy propulsions, pushing the effects onwards through spirals of higher learning experience, seeding the new versions of whatever is to evolve and what one must grow into. Eventually the various Bodhisattva *bhūmis* are trod.

Causes and conditions can never be truly independent of each other, though an originating cause can be free from the environment that its subsequent effects find themselves in. The causes can come from beyond or above the effects, or be a part of the continuum of the same stream of expression as the effects. The effects can outgrow the status of the originating cause. Causes are not determined by the after-effects happening subsequent to the originating cause (the rivulets of subsidiary causes), which produce further actions. The effects, however, carry the seed of the originating cause wherever they go. The cycles repeat themselves through ever vaster spirals of inclusive Identification with the All.

The action of *karma*

A cause acts as a conditioning law for all the effects. This means that the originating cause interpenetrates the subsidiary causes and effects, which are thus held within the protection or emanatory (multidimensional) sphere of actuality of the cause. This 'protection' produces or tends to produce an expected or visualised outcome. (The terms expected or visualised implicate the energy qualification associated with the empirical and abstracted minds.)

A consequence is a rippling bubble of cause-effect emanating outward in all directions of space from the originating cause. We visualise it thus because as an effect travels out into space it is acted upon by other causes coming from different sources (e.g., other minds) which deviates it from its path, and so forth. The overall effect, when viewed from a distance, is seen as a ripple in the *ālayavijñāna*. We could say that when the ripples criss-cross each other they form the warp and weft of the fabric of *manasic* space. It can also be viewed as the way *karma* manifests within a limited zone of expression bounded by consciousness. The true effects of *karma* are those affecting consciousness. (Pain-suffering, etc.) This fabric has a karmic pattern woven into it that delineates the overall picture of a sphere of karmic interaction. The fabric extends through the three times and inevitably imprints patterns into *maṇḍalas* of mind/Mind. The thickness of the fabric depends upon the levels or layers of consciousness woven into it, from the concrete (or desire-mind) to the abstract Mind. Thus the *ālayavijñāna* can also be viewed as a *maṇḍalic* tapestry.[18]

The furthest extent of this rippling effect for any thought is the outermost boundary of the associated *karma*. (This depends upon the nature and intensity of the energy expressed by the originating cause.) One can thus coin a phrase: 'rings of *karma*', indicating the limits of this boundary binding the progenitor of a particular type of action to its reciprocation. Such boundaries of karmic expression allow one to annul the effect of the originating cause, which is needed if *śūnyatā* is to be the 'ultimate' effect. All of the moving strings of cause and effect are tied to the perpetuator and must be annulled by the reciprocation of an exact countering force to the originating cause. Consequently the effects must rebound upon the originating source, so Nature's balance score, the esoteric Gibb's Free Energy account, is equilibrated, because the rings of *karma* make it a closed system. It is not open ended, which would allow the karmic effects to travel forever onwards into space and be dissipated. If dissipation would happen, then we would have true annihilation and no karmic law.

We are not just concerned with impartial 'blind' energy here, but with effects manifesting within substance *(manas)* that is awake, sentient, of a parallel stream of evolution to the human, the feminine *devas* (such as are the *ḍākinīs)* that embody substance, making our universe hylozoistic. They are consequently agents of *karma,* and act to rectify the imbalances ('ripples') in their bodies of manifestation so that equilibrium is achieved. This is a vast subject, introduced here, but will be further explored in this *Treatise on Mind,* specifically in

18 This esoteric subject hints at a fruitful field of research for a prospective Bodhisattva of the future.

Volume 5A, where the role of the Consorts to the Deities of the *Bardo Thödol* are explained.

There are thus natural limits as to the way that *karma* can manifest and travel, according to the nature of the substance that is moved, and the energy put into the propagation of that action. These two determine the power and extent of the effect(s) and the attributes of the energy that drives them back to their source. *Karma* is like a rocket that travels upwards in the earth's atmosphere towards escape velocity, but never quite makes it, with gravity then pulling it back when the energy put into its forward momentum is exhausted. If the rocket actually reaches escape velocity, then this symbolises the attainment of a consciousness that is able to break free from the bonds of *karma.*

The law of *karma* is very much like gravity. They both act upon material bodies, across space, and are not conditioned by any other natural phenomena, and there is a limit to their expression.

For gravity, its effects work through space helping to delineate the motion of bodies, from whence time can be reckoned, and diminishes according to the square of the distance that separates the attracted bodies.

For *karma* the limitation concerns the field or nature of consciousness that must experience its effects. The more sluggish or dense the consciousness, the more limited the effect of karmic interplay; for increasingly refined and subtle consciousnesses, the further reaching the possibilities of karmic expression are. Such a consciousness quickly moves (and penetrates deeper) the substance it contains in order to achieve its effects. The substance consciousness incorporates therefore determines the nature of the experience of *karma*. The overall effect diminishes according to the density of the consciousness involved, if more concretised, but the frequency of karmic interaction is increased, as well as the intensity or violence of the interplay. Thus dull emotional consciousnesses are attracted to each other to produce more forceful or violent karmic interplay (like large bodies close to each other in space with respect to gravity), but the effect of such activity in the overall scheme of things is not large. It is generally limited to the proponents of their immediate families or environment. A highly refined consciousness on the other hand manifests great effects in the realm of ideas that can affect billions of people for generations to come. *Karma* works through time by organising formed space via the effects of past eventualities.

It should be noted that if causes do not act as a conditioning law for all the effects, then the later causes would be freed from the pull of *karma*. There would be no links to the environment of the original causes that produced them. This would make an original cause cease to exist, because the environment wherein it was to act had changed. Thus the subsequent causes and effects could not happen, because what created them had changed, as it was not stable or defined. The phrase 'cause and effect' would then be meaningless, *karma* would not exist and ordered events could not eventuate.

We can therefore postulate that if there was no proportional limit on the capacity of cause and effects that could be made upon the original cause that created all and its effects, then the progress of evolution would be uncontainable. This means that (the effects of) each further cause would not be able to create a boundary sphere (or spheres) of influence, to maintain the effects of the originating cause. It would allow each smaller effect to deviate from the originating effect, and eventually dissipate its energies through widespread dispersal of activity. Consequently a ring of containment, a cellular wall or skin, must manifest to delineate the extent of the space expressed by one sequence of cause and effect. The earth has such a boundary exoterically in the upper reaches of its atmosphere that distinguishes it from outer space. Subjectively the boundary is the tapestry of the woven karmic threads created by all upon earth within the domains of mind/Mind. A Buddha is one that has evolved Mind to the extent that this boundary no longer serves to provide any basis for further experiential growth of Mind. In order to progress, he has freed himself from the cause-effect sphere of activity, the 'bubble' that is the cumulative mind-space of all upon the earth. He thus is free to create a new set of causative conditions within a far vaster Mind-space *(dharmakāya)* than encapsulated by the karmic zone of the earth-sphere. Hence entirely new strands of karmic interrelations are established between those in cosmos which he will now share causative effects with.

One of the problems with everything existing in the mind of the thinker, as Yogācāra doctrine presupposes, is that if this was so it could change the originating causes of what exists *in situ* within it. If it could alter the originating *bījas* of its own thoughts, rather than to simply build upon the paradigm previously established, then automatically the thinker would incoherently transmogrify into the previously established and the entire basis to logical thought would disappear. Over time the sequences would no longer be available to give stability to anything. Also, one could speculate whether the phenomena of the external universe could be altered with his thought, as that phenomena and the mind are one, hence the functioning of time could not manifest therein, nor the law of *karma*. Everything would be skewed according to the nature of the images created in the mind. Though the phenomenological appearance of our planet does change, to an extent via the effects of the mind's exertions, it is not an exact demonstration. The fact is that the mind cannot change the originating causes, which it must be able to do if everything exists (only) in the mind of the thinker. This shows that there is more to the nature of the appearance of phenomena than the mind of the human thinker.

Other factors are involved that safeguard the inviolability of what is stored in the *bījas*. One is the activity of the Sambhogakāya Flower, which because it exists in the domain of the abstract Mind, regulates the storage of the *karma* associated with each seed. Also, we have the Lords of *karma,* the higher *devas* (incorporating *ḍākinīs* and the Consorts of the Buddhas and Bodhisattvas) that regulate the overall expression of *karma* through the passage of time. They control the substance of the planes of perception via which all karmic forces manifest. They work under the Ādi Buddha, constituting part of his retinue, being but force factors within the Mind of such a One.

The fact is that the originating causes cannot be modified. The images of the mind have been fixed in space (of the consciousness), because of conditioning law and hence can be recalled, once the proper processes have been undertaken to do so. Recollection is possible because the environment of the originating causes have *not* changed. It is not possible for consciousness to do so, though the imagination could impute changes to have happened. Such changes may appear to override the old images, but the consciousness has simply created a new set of originating causes for itself, without changing the originating one(s). The originating paradigm may have been extended or altered to suit the new images, but still the original exists in pristine condition. Thus it is in Nature and with the laws of *karma*.

The adamantine unchangeability of past actions is what the Lords of Life use to maintain a steady process of cause and effect to produce the effect of the evolution of all consciousnesses to liberation without the nullification of existence. Stability is needed for the projection of effects into the future. Such logic explains the laws of life and presupposes a larger, vaster form of Mind outside of the human mind, that regulates the flow of all that is and is not, according to the impeccable law of cause and effect. It necessitates the maintenance of a time line, a sequence of goalposts, whereby the past can be remembered and the resultant formations projected to the future in a progressive way, allowing an enlightened being to predict what should be.

If the consciousness of the thinker alone, its willy-nilly peregrinations, ruled the illusionality of what is, it would spell utter chaos in the order of Nature. If the past can change then nothing could exist to make a lasting impression upon any consciousness because it can be completely annihilated by any thought desirous of changing what once was. If the past is unmovable then it produces calculable effects that serve as laws for the smaller outcomes. If the effects were not held within a stable frame of activity then all effects would be unaccountable and could appear everywhere to affect every moment of the whole picture for everything existing.

The past exists in the future expression, thus the past can be examined. The future tendencies are constantly changing because the past is always being added to. Stability is however needed for rationality to rule the mind. Consequently, consciousness can at any moment evoke any image or *saṃskāra* that has been stabilised in the past and alter it by adding to it, to cause a new event. All people do this as part of their everyday existence, but they do not alter the past. Instead a new moment in time, a new picture image registered by consciousness is eventuated, which then becomes a past moment that can be remembered and accordingly altered. Consciousness contains a myriad of such sequences of image-making, all stored in the recesses of memory, where past images are added to, making a new past image, the originating one and the one created, and so the process continues.

This introduces the concept of evolutionary progression, because people generally alter past images in such a way that the new one serves them better. They adapt what was and add to it so that what is formed equips them better in life. Consequently, a baby grows into a child, the child into an adolescent, and the adolescent (meaning that the emotions are the mainstay of life) to a adult (where emotions have been supplanted by logical thought). Evolution proceeds thus all the way.

The present conscious moment changes appearances of recalled images through modifying what appeared. They are part of a continuum of such change, and these projected changes are harbingers of the future. The future tendencies become the store of the information of what will be, before becoming the past.

The patterning or overview of all such tendencies towards the future represents the mechanism governing the way information is stored and categorised so that it can be retrieved by consciousness for any future outcome. This necessitates a container of the images constituting the trends to the future that incorporates the continuum of the streams of lives that evolve towards Buddhahood. We thus have a subtle 'soul' concept that incorporates such a function.

A cause may have passed, yet it can be retrieved to produce a reinvigoration of possibilities within the memory banks of the present-future. The layers of memory stabilise what is happening and account for the possibilities of future endeavour that will record the content of the past and present actions. Strands of *saṃskāras* move towards the future. Collectively they produce a paradigm of possible future events because the tendencies are already there *in situ*. The future potential thereby manifests as a *maṇḍala* of the sum of the pathways of the past manifestations producing the present. The potential exists for the future to utilise any aspect of the past for the present display so that an envisioned outcome of the life of the personal-I can be accommodated. Here we have the action of the Sambhogakāya Flower implicated, which consciously directs all such future potential.

The *maṇḍala* is a completed structure that holds all that was, is, and is to be in its cognisance. It exists and acts thus to ensure the future evolution of what must be. For instance, in the child exists the *maṇḍala* of all future potential of the person. The potential has been laid, and given the right conditions, the child will grow along predetermined pathways; biologically, socially, and in the development of consciousness. Nothing will stop this process, short of premature death.

If there was no proper ordering of the consequences of cause and effect in a progressive manner then the opposite to evolution would occur with far greater frequency than is presently possible. The attributes of avarice, separateness, and sexual potency of most people would drive them deep into self-serving arenas of perpetual indulgences and materialism. Inevitably the great bulk of the human race would evolve towards being abject sorcerers, bent upon the acquisition of *siddhis* for selfish purpose and power in *saṃsāra*. This is because the forms of activity producing black magic is the line of least resistance for incarnate humanity. This concerns the development of extreme selfishness, the ruthless projection of the self-serving nature of the desire-mind in the quest for sexual and sensual gratification, money, material possessions, and power. The next step is psychic manipulation over others, the full unbridled unleashing of sex-yoga; the consequent manifestation of gross psychic passions, manipulative scheming to dominate all, and ferocious war-like tendencies. These are qualities which people would most certainly manifest if left to their own accord without the impulse of an evolutionary push of a compassionate Mind (the Sambhogakāya Flower) subjectively guiding them. This should be evident to any who would carefully ponder upon the subject, especially if consideration is made of the effects of the arousal of psychic powers, producing the black *dharma* (the left hand path).

Despite the iniquities of the inequality of resource sharing upon our planet, and the cupidity seen everywhere amongst people, there is actually a progression of the quality of human civilisation over the millennia, because *karma* is metered out in order to produce evolutionary purpose. Such a progression is clearly evident if we look back but a few hundred years in Europe, where every nation was ruled by despots, with serfdom and slavery being commonplace, whilst in religious affairs the Inquisition ruled nations.[19]

It should be realised that *karma* is inviolate, therefore the sum of the evil doing of the many groups of humanity have to be arranged in such a way that inevitably good evolves from human selfish proclivity and avaricious predation. Their massed cupidity is rampant and a most

---

19 The study of the psychic history of humanity would be a fascinating study for anybody with the opened Eye to be able to do so. Human civilisation has actually passed through periods of widespread sorcery, and much pain, suffering, and abject poverty in our civilisation today has its roots in such human psychic predation of the past.

destructive force upon the planet. People however cannot be forced to act right, thus if they transgress again and again, the resultant *karma* of evil doing will follow them until the reciprocal of the factor of the pain they have caused others educates them on what not to do. When the billions of incarnate and disincarnate humans upon our planet are accounted for, we see that many millennia must pass before a clear evolutionary progression of some desirable trait amongst humanity is seen.

The existence of the white *dharma* on the planet proves evolutionary law to be in place, thus to be functioning according to the meditation of a great Being (Ādi Buddha), who controls all in His compassionate stance. Also, such a Being needs to act via mediators, Bodhisattvas that work to sanctify the all by lassoing the mechanisms into place that will allow each human unit to gain liberation. They also direct the consciousness of human groups and disciples in such a way that it is in accordance with the meditative construct of this 'All-Creating-King' that is *guru* to all. Such activity happens in coordination with the kingdom of the Sambhogakāya Flowers, who direct also the *karma* of individual human units.

If such constructs were not in place within the human psyche then internal wisdom, *bodhicitta,* could not arise for them to recognise whatever it was that a Bodhisattva would try to say or show. Humanity would be too focussed upon determined materialistic ambition, the pursuit of sensual pleasures, power and wealth. For the lower empirical mind the benefits of a life set on pleasures and materialistic ambition are too obvious for it to seek change. Thus the words of a Bodhisattva (no matter how skilful his means) are too far away from the 'reality' or mind-space of such people. The Bodhisattva would more likely be psychically or physically attacked than listened to. With respect to this, much more needs to be understood concerning the functioning of the psychic protectors (as well as of the nature of the massed psychic projections) of the human race. They are *more* than just mind-conjured entities.

Evolutionary law

The points made concerning the direction that mind would take if left to its own devices may be debated by some because the evidence from the people around them appear otherwise; that they are surrounded by loving, receptive people. Nevertheless, the points made do show the true nature of things relating to the human condition. Those who would argue to the contrary comprehend not that their observations arise because evolutionary law is in place. Too many are glamoured by their concepts of the real, of what for them constitutes the nature of truth, personal, or otherwise. *Glamour* consists of a thick cloud of *māyā* surrounding the perceptions of an individual, which instantly colours his/her thinking according to the nature of the object of desire. The five factors utilising evolutionary law are:

1. The overshadowing Mind of an Ādi Buddha directing evolutionary purpose for this planet, who works with other Primordial Minds manifesting a similar purpose for other planetary systems. They are part of an integral body of manifestation, a cosmic *nāḍī* system, that incorporates them in an omnipresent arena of Beingness. Cosmic *karma* is thereby directed to govern the sum of the evolutionary space constituting their Bodies of manifestation.
2. Bodhisattvas working as mediators between the Buddha-Mind and the Sambhogakāya Flowers. They endeavour to assist the resultant incarnate personal-I's to look inwards so as to receive impressions from higher sources as a basis for their path to liberation. This inward contemplation, right concentration, etc., coupled with a heuristic approach to life, awakens *bodhicitta* and generates the needed wisdom that is the keynote of enlightenment.
3. An entourage of *devas* constituting the sum of the substance wherein *karma* plays its role.
4. The Sambhogakāya Flowers directing the *karma* of individuation or continuation of lives according to the dictates of evolutionary law, as it exists in the realm of consciousness.
5. The life of the personal-I evolving consciousness and developing compassionate understanding in the realms of illusion.

Humanity has travelled for many cycles of millennia under the influences of the above-mentioned factors, and this has generally made them loving in disposition. If one looks to the future, then we see that there is the possibility of all outcomes, and is also a record of the memory of the past. Thus, if these memories of the past are brought to the surface in the right sequence, then the outcome will be towards that desired by the indwelling Sambhogakāya Flower. Memories, even from past lives, can be rightly *seeded* in the personal-I's mind, so that it pushes awareness in the direction desired, towards loving actions and not those empowering the 'I's' forms of selfishness. The receptivity of a personality to impressions indicates the ability to manifest the purity of mind to be able to listen to Bodhisattvas. Many lives of development of such receptivity generates the path to liberation.

The recollection of the right experiences, including from dreams, all help to influence the personal will to act according to the progression of evolutionary law, rather than the way of the base self. Without such evocation of memory and inner promptings (the inherent memory or acknowledgement of karmic lessons learnt from bygone eras), the personal-I would find it difficult to travel any direction other than that of accruing sensual experiences and seeking personal gain. No reason would exist to question why such pleasures should not be indulged in. There would be no inner promptings, conscience, ordered timely appearance of memories, or necessary past life *saṃskāra* appearing, teaching otherwise. The grounding for the development of compassion, of *bodhi*, which is the way of evolution, will have not been established.

It should also be noted that the *saṃskāras* recalled in normal human evolution are sequenced and timed in such a way that the person can gain something from their social or environmental intercourse. That many do not do so is because of their free will. The inevitable outcome of not following the purported patterning of their life, of the inner promptings to be more loving, is further pain, sickness, losses of various types, and inevitable death so that one can start anew.

Saṃskāras are also often the expressions of past lives of human selfishness, coarse desire and hatreds. Though they again produce tendencies towards such activities is true, but always the Sambhoghakāya Flower directs the sequence of the retrieval of available *saṃskāras* so that some, even minutely incremental, gain happens along the road to development of *bodhicitta*. This happens for individuals and also for all factors of civilisations. The way is slow at first, as the personal-I has many desires and self-deceptions, but as each little increment to *bodhicitta* is developed, so they build up, making a fresh course of compassionate *saṃskāric* impetus. Eventually a cavalcade of such *saṃskāras* manifest, pushing the person far and fast along the Bodhisattva path. This development needs proper organisation; it will not happen by chance, which the Buddhist philosophy seems to indicate. Everywhere the ordering of Nature is evident, and so it is for the evolution of human consciousness.

With respect to the concept of the 'past' one should also note that whenever *saṃskāras* are called forth and modified in some way, making a new past, then this past is constituted of many seeds, any one of which can be recalled and modified. A new seed pattern therefore forms, and can awaken a *laya*-centre containing many *bījas* for the future. Thus *saṃsāra* unfolds, containing as its foundation, many such centres of potential activity, forming the complete picture of all seen around us. Because *laya* centres *(chakras)* pre-exist, future events can manifest in the way they are pre-ordained to happen. The awakening *chakras* constitute a universe of possibilities.

One could also deduce that if *śūnyatā* and *saṃsāra* are one, then *saṃsāra* represents the past that is the foundation of all, and *śūnyatā* the (indeterminate) future. 'Indeterminate' because it is the future, therefore by definition not yet manifest, and exists as an 'ultimate'. Therein past tendencies do not exist, hence *karma* is not expressed. Nevertheless, one who has attained *śūnyatā* can still recall past lives (like the Buddha), as well as details of volitions enacted by others. This means therefore that the past is real, indestructible. Therefore Nāgārjuna's famous *catuṣkoṭikā*; 'is, is not, both is and is not, neither is and is not' can be applied to it as it evolves to a future ultimate. It 'is' (the past), 'is not' (because no longer manifesting), 'both is and is not' as the *saṃskāras* of the past are experienced in the present, and 'neither is and is not' in the future when past images can be recalled, and yet the *karma* of its expression has been extinguished.

Those upon the path to enlightenment will do well to study future tendencies (of all around). Also, one can say that the enlightened totally live in the future. They are agents of it, and consequently of *karma*. They mould past effects in order to make the future 'real' for humanity. In studying the future one becomes concerned with the eternal ever-present NOW, which is the state of observing the process of the past moving to the future, and it slipping into the past in terms of total conscious recollection.

Anyone who can reside in the future tense does so from the stillness of the NOW. Such a one has transcended time, looking at the three times from a point above or beyond in space. Timelessness is therefore one's mode of being, yet the process of evolutionary time is the consideration when observing *saṃsāra*. One then, like the Buddha, attains the attitude described in the *sūtras* that state that the Buddha is atemporal and timeless *(Aṇguttara-Nikāya IV)*, that he transcends the aeons *(Sutta Nipāta)*, indicating that he has transcended the cyclic flux of time. Thus for the Buddha, all times are made the present, and there exists neither past nor future. Some commentators impute from this that for the Buddha time is static, eternal, nondurate and immobile. However, terms such as stasis, non-duration, or immobility are incorrect when depicting the state of being of the enlightened. *Serenity* is more accurate, because serenity is inclusive of all of the modifications of existence, but the mode of observation is without reaction of any type, other than clear instantaneous deduction that disturbs or modifies not what is observed. Such 'clear instantaneous deduction' is the opposite of immobility or stasis.

Oṁ

8

Signposts of consciousness

From a driver's perspective

The stages delineating the separation of cause and effect constitute the *signposts of consciousness*. This is likened to a car moving slowly along a road, with signs appearing in a continuous stream with symbols and words upon them depicting road conditions, danger spots, etc., ahead. The car driver (symbolising the consciousness residing in the personality vehicle) has opportunity to respond to the signs. They are major *saṃskāras* coming to the surface of the mind during important stages or events in the person's life. Each sign has an effect on the further development of consciousness. Therefore the driver can turn left or right upon a differing stream of experience contained within the same road system of possibilities, i.e., a certain area patterned by various potential avenues of possible travel. The sign might also be a piece of spiritual advice, such as a caution; there being wet weather, or bends in the road, necessitating the driver to slow down.

Other examples would be a single road exit, a dead end, multiple exits, or an accident. Consciousness can then choose to heed the support sign, and act accordingly, thus following a different set of circumstances than that originally planned. The signposts of consciousness generally manifest in a coherent, recognisable pattern that can be comprehended in time, so that steps can be made to utilise the information properly to advantageously benefit the personal-I's evolution.

The simile of the five examples provided regarding traffic can be developed in the field of consciousness thus:

1. *A dead end.* This action produces no spiritual possibility. It means reversing (karmic retribution) and trying another way.
2. *Wet weather, or bends in the road,* refers to a situation that involves emotions, or mental-emotions, meaning further muddied *saṃsāric* activity. Here one must take caution and calm the Solar Plexus centre, the central store of all the animal-like (emotional) energies of the minor *chakras*. It necessitates proper control and slowing down of one's emotional, desire-filled approach to life.
3. *An accident.* This refers to a non-heeding of the signs and as a result experiencing the consequences, affecting the personality in an often painful manner, by means of which lessons can be learnt.
4. *A single road exit* refers to a strict regime of conscious undertaking to be followed. There is only one road ahead away from disaster to success.
5. *Multiple exits* refer to the multiple choices in life, to travel the left or right hand pathway, or straight ahead to quickly achieve enlightenment. (The ultimate goal, or home destination.)

Within consciousness there are different currents and speeds of accumulation (the way the car travels). These speeds rarely transgress the bounds of the various normal forms of manifesting consciousness. They are conditioned by cycles, seasons, and life span. If these conditions are eclipsed then one may either head towards disaster or else towards obtaining enlightenment, depending upon the skill and wisdom of the driver to undertake new possibilities. If there are different speeds it means there are different potentials in human consciousness, as the quality of the mind and experience of an individual are factors to be considered for the time it takes for any one to become enlightened. Not only are the cars (personality vehicles) all different, with different capacities on the road, but they also have different functions, some are speedsters, some are goods carriers, some specialise in moving the family to which one belongs. Even if some appear the same on the outside, e.g., Buddhist monks, the drivers (the consciousnesses) all possess different capabilities. Individuality is all we see in the human world, though there is much emphasis to conformity in some societies, as all travel on the roads provided for them by the society of which they are a part.

Individuality must be seriously taken into account by teachers of meditation. All must follow their unique paths to enlightenment, though all paths follow the same general guide lines. Similarly motorists must obey the same road rules if the roads are to offer safe passage for everyone. Little consideration for the inner conditionings of the nature of manifesting *saṃskāras* and impacting *karma* of their students is one of the major failings of many meditation teachers. Due to the nature of *saṃskāras* and *karma* an individual consciousness can flourish and travel far upon the path, whilst others lack. Individual *prāṇas* of various qualities (similar to different cars on the road) flow and ebb within consciousness, indicating the rate by which individuals can progress. Why some can take enlightenment in a life, whilst others take lifetimes, depends upon choices that determine differing circumstances, which appear as signs from principles formerly developed. The signs are the causes of situations that affect, or can affect, the future outcome of any situation. Other signposts help determine the means to process hindering, obscuring *karma*.

The internally recognisant consciousness may also have the ability to react in a wide range of ways to the external stimuli. (Signposts on the road that indicate cause and effect.) But by driving along the way they can flow into different streams, (diverging roads or pathways in the larger overall consciousness of which they are a part), whether it be in good or positive currents or into negative ones. Hence the life experiences appear as a series of patterns of culminating *karma* based on former choices. They represent the response made to the previous signs, noting that the signs here were formed from an effect of a former response. Signposts created by former events are part of the organisational structure of the all-encompassing consciousness. The fact that particles, *i.e.*, individuals, can choose to go with or against these signposts is what creates individual *karma*. Hence individual *karma* is created by the force of free will, as to which way to drive within a set of circumstances. Gradually one can move out of these circumstances and become a causative principle for all around, directing the streams of appearing sentience and awareness. One will then manifest with the higher or greater streams of cause and effect, as produced by universal consciousnesses, and respond in unison with that state of awareness. Such beings assist the mechanism whereby *saṃskāras* can be cleansed.

Signposts change, as the type of philosophy that once was the sign or guide to the way no longer serves that purpose, for the entire landscape to which they are pointing to has changed. New cities (of revelations within consciousness) have sprung up, with new levels of information encoded therein to be digested by consciousness. This is clear if we study the history of the *buddhadharma* from the Theravādin doctrines, to the necessity of the rise of the Mahāyāna, then Tantricism. It should be obvious that this forward-progressive march cannot stop, therefore this present era needs new directions, new signposts, to rightly accommodate the West and its contributions to the arena of Buddhist philosophic debate. 'New' teachings of the *dharmakāya* can thus be given. They are not new, in the sense that they have never existed before, for indeed, the appropriate signs were there in the past for their recognition, but few knew how to read them. The wisdom presented is truth, or the foundation for higher revelations, and has therefore always existed, long before the earth was formed, long before the present humanity individualised to register the fact of consciousness and higher law.

Words are the limiting factor in any presentation, they limit the ability to put sentences together in such a way as to adequately explain the nature of revelatory vision. Despite all their limitations, however, words do serve as signposts. Other insights to higher truths can form in the consciousness of the aspirant. They are necessarily wordless, and reveal the way to the other shore of *saṃsāra*. Some signs are very subtle indeed, such as those relating to the intuition and which lead to high revelations. Observing such signs will obviously produce high rewards. Other signs can be blazingly conspicuous, such as those leading to excessive carnality. Following these can produce much attendant trouble. Clearly, therefore, it is important to know which signs to follow, to develop the level of discernment to be able to read and follow the subtler signs that appear in consciousness, that point the way to liberation. Not only must they be read in the right sequence, but one must also hear the subtle voices of the intuition (the important sounds amongst the general din of the traffic), which will produce great revelatory experiences, helping one to arrive at the objective of the journey.

Signs according to literature

The concept of signs is a subject also known from the Buddhist perspective. Donald S. Lopez, Jr., for instance states:

> Many of the most important phenomena in Buddhist philosophy fall into the category of hidden phenomena, such as subtle impermanence, the existence of former and later lifetimes, liberation from cyclic existence, the existence of a Buddha's omniscient consciousness, and emptiness. The definition states that such phenomena must *initially* be realized in dependence on a sign. This refers to the important tenet that phenomena which are ordinarily inaccessible to direct perception can eventually be directly perceived by gradually transforming the imagistic perception by thought into yogic direct perception *(yogipratyakṣa, rnal 'byor mngon sum).* It is this yogic direct perception which, in the Mādhyamika school, directly realizes emptiness, a hidden phenomena, and destroys the seeds for rebirth...[1]
>
> A sign is one component of a syllogism *(prayoga, sbyor ba),* the other being the probandum *(sādhya, bsgrub bya)* or that which one is seeking to prove[2]...In order for the syllogism to be correct, thereby yielding an inferential valid cognizer, the sign must be correct. A correct sign in a particular proof must be the three modes *(trirūpa, tshul gsum)* of that proof, in fact, a correct sign is defined as "that which is the three modes." The three modes are three relationships of the sign to other elements of the syllogism.
>
> The first mode is the property of the subject *(pakṣadharma, phyogs chos),* which refers to the presence of the reason in the subject; in order to be a correct reason, that reason must be a property of the subject[3]...The second of the three modes is the forward pervasion *(anvayavyāpti, rjes khyab)* which is defined as that ascertained by valid cognition as existing only in the similar class in accordance with the mode of statement. The similar class *(sapakṣa, mthun phyogs)* is that class of phenomena of which the sign must be a member in order for the sign to be correct[4]...The third of the three modes is the counterpervasion *(vyatirekavyāpti, ldog khyab)* which is that ascertained as only non-existent in the dissimilar

1 Donald Lopez, Jr., *A Study of Svāntantrika, (Snow Lion, New York, 1987),* 61.

2 Ibid., 62.

3 Ibid.

4 Ibid., 63.

> class in accordance with the mode of statement. The dissimilar class *(vipakṣa, mi mthun phyogs)* is that class of which the negative of the sign must be a member in order for the sign to be correct.[5]

The information presented here concerning the use of a sign can also be applied to the river simile. The 'hidden phenomena' refers to that which is veiled by consciousness. What is it, exactly, that is thus 'hidden'? The list given is: 'subtle impermanence, the existence of former and later lifetimes, liberation from cyclic existence, the existence of a Buddha's omniscient consciousness, and emptiness'.

The list should be rearranged to put it into correct order. We thus have:

1. The existence of former and later lifetimes. This concerns the complete teaching of the nature of the law of *karma,* and of consciousness unfolding via the law of cycles according to evolutionary plan.
2. Subtle impermanence, which concerns the impermanence of *saṃsāra,* producing the sum of the doctrines developed from the Four Noble Truths, plus the doctrine of the nature of the sheaths of consciousness (of the *rūpa* and *arūpa* levels) that one evolves through. Here the teachings on meditation come into effect, so that liberation can be attained.
3. Liberation from cyclic existence. This necessitates a correct understanding of the Bodhisattva path, which therefore includes comprehension of the nature of the Sambhogakāya Flower.
4. Emptiness. This concerns the understanding of higher Buddhist metaphysics. The doctrine of *śūnyatā* is taught, but needs to be experienced.
5. The existence of a Buddha's omniscient consciousness. This necessitates understanding the nature of the Dharmakāya Way, then following its dictates, leading inevitably to treading cosmic paths as a 'thus gone one'.

Signs are needed in the deductive process, as outlined above concerning syllogisms, because human consciousness is normally unfamiliar with the forthcoming impressions, such as those relating

5 Ibid.

to subtle impermanence and liberation, because they do not fall into people's general experiential range. The signs translate what is generally not interpretable, because they help reveal what is yet to be experienced. The assistance of Bodhisattvas as guides to gaining enlightenment is specifically helpful because they have already travelled upon roads where the signs exist. What is unknown in a life can thus begin to be cognised in terms of interpretable symbols and images, which hint at what can be experienced and revealed to the personal-I. 'Subtle impermanence' for instance, does not just refer to things pertaining to the material world where it is relatively easy for most people to acknowledge the ephemeral nature of all around them because of their continuous attachment to aspects of it. Rather, it refers to the types of phenomena exhibited in consciousness, of emotional-mental concepts, indoctrinations, and psychic impressions, which people often latch on to as real. At the appropriate cycle in their lives signs or impressions come into consciousness indicating that their beliefs may not be true. Sometimes the accompanying realisations produce much internal agonising as one undertakes the process of discarding what was once cherished.

The question unanswered in the above quote however, is where do the signs or subtle impressions come from at the crossroads of one's personal life? They are not something that the person has dreamed up or thought of before. An answer may lie in the fact that they are *karma*, i.e., *saṃskāras* from former lives coming to the fore at a reciprocal moment in one's life when one is experiencing a happening akin to what was experienced before. The impressions are simply waiting in potential to enter the consciousness at the explicit moment. 'Waiting where?' we can then query. 'In a continuum of thought moments from the former life' may be the Buddhist response. But then the questioner might ask 'how does *karma* select the specific thought moment needed for that individual at exactly the right moment?' A plausible explanation in the orthodox Buddhist accounting is now considerably more difficult. There must be a mechanism that facilitates the instantaneous appearance in consciousness of the necessary sign at exactly the right moment. Such a mechanism is not found in the general Buddhist ontology or syllogisms. We must therefore clarify and improve the context and content of such logic.

The question actually presented is 'how does the personal-I recognise what it has never consciously experienced before, i.e., recognise that which is intrinsically alien to the present circumstance?' How does, for instance, the impressions from a former lifetime actually become realised to be that from one's former life, especially if observing the apparel of a different sex, wearing different costumes, and appearing in a totally alien civilisation and cultural situation? What signs appear in consciousness that allow one to so identify? The concept of an amorphous life flux cannot answer this, because if such a flux existed it would simply flow into a person's consciousness, where the flow continues in the form of new impressions being created.

If parts of the stream entering into that mind flowed faster than other parts, then we would have a schizophrenic effect because the flow would be unregulated, causing imbalances in perceptions happening at any time. Even so, consciousness would contain nothing in it from a far earlier part of that stream, for example, as a Buddhist monk ten lives ago, or of being the participant of a brothel in ancient Egypt. In such a scenario there are actually no mechanisms to pin such an appearing image to the intellect as actually being 'his' in a former life. How can there be if that intellect was developed from attributes pertaining to that life only, or with some input from the immediate previous life? However, *saṃskāras* from much earlier lives are normally (unconsciously) recalled to condition the present activities of a person. It must be so for *karma* to manifest.

Memory is generally considered as an expressed product of a particular life's aggregates developed from early childhood through to old age. Viewed in isolation, in this way impressions from a past life experience are an impossibility, as no mechanism exists in the mind which has subsequently developed allowing interpretation of the impressions that might appear from past lives as one's own. Consequently, a normal person does not remember former life experiences, neither do people take past life experiences into account in societies where rebirth philosophy is not taught as fact. Moreover, if normal people did acknowledge such experiences as possible they would still not know how to analyse properly what they might experience. In this context there are no roads or pathways in their present consciousness leading back 'there' for them to discern what is being perceived as a real past life experience, or simply an imagining. There is generally little or no understanding of the nature of the cultural situation, or even to when or where in time they are looking to in the past life experience. Signposts for understanding there may be, but they have not yet developed the capacity to recognise them, or to properly interpret.

Though he may be thoroughly ignorant of past cultural situations in the world, a Buddhist nevertheless accepts the factor of past life experiences and therefore will look to the possibility that he may have experienced a past life impression. An ordinary materialist from the West does not believe in such a possibility, and thus will normally relegate the possibility as imagination. Because the thought of past life experience has not entered into his consciousness, he therefore does not even recognise the most elementary sign of what was experienced. Similarly when it comes to intuitive impressions from sources above the empirical mind. Nevertheless, impressions and visualisations of past life activities can and do appear, especially in meditation, to which myriads can testify. Hence a valid method of accounting for such impressions must be made evident, and here we have the doctrine of the Sambhogakāya Flower as explained in this treatise.

The role of the Sambhogakāya Flower

The Sambhogakāya Flower provides the possibility of the intellect recognising the signs of past-life experience. It contains all of the quantified experiences of the past within its mechanism, thus can remember and recall because it contains them in a retrievable form, and has pathways that lead to the relevant information. Moreover, the mechanism is established by means of its link to the personal-I to present the signs in terms of images that the person can register as something that actually happened and was 'him' in the past through intuitive knowingness. He may not have the words to properly explain to others (they have not experienced what he has), but he intuits the truth, or internally sees images, producing a knowingness that what was experienced in consciousness was factual. This knowingness is the silent voice of the Sambhogakāya Flower speaking, and provides a proof establishing the factuality of the existence of a subtle soul, a consciousness container.

The ability to experience such knowingness takes time to develop, because the intellect must be slowly moulded by the Sambhogakāya Flower to recognise the signs from the subjective world that are worthy to be noticed as being valid pointers for the life experience. If the personality is too engrossed in the sensual pleasures of this world, for instance, or is an outright materialist, such signs of higher conscious identifications are generally quickly stifled, preventing the Flower from utilising the appearing form. The desire-mind substance is then too gross to be able to receive very refined subtle impressions. A life of dissipation of energies and *karma*-producing activities is manifested instead. Thus the consciousness is tied even closer to *saṃsāra*.

Even a high-grade consciousness, with strong links to the Sambhogakāya Flower, that has developed a capability to consciously receive the very subtle signs along the road to higher awareness, will find difficulty recognising exactly when or where the recalled past life experiences may have happened. This is because such a one needs to be a student of history to recognise the costumes and basic historical events of the particular country (which may no longer exist), concerning the time period from where the impression came. The person should, however, cognise the context of what he is experiencing and why, because his *karma* is involved. All happens within the auspices of the present *karma* manifesting. This *karma* is the reciprocal of the former happening. It represents the higher cycle of what was earlier sown that is now perceived consciously whilst it is being reaped for its cleansing or transmutation.

The signposts of consciousness producing remembrance of past life experiences, of internal recognition that they are from one's past lives and not just imagination running riot, are different for each person, though the process of their manifestation is similar. Differences manifest because the conditioned minds are different in each case. Similarities arise because the mechanism of expression is the same, via the *antaḥkaraṇas* (consciousness-links) projected from the container of all past-life experiences, the Sambhogakāya Flower, to the personal-I. The personality must learn to travel along the same pathways *(antaḥkaraṇas)* to the Flower on the road to liberation, and in doing so become a Bodhisattva.

A Bodhisattva can manifest altruistic purpose from life to life because the pathways to liberation have been established in former lives, and he/she must simply learn to reconnect with them in any new life, and go from there. This must happen in accordance with the new conditionings manifesting in that life, and the plan that unfolds from the liberated realms for a sequence of lives. The Bodhisattva learns to recognise the signs producing the ability to envision the future as he/she invigorates the links to the domain of the *ālayavijñāna,* where the Sambhogakāya Flower resides.

Signs of progressive awakening

The signs that lead to liberation from cyclic existence always exist in consciousness. The process pointing to the way out of *saṃsāric* mire exists even for the grossest consciousnesses. The signs for such people may simply manifest in the harsh effects of *karma* teaching the lessons, or to the process happening within their desire-minds, leading to a subtler level of desire that, for instance, may not be totally engrossed upon sensuality. Small, further steps along the way will be built in the succeeding lives. However, if the concept of no soul-form was a reality, then one would have to ask where in fact these little consciousness-pointers come from? They cannot be explained by means of the law of *karma*, because they are something *other* than *karma. Karma* stages the events, but this 'something other' speaks to the individual and presents relevant related images. Sometimes these pointers are not so little, but are rather momentous, such as a sudden realisation, a flash of revelation that a path of action that one was engrossed in was wrong. Often a sudden substantial physical plane hardship can act as such a cue.

The religious texts present numerous such examples in the stories of their saints. Their entire life then changes, as it did for Milarepa when he decided that the path of sorcery was not the right way; or for the Buddha when he saw the living images of old age, sickness, the crippled and the dead. Overwhelming flashes of revelation or inspiration do not come from nowhere, and they are certainly not explained as being part of the aggregates, as they are not. The aggregates cannot produce a revelation of something new.

Such signs come from somewhere other than the intellect. What's more, they are progressive in nature, such as the series of revelations that led to the Buddha's enlightenment. Most people have had them in one form or other. So once again we are left with the conclusion that something greater than the incarnating human unit and his/her intellect exists, directing the events associated with a human life to its conclusion, and so on through to the succeeding lives.

We also have signs of 'emptiness'. The texts give enough information concerning the nature of such signs that lead to the condition of the 'signlessness' that *śūnyatā* represents. However, when one visions through the Śūnyatā Eye, then further signs appear that are productive of the Dharmakāya-Mind.

Obviously, the signs pertaining to proving 'the existence of a Buddha's omniscient consciousness' can only appear to a Bodhisattva well travelled along the path. They manifest as yogic direct perception, as they can only be understood by one who is on the verge of liberation. Consequently, they are necessarily of an esoteric nature.

Desire based thoughts strengthening concepts of 'self', such as the amassing of money, are produced by those with a narrowly directed control over the attributes of the mind. Many lives are squandered when the influx of mind is added to desire. Base *saṃskāras* are developed, and a low quality of information is preserved from previous experiences, because the intensified self-concept of such a one projects what it has gained exclusively for the empowerment of the transient, petty 'I'. An intensification of subsequent chained thoughts is produced that manifest like the branches of a tree which continue to be added with time. Such 'branches', however, introduce the concept of a hierarchical structure in the field of consciousness, allowing thoughts and images to be quickly retrieved from memory. They also offer opportunity for the indwelling Sambhogakāya Flower to gradually introduce less selfish ideas to such a one.

There are signs leading to major highways of information and concepts, and others to lesser known and travelled paths, like the smaller branches of a tree. The branches lead to a central processing unit, such as a major city in the case of the roads, trunks in the case of the tree, and the Sambhogakāya Flower in the case of human thinking processes. There are well known routes to higher realisations that the person has spent much time building in past lives, and much smaller pathways along unfamiliar avenues of thought, yet to be fully developed. Some pathways may lead to the minutiae of investigation, like the leaves on a twig, and then the leaves can also be open to microscopic analysis. Whatever the pathway chosen, there is always the link to the central processing unit, and there are signs all along the route pointing out the way. It is so in all of Nature (though sometimes such links may be subtle), and also with human consciousness, and this is the reason why consciousness manifests as efficiently as it normally does.

Faith, devotion, and aspiration

Many thoughts can manifest to intensify an original idea, unless an experience occurs that the individual decides to pursue, which then alters the course of thought in a different direction, hopefully for the better. By utilising free will we all have such abilities for decision making. In time, free will can produce a revolution in thought. It may steer away from the pain caused by the consequences of attachment to transient things. Many incarnations may, however, pass before the causes are seen to be the consequences of attachment to the concept of a personal 'self'. The solution can then be discovered through developing *bodhicitta*. Many lives of transition will pass before the way of *bodhicitta* produces Buddhahood.

The transitional phase will produce many attachments to devotional or aspirational concepts. Concepts will be produced similar to, or as that of theists that faithfully manifest a belief in 'God', and devotedly offer their life for the grace of the Divine Will. In order to thus devote oneself, one must have a belief structure, a faith that is attached to something that is beyond or greater than the 'I', and which can produce salvation for that 'I' from this world of suffering. The devotion represents a belief in something that is capable of performing miracles with respect to the 'I'. It assumes a faith in the liberating properties of that which is 'greater than', with its perceived miracle-making capabilities. Devotion can be likened to the desire to be able to breathe under water. If one can do so then an entirely new universe (of the watery world) opens. If that which one is devoted to represents the truth, then such may be possible, just as it has become possible to experience the watery world via the help of an aqualung.

Faith in the 'other' means a corresponding relinquishing of self will, of the I-concept, so that a greater 'I' can assume control. It is one method to liberation, if that greater 'I' has attained the omniscient Buddha nature in a universal manner, manifesting so for the macrocosm. The other method is the one espoused by the doctrine of internal meditation and introspection of the nature of the personal-I, and thereby its elimination. The one who is full of faith is ever ready for the appearance of signs to help his/her sense of right direction.

When devotion turns to faith, it produces ardent aspiration on the path. Aspiration is also the driving fuel of *yogins* until they have reached their purported goal of liberation, or union with the All. Devotion can mean a steady adherence to ritual, to daily ablutions, and has its own rewards, but aspiration necessitates a steady driving will that leads the practitioner on to gain the goal. The aspiring one generally has a well-mapped road to follow to an ultimate destination.

Often with devotion, the desire-mind is also attached to what the devotee is focussed upon, thus the devotee will ignore contradictory experiences because of attachment to that idea. Devotion can thus produce many obscurations of mind, but is the foundation for the later expression of *bodhicitta*. Through devotion, *kliṣṭamanas* can be used to uplift Watery substance (of base desire) to a higher level of energy qualification, of *prāṇic* vitality. The personal will is then invested with brightly coloured, refined defilements, according to the quality of the devotion. It is thus deemed imperfect by the higher reason. The devotee always has the image of his major 'sign' (of divinity) before him, to which he pays obeisance.

A higher reason is incorporated in the devotee, for it is the antithesis of the critical concrete mind, which will not deem devotion as worthy of expressing, unless it increases carnal or sensual pleasures. The critical mind has its basis in classification and segregation, not in union, which is the objective of the devotee. Devotion generates a will directed to self-abnegation, but in a sense, at first it intensifies the I-concept, producing a sharp cleavage between the devotee and that which is devoted to. There is a dramatisation of the personal-I with respect to the more desirous 'other', the image of the 'beloved'.

The devotee applies him/herself in a similar way that most people aspire for money. The entire thought life is prostituted for this aim by the personal will, with images produced of what money shall do for the person. The devotee uses emotional energy as his money and fills the mind up with images of the objective of the devotion. The quest for personal wealth is therefore the lowest form of devotion (apart from basic sexual gratification) and is the murky breeding ground of the most basic *saṃskāras* of *kliṣṭamanas*. Here, all the resources that can be possibly amassed in the material universe, which are deemed worthy for the adornment of the needs of the 'self' concept, are rigorously sought after. The personal-I is embellished thereby with every form of attachment, fetishes of devotion to material comforts and personality indulgences.

In such base reasoning the personal-I tends to ignore any contradictory experience, or sign, and place it under a miscellaneous file of non-desirables, a type of cognised rubbish spot, or even blame others for any bad situation incurred, depending on the circumstance. This is because so much personal will has been invested upon the object of desire and the imagined images of the outcome, that the personal-I fears the loss of so much investment, and will do almost anything to prevent this loss.

The continuous fettering of attachments to all types of transience eventually produces the painful experiences that make the person wish to be freed from them and to seek salvation by attachment to concepts of divinity. The ways of union thereto are then sought, for which signs are continuously looked for. Thus, we see that the transition from desire for personal wealth to devotion for divinity, of the *dharma*, is a relatively simple step. It necessitates the painful interlude in between, of nonattachment to transience on the one side, and a consequent reattachment to things deemed permanent, e.g., concepts of Deity, on the other.

If higher abstract reasoning acts upon the personal will to curb glamours (the expressions of the extremes of the emotions generated via the Solar Plexus centre, governing the Watery Element), then a crisis situation occurs. It necessitates the consequent conversion of the thought life of the personal-I, where the bonds to long standing attachment and desires must be broken, and the right signs heeded. The state of crisis continues until what the 'I' identified as itself (its mind) becomes stabilised in the new direction of the more enlightened thoughts. All thoughts that were enchained to desire must be freed. The life process therefore changes and the purpose for life re-evaluated. Consequently, new signs (revelations) are looked for in consciousness.

Originating thoughts can help the person effect all further ideas by linking up the categories of thought into a correct sequence, engendering further light upon any subject, leading eventually to enlightenment. This necessitates above all choosing to link together unselfish thoughts, to fix them to the main trunk of the tree of life. All ideas will then be conditioned by the action of manifesting the overriding unselfish energy pattern.

If a complete revolution of thinking has manifested, because of a crisis (that changed the patterning of the entire life), then the person is much more consciously aware and weaves the lesson gained from having mastered the crisis into all future actions. The original structures of the desire-mind are consequently uprooted. The simile is that of destroying a forest of ungainly, sickly trees of thought-patterns, with their trunks of consolidated desires, main branches of subsidiary desires, twigs of various image-responses, and leaves consisting of bits of desirous information. In the new system thoughts are more streamlined, with vibrant tracks of information. They have become cogently ordered.

Sickly trees manifest because they have grown over many lives of ungainly mental activity. Their *saṃskāric* roots may be deep, but are embedded in soft soil, easily pried loose by correct enlightened activity. The trees grow in the inhospitable desert-like conditions of *saṃsāra*. The 'roots' of the Sambhogakāya Flower, on the other hand, are inverted, in that they are turned upwards into the *dharmakāya* for nourishment. That which feeds the main trunk (the Śūnyatā Eye) is therefore the Real, being the sustaining food of the imperishable *dharma*. Its main attribute is the Flower, which is accompanied by the *nāḍī* system and lesser flowers *(chakras)* of the personal-I.

The new thought-streams consist of heightened energy states. The avenues of assimilated experiences become broader and much brighter, with more intensified concepts. Once the mind has analysed the ramifications of the new thoughts, then a vastly expanded understanding radiates, branching out from the root thought. Time is needed for such a revolution in thinking to manifest, as each affected thought must be understood and each change carefully imprinted in consciousness.

Devotion leads to *aspiration*, which necessitates the use of the personal will to sacrifice things no longer needed in the life of the personal-I, so that higher identifications with divinity or enlightenment states can be made possible. We therefore have the engendering of *bodhicitta*, which from this perspective is the child of *kliṣṭamanas*.

Sacrifice sanctifies and makes engendering refined types of *prāṇas* possible; eventually even those stemming via *śūnyatā,* that cause the destruction of all ego-clinging, the concept of the 'I'. The I-consciousness then stands in its place, and this consciousness inadvertently experiences the reality of the Clear Light, which inevitably leads to its own death. Consciousness has become supplanted with something far vaster, the universal Mind of *dharmakāya.*

Signs can also be created by the thinking person. They are seeded to take root and flower in a future life (even if one is not aware of the process). They are patterns of thought on a given subject that change the habits of a person.

An example that can be given concerns a person who found that when he walked down the street and saw a particular gnarled tree, it would generally prompt him to worry about the need to possess much money, because of the power and material comforts money brings, for which ever more resources are needed. Later however, he seeks to eliminate such concerns. For one reason or other his thinking has been revolutionised via a crisis that instigated a revelation that little is needed apart from basic survival needs and for shelter, that instead of avaricious pursuits time should be devoted towards religious and altruistic activity. Now when looking at that tree it helps stimulate the new thoughts. The room in his mind is spacious enough to hold many lofty ideals if his thoughts have been uplifted by faith, devotion, and aspiration.

Inevitably there are drastic effects upon his daily life and changes to his immediate environment to take into account when unselfish attitudes manifest. This will affect the nature of the way resources are manipulated, depending upon the degree of his newfound dispassion towards money. A crisis situation has been mastered allowing the former lifestyle to be sacrificed to build the new, whilst evoking love for images of his perspective future and possibility of success.

In a future life his reincarnation may see a similar type of tree, and this may spark in that consciousness a remembrance (signs) of altruistic thoughts, now relegated to the new life circumstances. The tree being a spark awakening the image sown from the former life when consciousness was transformed, and now bears fruit as a sign, a voiceless command, signifying great beneficence or change in that life.

9

The Nature of Light

The intensity of light

The meaning of light in relation to sight is important in the study of consciousness. When we are vivified by experiences we move from a point of dark existence (our ignorance) into forms of light. The light increasingly grows around the point we represent, so that inevitably the domain of the dark breaks down. Light consumes the darkness of space. Because darkness shrinks whilst light grows, it can be assumed that an evolutionary relationship exists between the two qualities. Light evolves from a point in the past to future radiant glory. The accumulation of awareness brightens up the whole.

The emanation of light can be considered as an ability to consume darkness. If that darkness is defined as ignorance, then the projection of light is the annihilation of ignorance, which concerns the accumulation of knowledge. As knowledge necessitates gaining experiences, so the emanation of light represents the progress of the experience that delineates consciousness. The strength of the consciousness thus concerns the amount of light that it contains. The stronger the vibrancy of light, the more intense the consciousness. Intensity concerns resoluteness, the amount of energy or force one possess to overcome anything.

The intensity of light possessed by a Bodhisattva that is utilised to overcome the ignorance around can be considered a *saṃskāra*, in the sense that the pathways for its development can be recalled from a past life in the way that the emotions are. Such intensity is not the normal equipment of an average person. Strong desire or personal will is evidenced instead. Intensity is a strong motivational force that overcomes all adversity preventing the liberation of consciousness. In a normal mind such a force would intensify fanaticism and desires; the substance of such a mind being too dull to handle the potency concerned. Normal people can, however, hold intelligence and strong emotions. Vacillating mental-emotions are then what is normally reckoned with. (There are always exceptions to the norm.) The difference between strong emotions and intensity is that the emotions are generally forceful, turbulent forces that manifest rather erratically depending upon stimulus, whereas intensity is a strong, steady, continuous pressure towards rarefying consciousness.

Intensity is an energy descending from the *ārupa* (formless) levels of perception. The Bodhisattva has spent many lifetimes in meditative equipoise, projecting links upwards to higher consciousness states, and receiving the descent of refined spaciousness that transforms consciousness. Increasingly refined consciousness-expansions produce contact with intense energy sources. They pour through the meditation-Mind, allowing it to be self-sustaining because their intensity produces an easily maintained stabilised *dhyāna*. This allows *yogins* to sit for long periods of time without distractions interfering with their meditation. When directed to the *chakras* the energies dynamically expand their scope of activity and increases their receptivity to subtler perceptions. The energy awakens their inherent powers *(siddhis)*.

Such meditators have projected consciousness-links *(antaḥkaraṇas)* upward to the formless realms, producing a downward response of energies and revelations. The intensity, quality, and quantity of such responses directly relate to the degree of attainment of the Bodhisattva. Thus they govern the extent of the Bodhisattva's ability to serve all beings.

Though such links are eliminated upon the death of the physical vehicle, what has been gained by them is retained by the Sambhogakāya Flower that qualifies the Bodhisattva's consciousness. When that Bodhisattva reincarnates, the Sambhogakāya Flower gradually projects into his/her mind the consciousness-links that were developed in former lives. Through these links the Bodhisattva then gains the force of driving energy and revelations that push him/her onwards upon the new course of this life, which is a continuation of the past life's endeavours.[1] Thus the Bodhisattva's intensity is another factor signifying the existence of a soul-form. What is projected differs somewhat from a *saṃskāra*, as a *saṃskāra* is viewed as a bundle of aggregates (an appearance of phenomena), whereas the purpose of the intensity is towards the transformation (or destruction) of such appearances. The Bodhisattva then builds upon what is already strongly established, thereby progressing along the upward way (*bhūmis*) to Buddhahood.

Light can be perceived as an energy that integrates the separated parts of a *maṇḍala* into unity. In producing the complete picture it colours those parts with the characteristics that distinguish them, by which their qualities can be analysed. The knife of right discriminatory awareness utilises light to segregate images of the past so that the undesirable ones can be transformed, facilitating the production of revelatory awareness. Inevitably, light eliminates *saṃskāras* that do not produce enlightenment. The tendency of light to produce the revelation of future forms that can be known manifests as symbols of life. Pictures in the mind are created of future possibilities, causing arenas of ignorance to be illuminated, allowing more intense forms of light to eventually prevail. Forms of darkness (of grey or darkened thought) recede into a void as greater intensities of light are projected to arenas of consciousness that were dimly lit. The resistant substance of ignorant, reactionary and rigid thinking, need intense forms of light to overpower it. As consciousness is accordingly illumined, then conscious expansion into arenas not dreamed of before becomes possible, allowing more darkness to be conquered. The progress to enlightenment thereby ensues.

The Void is thus ultimately illuminated, according to the extent that darkness receded. *Śūnyatā* is revealed in the Clear Light of the adamantine vision that remains. The Void can be visualised with the Eye that has developed the capacity to withstand its potency. What once was in darkness is now embodied Light.

---

1 Note that the Bodhisattvas of the higher *bhūmis* have evolved past the stage of needing to possess such a Flower, nevertheless the same principle applies. In such a case it is the Mind of the Bodhisattva itself upon the *dharmakāyic* realms that projects the impressions through the consciousness-links. Such a one therefore creates a *sambhogakāya* form to manifest purpose for any incarnation.

In developing the intensity of practice, the process of clarifying the mind proceeds with increasing fervour. An accelerating momentum proceeds as the armies of light self-replicate in increasingly greater numbers to counter the darkness. The more one truly knows, the faster information is revealed to the mind and the quicker the mind can build bases for further vaster expansion into revelatory truth. The process continues until there is no further need for such expansion and the Space then revealed is the Void.

Light, Love and *citta*

The abovementioned intensity is the energy fuelled by the characteristics of *Love,* viewed as a compassionate though dispassionate force. Clarification proceeds apace when engendering the qualities of Love, as Love is 'unobscured and not a subject of moralizing'. The Love developed therefore produces unadulterated truth. Mind (the quality of light generated) and Love must awaken together to produce liberation. The intensification of the energy of Love therefore eventually produces the Clear Light of Mind through which all can be revealed instantaneously, once the mind has been sufficiently developed to hold the vision. The mind is needed for right understanding, to eradicate the darkness of wrongly sequenced *cittavṛtti,*[2] and the Heart's Mind is needed to integrate all separate parts into unity. Love is produced through right action, skilful means in the field of service work, based on meditative insight. Together Love and light generate *bodhicitta,* the basis of enlightenment.

The process here outlined therefore concerns the way *bodhicitta* is evoked. Meditative concentration is necessary to keep the mind steady in such a way that one can see in light the revelation of what needs to be done. The developed intensity of the mind facilitates the process. If there is little or no intensity, then the substance of the mind can be too sluggish, changeable, turbulent, wispy or distracted to be controlled. Ignorance, and the related darkness are then the dominant factors. If control is for only relatively short periods then not much can be revealed.

We should look deeper into the concept of the meaning of light and its relation to consciousness because of its importance in the process of

---

2 Modifications of mental substance.

gaining enlightenment. The concepts should be made lucid, to hopefully eliminate many controversies in Buddhism. Here a quotation from the book by Marion L. Matics may be useful.

> Without an object, reasoned Candrakīrti, what can thought (Citta) know? No thought is known which is not caused by an object, no object can be known without thought. If thought claims to know thought—to be self-known *(svasaṁvitti),* division is made between knower and known, between cause and object. "Even the sharpest sword cannot cut itself; the fingertips cannot be touched by the same fingertips. Citta does not know itself."[3] This is the argument repeated by Śāntideva, and, in addition, since the Vijñānavāda especially compared the self-luminous Citta to a lamp which shines in darkness, he may very well have had in the background of his learning this more ancient statement from the Pali Canon, one of the many wherein the Buddha declared the unreality of the *skandhas:* "Depending on the oil and the wick does the light of the lamp burn; it is neither in the one nor in the other, nor anything in itself; phenomena are, likewise, nothing in themselves. All things are unreal; they are deceptions; *Nibbāna* is the only truth."[4]
>
> Likewise, one's 'self' (the false unity dependent upon the combined *skandhas)* is not self-conscious without objectification. The Vijñānavādin thesis that "the self is like a lamp which illuminates" cannot be maintained.[5] The flame of the lamp causes light in darkness or it does not cause light. If the lamp is not in darkness there is nothing to illuminate, so it does not cause light. If the lamp is in darkness it still does not cause light, because darkness cannot make itself light and still be darkness. Light is light and cannot make itself dark; dark is dark and cannot make itself light. If, on the phenomenal plane, one sees that a lamp illuminates, this is affirmed by knowledge, or by consciousness of an object to be illuminated, but to say that intelligence *(buddhi)* illuminates, is meaningless in that it is affirmed by nothing, i.e., it has no cause or object. "That it is illuminated or not illuminated, as long as it is seen by no one whatsoever, is as uselessly affirmed as the charm of a barren woman's daughter."[6]....The statement that the

3 Quotation given: *Mūla-madhyamaka-kārikā-vṛtti,* 61 ff.

4 *Majjima-nikāya,* III, 245, Dialogue 140, edited by Murti, 50.

5 Footnote given: *Bodhicaryāvatāra, Ch. IX, v. 18.*

6 Marion L. Matics, *Entering the Path of Enlightenment, The Bodhicaryāvatāra of the Buddhist Poet Śāntideva,* (George Allen & Urwin. London, 1970), 115-116. Footnote given: *Bodhicaryāvatāra, Ch. IX, v. 27, et passim.*

mind is or not as a blazing lamp is in itself of no significance. If no one has knowledge of it, how can it be said to be? Why should it be affirmed at all? Yet it is noteworthy that the very point which is denied by Śāntideva is capable of interpretation as *Tathatā* (Such-ness) in the *Mahāyānaśraddhotpāda-śāstra* of Aśvaghoṣa, and in Ch'an it becomes the very key to reality[7]...Regardless of inconsistency, however, Śāntideva's method is that which is clearly stated by Candrakīrti: "The adversary, accustomed to think that the eye sees, is refuted by his own proof—even by inference."[8] The only possible justification could be the arguments cited in favour of *upāya.*[9]

In any case, it is not the *pramāṇas* which are the principal victims of Śāntideva's criticism of the Vijñānavāda, but the concept of the Citta itself, the psychic apparatus which is the source of logical thinking, and which is supposed by the Vijñānavādins to be self-evident. In various forms he repeats his basic argument that Citta is only Māyā. If there is no object of thought, there is no thought. If one says that the thing that is not Māyā is thought, then thought is made to be non-existent. If that which is seen is Māyā, then so is the one who sees, for the one who sees (or, for that matter the one who thinks) is made to be dependent upon the non-existent. When causes are cut off, there is no more Māyā, no more Saṁvṛtti. "As soon as there is no moving to and fro, by what means is Māyā perceived?"[10] In this way, Enlightenment is discovered to rest far beyond the illusionary power possessed by Citta, and what is called logical thought is superseded by Prajñā.[11]

First in relation to the statement:

If thought claims to know thought—to be self-known (*svasaṁvitti*), division is made between knower and known, between cause and object. "Even the sharpest sword cannot cut itself; the fingertips cannot be touched by the same fingertips. Citta does not know itself."

The error here is that one cannot really compare the process associated with thinking to mere physical objects. They can only be

7 Ibid., 116-117.

8 Footnote given: *Mūla-madhyamaka-kārikā-vṛtti,* 34.

9 Note that *upāya* means skilful means.

10 Footnote given: *Bodhicaryāvatāra, Ch. IX, v. 15.*

11 Matics, 119-20.

partially correlated. It appears that Candrakīrti also assumes that the substance of the mind (i.e., of thoughts) is homogeneous, when it is not. If the mind was homogeneous, i.e., there was no differentiation of thought-forms, or levels of the substance *(citta)* contained within it, then his assumption would be correct. However, it is composed of myriads of little 'unitaries', the images (thought-bubbles) that can be considered 'selves', and any of these can be utilised to 'know' the other. Thus one aspect or portion of *citta* can be used by the mind to analyse the contents of another aspect. This means that *citta* can come to 'know itself', providing that there is a higher consciousness directing the process of recalling past thoughts (streams and pools of *citta*) for the 'knowing' of thoughts. *Citta* may indeed be an attribute of *māyā,* but it has a duration of existence, thus an 'object of thought' for that duration, allowing valid experiences (cognition) to be derived. Without it there can be no quest for enlightenment. Consequently *citta* is the basis for the derivation of *śūnyatā,* hence cannot be arbitrarily dismissed.

There are two distinct divisions of mind dealt with earlier to take into account. First we have the lower empirical mind, organised according to patterns of the *cittavṛtti* (modifications of the mind) that it is composed of. It is to this substance that Candrakīrti's arguments are directed. He is partially correct here in that the mind utilising this substance has limitations in its ability to self-analyse to gain an overview of itself. It reacts to sense impressions and can order the sequences of sense-impressions as it desires, as well as recall those from past actions. It cannot rise above itself to view the entire process *in toto,* the higher abstract Mind however can and does. It is not conditioned by this *cittavṛtti,* its substance is *manasic* and conditioned by *svabhāva* as explained earlier. This refers to the 'intrinsic Fiery substance that is Void of the vicissitudes of mind' and which is the subjective foundation of the *ālayavijñāna. Manas* clothes *svabhāva* with the attributes of Mind, whereas *cittavṛtti* is the substance of sense-consciousness modified as a consequence of the activity of *pravṛttivijñāna* (intelligence). The gain of both types of activity is stored as the *ālayavijñāna.* This gain is that obtained via sense-consciousness, plus that experienced via the *śūnyatā-saṃsāra* nexus. This constitutes the dual aspect of mind/Mind and makes enlightenment possible, translated here in terms of the all-knowingness of a high level Bodhisattva or the omniscience of a Buddha.

The overview is instantaneously seen in all things by an enlightened one, certainly of the concrete vacillations of the substance *(citta)* of an ordinary mind. *Manas* is constituted both of *kliṣṭamanas* and *pravṛttivijñāna* in the lower strata of mind, the distilled aspects ('perfumes') of which are then integrated with aspects of the *dharmakāya* within the abstracted strata of Mind. (The *dharmakāya* hence is carried by the *svabhāva* as it conditions *manas*.) The sum then is incorporated in the store *(ālaya)* of consciousness (*ālayavijñāna*). As well as the two major divisions, one can also discern seven different densities (layers) of mind/Mind, to take into account.[12] Four are concrete and three are abstract. These layers can be considered 'fingers' of the same hand of *manas/citta* that can touch each other. The higher three strata of Mind can be considered to function as the ambidextrous thumb, and the lower four concreted empirical layers as the remaining fingers.

There is thus definitely a division made between knower and known, between cause and object, because one aspect of the mind, one unitary thought stream, takes on the attributes of the analyser, the knower, and the other to be analysed, the knowable. That which is knowable can extend to the domain of the sense-perceptions. The gain in knowledge is then correlated by the mind, or the I-consciousness (Mind) if need be, with respect to what is of value to it, or whether it is to be disregarded. Because different thoughts can interrelate via the different layers of substance constituting the thought-bubbles, some thoughts can be discarded, others added on to or refined. All philosophers work in this way, and Candrakīrti certainly did, otherwise he would have very little of value to say to any other thinking person.

If there was no differentiation ('division') of thought-forms[13] (noting also that thoughts are things) then there could be no individualised thoughts about any subject. Ideas could then not arise and be thought out to a conclusion, nor could there be memory of particular images or scenarios of the past. Then all would be but a blur, a meaningless

12 See Volume 4, chapter 1, entitled 'Layers of Mind' for detail.

13 Commenting here upon the statement given above: 'No thought is known which is not caused by an object, no object can be known without thought. If thought claims to know thought—to be self-known *(svasaṁvitti)*, division is made between knower and known, between cause and object'.

running commentary of a mind-continuum, from which the mind could retrieve nothing at all, because to be able to do so necessitates individuation, clearly defined thought-forms and structures built into the mind, i.e., non-homogeneity. Indeed, the prime function of the mind is its categorisation ability—to be able to put things into hypothetical boxes, clearly labelled as being this and that. Thus it names the things it contains, and it does so for physical plane objects too. The analogy used of the sword cutting itself, or the idea of the same fingertip touching itself, thus does not work with the mind. Rather, the truth is that it is more like two fingers (different thoughts) touching each other, that can also touch the thoughts ('fingers') of any other human being if it needs to. (The function of telepathy.) Also, the sword (of discursive mind) need not cut itself, as it can be presented with a host of other things (thought-bubbles) to cut (analyse).

The reality is that thoughts can thus analyse other thoughts and come to know their meaning, even the thoughts of other's presented to it, such as those of Candrakīrti. However, to do so a prime director is needed, an organiser of the thought-streams and the 'bubbles' within them. Such is organised by the Sambhogakāya Flower. Candrakīrti is correct in his assumption that thoughts by themselves can do nothing, but if an overriding Mind exists, even an organising empirical mind, information can be extracted from the *citta,* and thought-bubbles reorganised according to the will of the organising entity. Such an entity can be considered a 'self'. Without the existence of such 'selves', no one would be able to think. That people can think therefore proves the existence of a 'self', even if governed by the laws of *māyā.*

Through analysis of 'the other' in this way an organising mind also gains the ability of self-analysis. It utilises the gain from analysis of categories of things, which it then projects via its own *cittavṛtti* in order to analyse it. However, as stated, to gain a complete view it must stand above its streams of *citta* and bubbles of thought by utilising the abstracting function of the higher Mind. Mind builds a compound image for this complete view (qualified by differing categories of light) by experiencing the *citta,* and thus it comes to know. Analysis can consist of more than just utilising what is directly 'caused by an object'. It constitutes projecting the information from such perceptions into domains or realms far beyond the image of what was directly perceived: the realm of the imagination, to the *sambhogakāya* forms of manifesting divinity, or even to the foundation of experiencing the *dharmakāya*. Thoughts consequently can be transmuted or transmogrified.

It should also be noted that the substance constituting the things composing a thought is different from that constituting the objects that are said to cause it, unless that object be another thought. Therefore just because an object is said to cause a thought, there is no reason to presume that they should not be separate. Once the mind has cognised the existence of an object it catalogues it in terms of the nature of the substance of its own composition, not that of the object. The two forms of substance are different, they obey different laws. Physical substance cannot move with the speed of thought, the substance of thought is not bound by gravity, etc. The mind can also instantly modify the substance (images) contained in its domain, but cannot do so with respect to physical plane objects.

The Vijñānavādin thesis that 'the self is like a lamp which illuminates' therefore, *can* be maintained. Here the term 'the self' refers to the organising mind and its contents. From the analysis of the nature of light above, we can see that each thought-form is really lighted substance that obliterates an arena of darkness, with respect to that which the content of the thought-form reveals. The substance that 'burns' is the *citta* itself. It is the fuel for the Fire, but rather than being consumed (as energy cannot be destroyed), it becomes more refined, thus entering a higher strata of the domain of mind/Mind, if it is fanned with energy (lighted substance) from above. The entire mind structure therefore is illumined, because all of its myriad thoughts are interrelated and coordinated within the boundaries of the thinking process of that mind. Furthermore, that illumined mind can analyse things, other thought structures, and also itself, and is free to reject therein arenas of (relative) darkness, so the light that shines from it becomes brighter, like a 'lamp which illuminates'. There cannot be any other way for it, otherwise no light could exist anywhere, and ignorance cannot be defeated. Therefore no evolution could proceed from which a Bodhisattva could arise.

It is the quality of the light emanating from a mind that allows another mind structure to quickly determine its degree of attainment, and its major characteristics or qualifications. The light of the mind continually grows, because for humanity one of the fundamental instincts is that of growth towards knowledge. When the needed intensity of the mind is eventually reached, we have more than a lamp, we have a blazing sun beaming out its revelatory awareness in the realms of Mind. This does not deny the statement 'All things are unreal; they are deceptions', because the nature of such deceptions are then revealed in the light, which is the only way anything can be seen. Light may be 'neither in the one nor in the other',[14] with respect to 'the oil' (here referring to phenomena that stimulates mental images) or 'the wick', which refers to the sense-perceptors that bring the impressions garnered from phenomena to the mind (the lamp). It simply *is* the actuality of the substance of mind.[15]

Degrees of darkness

Next I shall analyse the statement:

> The flame of the lamp causes light in darkness or it does not cause light. If the lamp is not in darkness there is nothing to illuminate, so it does not cause light. If the lamp is in darkness it still does not cause light, because darkness cannot make itself light and still be darkness. Light is light and cannot make itself dark; dark is dark and cannot make itself light.

This simile of the lamp should incorporate (when comparing it to *citta)* the fact that *citta* is self-illuminating, and that it can grow brighter as needed, thus overcoming different degrees of darkness. The statement 'Light is light and cannot make itself dark; dark is dark and cannot make itself light' needs to account for the different intensities and hues of light that can manifest. The expanse of darkness automatically changes as the light changes. The darkness is all pervasive until the appearance of light. Then the extent of the darkness depends upon the light's intensity or hue and to the degree that it might change, which in

---

14 With reference to the phrase 'Depending on the oil and the wick does the light of the lamp burn; it is neither in the one nor in the other'.

15 There are substantial ontological implications here if physical plane light is included in the definition.

the case of our analogy represents the activity of the mind. It determines how much light enters its arena of darkness to counter ignorance. In fact, the mind can generate light from out of the relative darkness of its own substance. The phrase 'darkness cannot make itself light and still be darkness' is correct as darkness simply cannot make itself light. Darkness is defined as a partial or complete absence of light. Darkness can do nothing to cause the appearance of light. The nature of such an appearance determines the extent of darkness. The candlelight simply transforms the darkness, to reveal what it veils by means of light.

Just as there are differing degrees or intensities of light so there are differing forms of darkness. As a candle light appears dark in the light of a 1,000 Watt neon arc light, so the phrase 'Light is light and cannot make itself dark' is conditional, as it depends upon where that light is situated and the factors that can change the degree of its intensity. Its intensity can be dimmed through lessening the energy input. Similarly, a formerly bright consciousness that undertakes a course of sensual intoxication or ignorant presumptions becomes thereby dimmed. The light of the consciousness of an intellectual person is 'dark' when compared to that of an enlightened being, yet to his contemporaries in normal human society (with their dull consciousnesses) this intelligent person is a great luminary.

Darkness is consumed by light, relatively so by a candle flame, giving a weak yellow-orange light, that has a limited range, according to the intensity of the flame. When the flame is extinguished then the darkness resumes its former territory. However, as above-stated, one simply cannot relate the imagery of the dense physical world to the field of consciousness. There are different laws and processes at work. For instance, if a candle is snuffed then darkness again appears, but with consciousness this is not the case, consciousness persists (for instance at the death of a person) and can remember what was formerly illumined when needed. Therefore the light of the candle can never really be snuffed in consciousness. Even in the natural world the energy that the candle emitted still persists long after the candlelight was extinguished, and there is always the possibility of relighting it. In any case, the consciousness knows what the light had revealed and no longer needs that light if it merely wishes to remember what was before that candle was snuffed.

One can perceive relative degrees of darkness. Thus there is the darkness of a moonlit night, the darkness of a star-filled night, the darkness of a cloudy night, and the complete darkness inside a locked, windowless room at night. The degree of darkness depends upon the nature of the receptors one possesses to perceive. It also depends upon the nature of the consciousness one has to translate the impressions into images whereby one can see. A bat can 'see' even in the pitch blackness of a cave with its sonar mechanism. To humans the cave is black, but not so for bats. The 'darkness' does not need to make itself light in order for us to perceive light; simply the faculties of consciousness must have some mechanism to perceive what it is that the darkness veils. The mechanism of the appearance of light or sonar both work to overcome darkness. *Siddhis* that transcend the limitations of physical plane eyes could also be developed for such a function. As consciousness is lighted substance, the faculty of consciousness can illuminate darkness, or any arena of it, if it so wills.

From the above perspective, the Buddha's statement: 'Depending on the oil and the wick does the light of the lamp burn', can be interpreted differently than before. Consciousness here ('the light of the lamp') utilises the 'oil', the substance of the mind, which is lighted, and the 'wick' is the carrier of the perceptions to be analysed, be it of physical plane phenomena, or another thought. The wick consuming the oil refers to the process that allows consciousness to understand the nature of what it is perceiving. When done to completion, where nothing more can be learned, then the wick is redundant. The lamp here represents the brain, the container of the oil and wick, and being 'in darkness it still does not cause light'. Of itself it can do nothing, because consciousness is the light, the 'hand' that strikes the match to consume the darkness, to thereby intensify its own quota of light. From this perspective we see that light feeds upon darkness, and it grows in strength as the darkness recedes.

With respect to thoughts, it can also be said that being phenomenological they are but signposts upon the road to enlightenment and form a support or basis for its functioning. They are neither the enlightenment, or the *māyā* per se if they eliminate ignorance, but are also 'not anything in itself', if they are perceived as part of the illusionality of *saṃsāra.*

Śāntideva misses the point in this extract:

> If, on the phenomenal plane, one sees that a lamp illuminates, this is affirmed by knowledge, or by consciousness of an object to be illuminated, but to say that intelligence (*buddhi*) illuminates, is meaningless in that it is affirmed by nothing, i.e., it has no cause or object. "That it is illuminated or not illuminated, as long as it is seen by no one whatsoever, is as uselessly affirmed as the charm of a barren woman's daughter."

Superficially he is correct because if there was no consciousness then it does not matter what is happening anywhere in the universe, if nothing is cognising it then it equates to not having happened at all. The fact 'that intelligence *(buddhi)* illuminates' is however meaningful in itself. It does not need another mind to perceive it, just as the sun's illumination of all upon the earth does not need the presence of eyes to notice it. It goes on illuminating whether there is night or day upon the earth, and the portion of light that happens to strike the earth at any one time is only a tiny fraction of its output of light. Likewise, if Śāntideva's consciousness is too dull to perceive the illumination of an intelligence functioning elsewhere, it does not mean that that particular mind is not spreading light. It does not need to be affirmed by anything or anyone. Also, how does Śāntideva know that 'it is affirmed by nothing, i.e., it has no cause or object?' From what level of darkened sight is this cognised? Just because he was standing in comparative darkness behind a closed door, where there was light (of *buddhi*[16]) striking it, and he perceives it not, it does not mean that it is not there. Maybe he should learn how to open that door. That it has 'no cause or object' may evoke the doctrine of absolutes, but it is a spurious statement, because 'nothing' implies annihilation, and if this is not so then a 'something', such as an enlightened Mind, can affirm it.

The fact that *buddhi* illuminates can be affirmed by those with the sense-receptors, the consciousness awakening factors intact, and the *siddhis* developed, that will allow them to see the light, if they look that

16 Later this term shall be analysed and in my rendering it will be shown to mean more than just 'intelligence'; rather it signifies the nature of the illumined, enlightened mind, which exists at the *śūnyatā-saṃsāra* nexus. *Pravṛttivijñāna,* the consciousness that discriminates the sphere of objects (the intellect), is a better term to use here.

way. Just because one momentarily closes one's eyes upon something does not mean that thing does not then exist. If one does not want to see something, or can't because of dullness of mind, ignorance, or because of the fact that they have impaired sense-receptors, then indeed their affirmation of something not existing may be as useless as 'the charm of a barren woman's daughter'. For Śāntideva it may be this way with respect to his ability to vision an illumined mind, but he should not project his shortcomings in this respect upon others. All appropriately illumined minds can 'see' this light if they wish to.

An illumined mind is illumined because light is the fundamental quality of its Fiery base substance,[17] and it has both 'cause' and 'object' in the function of perceiving. The cause is the steady evolutionary growth of the Fiery principle of mind by means of the law of *karma*, the development of the related *saṃskāras*, and the mode of expression of developing intensity. The object is whatever is perceived at any time. The inevitable objective is the attainment of Buddhahood by means of the proper utilisation of the mind's functions. Indeed, this is the only way that Buddhahood can be obtained.

If Śāntideva wants to look just at the principle of absolutes (*śūnyatā*) and state that just this exists, therefore nothing in *saṃsāra* exists, or has functionality, then he is denying the basic identity of *śūnyatā* with *saṃsāra* and of his own existence. In such a case it is pointless for him to have written one word, and indeed naïve to have done so.

The relativity of *māyā*

The question 'As soon as there is no moving to and fro, by what means is Māyā perceived?' is valid. What is also implied in the question is the fact that *māyā* exists as long as there are minds existing that are willing to reason between this and that, i.e., utilising mind-substance moving 'to and fro'. Whilst *māyā* exists we must reside in it, evolve through it, and come to an enlightened stance once we have transformed it. Thus the conventional truth of the evolution of mind and its relation to *māyā* is acknowledged, but the essential role *māyā* plays in the inevitable experience of *śūnyatā* is normally quickly glossed over by the theoreticians.

17 Similarly the sun is autoluminous.

To those that think like Śāntideva, I say that you are killing me and all others with this form of Buddhist philosophy. This is because the logic effectively denies our endeavours to live, to gain experiential growth, to develop *bodhicitta*, to strive towards becoming a Bodhisattva. You deny the existence of our developing minds that must register all of this as it greets the *māyā* of our lives. Without human minds there is no humanity, but you refute the mind, with your human minds very busy advocating your thesis of absolutes. You try to tell me that what I have been learning throughout my life, all that my developing mind apprehended was in fact *māyā*. This may be so, as *māyā* is incorporated in any state of enlightened perception that I may have developed at any time.

The fact that something is or stands in *māyā* does not invalidate its usefulness or necessity along the path of gaining enlightenment. One can strive to overcome, to attain clearer insights into the nature of reality, and to do so, one must compare the relative *māyā* developed in the past with what is possessed in the now. *Māyā* is an essential ingredient for the attainment of enlightenment. What I now posses was what twenty years ago stood in the future. What was then apprehended was still a form of light, though relatively in darkness. My consciousness was further from the truth than it presently is. Although my experiences then where not as cogently perceptive as now, does it make what I am now experiencing still *māyā* in relation to then? The present lucidity of consciousness was not known. Certainly my consciousness has considerably developed during the subsequent twenty years of meditation. In fact, all we see is part of an exponential growth from a state of relative darkness to one of a more intense form of light. We have a process of the lessening of darkness, where darkness is equated with *māyā*.

What is being perceived now and what was perceived then are not the only possible realities needed for attainment. Outside of this there is that which consciousness has not experienced, hence comprehended, and therefore cannot truly acknowledge to be real. What has not been experienced does not presently exist in consciousness, but there lies the immanency of an ultimate reality. In comparison to my former state twenty years ago, the intensity and clarity of the blaze of light of the mind has developed, and has been held steady for the revelation of all that yet remains hidden. Still, what is *outside* of what I perceive now, being different in certain respects to what I do perceive and that which may be perceived in the future, is a further 'ultimate reality', where *śūnyatā* is but a foundation. It is pure potential of what has not been discovered in this moment but may be in the future. Though I may be fully enlightened ten years from now, still another ultimate reality will then exist in the future. The signposts of what is ultimate reality will have shifted accordingly. There consequently is no 'ultimate', only a moving scenario of relativities. The concept of *māyā* can therefore transmogrify in line with that moving scenario.

The perception of *nirvāṇa*

One should beware of perceiving *nirvāṇa* (or *śūnyatā)* as a zone of passivity, a type of blissful experience of nothingness. This is far from the truth. An example of such interpretation is found in the introduction to Obermiller's translation of the *Uttaratantra of Maitreya.*

> Although a Bodhisattva has in principle fulfilled all the requirements and has realised the Ultimate Truth, he does not wish that his altruistic activity should stagnate by his entering the eternally blissful but passive state of *nirvāṇa*.[18]

Nirvāṇa[19] is not a place of stagnation where a Bodhisattva rests from compassionate activity. For a Bodhisattva it may represent an interlude wherein the necessary forces can be brought together prior to the next cyclic manifestation. For others, *śūnyatā* represents the Void experienced as the natural state of Mind whilst being compassionately active. Therefore it is not a state of passivity, but rather of dynamic serenity. It may be 'eternally blissful', but such a concept loses its meaning therein. When a Bodhisattva enters *nirvāṇa per se,* it means that his/her focus of compassionate activity has moved away from being purely concerned with humanity, and can look to cosmic vistas. This is a far greater field of service than hitherto possible, for which an extended period of *dhyāna* is needed. Consciousness has been

---

18 E. Obermiller (trans.), *The Uttaratantra of Maitreya,* (Sri Satguru Publications, Delhi, 1997), 18.

19 Here the term *nirvāṇa* is used in lieu of *śūnyatā.*

transcended. However, if *śūnyatā* is the conception here then it refers to a dynamic state of intensely radiant blissful awareness that is detached from *saṃsāra*. This 'ultimate truth' manifests in relation to human consciousness, which is what Buddhist philosophers of the past thought in terms of. This was the limit of their field of experience, explainable in terms of words and concepts related to the interested populace.

Śūnyatā is at-oned with the omnipresent All, and *nirvāṇa* represents the means to further explore the dimensions of such a multidimensional Space. *Nirvāṇa* consequently refers to what must still be experienced, but cannot be done so upon earth, hence a Buddha evolves to travel thus to overcome further ramifications of *māyā*. (There are different types of Buddhas, not just *mānuśi* Buddhas that incarnate to teach humanity.) What has not been experienced in cosmos still exists as a potential, for which a Buddha 'strives' to Know. As a human unit upon earth strives to know more, so it is for a 'thus gone' one embracing *parinirvāṇa* as he travels through cosmos. Ever higher enlightened states await. *Śūnyatā* can be conceived of as the base substance allowing further expansive embrace of a Buddha-Mind in cosmos.

Buddhists are not accustomed to thinking in such terms, but must broaden their epistemic and eschatological thought to accommodate further revelatory concepts concerning the nature of ultimate truth and its relation to cosmos and the Dharmakāya Way.

For the ability to inevitably travel through cosmic space all humans possess a *tathāgatagarbha,* a Buddha-germ, within them. This unrealised potential is an inevitable revelatory experience. The future holds the potential and the ultimate consciousness states of reality. It contains all that is outside of what is presently perceived and therefore represents the real in terms of a vaster, more intense quality of perception than what one is presently perceiving. Therefore much exists that is outside the present categories of the perceiver and the perceived. What exists outside that which one is perceiving and which is still the object of perception exists as an effective ultimate in relation to the present. Ever vaster are the bounds of the experienceable. When one boundary (such as the earth sphere) is pierced then another subtler, vaster one appears on the event horizon. Consequently, any zone of apparent finality, such as *śūnyatā*, represents a boundary in the process of being pierced, and once 'pierced' the enlightened one moves on. Similarly for an incarnate being that moves from one experiential level of attainment to a higher one, until enlightenment is reached.

It can be said that the Mind of a perceiver that has transcended the state of perception that others are engrossed in is comparatively enlightened. That person represents the future for them, wherein the transcended part of their minds can be considered to exist as part of his/her contemplative unfoldment. This is but an extension of the philosophy regarding the doctrine of the Bodhisattvas, who are continually meditating upon our salvation from *māyā*. The more advanced the individual seeking enlightenment, the greater the level of attainment of the Bodhisattva needed to help liberate such a one. Inevitably, Buddhas appear to assist the most advanced Bodhisattvas to overcome what represents *māyā* for them. Having entered *nirvāṇa,* many are the paths that lead from that zone of bliss to conquer vast domains governed by transmogrified *māyā* in cosmos.

From the perspective that the *buddhadharma* is normally observed, it might be said that the ultimate compassionate entity that could lend a hand here is a Buddha. But an enlightened being can perceive vaster, greater 'thus gone' ones that had attained Buddhahood from ineffable past cycles long before our Buddha was even human. The inadequate term Logos (meaning 'embodied Word') is given to such a being in this treatise, be this the Logos of a planet, one who has taken a whole solar system in his field of embrace, or of a constellation or galaxy of stars. Much still needs to be revealed concerning this field of 'relative ultimates'. There are other categories of great Ones in cosmos, both male and female, for whom terminology has yet to be developed allowing proper description of the nature of the attainment or qualities developed by such Ones, and the cosmological worlds they reside in.

One cannot say that such vast meditative Mind spaces do not exist right now, it is just that 'I' (e.g., the Buddhist philosopher) is not aware of it. It may exist in my future, because the future contains the pure potential of all that is. Then I will be Realised, Awakened, thus the future holds the ultimate key to reality. A person in fact manifests self-deceit if he states that what he knows and is experiencing now is the only reality, that everything outside of his present deductions is void of truth. It may be so for that individual that admits of nothing else, but not in terms of the reality of what actually is. Certainly so if the concept of Logos is automatically denied, not because of what may or may not be perceived, but because of dogmatic assertion. Inevitably all will be revealed because the future holds the pure potentiality of the All.

Further considerations of darkness verses light

One can say that light essentially stems from darkness, because eventually darkness (ignorance, *avidyā)* evolves and transmutes into the illumination of the Bodhisattva. Such is the way of evolution. With logic such as Candrakīrti's and Śāntideva's we will find that such a being as a Buddha cannot evolve from out of the darkness of an ignorant mind, thus teach humanity anything, for they say that darkness does not have the germ of light ('dark is dark and cannot make itself light'). This is the prima facie interpretation, if ignorance is equated with darkness. It is clearly antithetical to the Buddha's teachings concerning the human ability to conquer ignorance. However, one can conclude that these eminent philosophers only had physical plane darkness in mind and not its subjective correspondence.

In reality, everything manifesting as light originated from darkness. Everything that is in darkness shall eventually be infused in light, like the cosmic dust that agglomerates to form the substance of future stars. Darkness inevitably becomes light-filled because it contains the accumulative substance that has the capacity to evolve. It represents that which can be utilised by a conscious source and converted into forms of luminosity, the attributes of the Element Fire. Darkness is not totally still or stagnant. All is in ceaseless motion, therefore darkness has movement, and movement has inherent within it that which inevitably produces light. The internal motion has an inherent radiatory effect, the atoms of substance are energetic and hence emanate the wavelengths of light, spectrums, which are their fingerprints and which can be utilised by scientists to distinguish one from the other. Photons, the elementary particles of light, can be considered to traverse the vistas of the black of space.

It should be noted that what is seen as a green chair is not green, rather every colour other than green. Being darkness, it absorbs all colours but reflects that which we see it by, but what it is not in reality, hence we see the reflected green. This type of illusion indicates the nature of the sum of *saṃsāra*. That which is black contains all colours and reflects none, so we have the colour of darkness. This is a scientific observation of the nature of *māyā*.

The Secret Doctrine by H.P. Blavatsky, an exposition of 'The Stanzas of Dzyan' (stanzas of meditation), states that at the beginning of the Universe 'Darkness alone filled the Boundless All'.[20] This 'Boundless All' being all that could be in the beginning of all things. At that time there was nothing that emanated light, just that which was proficient in the containment of all energy states within it. (This can also be another definition of the term Void.) Therein the natural interrelation between the particles of matter at first causes heat, light, then mind. The emanation of light originally concerns just a dull infra-red glow, moving to orange, then yellow and all the way to brilliant silver-white as the evolutionary epochs unfold through time. It involves the inevitable appearance of human minds, which then convert darkness to lighted substance—enlightenment. Thus is summarised the entire purpose of evolution (as far as the formed side of things is concerned). The night sky is dark space, and in it are the enlightened spheres of light (stars) that have evolved to convert dark matter. Mind has evolved from out of the darkness, being naturally segregative and collative it needs to name and categorise what it collates, and illuminates the darkness as it projects itself to know. This is an exceedingly brief account of the beginning of things. I need not delve into detail concerning this subject here, as the process of planetary formation, and the nature of evolution within our solar system is presented in *The Secret Doctrine,* but the stanzas should be properly analysed and decoded, utilising the seven keys explained in my book *Karma and the Rebirth of Consciousness.*[21]

Darkness equals ignorance, and the evolutionary process concerns the conquering or 'devouring' of ignorance, which is but the effect of the yearning to know whatever can be known.[22] All within a solar

20 H. P. Blavatsky, *The Secret Doctrine,* (Theosophical Publishing House, Madras, 1971), Vol. I (of the six volume set), 113.

21 I will later publish a treatise on the cosmological part of these stanzas.

22 The 'God' of the Christians and Jews is 'a devouring Fire', so says the Bible *(Exodus 24:17).* This 'God' is Mind, is Love, is pure radiatory energy also, for how

sphere evolve together as one, and move onwards through space. As one evolves, all inevitably must be pulled all along with that progress, be this 'one' a Bodhisattva, or a 'God' of whatever is manifest. This is the nature of the law of Love that sustains and coheres all into a unity, and the law of Love is *karma* in action.

Human evolution parallels and mimics cosmic evolution, being but a child within it. The process can be described via analogies and symbols, especially when observing the nature of the evolution of consciousness. That which nourishes and grows is conceived of in terms of light, of evolving suns (as can also the Sambhogakāya Flower be considered). Opposed to this is the material phenomena to be transformed, which disintegrates, degenerates or is resistant to evolutionary change, and which therefore can be considered aspects pertaining to darkness. The dark of the now is found in dark space, sluggish phenomena, the unenlightened brother, and intensified in the 'brother of dark face', who propagates evil as a way of life. ('Evil' here being defined as the darkness that should have been transcended but is still perpetuated.) All are yet to be converted to enlightened states of being. The process is immense and aeons pass in the conversion process upon planets such as ours.

The further light advances, the further back into the past darkness (or the origin of it) recedes. This advancement of light (with respect to consciousness) is not just how it has moved through time, but also its increase in intensity. The way things move concerns the process of transformation through time. The ability of consciousness to consume base substance with *manasic* Fire, and hence to convert darkness to light is the driving force of evolution in cosmos. Every atomic sentience is inevitably transformed thereby, as all are incorporated in either the mind of a human unit, or else in the Mind of a Logos. Through time the little sentient rivulets flow into greater sentient states until eventually rivers of consciousness are formed, allowing the actualisation of the faculty of memory and thus the ability to register time. They carry with them 'sediments', concreted thought-structures. This is one way of describing the evolutionary process.

---

else can such a being convert the substance of the all into light, in order to conquer the ignorance of the darkness in all being? Here I am utilising the adjunct that such a 'God' is but a Jina from a former cosmic evolutionary epoch.

If one travels back through the flow of time, from arenas of strong light to darkness, one gets closer to the power base of this darkness, the beginning, or originating cause of whatever is. We can then see where the currents (the *skandhas* and *saṃskāras* of origination) begin. There are five main types, associated with the five Elements and instincts.[23] The instincts are basic to all of Nature, and can be applied from the atomic realm right through to the human kingdom. (Thus for example, the laws of valency, governing chemical union, are but an expression of the instinct towards sex.)

Inevitably however, all will be seen to derive from the primacy of the fundamental energy states, of which there are three, expressed in terms of the three *guṇas. Sattva,* rhythm, dynamism, *rajas,* activity, mobility, and *tamas,* inertia. The motion is at first lethargic, cyclic and self-contained *(tamasic),* and later spiralling (as light is further engendered—*rajasic),* then the bounds of an originating cause (for any form of action) are broken with a forward progressive motion *(sattva)* that can interrelate with another such 'cause'. When such a cause comes from another external source, then this produces a reverberating pattern, so what was once producing cyclic rhythms now produces eddies in currents, in the flow of time. The greater patterns in the flow of life consume the smaller ones in their embrace. They are larger and of longer duration.

As consciousness develops, the future is gained. The cycles of activity that are not relevant in terms of the patterns of the now are dimmed in the arenas of consciousness. What is unessential recedes into darkness. Aspects of what we once knew can also be exposed to greater light, thus consciousness is raised. The rate of awareness grows as experiences increase, giving the perception that time quickens.

The energy constituting the sum of people's intellectual capacity has increased exponentially over the earth during the past century and a half, increasing people's power to think. Consequently what was once known as the highest type of wisdom, the point that had to be made, fades into the background of new advances of thought. Thus much that scientists, philosophers and sages of the new era offer has perceptively improved what was presented in earlier epochs. All is however moulded upon the paradigms of the past patterns of knowledge. The hold of

23 The five instincts are explained in Volume 5A, chapter 5.

concreted empirical information upon the consciousness of humanity must yet lessen and greater fruits of subtler, esoteric revelation be made manifest within the present momentum. The entire earth system thus evolves. Evolution means that the energy level of consciousness continually heightens. Thus computers have replaced the stone age and mechanistic implements of the past.

The substance of the mind accumulates, intensifies and becomes more vibrant as consciousness advances, and integrates with the forces from the Heart. This quickens the speed of activities upon the physical domain. The progressive evocation of light produces the awakening of consciousness, as it first illuminates all arenas of the darkness, and then eradicates it, like the blaze of a fiery sun that eliminates the night. Each point or stage in the development of consciousness can be considered to exemplify a step of history for humanity, and the steps will continue far into the future.

One's mental accumulation can liberate thought or imprison it, depending upon how the mind is used. Either way it can produce accomplishments by the personal-I on the physical plane, or in terms of pure mind stuff *(citta)* on the mental realm. We must therefore properly formulate ideas before we activate *citta* into concepts that are acted out with the skills and tools at our disposal, because there is a danger of reification, forcing thought into darkened domains. Increasing the density of pure intellectual pursuits for the aggrandisement of the 'self' concept is not advisable. It produces a *tamasic* blockage to the quickening pace of evolutionary progress, and stifles the movement for all towards greater light. This tendency must be countered with broadminded gifts of sharing. As time progresses people then become more intelligent, with greater capability of commanding rational thought in any chosen field of activity. Consequently, we can manifest physical creativity at a far faster speed, and with greater ingenuity. Accordingly, our civilisations become more complex and enlightened.

Considerations of time and mendacity

When one holds on to the past, socially or mentally, one's mind becomes 'darker', less able to command a proper train of liberating thought, to establish a clear mind. One's progress is consequently stifled. Humanity inevitably moves on, but is it not the relatively enlightened renegades that stimulate the general (base) intelligence level of humanity to rise? The majority who lack much light, who cannot bear the progress of lighted substance, generally ardently resist such endeavours, castigating and condemning such lights on their path. They often imprison them and seek their death. Thus the various levels of thought of the conscientious intelligentsia and the general work of Bodhisattvas is often doomed to abide in obscurity until a future time when the base level of the populace has risen sufficiently to accept their light. The light bearers are the residents of future potentiality for the average thinkers. The lack of clarified light in general human thought can be compared to a great nemesis or millstone upon our societies. Thus we have intolerant people possessing dogmatic, selfish, avaricious, fanatical and bigoted ideas, fed by social, religious, philosophical, and political indoctrinations.

As the future carries the general populace on to greater revelatory heights we have within that general space sluggish minds living in past time zones composed of groups of recalcitrants who hamper the process. They keep darkened areas of past reasoning alive with outmoded social mores, customs, forms of religiosity or philosophic doctrines that should have been abandoned long ago. They thereby hamper the progress of the all that try to move ahead into a progressed, speeded up time zone of consciousness momentum.

The 'past reasoning' refers to the characteristics still possessed and exaggeratedly utilised that one should have surpassed. Such characteristics (fanaticism, bigoted attitudes, etc.) are not light-engendering because they foster ignorance rather than countering or conquering it. They refer to any habit of thought, word, or deed, that has not progressed into a new, higher expression during the cycle set for it to have accomplished such action. All such qualities can also be exemplified in many of the attributes of our societies, such as to the way that the mass media works, and in general how people are spoon-fed political agendas, falsehoods and sensationalised information. Such information does not produce clear-thinking, independent thought, or a sense of compassionate responsibility.

The flippant demands of most humans have also been the downfall of many an enterprise deemed to serve the common good. The force of such demands display avaricious, emotional and sacral desires that do not permit the proper display of truth. Television, for instance, demonstrates the way that people actively assimilate large amounts of triviality made out to be all-important. The little knowledge of true value being swamped by such fare. Television replaces the clairvoyance that many possessed in ancient societies. The intelligence quotient in television programs provides little time for factual information, with the presenter inanely chatting to appeal to people's emotions. Superficiality, violence, sex, comedy, money and fiction, is the order of the day. What could have been a prime educational tool is instead used to amuse. Rarely do any programs reflect the leading edge of thinking, producing the revelations that are at the forefront of any evolving change. Attitudes must change, and hopefully our technological age will someday deliver a mechanism to divert people from sacral and emotional concerns into the higher centres demonstrating beauty and light. Such a diversion needs a future cultural revolution. People will then not be fed images based upon the lowest common denominator that the least intelligent masses want, but rather proper educational values will be sought, especially for children.

For a society where such change is possible, then selfish attitudes and common human avarice would undergo a transformation. This cannot happen with the images of the future presented by mass marketing of technological advances running riot in a violent amoral society, or what a morbid post third World War future might represent. Developed, cogent ethics for humanity is the way that civilisation's finest edifices can be sped up. Computer technology has, however, presented a means to this end.

For many, selfishness is a form of 'modernism' that bloats up their self-esteem. It is seen in the trend towards desire for more consumer goods, fashionable and expensive possessions, trendy cars, houses, clothes, technological innovations, and the like. Many think they are following a future trend, but in fact they pull into the present the tendencies (*saṃskāras*) from past epochs, of such things as possessing slaves (which modern appliances represent), various magical practices and incantations to possess power over objects and people.[24] (The power the wealthy have over all aspects of our societies.) Old avaricious

24 *Siddhis* were relatively easily developed without the forms of modern distractions we now possess.

fashions thus come to the fore with a modern dress. So darkness is perpetuated, and evolutionary progression stunted. Distortions and contortions of ungainly forms of human consciousness abound in these darkened consciousness realms.

By reiterating attitudes of the past people prevent the evolutionary flow. Ungainly aggregates congeal and hamper progress. A bright future will manifest when governmental laws are enacted that genuinely produce true equanimity in our societies, and which do not reward the avaricious in any way. Governments must actively discourage human greed, the cause of much suffering and human iniquity. (The opposite to how our societies nowadays generally educate children.) It necessitates proper proportionate sharing of the wealth of nations to the needy and the dispossessed. Thus true compassionate spirituality is engendered in our societies. Religion is of little consequence or meaning if it does not actively work to eliminate avarice in our civilisation by rightly educating people as to how it works. Here also many Buddhists are found lacking. We see ever more luxurious Monasteries and shrines built but little is actually done for the genuine welfare of the people around. Monks should learn to properly serve, to farm the land of compassionate conscious awareness for the benefit of the many.

Compassion provides the answer that alleviates the suffering of the many, whereby the present quota of multimillionaires (in their steely cages of intensified desire-mind) will become a thing of the past. The engendering of multimillionaires must become as frowned upon in the same mode as we now look upon the slave owners of the past, as dispossessing the labour of their captives. This is because no matter how it is dressed up, the amassing of such wealth in the face of the world's poverty is really manifesting forms of thievery and rapine of the wealth of the nations, a legalised theft from the common purse. Capitalistic, and our increasingly fascist societies, extort the wealth of the planet for the gain of the very few, where the common worker is forced to pay excessive rents to a rentier class, and to be debt slaves to those controlling the money supply, because of the iniquities that abound in our societies.

We have vast resources prostituted to producing war machines, and an entrenched corrupted legalistic and legislative system, keeping the extremely wealthy in power, allowing them to exploit the masses of dispossessed people. The money markets, with America being the true modern guru of this form of black magic, control this empire of greed. Militaristic might is used to bully or invade resistant nations of an imperialistic hegemon. Thus is stolen the oil, trees, natural resources of the world; impoverishing and keeping the masses destitute. The true value of the labour of the multitudes and of farmers (especially in the Third World) is also stolen, so that goods can be produced at very little cost to entrepreneurs. This allows the capitalistic elite to continue bathing in their ungainly wealth. Thus the darkness, the habit-patterns of past societies, such as the Roman empire, reinvent themselves anew. The only real change being the technological forms, and psychological or scientific jargon that disguises the old avarice. Whole societies have thus reincarnated, perpetuating old attitudes in modern garb. Buddhists specifically, and all other religiously minded people, need to seriously look to the compassionate tenets of their doctrines and begin to act like Bodhisattvas to effect the needed changes in our societies. They need to overcome their forms of complacency and insouciance, to make their religions alive in the *dharma,* by taking proactive steps to move people's minds away from the past and into the bright future of enlightened possibilities.

From an amoeba to the universe of time

Time relates to the relationship between the microcosm of consciousness and the macrocosm of Being. Time is a determining factor between cause and effect. Time expresses comparisons in consciousness. Time delineates the interrelation between individualities. The human unit can speed up the processing of time when consciousness strives to incorporate the higher strata of Mind. Lightning fast can ideas then be processed and the main event quickly analysed. Individuality then merges into the universality of the omnipresent whole. This is measured in relation to the snail-like events happening in the physical domain, yet when consciousness is abstracted elsewhere such events can be very fleeting indeed. One nevertheless enters a timeless state in the after-death because then one resides purely in consciousness, where there are no physical plane events to identify with.

The concept of time cannot, however, be denied and must be utilised in all temporal considerations, even as the Buddha did. As David J. Kalupahana states:

> The Buddha described time and temporality in a more empirical way when he said that the arising of phenomena, the change of what has come to be and their cessation are evident. The three temporal periods of past *(atī ta)*, present *(puccuppanna)*, and future *(anāgata)* in relation to phenomena were thus recognized. To refer back to the discourse on "Linguistic Conventions" *(Niruttipatha)* mentioned earlier, the Buddha even examined the three linguistic conventions *(adhivacana)* such as "existed" *(ahosti)*, "exists" *(atthi)* and "will exist" *(bhavissati)*, pointing out that these should not be ignored.[25]

An integrated whole evolves from an amoeba-like sentience to the intricate human mind. Time affects the human mind, but not the amoeba's sentience, yet the amoeba evolves through time. When it needs to progress it morphs into a more advanced entity. It represents but a stage in the development of mind. A considerable number of amoebic life-cycles happen during the course of one human life, therefore if amoebas could record time they would do it differently than us. They would look to something like a minute for us as a standard day. Our reckoning of time is consequently at a much slower rate than theirs would be, but can it also speed up for us? The answer lies in how the mind is used, and how time is defined. The mind can choose its pace of activity, or whether it wishes to register the passing of time at all. It can choose to enter into an amoeba's world or race ahead beyond the states of sentience it will morph into. It then represents the far-distant future for that evolving spark of mind, and so moves very fast indeed for that entity. Millions of amoebic lives may have to pass by before the next stage of its development is accessed. The human mind can access the same in a millisecond. From an amoeba's perspective, therefore, a human's time has considerably sped up.

---

25 David J. Kalupahana, *Mūlamadhyamakakārikā of Nāgārjuna,* (Motilal Banarsidass, New Delhi, 1999), 35. He delves deeper into this subject in his article 'The Buddhist Conception of Time and Temporality', published in *Philosophy East and West,* ed. Eliot Deutsch, Honolulu: The University Press of Hawaii, 24 (1974): 181-191.

The effects of the activities stemming from human consciousness are obviously much vaster in scope than that of an amoeba's world. Considerations of the process of time are also due to the methodologies and activities of human individualities in our societies. Thus human consciousness has grown to activate thoughts faster, which are also vaster in range than in primitive societies. These societies had no clocks to measure the passing of minutes and hours, hence lived comparatively sedentary lifestyles. Our present civilisation is now slavishly regulated by those time sequences. Hours and minutes matter considerably to us, and life upon the entire planet is affected by the way we are conditioned by our concept of time. The high value we place on all time considerations causes us to strive to achieve more within certain time limitations. Each new generation of humans must therefore cope with an increasingly perplexing complexity and variety of things, for we have travelled from the horse and carriage age to the computer age in less than a century. With this progress comes a concept of the pace that time travels, not that the duration of an hour has changed, but rather the perception of what needs to be accomplished in that time. Effectively, time has sped up for those with such perceptions.

The beginning of a world sphere, star or universe can be considered a sphere of self-contained activity, with a central dot signifying the incorporation of the originating Thought, from which comes the streams of fluxial progression causing the animation of things. (This is symbolised by the space from the central point to the circumference of a sphere.) These lines of activity have many interpretations of time as the evolution of consciousness progresses from an amorphous whole to a marvellous diversity over time. One set of circumstances become dependent upon another in sequence, thus a set of past circumstances make a new set, and as the present is reached a line of progression has been formed. This makes up time, the order of being and appearances, of consciousness evolving. All becomes part of a pattern, a rhythm, and it is a cyclic rhythm with which we associate that is measured, that becomes our concept of time, making the fabric of our knowingness.

The nature of this fabric changes according to the perceptions of the viewer, and so also the concept of time. The quality of perception therefore constitutes the comprehension of time and is concurrent with the evolution of a person's consciousness. For a lethargic consciousness the appearance of time has slowed down to be barely perceptible. From this perspective, birth into animal forms may hypothetically be possible (hypothetical because other factors prevent such incarnation) because, if consciousness was slowed to the point of being barely active at all, similar to that of an animal's, then the animal and human consciousness would be similar enough for such an incarnation. Not possessing consciousness is a major reason why animals do not have a concept of time, apart from the effects of the seasons upon them, and of day and night. Time is stretched from the seconds and minutes that govern human thinking to diurnal and seasonal considerations. The evolution of consciousness and its rate of progress is exoterically reckoned in terms of time, and esoterically in terms of cycles of accomplishment denoting mastery of heightened rates of perception.

The speeding up of time can indicate the creation of materialistic thinking, of a very busy active intellect continuously concerned with concepts of seconds, minutes and hours. If time is transcended, then we have the eternal Now, where all of the rhythms and cycles of life are seen in context, as part of the patterning of the overall view of the schema of life. This is true timelessness.

A rhythmic action of consciousness integrates the conflict of opposites, producing a spaciously evolving time line. It allows consciousness to move according to the pulsations of a heartbeat, and accordingly to experience the greater cycles of space, the overriding cycles of time which condition the all. The enlightened Mind is thus attuned to the pulsations of the universal Heart that governs all life in *saṃsāra*. Consequently, the conditioning *karma* can be comprehended and directed.

The universe unfolds according to the rate of its own cycles of progression. Separation (individuation) manifests first and then order, the bringing together of all into a unity. The Buddhist concept of non-self evolves from considerations of such unity. Even a lion-like consciousness couldn't evolve without the occurrence of the repetitious cycles whereby time is measured. The lion stalks the attributes of the separated units of consciousness that are its prey, and over time integrates them into the oneness that is its pride.

For awareness to evolve, certain requirements are necessary. *First* you must have the lifespan manifesting for it to develop. *Second,* you must have the receptors whereby experiences can be observed and assimilated by a consciousness. *Third,* there must be a progression of experiences manifesting over time from which one can learn. *Fourth,* the nature of the environment wherein one is endeavouring to experience must also be considered. *Fifth,* how much time one has to assimilate new experiences to validate thought-forms, thus if one is in a dangerous situation there may not be the time to make conscious aspiration possible. *Sixth,* there must be a 'self' or mode of containment of those experiences in such a way that successive incarnations or generations of that experiential line can progressively accumulate experiences. *Seventh,* there must be a goal or conclusion to every line of experiential endeavour. This implies a transmutation or projection of that experiential patterning to a higher level, once that goal has been reached, leading eventually to an ultimate goal. Hence we have the concepts of *śūnyatā* and of enlightenment, where the 'self' concept is transcended.

Whenever one thinks, it implies that there is an established reason for that thinking process. If little or no reasoning capability exists, then very little can be deduced. Scattered thoughts would be blown like leaves in the wind. An established reason implies the use of a will to assert oneself in the thought environment. This is a reason that an elephant with a possible longer life span than humans, does not muster the equivalent thoughts. There are, however, cases when its instincts are sufficiently violated to generate the rudiment of thought, such as the decision to charge a human being who has provoked him in some way. The elephant doesn't have the mental aura, the basic mind-stuff, the elements of consciousness linked to the brain mechanism, that allow it to think, except in the most rudimentary way. Such substance has not yet been developed and accumulated by the evolutionary capacity of his species. Its elemental formation, or quality of its evolved sentience, has not yet reached the needed intensity for thought. Even if it could think, it would lack human volition, human ability, with fingers and toes. The elephant lacks the means by which it can discover enlightenment, and so its mental body is in an auric state of relatively unorganised particles. There is no will directing mental particles into a proper, ordered pattern of time sequences.

Some of the fundamental differences between human cognition and that of animal sentience thus come to light. We organise the particles of our minds into sequences that we remember in context of time, and upon which we can build with our imaginations, and this gives us coherent thoughts whereby we learn in relation to what we cognised from the past. This process intensifies our mental aura and makes it bright. Animals do not have the content of such organised, intensified thought-forms, making their mental auras dull, lacking of any refined quality, though they do have the capacity to remember. This ignorance state then is reflective in their lack of the sense of time, or right timing, other than that which relates to basic bodily needs and instincts, such as needed for reproduction of the species. Technically, they live in a three dimensional world with respect to our fourth. (The addition of time to the three co-ordinates of space.)

This is another reason why it is not possible for human consciousness to transmigrate into animal bodies. The animal consciousness has not the same time frame references as the human. The ignorance state, or 'light quality' of the animal-mind is too dull, too far back in the time sequence of events we call evolution, for the human consciousness to be able to utilise it. The auric state of the human consciousness, or even the intelligence level of the most base human, is simply too bright for the animal sentience, too far into a future time zone, for the two to interrelate. The relative awarenesses do not function upon the same time line, and therefore any possibility of karmic connection must be specifically adjusted to take this into account. Certain levels of substance interrelation can be adjudicated between them, but not that which relates to the sharing of our consciousness-space. An animal does not have the imaginative facility of a human being, our suffering levels, nor the ability to experience the bliss of exalted consciousness-spaces, because these types of karmic interaction are too far into the future for them. The movement of the related human volatile substance occurs at too fast a frequency for them to capture consciously. The animal 'mind' resides in a state of relative auric non-energisation that cannot accommodate the intensified blaze of human thoughts. This however does not deny the animal's ability to live in a psychic continuum, to possess clairvoyant and clairaudient faculties, as neither of these require intelligent cognition.

It has been noted that time does not ultimately exist, as it is part of *saṃsāra* and hence is an illusion. The fact is that it makes all things exist relatively, and that is why we say time exists. Our consciousness is designed to perceive the relativity of things. It exists, therefore, with regard to physical incarnations relative to human experiences in *saṃsāra*. It does not exist in *śūnyatā* because therein consciousness does not exist. The truth of relativity, however, persists as the *Dharmakāya* exists relative to *saṃsāra,* and *śūnyatā* is relative to both. From the perspective of *śūnyatā,* the flow of time-spaces can be observed because *śūnyatā* is freed of the impediment of the substance that is incorporated into things, but not of the substance that delineates the space between things. *Śūnyatā* is not a state of complete annihilation.

Many Buddhists reside in a slow time flow, as their thought accumulations are meditative and restricted to the statements of *sūtras* or *śāstras* generated in the distant past. Conditioned suppositions make them put too much emphasis upon the forms they are taught that exist as an expression of their meditative minds, and they cannot quickly let go of these mind-constructs. Their consciousness is too occupied by the accumulated weight of conceptualisations derived from scriptures. Such concepts are 'things', and they cannot view the reality of the nature of the spaces between those 'things'. They have not built the intensity of Mind that allows them to hold the Clear Light in place so that instantaneity of spacious movement in the Void is possible. Clearly, methodology that breaks down the barriers of the old congealing concepts is needed, allowing thinking to speed up to ascertain the new. The *dharma* does not stagnate, but moves on with the accelerating pace of the time flow. Liberation is inclusive, not exclusive of the all, and intensity is built through overcoming the sluggishness of past reticulations of thought, allowing the all to be experienced for what it is. Intensity becomes a springboard to dive into the clear serene pool of enlightenment that is the future's bequest. Astounding is the instantaneous, spontaneously revealing ideation of the epoch of enlightenment's progression.

Oṁ

The Jungle

While sitting in a suburban
room yard jungle,
I escaped in my mind
with a volley of remembrances
of yesterday gone by
re-enacted today,
in seeing those around me play games
in a cycle of returning,
and walking in feet
that must pass
many a graveyard of tears.

In vacuous space
my mind is unfolding,
its something that is
returning again and again.
Encompassing the vast extent
of the vision I'm holding,
silently brooding, enlightening,
always returning,
always journeying
to the central Heart.
Life's radiant jewel found.
Unlimited space-time insight,
the Mind in clear Cold Light.

10

Commentary on Ālayavijñāna as Seed

Some key terms

The *ālayavijñāna* doctrine of the Yogācāra-Vijñānavādin School provides a detailed, generally accepted explanation of the Buddhist concept of the causes of things, from the perspective of mind. (Though various Mahāyāna schools hold different views on the subject.) The *ālayavijñāna* is defined as the store-consciousness, the mind-basis-of-all. *Ālayavijñāna* is composed of the Sanskrit words *ālaya* and *vijñāna*. Here *ālaya* is a store of mental images. Strictly speaking, the *ālaya* is not a *vijñāna*, as it has no discerning power and it indiscriminately harbours everything poured into it through the channel of the sense-perceptors. The *ālaya* does not judge, it has no independent discernments. *Citta* (basic mind substance) as a cumulative mental faculty is identified with the *ālayavijñāna*.[1] All the *vijñānas* are evolving and deed-performing except the *ālaya*, which always abides in its self-nature. Thus the *vijñānas*[2] may cease from evolving and acting out various impressions, but the *ālaya* always remains as itself.

---

1 The above is adapted from Daisetz Teitaro Suzuki, *The Lankavatara Sutra*, (Routledge and Kegan Paul, London and Boston, 1973), xxii.

2 Suzuki states: '*Vijñāna* in Buddhism has a technical sense; it is not mere cognition or understanding, it is a sort of principle of conscious life as distinguished from the body, and also the power or faculty of discrimination. It has however, an essentially intellectual connotation, faithfully retaining its original sense. In the case of the Ālayavijñāna, there is no discrimination in it, no intellection; for it simply accumulates all the impressions, all the memory-seeds *(bīja)* that are produced and left behind by the activities of the other Vijñānas'. D.T. Suzuki, *Studies in the Lankavatara Sutra*, (Routledge and Kegan Paul, London and Boston, 1975), 176.

Suzuki states (quoting from scripture) that: 'Citta gathers up karma, Manas inspects, the Vijñāna distinguishes, and the five Vijñānas discriminate the visible [world]'.[3]

According to *The Laṅkāvatāra Sūtra,* the *ālaya* has two aspects: the *ālaya* existing in itself and the *ālaya* as a mental representation. These aspects are also known respectively as the incessant (*prabandha*) and the manifested (*lakṣaṇa*). The *ālaya* is incessant because its activity is perceptible by the mind.[4] Therefore we can see that the *ālaya* can be conceived to be ever-present in one respect, and also as being subject to evolutionary progression (*pravṛtti*). This evolving aspect of the *ālaya* is produced by the activities of *manas*. The *ālaya* that remains in and by itself can also be considered to be an aspect of the abstract Mind. It can be equated with the concept of a 'World Soul' (*anima mundi)* when extended to represent the cumulative mind of all of humanity.

Suzuki's definition of *manas* is quite illuminating:

> Manas roughly corresponds to mind as an organ of thought, but in fact is more than that, for it is also a strong power of attaching itself to the result of thinking. The latter may even be considered subordinate to the power of attachment. The Manas first wills, then it discriminates to judge; to judge is to divide, and this dividing ends in viewing existence dualistically. Hence the Manas' tenacious attachment to the dualistic interpretation of existence. Willing and thinking are inextricably woven into the texture of Manas.[5]

From this perspective, *manas* incorporates the intellect. As stated in chapter five, I identify *manas* with *manovijñāna* (thought *vijñāna),* which is sometimes also considered as the sixth sense (as the five

---

3 Ibid., 172. He further states that *'Citta,* according to the sutra, apparently comes from the root *ci,* which has two senses, (1) "to gather," "to pile," "to acquire," and (2) "to perceive," "to look for." *Citta,* therefore, may mean either "collection" or "perception," and in the present case, that is, when it is identified with the Ālaya, Buddhist scholars take it in the sense of accumulation. So we read in the *Laṅkāvatāra,* "Citta gathers up karma," or "karma is gathered up by Citta." Ordinarily, it may correctly be rendered "thought," or "mind." The great source of confusion, however, comes from Citta being used frequently for the whole system of Vijñānas as well as for the Ālaya alone.' Ibid., 176.

4 Adapted from Suzuki, *The Lankavatara Sutra,* xiii.

5 Ibid., xxi.

vijñānas are the five sense consciousnesses). *Manas* is a shortened version of *manovijñāna,* where the fact that it is a *vijñāna* is implied. *Manovijñāna* signifies the manifestation of thought, and *manas* is the will to produce such, incorporating also the attributes of the creative imagination. I normally dispense with the term *manovijñāna* in this treatise, hence when 'the sixth sense' or the intellect is referred to, as well as all aspects of the functioning mind, the above connotation of *manas* is implied. Another Sanskrit term used for the intellect is *pravṛttivijñāna,* meaning the discriminating consciousness.[6] In this treatise *citta* is relegated as the basic substance of mind, whereas *manas* is that attribute (the thinking principle) that utilises this substance, taking both the empirical and abstract minds into account. (In which case the terms lower and higher *manas* are utilised.)

The *ālayavijñāna* and *kliṣṭamanas*

To obtain a deeper understanding as to the nature of the *ālayavijñāna,* I shall utilise the writings of Tsongkhapa, as he presents an acknowledged, excellent account of all Buddhist doctrines. The text translated by Gareth Sparham is utilised here. The presented quotation contains many Buddhist technicalities, which hopefully will be explained from a meaningful perspective to the reader:

> [The seed *ālaya-vijñāna]* is that potential—the seeds of virtue, nonvirtue and of what is not the subject of moralizing—placed on the location of perfumes by the perfumer. [The so-called perfumer] is the set of seven-consciousnesses, at the time it is ceasing. The set of six consciousnesses [i.e., excluding *kliṣṭa-manas* and *ālaya-vijñāna*] places the seeds of both virtue and non-virtue and also what is not a subject of moralizing. This is because in this group [of six] is found all three [types of minds], such as a virtuous [mind], etc. The *kliṣṭa-manas* and its associated [mental factors] only leave neutral perfumes since they always remain, in essence, what is not a subject of moralizing.
>
> Question: How is it ascertained that the perfumer is the group of seven [consciousnesses] and their associated [mental factors]?
>
> [Answer:] Entering *(pravṛtti)* consciousness and the *ālaya-vijñāna*

6 In chapter five I related it to the *iḍā* aspect of *manovijñāna.* Throughout this series I use the terms intellect, concrete mind or empirical mind, for *pravṛttivijñāna.*

continually adhere to each other, each functioning as cause and result of the other. For, all such entering consciousnesses, by nurturing the older seed, function as the empowering condition *(adhipati-pratyaya)* of the seed part of the *ālaya-vijñāna,* by placing a new seed, as its causal condition *(hetu-pratyaya)*[7]...This explanation is from the point of view of simultaneous cause and effect. From the nonsimultaneous point of view, [the set of six consciousnesses] also place the seeds which give rise to the maturation part of a future life's *ālaya-vijñāna.*

Moreover, the perfuming occurs as the basis is ceasing and the perfumer arising. This is simultaneous. It is like, for example, sesame *(tila)* and the sesame flower which are there together, one arising as the other is perishing, so that later on the flower does not exist, but its fragrance is left, placed in the sesame seed. Thus it is also said:

> Here, the entering consciousness functions in two ways as a condition of the *ālaya-vijñāna.* It is posited [as a condition of *ālaya*] from the point of view of nurturing seeds fully in this life and, since in a future life it [the *ālaya*] is caused to become manifest, from the point of view of directing (Tib. *yongs su'dzin pa*) the seed. For this reason, just as, with the full expanding of the seeds in this life, virtuous, nonvirtuous [minds], and those not the subject of moralizing arise contingent on the *ālaya-vijñāna,* to a similar extent, by way of a simultaneous coming into being and ceasing, they perfume that upon which they depend.[8]

Here we see that the (originating) seed, the *ālayavijñāna*, is the potential of all possibilities of the evolution of consciousness, but it is the six consciousnesses (the five sense-consciousnesses, plus the coordinating intellect) that actually sow it. (That which 'give rise to the maturation part of a future life's *ālaya-vijñāna'.*) Thus these qualities arise out of the manifesting personal-I through conscious volitions.

That the *kliṣṭamanas* (defiled-mind[9]) only leaves 'neutral perfumes', that are 'not a subject of moralizing' needs commentary. This means that

7 Gareth Sparham, *Ocean of Eloquence, Tsong kha pa's Commentary on the Yogācāra Doctrine of Mind,* (Sri Satguru Publications, Delhi, 1995), 65.

8 Ibid., 66.

9 Explained in detail later.

which it sows: the desire principle, and associated emotions (allied to the Elements of the five senses), are technically not a mind (not a *vijñāna*), and they cannot moralise, as no thought process is there. Rather, they are the principle of attachment to things; at first for pleasurable concerns, and later for the building of the empire of the 'self' concept. When it attaches to the mind *per se* (the 'sixth consciousness'), then we get desire-mind and all the forms of selfishness so well known to humanity.

The gain of such sowing via *kliṣṭamanas* is the evolution of the principle of Love. At first we have a higher form of attachment to things glamorous, and to the concept of union with another, and later to the Love that detaches, for the sake of truly helping the 'other' on the quest for liberation. This awakens the qualities of *bodhicitta*.

We can see here that when the *ālayavijñāna* and *kliṣṭamanas* act to seed 'the perfumes', then this is a case of an evolutionary process, explained above; which in time will evoke a response from the set of six consciousnesses that have been thus perfumed. Evolution necessarily presumes an involutionary (descending) process, where we have:

a. A *descent* from something (represented by the 'seed *ālaya-vijñāna'*) and then an ascent. Here the 'thing' descending from the potential that is the *ālayavijñāna* is the substance of consciousness, manifesting both virtue and non-virtue, as well as that which doesn't moralise. The principle of ascent represents refined attributes of consciousness and the transformed *kliṣṭamanas*, which I have termed Love.

b. The Sambhogakāya Flower within the *ālayavijñāna* controls the entire process. It seeds the 'entering consciousness', which must eventually return to it with a consequent gain. Also, the law of *karma* must be directed to play its appropriate role. Thus the *ālayavijñāna* veils the Sambhogakāya Flower, as per the phrase 'from the point of view of directing the seed', because the *ālayavijñāna* on its own *can direct nothing.* How can it do so if it in itself possesses no organising conscious will incorporated within it, according to the extant philosophy? This can be inferred because if there was such a will then we would have a 'self' concept. However, some conscious entity must direct the seeds that represent the elements of consciousness for a new personal-I. Such a will is provided by the Sambhogakāya Flower. Consequently, the seeds (*bījas*) perfumed can manifest the empirical consciousness of a personal-I, and the appropriate destiny *(gati)* unfolded.

In terms of the terminology I have presented, we thus have a process involving:

1. *Ālayavijñāna,* which (via its inherent *citta)* is the store of *manas,* the attributes of mind that can be incorporated into a new personal-I.
2. *Kliṣṭamanas,* via which the desire factor and the emotions are seeded.
3. Continual evolution from the corporeal mind by further refining and elevating the six consciousnesses, which sow the seeds of all further impressions. This is implicit in the words: 'from the point of view of nurturing seeds fully in this life and, since in a future life it [the *ālaya*] is caused to become manifest'. The entire point of directing the evolution of the seed through many lives of expression is, by inference, the growth or maturation of the *ālaya* itself. Otherwise the entire process would be pointless. It is the *ālayavijñāna* (or more specifically the Sambhogakāya Flower therein) that benefits from the process of the growth and maturation of the seed. Consequently it evolves, which is the point of it all. Such evolution in itself is meaningless, unless we are concerned with something (the Buddha germ, or *tathāgatagarbha*/Sambhogakāya Flower[10]) which can inevitably evolve into a Buddha.

   This Flower gains its fragrance by means of:[11]

   a. *Colour*—The distinctive radiatory characteristics of the various states of consciousness it imbues.

   b. *Expansiveness*—As more qualities of mind are absorbed into the *ālayavijñāna* from what it has seeded, so its size expands to

10 Suzuki points out that '*Tathāgata-garbha,* which is another name for the Ālaya, is also a sort of store-room or receptacle where the seeds of Tathagatahood are retained and matured...we are all possible Tathagatas except that we sit generally bound like mummies by the heavy intellectual and affective coverings known as *jñeyāvaraṇa* and *kleśavaraṇa'*. *Studies in the Lankavatara Sutra,* 177.

11 The term 'fragrance' is here used because it refers to the most subtle essence of a flower. In the case of the Sambhogakāya Flower, it extracts the fragrances from all of the *chakras* of the constitution of the personal-I.

include more space. The boundaries of its possible affiliations in the realms of consciousness grow.

c. *Perfume*—This concerns its emanatory energy as perceived by others, and that which allows it to seed the personal-I with specific characteristics that makes it different to other 'I's'.

d. *Intensity*—The heightened energy qualifications of the more refined and energetic *saṃskāras* produced and stored as *bījas* provide a broader propensity to be able to act decisively in the gross phenomenal realms. This is reflected, for instance, in the ability of the personal-I to tread the Bodhisattva path.

e. *Internal motion*—This is the way that consciousness moves within itself to become much faster as its substance is refined. The process continues until the retrieval of wisdom happens at lightning speed, and is instantaneous at many levels at once. Thus enlightenment has proceeded from the Clear Light, where there is no resistance at all from its own substance. Consciousness has achieved fourth-dimensional motion, transcendence, from the point of view of its own level of being.

4. A *point of extinction or cessation* of all forms of such activity, implying the gain of evolutionary perfection, thus *śūnyatā*.
5. A *resurgence* of expressed wisdom upon the transcendental level embodied by the Dhyāni Buddhas, beyond the ken of mind.

The meaning of the statement 'the flower does not exist, but its fragrance is left' implies that the past has left its imprint (the 'fragrance') in the future. The fragrance is the distilled extract from the life of the personal-I. This then is seeded in the future by the Sambhogakāya Flower into another personal-I so that the unfolding destiny (the march to Buddhahood) can occur.[12]

The statement 'Entering *(pravṛtti)* consciousness and the *ālayavijñana* continually adhere to each other, each functioning as cause and result of the other' also implies an evolutionary process (i.e., 'the maturation part of a future life's *ālaya-vijñāna')*. Here something

12 One can speculate here that the author has used the simile of 'the sesame flower' here as a hint, a veiled reference to the doctrine of the Sambhogakāya Flower.

from 'above', the *ālayavijñāna* (i.e., the Sambhogakāya Flower), continuously works with and upon something below. Thus the 'entering consciousness', works upon the mind of the personal-I. (That portion of the *ālayavijñana* that is incarnate, hence 'below'.)

If the *ālayavijñāna* did not function thus, the consciousness of the personal-I would not evolve, as there would be no two way interrelation between the mind of the personal-I and the *ālayavijñana*. There would be no capacity for mental growth beyond the life of the personal-I and when it died then all mental formations would dissipate totally (be annihilated). This appears to happen at the death of a person, however, the mental *saṃskāras* are retained in the *ālayavijñāna* for a future life's usage. We thus have a progression, an adherence of consciousness states throughout the successive rebirths of the consciousness-stream, through to the *bhūmis* of a *bodhisattva* to Buddhahood. Such a line of reasoning implicates an overshadowing consciousness, which has a purpose for working thus, for manifesting the form of limitation of its freedom of expression, denoted by the term 'adherence' above. It would not do so unless there was a gain for it. The gain is wisdom, and eventual liberation from the need for formed expression once nothing more can be gained from *saṃsāra*.

If the 'entering consciousness' that conditions the personal-I dies with the death of the person, so logically the *ālaya* should also 'die', because it has been 'caused' by the entering consciousness. (They 'continually adhere to each other, each functioning as cause and result of the other'.) If this happened, then it would indicate that there could be no continuity of *saṃskāras* into future lives, as the *ālayavijñāna* would then be no more than a mind state of the personal-I. In fact, the *ālayavijñāna* is continually 'seeded', or 'perfumed' with impressions, images, from the 'entering consciousness' as it grows with the mental development of the personality. The *ālayavijñāna* is caused by the sum of such impressions, stemming through many cycles of experience of births and deaths of 'entering consciousnesses', because it persists after the death of each personal-I.

What is subtly avoided here by the author, but is implicit in the statement, is that the *ālayavijñāna* must be organised in a way that will accommodate the progression of billions of individual human unit minds upon the earth, and those disincarnate. The observation here concerns the collective *ālayavijñāna* as a unity, not as individual entities of expression, for indeed, all are integrated thus in the realms of mind/ Mind, as all people share ideas with each other. The commingling of human thoughts must also be contained in the *ālayavijñāna*. It means that it acts as a universal store of consciousness that is organised so that it can appropriately accommodate all individualised units of consciousness. Incorporated within the *ālayavijñāna* are the Sambhogakāya Flowers. Each Sambhogakāya Flower is responsible for the karmic output and destiny, the programming of future tendencies, for each human unit that individuates out of the consciousness-stream it directs.

There also needs to exist that which is responsible for the karmic destiny of this collective mind/Mind. This means that an amorphous structure of the *ālayavijñāna* does not exist, otherwise the billions of human units could not be accommodated to evolve compassion. Neither could their minds be directed away from the self-concept. The appearance of tribes, racial groupings, the customs and manners they are governed by, social groups, cultural and national identities do not appear haphazardly. They may be affected by conquerors, such as an Alexander, Ashoka or Caesar, but such ones incarnate according to an overriding plan that has the evolutionary progress of humanity in mind. Nothing is left to chance within the compassionate Mind of an Ādi Buddha and his retinue. The billions of human units are thereby accommodated to ultimately evolve compassion. Hence the *ālayavijñāna* is structured by Mind to accomplish the eventual gaining of Buddhahood for all. Not only the *karma* directed by the *tathāgatagarbha* that utilises the karmic attributes organised by the *citta,* but the entire flow of the externalised *dharmakāya karma* works this way.

If there was no structure to the *ālayavijñāna,* there would be a chaotic admixing of all mental formations developed by human interrelationships whilst incarnate. Their future then cannot lead to Buddhahood, as there would be no fabric *(maṇḍala)* of *manasic* space that could accommodate a drive thereto, for nothing could sort out the chaotic mess. For a great one such as Gautama to have appeared and to have a vast effect upon human civilisation, it necessitates his foremost disciples, those karmically associated with, and who were educated by him over aeons, to have incarnated with him, so that they could appropriately respond to his teachings, with the religion we call

Buddhism today being the consequence. If he had incarnated in another part of the word (say South America) where the social structure did not support yoga-meditation or wandering *sadhus,* where the concept of liberation was non-existent, or in an area wracked with internecine or tribal warfare, he could never have succeeded. There simply would have been no *manasic* support in the *ālayavijñāna* associated with that area of the world for a Buddha to have appeared. The subject hinted at here is vast and incorporates the philosophy associated with an Ādi Buddha and retinue, introduced in Volume 5A, and from a more detailed perspective in Volume 7, incorporating the functions of Shambhala.

Continuums of mind need to exist from one particular thought life of an individual to another so that at the right thought sequence the drive to Bodhisattvahood, say ten lives into the future can be achieved, or any other necessary empirical evaluation.[13] (*Karma* alone cannot work without a highly organised structure in place to unerringly effect such retrievals with adamantine assurance.) Also, the entire process of the 'entering consciousness' and the *ālayavijñāna* adhering to each other would be pointless, purposeless, apart from maybe the growth of the *ālaya* itself as it absorbs the conscious identifications of the personal-I, but again, for what purpose? The *ālayavijñāna* does not evolve a drive to Buddhahood on its own, as it is a principle, not an entity.

There would only be a purpose if:

1. The *ālayavijñāna* contained individualised units, each of which were tied to a stream (*santāna*) of interrelated personal-I's that are responsible for bringing to maturation needed principles (the evolution of wisdom) over a series of lives. 'Maturation' means, therefore, the development of aspects of a Buddha-Mind. The manifesting personal-I then becomes the *nirmaṇakāya*, the *ālayavijñāna* the *sambhogakāya* aspect, and this is responsive to or identified with its *dharmakāya* aspect via the *Śūnyatā* Eye. The individualised *sambhogakāya* aspect can thus be termed a 'soul', but this 'soul' is not eternal or unchanging. It changes with respect to the perfumes abstracted from each successive personal-I that

13 One could extend this concept with consideration of the vaster Space associated with the *dharmakāya,* but to do so one would have to speculate upon the content of a Buddha-Mind.

has evolved the ability to leave such essences. It also ceases, when *śūnyatā* is attained by the I-consciousness-personal-I fusion.

2. The *ālayavijñāna* is part of the Mind-structure of a great evolutionary Being, an Entity evolving in its own space-time zone with respect to humanity, and with a far vaster agenda, being inclusive of the sum of all human consciousnesses and their aspiration to Buddhahood. If in this scenario the human consciousnesses are not individualised, and have no prospect of a 'subtle-soul', as is indicated in general Mahāyāna ideology, then there is no true mechanism to explain the process of rebirth of an individual consciousness from its previous one. That is, something must hold consciousness in place in the after death state in such a way that all of the elements necessary for the new life can be resurrected, producing a proper continuum.

   If a person dies and that consciousness is eventually absorbed into the general Fiery lake of quietude that can be considered the *ālayavijñāna* on the abstracted mental realms,[14] then what? It appears, according to current Buddhist ideology, to become a part of an amorphous mass of mind, to be somehow resurrected and reconstituted at the appropriate time. It is therefore obvious that in the above scenario no Buddhahood is possible for any consciousness-stream therein, as nothing can be particularised in such an environment to evolve. How can individualisation (wherewith a striving for Buddhahood can be achieved) be possible here? The only possibility is that it is the *ālayavijñāna* that gains Buddhahood, but again this is not possible, unless that *ālaya* is part of the Mind-structure of a vast Entity. Then there is inevitably no such thing as a human unit, and human evolution and aspiration itself is purposeless, except for that Entity.

3. A combination of both these factors. Here we have the expression of the human 'soul', which contains or holds consciousness in individualised forms, as part of the compassionate concern of an embodying presiding Buddha. If there was just the second point, as explained above then we saw that humanity would be expendable, they would vanish in time, and just the enormous Mind-structure

14 On the concreted mental realms we would more specifically see torrents and eddies of fiery energies.

would be left as a consequence of the entire former *saṃsāric* play. Thus humans would not attain Buddhahood, only the Being whose Mind was the *ālayavijñāna*. All human essences would but be an aspect of That Mind.

The point to be made here is that if there is no individuation, there is no possibility for evolution for any entity, no matter how vast or minute it is, and no matter if it is a sentience, or mind, or constituted of pure consciousness. It must have a particularised form with which:

a. To firstly develop knowledge of something 'other' than itself, and thus improve the quality of mind or sentience it possesses.

b. To correlate all such knowledgeable impressions in order to get an understanding of balance in the environment of which it plays a part; thereby to manifest the proper role that *karma*, or the Lord of Nature has assigned to it. The sentience of forms of life lower than the human is conditioned by instinct, which predetermines the way that each species of lives must interact.

c. To gain higher principles, through contact with other more exalted forms, and to interrelate in some way (e.g., to 'adhere to each other, each functioning as cause and result of the other'). This allows it to aspire to something greater or beyond it.

d. That form must be able to be transcended when the something greater or 'beyond' is reached.

e. Ultimately, there is the fusion of all such awareness or experience into a unity, a synthesis of comprehension, as is expressed by a Buddha-Mind.

The first postulate works for the evolution of each human to Buddhahood, but then the incorporating *ālayavijñāna* would still have to be accounted for, of what it has gained through the entire process, and why it has done so. What then becomes of it must also be explained.

The third postulate is the favoured one because it introduces the idea that the entire *māyā* of human evolution and interrelation is part of the compassionate meditation of a primordial Buddha from a former aeon of evolutionary growth. This Buddha gains further advancement upon his path by the sacrifice of an aspect of Himself (hence constituted of Mind) in order to convert units of cosmic darkness (what humans were before there was a humanity in our equation of life) to light (the consequential evolutionary push to Buddhahood for each human unit). This can be considered an aspect of the *dharmakāya* view, the Dharmakāya Way that must yet be meditated upon by the world's aspirants.

The five qualities needed for perfuming

Concerning the 'Mechanics of seed formation'[15] we are told that the 'location of perfumes is posited as having five qualities', the first of which is given as:

> a) It is stable. This means that it must be something like a sesame seed, etc., the continuum of which is ongoing. It cannot be like sound or lightning which is unstable and not suitable to be a location of perfumes. Such things are not accepted to be imbued with any residual impression. They are phenomena which lose whatever they are imbued with. This [word 'stable'] teaches [14a] that the set of seven consciousness and forms cannot be the location of perfumes. For [the *Triṁśikā-kārikā]* says of these:
>
> > The arising of a mental consciousness takes place continually, unless in a state without thought processes, in one of the two absorptions, in a torpor, a faint or a state devoid of mind.
> >
> > But it [*kliṣṭa-manas*] does not exist on the transcendental paths or in the cessation absorption.
>
> Thus, because [forms] are not in the form or formless realms, and because [the set of seven consciousnesses] sometimes cease, they cannot be the location of perfumes.
>
> Question: In this case the *ālaya-vijñāna* also cannot be the location of perfumes because it also sometimes ceases, as it is said [in the *Trimśikā-kārikā]:*
>
> > After the state of the Arhant it turns back.
>
> [Answer:] There is no flaw here. It is enough that [the *ālaya*] remains without break for as long as there are perfumers.[16]

15 Sparham, *Ocean of Eloquence,* 66.

16 Ibid., 66-67.

We should note that the *ālayavijñāna* does not 'cease' because a being has attained the *arhant* state, it is just that the *arhant* is so thoroughly identified with it that there is no difference between it and him. It ceases to become a realm to strive for. He has achieved a cessation of the concept of 'self' (hence *ālayavijñāna* may be considered to have turned 'back'). The *arhant* is not at the end of the road to bliss, he still has the higher stages of the Bodhisattva path to follow, hence the true *śūnyatā* abstraction still lies ahead. Consequently, the *ālayavijñāna* persists for him. *Saṃskāric* transmogrifications and transmutations must still be accomplished in a future Bodhisattvic life. They come to conclusion within the five wisdom groupings of the Tathāgatas.

The *ālayavijñāna* is a universal store of consciousness, which means that it is omnipresent for all humans. When somebody is not directly perceiving something because he has looked away from it, it does not mean that the thing has disappeared, or has been obliterated. It is still there, it can be perceived by any other being with the sense faculties intact. The same goes for the *ālayavijñāna,* with respect to thc *arhant.* It may be said that all that he has achieved is the extinguishing of his thought patterns for that life. It may mean a type of death of the portion of the *ālayavijñāna* created by him for that life, but in reality his mental *saṃskāras* have been converted to *bījas* and absorbed in the continuum of the *ālayavijñāna,* to be activated in a future life. Thus the statement given above, 'After the state of the Arhant it turns back', may be true only for the individual *ālaya* for a particular life, but for the universal *ālayavijñāna* it is not so; at least not until all of humanity have attained Buddhahood. An *arhant's* mind has been absorbed into that portion of the universal *ālayavijñāna* contained by the Sambhogakāya Flower. His mind therefore has become universalised, thus freed. The *ālayavijñāna* that was contained in that mind has effectively been 'turned back' to its originating store.

By a similar reasoning, just because the Buddha has taken his *parinirvāṇa,* it does not mean that the world has ceased to exist for him, or that the *ālayavijñāna* has, for that matter; it is just that he is not attached to any portion of these states of being, and knows all their mysteries in their entirety. He has outgrown their usefulness for his further development and thus has moved to another 'shore' of being/non-being.

What is posited in this discussion is that only in the *ālayavijñāna* can the perfumes be located. This assumption is reasonable enough, as these perfumes are the gain of the evolutionary experiences of the various personal-I's, and can only be stored under the conditions met by the *ālaya*. This happens because the *ālayavijñāna* can be considered to be stable, existing over the millennia of the incarnations of the personal-I's. In fact, the perfumes are stored in the Flowers that organise the *ālayavijñāna*. Ostensively, the store is the Sambhogakāya Flower for the personal-I, whilst the *chakras* embody a similar function in the human body with respect to the *prāṇas* of the particular Element each processes. The Flowers are stable enough, and constituted so that all aspects of consciousness can be stored by them. There is also a process needed to awaken the *chakras,* but nevertheless they act as containers of all aspects of mind for its interrelation with *saṃsāra.*

It should be noted that these 'perfumes' are but refined *prāṇas.* They are categorised according to the action of the originating sowing of the seeds that develop the five sense consciousnesses. This also necessitates a mechanism whereby the individual *karma* of each successive personal-I can be accounted for within the continuum of consciousness. Such *karma* also includes the nature and quality of the perfumes seeded. They need to be appropriately organised and directed through a mechanism that allows the perfumes to be experienced by the right recipient, the successor 'I' that has the *karma* of earlier sowings. Again we see the necessity for *karma* to have a mechanism whereby it can work efficiently, otherwise it would be but a blind law. If no such mechanism exists then the perfumes stored in the *ālayavijñāna* would haphazardly perfume any person's mind that happened to be receptive. Any of the billions of images created by humanity over aeons could then enter our minds, with little or no ability for us to be able to block them out. The thoughts of another, of all other beings, would be ours, and a form of insanity would be the result. Indeed, we can postulate that many insane people have had the normal checks and balances of their minds broken down to an extent that they receive a vicissitude of mental impressions of this type, for which they are not *karmically* held responsible.

Also, if there were no mechanism for the appropriate storage and retrieval of *bījas,* there would be no stability in consciousness. The *ālayavijñāna* may exist for the duration, but the way that its *bījas* and perfumes are stored would be chaotic.

With respect to the concept of what is formed or not formed it should be noted that because all things are relative to the angle of vision of the perceiver, what is known as the *arūpa* (formless) universe actually has form from the perspective of the view in *dharmakāya*. The forms are only intangible to normal human consciousness. Because of the factor of human eyes, only gross forms are noticeable, and the psychic universe appears in response to the *chakras* being awakened. This is because the substance of the body, of the eyes, or the mechanism of the lower *chakras*, have not been sufficiently refined or cleansed of grosser lethargic energies, to perceive the forms of ultra-high energy states of the *arūpa* realms. Such forms then are formless. When a *yogin* has cleansed his/her sheaths appropriately and consciousness has transferred to the higher, awakened *chakras,* then the true forms of those existing in the *arūpa* realms can be seen, and also the forms consciousness takes. Such a person has attained what may be described as 'satellite technology' in relation to normal earth bound visioning. It is all a matter of the quality of substance with which and through which one perceives, and also at the distance, i.e., elevation or height, esoterically considered, from which one views something. In terms of perception, this concept of height concerns how all-embracive or vast a consciousness is in relation to that which it is perceiving. In a similar vein, the earth appears flat to those upon it, but from a distance it is seen as a sphere, with the haze of an atmosphere around it.

Continuing now with the list of the five qualities needed for 'the location of perfumes':

> b) It is not subject to moralizing. Strong (Tib. *mi mnyam pa)* smells like garlic and sandlewood cannot imbue all seeds while bland smells like sesame can do so. Thus, something not the subject of moralizing, with a bland type of smell, is not incompatible with extremely clear virtuous and nonvirtuous minds. This [not being a subject of moralizing] teaches that virtuous and afflicted minds cannot be the location of perfumes.[17]

Smells like garlic and sandlewood cannot imbue all seeds because they represent forcefully opinionated minds, be this religiously or materialistically focussed. The natural intensity of the thought currents

17 Ibid., 67.

will reject the seeds of alternate views from entering. Where no such forcefulness of view exists (a 'bland type of smell'), and the mind has been made clear, then all types of seeds can enter, which can produce both virtuous and non-virtuous effects. The type of effects depends upon the tendencies already existing in the mind.

With respect to *prāṇas* coming from the personal-I to the subtle soul-form, we see that this form must be able to store all types of *bījas*. They must be seeded in an appropriate way for future personal-I's to experience so that eventually there is a liberating outcome. It must be able to select which of all of the billions of *bījas*[18] in store are to be expressed for that life. Other than such selection, there is no moralising, otherwise whatever *karma* it selected would be slanted or perverted to produce something other than the true and rightful *karma* for that life. Moralising would not allow the self will of the personal-I a free reign to act according to its will, even if that went against the planned karmic expression for that life. There can be no other way—the good or true cannot be imposed against the will of the individual, hence there is 'no moralising'.

Karma, however, will later be adjudicated to account for the decisions made, and slanted (hence 'moralised') to assist better decision making at a later time. Consequently, each life should see a positive progression from a previous one, as the factor of suffering from the consequences of 'bad' decision making in past lives come to the fore. The succession, or streams of *bījas* to be dealt with, are chosen so that *bodhicitta* can be developed and explored by the evolving personal-I's. Buddhahood is then attained in the end. Once the *karma* for the greater patterning of lives has been selected, then free will must be allowed to reign for any individual life. The consequences can then be factored into the karmic process. Consequently, there is both a moralising and non-moralising effect for the Sambhogakāya Flower. However, it must be truly impartial as to concepts of suffering or joy, opinions, religiosity or atheistic bias, type of sexuality, etc., a personal-I may possess. It does not moralise on these grounds. All forms of gaining wisdom are beneficent and every type of experience is needed. It simply directs

18 Note that the term *bīja* (seed) used throughout this series is best thought of in terms of being part of an energy stream of characteristics that can be selected rather than as an objective form, such as a physical plane seed. Such characteristics can be quantified, from another view, hence the concept of 'seed'.

the available *karma* so that inevitably *bodhicitta* is produced. A reason why is because *bodhicitta* is the major energy qualification of the Sambhogakāya Flower.

The third point presented is:

> c) It is perfumed. This means it must have the capacity to be perfumed. This is saying, then, that impermanent, as distinct from permanent, phenomena can be imbued, and hence that noncomposite phenomena (*asaṃskṛṯa*) cannot be the location of perfumes.[19]

If something is alterable by being perfumed, then it is impermanent by means of it being altered. Only *śūnyatā* can be considered unalterable, noncomposite. The Sambhogakāya Flower, therefore, is also impermanent, but has a lasting permanence with respect to the lives of the personal-I's from which it gains impressions and perfumes. Hence it has a capacity to be perfumed.

Next we have:

> d) It is related to the perfumer. This means there must be a relation such that the perfumer is arising and the location of perfumes is perishing at the same time. This teaches a) that different streams of consciousness and b) phenomena which exist at different times cannot be perfumer and location of perfumes respectively.[20]

We can rephrase the above to state that:

i. Different streams of consciousness cannot be the perfumer, thus only one personal-I per life can perfume the Sambhogakāya Flower. Correspondingly that Flower can only perfume the personal-I that it embodies.

ii. That phenomena existing at different times cannot be both the perfumer and the location of the perfumes is obvious because the perfumer and the action of perfuming must occur together. The actor that perfumes cannot manifest at two different time sequences at once. The person follows the time line applicable to *saṃsāra* throughout. The Sambhogakāya Flower exists within a timeless zone but enters into time to perfume the personal-I.

---

19 Sparham, 67.

20 Ibid.

Being a unified consciousness linked to only one personal-I at any time, the Sambhogakāya Flower consequently cannot be seeded by other personal-I's ('different consciousness-streams') with whom it has no links. The laws pertaining to *saṃsāric* activity must be obeyed, thus the 'location of perfumes' constantly perishes with the moving time line (of the personal-I) as new locations appear and recede, whilst the consciousness of the perfumer continuously arises. As no concept of 'time' exists in the realm of the Flower, except that pertaining to the law of cycles, so the perfumes are absorbed by the Sambhogakāya Flower after appropriate cycles of activity have been pursued by the personal-I. This subtle 'soul-form' manifests as the location of perfumes because the personal-I's consciousness is linked to it. There is, however, no 'perishing' of the location when focussed upon the consciousness-space of the Sambhogakāya Flower. The Flower has absorbed the perfumes of the succession of personal-I's before the present one and will continue doing so for all succeeding ones until liberation is attained.

What is really meant by the statement 'the perfumer is arising and the location of perfumes is perishing at the same time' is the idea that as the perfumes move from one location to another they must cease to exist in the former location so as to appear in the other one. What in fact happens is that the refined *prāṇas* move from the mind of the personal-I to stimulate a corresponding growth of energy-pattern in the Sambhogakāya Flower. Conversely, when the Flower perfumes the personal-I it seeds images or produces an urge to act in some way. There is a movement of the energy of consciousness-attributes ('perfumes') in either direction, which can be perceived as an 'arising and perishing', but in fact the seeding process produces lasting attributes for both the Flower and personal-I. (At least for the duration of that 'I's' existence.)

The fifth point presented with respect to seed formation:

> e) It is a basis in its own right. This means it is a basis in its own right, [14b] not just one through the process of synonymity. This eliminates [the five omnipresent mental factors] such as contact, etc., associated with a main mind *(mūla-citta)*, from being the location of perfumes. For these [mental factors] depend on a main mind, the *ālaya-vijñāna*, and are not, therefore, a basis in their own right.[21]

21 Ibid.

The Sambhogakāya Flower is a 'basis in its own right', as all personal-I's of a consciousness-stream that develop these 'mental factors' arise from it. That which is seeded by it comes back in essence (as perfumes) as the most rarefied gnosis and spacious forms of *vijñāna*. There is thus an evolutionary gain, if the plan for the originating seeding has been fulfilled.

What is posited here is that the Sambhogakāya Flower is an attribute of the *ālayavijñāna* that acts to contain a portion of mental substance *(citta)* in such a way that a sequence, a stream of successive personal-I's, can evolve consciousness in a progressive manner. To do so it utilises its own particular attendant *karma*. The Sambhogakāya Flower acts so that eventually *śūnyatā* is ascertained as the doorway to the *dharmakāya*.

The five omnipresent mental factors

Next a question is asked:

> In that case, then, do these [the five omnipresent mental factors] such as contact, etc., perfume their constituent *ālaya-vijñāna* or not? If the former, then there will be a perfumer other than the group of seven consciousnesses. If the latter, these [five mental factors] will then have no cause.
>
> [Answer:] There have been two opinions, one saying: "They must perfume, for otherwise they would have no cause," and the other saying, "The [associated mental factors] are extremely indistinct and are not a subject of moralizing. Therefore they do not perfume. However, since they are a maturation of past action they are propelled [into existence] and remain until death." The latter [explanation] is better, otherwise the *ālaya-vijñāna* also will itself have to perfume and there will be the flaw of not finding the location of perfumes.[22]

Concerning these mental factors it is said:

> Always present with [*ālaya-vijñāna*] are five omnipresent mental factors:
>
> These are:
>
> a. contact *(sparśa),* because it is the cause of all mental factors,
>
> b. *[vedanā],* because all minds are concerned with one or another of the three sorts of [pleasant, unpleasant, or neutral] experience.

22 Ibid., 67-68.

c. a basic *(Tib. tsam)* delimitation of the object *[saṁjñā],*

d. a basic stirring [in the mind] relative to the object *[cetanā],* and

e. a basic turning of the mind towards its objective support *[manaskāra].*[23]

The attribute of 'contact' *(sparśa)* implies the ability to seed because that which is contacted is material in nature, hence seeded with the volitions to act, to experience. Of its own accord the *ālayavijñāna* has not this ability, however, the Sambhogakāya Flower can and does so influence the mind of the incarnate personality. Also, if one attributes thoughts as 'things' then it is possible for one aspect of thought to contact another to produce different ideas in the mind. This presumes that there is an incarnate thinker manifesting the volition to move the thoughts. Hence there both is and is not perfuming, depending upon how one views the *ālayavijñāna.*

Vedanā is feeling-perception obtained via the senses, but more specifically that governing the expression of the emotions, or emotional input to the mind. Again the *ālayavijñāna, per se*, is incapable of expressing such, but *vedanā* can be seeded by the Sambhogakāya Flower. However, this quality is normally developed by the personal-I with the input from such seeds, *saṃskāras* from the past lives, stimulated and further developed by the present life's activities.

Saṁjñā relates to the primary imagery of perception, the discrimination that delineates things, producing the flow of ideas. It is that which allows one to wholly *(saṁ)* know *(jñā)* something.

Cetanā is simply the driving force behind thought, a desire, urge and motivation to experience something, to know. It helps form our habits and aptitudes. It produces the potency of the resultant *karma.*

Finally we have *manaskāra,* the egoistic posturing of an 'I', 'me', 'mine', the central actor in the world stage of a personal-I.

These 'omnipresent mental factors' consequently are only 'omnipresent' when a personal-I is incarnate and focussed upon a 'self'. They are not factors of the *ālayavijñāna per se,* otherwise, as above stated, 'the *ālaya-vijñāna* also will itself have to perfume'. They are factors, however, utilised by a Sambhogakāya Flower whenever it needs to seed a new personal-I and to sustain its development, and also for

23 Ibid., 59.

that 'I' to develop further characteristics and to evolve. Consequently, one can query if they are 'omnipresent' at all, considering also that one upon the path to liberation is working to transform or transmute all of these into enlightenment-characteristics. Hence *manaskāra* must die to produce the true 'selflessness' of an enlightened one. *Vedanā* becomes selfless, impersonal Love, *bodhicitta,* to see the liberation of the all accomplished. *Sparśa* is no longer oriented towards sense contact, but towards the *arūpa* and liberated domains. *Cetanā* is no longer active in producing *karma*-producing modifications of the mind, but rather to still the activities of mind. *Cetanā* is effectively transformed into *vāsanā,* here interpreted in terms of a driving force to liberation. *Saṁjñā* then manifests as emptiness, the Clear Light of the Mind.

Having taken this into account, one can view the subject from a different perspective, of viewing the sense-functions causing the attributes of mind that delineate objects, etc., as being seeded by the Dhyāni Buddhas into Nature via their Consorts.[24] Their qualities are thus found implicit in all listings of five in this series of works. The attributes of mind can be considered omnipresent from a higher sense, as being the reflexes of the five transcendental wisdoms of the Dhyāni Buddhas.

This esoteric fact is brought to our attention because it exemplifies the nature of the Dharmakāya Way and of the Mahāmudrā, which concerns the integral fusion of the inner universe (of the *ālayavijñāna),* seeded by a Dhyāni Buddha and the outer universe of the sense-perceptors, governed by their Consorts. When this process is experienced in consciousness, then we have the expression of the highest enlightenment via the *śūnyatā-saṃsāra* nexus, the seed of the *dharmakāya.*

Also when focussing upon the abstract domain of the Mind, wherein the *dharmakāya* first impacts upon *saṃsāra,* we find therein the Sambhogakāya Flowers. Here the transmuted correspondences of the senses can be found in the following manner, utilising the key phrases given above.[25]

---

24 This includes the Consorts of the retinue of the Dhyāni Buddhas, the Dhyāni Bodhisattvas and Mahābodhisattvas, as will be explained in Volume 5A.

25 From one perspective the whorls of petals of the Sambhogakāya Flower can be arranged as three groups of five petals, as will be explained in Volume 3, chapter 7B. The five senses can therefore be relegated from the highest to the lowest petal for each grouping of five, for which the interested student can later do the correlation.

a. *It is perfumed*, refers to the sense of *smell.*[26] This is obvious enough, as the reference to perfuming is to the heightened essences of experiences. Similarly, smell detects the essences, the aromas of things. It elucidates the highest perceptions in the domain of mind/Mind. Here the principal 'perfuming' is via *śūnyatā,* to produce the abstraction of thoughts and the eventual demise of the Flower via the highest of the petals of each pentad of the Sambhogakāya Flower. The lower petals receive their perfuming from the results of the thought-processes of the personal-I.

b. *It is related to the perfumer*, referring to the sense of *taste.* Taste and smell go together. The sense of taste is heightened by that of smell, they both rely on a watery medium to function, in the mouth or nostril. 'Taste' allows the perceiver to directly experience the true nature of a representative portion of something; thus, 'a taste of enlightenment', of *śūnyatā.* It is also related to the personal-I, from which the most abstract impressions ('perfumes') are derived and absorbed into the second highest of each pentad of the Sambhogakāya Flower.

c. *It is a basis on its own right*, referring to the sense of *sight,* as sight perceives things with just a glance. What is perceived is then the basis for the information of all the images that together constitute consciousness, as consciousness is based upon the images it contains. The Sambhogakāya Flower needs to merely glance at its construct, the personal-I, in order to perceive the sum total of what the personal-I is experiencing, the available *karma*, and all future trends of any action. Here the middle petal of a pentad of five petals of the Sambhogakāya Flower is implicated, relegated to the major characteristics of this Flower. The Love-Wisdom pentad's Heart, for instance is the Love-Wisdom—Love-Wisdom petal.

d. *It is not a subject to moralising* refers to the sense of *hearing.* Sounds can come from any direction in space and manifest in all forms and intonations. With the eyes closed, it is often hard to know from where the sound containing bits of information comes from (i.e.,

26 Note that Volume 3, chapter 5, will delve deeper into an explanation of the five senses. (See Table 2.)

'not moralizing'). The context is important, however, both good and bad serve as the basis of building an information base needed in life for all future activity. The ears must thus resonate to all forms of sounds ('without moralising') if a true information base is to be established that will help one meet the needs of life. Hearing is the basis of speech, our major mechanism of communicating with others, and all forms of speech (crass and divine) are generally needed by all to communicate the facts of life. If one moralises with respect to sound, then much pertaining to what one has experienced, read, or viewed, becomes distorted, a lie. Consequently, for truth to be known moralising must cease. The intellect, however, judges what is to be said from out of the many sounds it has heard, and often moralises in doing so. Thus is *karma* created.

With respect to the Sambhogakāya Flower, the sounds that are heard are mantric and come from all levels of the realms of enlightenment. All manifest forms in Nature, as well as those which are considered *arūpa*, have their inherent sounds, their fundamental notes. (Which depict the essence of what they are.) These must be correctly heard in order to properly know their characteristics. This allows the Flower to work with what is to direct the *karma* towards the manifestation of what must be.

e. *It is stable*, referring to the sense of *touch,* as touch can only register forms that are stable, rather than mirages and the like (which are unstable, or non-existent), such as what the eye, or the other sense-perceptors, might perceive. To properly acknowledge the validity of something, it must be touched. With respect to the Flower, such touch manifests utilising the abstracted *manasic* substance of which it is composed. Being 'composed' means that it possesses a stable form circumscribed *manasically* according to the laws of Mind, that can be sustained thus for a duration of many millennia of incarnatory development of the personal-I's that are brought into expression so that Buddhahood can eventually be accomplished. What is 'touched' by the Sambhogakāya Flower is the attributes of mind developed by the incarnate personal-I. This is accomplished by means of the lowest of any of the pentads of petals of the Flower.

These senses are not experienced through localised sense-perceptors, as found in a human unit, but rather permeated through the substance of consciousness. Together they delineate five fundamental characteristics of the Sambhogakāya Flower. They can then project the five *prāṇas* of the *nāḍīs* that emanate from it in the form of an *antaḥkaraṇa* (consciousness-link) connecting it to the personal-I, through which energy (perfumes) can flow in a two-way stream.

Note that the sense of touch is normally assigned to the Element Water in this *Treatise on Mind,* and Hearing to Earth. From the above perspective however, the Watery Element has been transcended, referring to the higher abstract Mind ('not a subject of moralising'), and the Earth Element (touch, 'is stable') relates to the lower mind *(citta).* The mind/Mind is relegated to Fire. 'A basis' therefore here relates to the Element Fire, as an expression of the *dharmakāya.* The 'perfumer' then relates to the Airy Element, which carries the *manasic* impressions ('perfumes') either from the *dharmakāya* or from the mind/ Mind of the personal-I.

Further aspects concerning the *ālayavijñāna*

Other aspects of the *ālayavijñāna* doctrine can now be delved into, to complete the consideration of its nature. Quoting Sparham again:

> Thus the *ālaya-vijñāna* as a basis should be understood by these four: a) objective support (*ālambana*), b) form *(ākāra),* c) nature *(svabhāva),* and d) [the mental faculties] that accompany *(saṃprayukta)* it.
>
> First, there are the following three components to its objective support: 1) five objects, i.e., forms, sounds, smells, tastes, and feelings; 2) a 'sentient being,' which is five sense-faculties, i.e., eye, ear, nose, tongue, and body; and 3) the residual impression *(vāsanā)* [left] by settling on the thoroughly imagined nature *(parikalpita-svabhāva)* of persons and dharmas.
>
> Second, the form of the cognition is such that though the world and what is in the world appear, it is neither able to determine what is appearing, nor to give rise to certainty later [about what appeared].
>
> Third, the nature of the *ālaya-vijñāna* as a basis is unobscured and not a subject of moralizing *(anivṛtāvyākṛta).* [7b]
>
> Fourth, it is always endowed with feeling *(vedanā),* cognition

(samjñā), volition *(cetanā),* contact *(sparśa),* and attention *(manaskāra).* Therefore it is said [in the *Madhyānta-vibhāga*] that

> [*ālaya-vijñāna*] arises as the consciousness of the appearance of objects [of the senses] and of living beings.[27]

The *objective support* is the proper foundation from which the *ālayavijñāna* arises, and which supports all of its further beingness.

In modern terminology this *support* can be viewed as the environment one is in and from which one experiences things. Of the five objects given, all except one relate to the five sense-perceptions (i.e., the way that these senses receive impressions).

Forms relate to the sense of touch because we can properly experience forms only by touching them. Sight can perceive the forms, but it may be fooled by a mirage or image, but touch can't.

Sounds refer to the sense of hearing.

Smells refer to the sense of smell.

Taste refers to the sense of taste.

However, *feelings* do not directly relate to the sense of sight. One cannot see feelings, unless one is clairvoyant. One may observe a person that is emotional, but the sense of sight cannot make out what type of emotions are involved, or how the person feels about things. Here the traditional mistake is made of identifying feelings or feeling-perceptions as a consciousness, however they are not really consciousness, but rather modify consciousness. They affect the way one thinks. Feelings do, however, relate to the state of being sentient. The objective of the text apparently tries to identify the sense of sight (in the sense of the way one feels) with the mind, because that is the expression of the Element relegated to sight. Feelings, therefore, can here be posited as a form of mental formation that can be 'seen' by the mind. Each of these sense consciousnesses has its related Element, and hence type of *prāṇa*, as explained earlier.

We see, therefore, that the five sense-perceptions, i.e., their forms of experiences, as assimilated in consciousness and retained in memory, are the first of the major supports of the *ālayavijñāna*. This is obvious enough, if the *ālayavijñāna* is considered as mind-basis-

27 Ibid., 51-52.

of-all. Consciousness is derived from every phenomena it has come into contact with.

Next on thc list is *"a sentient being,"* which is five sense-faculties, i.e., eye, ear, nose, tongue, and body'. These sense-faculties are the mechanism that one can gain the necessary impressions whereby consciousness can perceive something phenomenal.

To this list of five I would add also two more:

1. The entire bodily form, incorporating also the internal organs, which integrates all of the sense-perceptors and assists in their functioning. (The concept here differs from the term 'body' in the above list, because what is there implied is the skin whereby the touch sense-consciousness manifests.) Without such a form containing the life-support mechanism of heart, lungs, etc., none of the five sense-perceptors could function and consciousness could not gain anything.
2. The etheric body, containing the *nāḍīs* and *chakras*, through which consciousness, *skandhas,* and *saṃskāras* function. This is the subtle mechanism of response, conveying the sum of the *prāṇas* obtained through sense-perceptions, merged with thought processes, and embodies their method of assimilation, storage and processing. It is also the mechanism whereby one expresses such manifestations as 'feelings'.

By deduction, therefore, we see that there are really seven Elements (of which two are esoteric), that are accommodated by the seven *chakras.* The five Elements given in the texts are those that are practically concerned with life associated with *saṃsāra* and liberation from it. The two esoteric Elements are experienced by liberated beings.

Next we have *'the residual impression (vāsanā)'*[28] that are left 'by settling on the thoroughly imagined nature' of 'persons and dharmas'.

---

28 The term *vāsanā* is defined as karmic predisposition driving the *saṃskāras* to come to the surface of consciousness. They are a driving force of *karma* and consciousness said to be generated or accumulated from within the *ālayavijñana.* The 'residual impressions' are thus *saṃskāras* driven into activity by *vāsanā.* This concept, therefore, is not concerned with the 'divisions of *vāsanā'* associated with the various seeds (see Sparham 68*ff.),* but rather the major sweep of this energy as a driving force of the entire rebirthing process.

This impression is really the force *(vāsanā)* of the *saṃskāras* yet to be dealt with by the succeeding incarnations of the personal-I. The impressions can be considered the tails, or ribbons of *karma* that follow every person, and which must be retracted during the normal course of the evolutionary process, if the person is to eventually become liberated. Their nature is 'thoroughly imagined' in conformity with the way that the Buddhist syllogisms and logic have presented phenomena of all types to be. To this we give the proviso that it is both 'imagined' because of fleeting transient phenomena, and yet 'real' because it can be experienced, and as a consequence forms the basis to the *ālayavijñāna.* In being consistent with the Yogācāra philosophy, it is also imagined because 'all things exist in the mind and are component parts of the mind' and are consequently stored as part of the *ālayavijñāna.* It is the mind that imagines and makes things real. It is 'thoroughly imagined' because the normal person is thoroughly absorbed into its illusion.

The *second* reasoning for the *'ālayavijñāna* as a basis' is 'the form of the cognition', which is but a description for the use of the intellect by the personal-I. This is logical, as the intellect is considered the sixth sense following the five so far given. It is also indicated by the statement, 'though the world and what is in the world appear, it is neither able to determine what is appearing, nor to give rise to certainty later'. In other words, it is not able to determine ultimate reality by itself. What it identifies as appearing is transitory phenomena, which it takes to be real. However, because it is illusional there is no 'certainty' as to what has *actually* appeared. The phrase, therefore, does not refer to the I-consciousness, which, complete with *bodhicitta, can* thus determine, because the intuition through which it functions (from the point of view of the personal-I) is the guarantee of certainty, as it stems from the highest spiritual faculty, the *dharmakāya.* It sees via the Clear Light of Mind.

When analysing the term 'basis', here the reference is to that which is the base or foundation of something, a principal component upon which something is based. What is presented as this 'basis' is the fact that the correlating and classifying tool that the intellect represents manifests the basic form of activity that sustains the *ālayavijñāna.* It should be noted that it is that part of the *ālayavijñāna* represented by the Sambhogakāya Flower that is implicated here. As such, it can gain nourishment from the intellect, as it had 'perfumed' it in the first place. The I-consciousness is the inevitable gain of the expression of the basis, because it is the directing principle within the *ālayavijñāna*.

Esoterically, the four aspects of the basis of the *ālayavijñāna* given above are expressions of the four petals of the Base of Spine *(mūlādhāra) chakra,* supporting the entire multifunctional nature of the *ālayavijñāna*. This *chakra* represents the foundation from which all forms of consciousness grow, and the sum of the *ālayavijñāna* can flower. This is because the *ālayavijñāna* outlasts the successive appearances of each personal-I, whereby these four petals are grounded. The part of the *ālayavijñāna* that is enclosed by the Sambhogakāya Flower incorporates, and is inclusive of, the remaining six *chakras* and the functioning of their petals. The teaching of how they function can only be revealed when detail of the true nature of the *chakras* can be given. Detailed analysis of the *chakras* is a most esoteric subject, and problematic, with karmic consequences when wrongly given to the profane that are desirous of psychic power. Clear undistorted information however needs to be appropriately presented, because of the necessary progressive release of esoteric information needed for the advancement of Bodhisattvas in this modern epoch, who can think with their hearts. The timely release of esoteric information assists them to gain ever widening arcs of revelation.

The four petals of the *Base of Spine chakra* help develop the qualities of mind/Mind, as governed by the attributes of the orientation of its petals. It is the base for all that will later transpire as the Head lotus awakens. From the perspective of the orientation of the fixed cross[29] we have:

- The southern petal points downward into the realms of form. To this direction, therefore, is allocated the basis of the five sense-perceptors, and the interrelation with the minutiae and vicissitudes of the form. This allows the appearance of the 'mental faculties' in the northern direction. Mineral kingdom Earthy *prāṇas* are here generated. This relates to the appearance of 'form *(ākarā)*'.

---

29 The way the *chakra* normally manifests in a person (as related to *prāṇic* circulation) is that the north-south orientation relates to the plant and mineral kingdoms, east-west to the human and animal kingdoms. See Volume 5A, where this orientation is explained with respect to certain Īśvarī that embody the petals.

- The northern petal points upward toward the *ālayavijñāna*. Here therefore, we have the form of cognition that the intellect represents. Fiery *prāṇas* of the human kingdom are generated. (We thus have the generation of 'the mental faculties accompanying it'.)
- The eastern petal points inward to the Heart of life, which expresses the quality that is not subject to moralising. Airy *prāṇas* of the plant kingdom are generated. This relates to the *prāṇic* foundation that embodies the 'nature *(svabhāva)'* of what is to be.
- The western petal points outward to the field of human interrelations. This is embodied by the fourth basis, given as feeling, cognition, contact, and *manaskāra* (mental aspects or engagements, which Sparham translates as 'attention'). Watery *prāṇas* of the animal kingdom are generated. These attributes represent the 'objective support' of the entire embodied form that evolves.
- The central point of this flower represents the attributes of the stem that has grown from the sprouted seed of the *ālayavijñāna*. Here we have the expression of Aetheric *prāṇas.*

The *third* 'nature of the *ālayavijñāna* as a basis' is presented as 'unobscured and not a subject of moralizing'. What this means is that what is finally integrated into the *ālayavijñāna* is true, factually as it is, without distortion or error; be this from good or bad actions, or forms of consciousness. If there was moralizing, then the *ālayavijñāna* could not function as a store-consciousness, there would only be a jumbled mess of mental determinants that change with every new seed impulse. *Karma* cannot be directed from such an environment. Neither can consciousness work, if the attributes of mind pertaining to the past continually changes with moralistic whims and judgements happening where they are stored. Instead they must remain in their pristine condition until called forth into the present mental-formations of a personal-I as a basis for future actions. This function of 'not a subject of moralizing' as an aspect of the *ālayavijñāna* is another proof for the existence of a soul-form, the Sambhogakāya Flower, because as previously stated, the impersonal *ālayavijñāna* cannot cause the rebirth process. It needs a conscious will that determines 'without moralizing' that what is seeded for each successive incarnation of a personal-I manifests truthfully, according to the *saṃskāras* and *karma* to be worked upon or developed by that 'I'. Such a function could not manifest from the *ālayavijñāna* alone if it were just an amorphous collection of mental images floating around in a stream of some sort, as orthodox Buddhism seems to suggest.

The *fourth* of the bases is presented as 'that it always endowed with feeling, cognition, volition, contact, and *manaskāra'*. These aspects were earlier explained in terms of the 'five omnipresent mental facilities'. They are also the higher correspondences of the objects of support for the five sense-perceptors.

Sounds—contact (sparśa) and the sense of hearing. Sounds are caused by physical things vibrating or resonating in such a way that they can be heard and the mind can deduce their nature. This can refer not just to contact with physical forms, but also to subjective entities. (Principally with various thought-forms.) Such types of forms might be imaginary, non-tangible to those in dense physical bodies, but when the physical body is eliminated, and later also the emotional body, then one resides in the realm of mind, and thoughts become real things. They can then be contacted by a mind in a similar way that physical objects can be touched by the fingers.

Feelings—feeling (vedanā). As well as modifying consciousness in the production of *kāma-manas,* feelings also necessitate us investigating the evolution of the qualities of *kliṣṭamanas*. The sense of touch is esoterically implicated here, allowing emotional interrelations between people. Such interrelation is by means of the substance of the entire subtle body. Similarly, the sense of touch is the only sense not localised as in the case of the eyes or ears. The sense of touch generally stimulates an emotional or feeling response to what is touched.

Forms—volition (cetanā). Only forms can manifest actions that cause karmic consequences. They demonstrate the appearance of the things that are moved and as they are moved they produce consequences. This is the position that I normally relegate to sight, the expression of which is the intellect, which causes the forms to move, producing volitions. The eyes direct all such action. Forms can consequently also relate to thought-forms, the images formed in the mind. The Yogācāra doctrine, in any case, states that all things, hence forms, are expressions of the mind. (One can see here that contact and volition, the physical and mental domains, have a strong interconnectedness.)

Tastes—cognition (saṁjñā). We taste things to produce subtle discernment of their true nature, hence the phrase 'taste of enlightenment'. It produces a subtle, refined or internal recognition of the qualities of a phenomena: bitter, sweet, sour, salty, or neutral. The associated Element is Air.

Smells—manaskāra. Smells stimulate the highest of the sense-perceptors, directly affecting the mind *(manas)* to produce its subtlest or loftiest impressions, abstract cognition. This is because what is smelled is instantly acutely analysed by the mind. It is therefore the highest of the senses, where the attributes of the abstract Mind is implicated. Here the entire personal-I, that postures an 'I', 'me', 'mine', is involved to master all of the other sense-perceptions so that the Mind can awaken. Many odours are pleasant, but others can present a serious danger to life, signifying the need for very subtle discernments in the path of life.

It should also be noted that the five aspects of *taste* relate to the five Elements, when viewed from the perspective of the type of energies they represent. There are two lines of expression to these Elements:

a. The Will or mind line, energising the *iḍā nāḍī.*

b. The Love-Wisdom line, energising the *piṅgalā* stream.[30]

The mode of expression of these aspects of taste relates to the intensity and effect of the energies of the five types of *prāṇas* conveying the Elements within *saṃsāra.*

Along the *iḍā nāḍī* line we have:

1. *Bitter* signifies the most intense form of *iḍā* energisation, thus it represents Aetheric energies. This *prāṇa* is directly concerned with liberation from formed existence. It is the gain of the most traumatic types of (bitter) experiences; the effect of what the personal-I sacrifices upon the path to liberation. Consequently, it can also represent the *suṣumṇā* energy.

2. Next we have the Fiery Element, represented by the taste expression *sour.* This refers to the discriminative, analytical, deductive, dissecting capacity of the mind. Proper logic sours one's enjoyment of

30 From the perspective of the doctrine of the Rays, the will line governs the expression of Rays 1, 3, 5 and 7, whilst the Love-Wisdom line the Rays 2, 4 and 6.

saṃsāra because the concepts of suffering, death and nonattachment must be reckoned into one's involvement with it.

3. The third *prāṇa* along the *iḍā* line is Earthy. This is represented by the taste expression *salty*. The term best describes the way one experiences *saṃsāra* of and for itself. It often enhances the other aspects of taste, in the way, therefore, that the attributes of *saṃsāra* are experienced to produce the five *prāṇas*.

Along the *piṇgalā* line we have:

4. The quality *sweet* represents the expression of Watery *prāṇas,* which refer to the way most people view their emotional interactions with others. Pleasurable, sensual pursuits and the devotional, affectionate aspects of their psychology are here implicated.
5. Finally we have that characteristic termed *neutral*. This refers to the Airy Element, which is closely affiliated with the expression of Love, with respect to its involvement with *saṃsāra*. Consequently, it is neither pleasant or unpleasant, but rather a means to gather wisdom-producing experiences. This Element is also a direct emanation of the Void, which is decidedly neutral in character. This neutral characteristic accommodates all of the other *prāṇas*.

The question now asked is 'How do the transformed aspects of the five sense-perceptors manifest in the *ālayavijñāna* when viewed in terms of the functions of the I-consciousness?' The answer is fivefold:

- It has the ability to make *contact* with other such bodies (Sambhogakāya Flowers) by means of *mantra,* emanatory sound. This qualifies each consciousness-form. By the quality of sound or note its entire history, where it stands upon the ladder of evolutionary being, can be gleaned. The sound is a resonant vibration that immediately qualifies what it contacts with the nature of the substance that it imbues. The experiencer can thereby immediately discern its quality and make instantaneous assumptions.
- The Sambhogakāya Flower is a container of the *ālayavijñāna,* and also is an embodiment of Love (for which the term 'feeling' has been used as a substitute above) and wisdom. Such Love will not moralise, as earlier explained, however, will inevitably endeavour to steer the

course of the decision making of the personal-I's consciousness-stream so that its evolution proceeds to Buddhahood. 'Good and bad' are therefore both seen as part of a process that lays the foundation for the development of the necessary wisdom that is the basis of a Buddha's enlightenment. Both are necessary, but the associated *karma* is relegated so that liberation from *saṃsāra* is eventually produced.

- That aspect of the *ālayavijñāna* expressed as the Sambhogakāya Flower manifests *volitions* in the act of perfuming every new personal-I that is to appear in the formed realms. It becomes responsible for the evolutionary progression of the succession of such I's. There is also the volition to make contact with all Sambhogakāya Flowers that are part of the group *(chakra)* it is a part of.
- It gains in *cognition* from the perfumes that have been seeded into the personal-I's, which it esoterically tastes and therefore assimilates the responses.
- It *'smells'* the perfumes from other Sambhogakāya Flowers and therefore manifests a form of transcendent, instantaneous communication with them. This sense of smell is used also to receive what is perfumed into it from the realm of the *dharmakāya*. The perfumes govern the way it expresses itself with respect to its group affiliations, and also to the course of evolution of the personal-I's.

The basis for comprehending the functioning of the Sambhogakāya Flowers has now been outlined, allowing further revelation as to the nature of the constitution of its form to be provided in Volume 3.

The *ālayavijñāna* and the formless realms

The next quote from Sparham's work:

> Even in the two upper realms there is no externally established form, only physical appearances in consciousness.
>
> Thus, it is the force of the meditation on formless absorption *(samāpatti)* that incapacitates the seeds that produce appearances of form in the *ālaya-vijñāna*. For as long as the person remains in the formless realm, nothing which has form can appear. It is like the

force of the meditation on the absorption of the thought process which incapacitates the seeds of the six consciousnesses in the *ālaya-vijñāna*. For as long as the absorption does not wane the six consciousnesses cannot arise.

Question: Would it not follow, however, that the formless *ālaya-vijñāna* becomes without any objective support? For the world and what is in it, which have forms, do not appear, and it is meaningless to posit residual impressions as its objective support. If one agrees with this one is led to accept a consciousness devoid of objective support [an absurd proposition].

Answer: there is no flaw in this. For it is said in the MSam:[31]

> When [consciousness of] the past, etc., dreams, and the two kinds of images [i.e., those which appear in certain samādhis and in a mirror] there is no actual objective support [but still one is conscious of them]. Therefore, since one can be conscious (*ā-lamb*) of these, [consciousness does not need an actual objective support].[32]

It has already been noted that the Yogācāra doctrine that states 'there is no externally established form, only physical appearances in consciousness' is incorrect from one perspective, but also correct from another view. The mode of error of thinking here has already been established. Briefly stated, forms do not need consciousness to acknowledge their existence, they are simply there, whether a being's sense-perceptors experience them or not at any particular time. Consciousness simply identifies them as 'things' and appoints them into categories of useful, maybe, or non-useful to it. Closing one's eyes to a chair in front of one does not mean that it has vanished. It simply means that the eye function is no longer registering the fact of its existence, but the brain logically assumes it is existent, and recognitions are made in consciousness of the natural outcome of walking towards it, for then the person *will* bump into it. Its physicality is already pre-established in consciousness because the experiential foundations for such assumption have been established. Consciousness cannot realistically do otherwise than to presume this. If the chair existed only in consciousness, then

31 The abbreviation refers to *Theg pa chen po bsdus pa (Mahāyāna-saṁgraha).*

32 Sparham, 54.

from the above postulate, consciousness would be able to create any thing and it would appear so on the physical plane, but this is not the case. Also, if it happened to be something dangerous, such as a speeding car on the road, and one closed one's eyes to it, proceeding to cross the road with the thought of its non-existence, then one would pay the inevitable consequence for one's folly.

This non-reciprocity proves, in fact, that the Yogācāra doctrine is erroneous in this respect. They do not incorporate the nature of the laws that govern the substance of mind in relation to the phenomenal appearance of anything. The substance of mind is far too tenuous and subtle to directly influence physical matter (except under certain circumstances). Their assertions, however, are based upon a certain logic, as has been explained. Such substance also exists as the 'objective support' for the appearance of dreams and the images in *samādhi.* Without substance *(citta)* of some kind, such images could not exist.

I have already commented upon the fact that the formless realms are only formless to considerations by the human intellect, because of the relative density of the substance of mind utilised. However, if that substance were refined to a great extent, and elevated to a high rate of energisation, then that which was once formless begins to appear formed, like the formless wind around one that is shown to have form at a great elevation. Such refinement of thought is what happens in *samāpatti,* abstract meditation, perfected concentration before actual *samādhi* is reached.

The Buddhist philosophers in both these examples have not informed us of the extent that substance of some sort pervades all of space, even that of *śūnyatā*, otherwise it could not 'be'. *Śūnyatā* cannot manifest as a total vacuum that represents the annihilation of everything. Wherever you have substance of some sort, there you have the possibility of forms appearing, and indeed their certainty. That one does not register such as 'real' at any time is simply because one has not yet developed the psychic-perceptors to do so. (In a similar way that normal humans have not developed the ability to directly experience the TV and radio waves that pass through them invisibly all of the time.) They have not yet refined and elevated their consciousness to the subtleties needed to experience the formless realms as they truly are.

What is being presented here to the Buddhist reader is the revelation that the abstract realms of the Mind are indeed the true *arūpa* or formless realms mentioned in their texts. They are beyond the formed conceptualisation of mental images. However, within these levels, forms as such do exist, constituted of the substance of pure consciousness and arranged as petals of the Sambhogakāya Flowers unfolding. (We could also consider other *sambhogakāya* forms, such as the depictions of Buddhas and Bodhisattvas.) One that is absorbed in 'formless absorption *(samāpatti)'* is really absorbed in the energy fields and patterns associated with such a Flower (wherewith everything concerning the past and future is stored). The energy fields are an 'objective support' for the existence of consciousness in the *arūpa* realms. The highest of the formless realms represents entering into the Śūnyatā Eye.

Therefore the query concerning consciousness being 'devoid of objective support' in the *arūpa* realms, which is 'an absurd proposition', is easily answered because therein consciousness is supported by the existence of the Sambhogakāya Flowers. It does not need a circular answer, such as provided in the *Mahāyāna-saṁgraha,* where it is stated that *because* one is conscious of things of the past in the *arūpa* realms 'consciousness does not need an actual objective support'. This is but saying that because it happens, or has happened, so there is no reason to explain how, just take it for granted that 'something' overcomes the 'absurdity' of the proposition.

Further quoting Sparham:

> All consciousnesses, therefore, are not necessarily contingent on an existing objective support. In particular, the *ālaya-vijñāna* is present through a propulsive force [which throws the living being into *saṁsāra*] and is not contingent on the appearance of an *ālambana.*[33] For the previous virtuous or non virtuous action brings forth this basis of a happy or bad migration that is not removed, even for one instant, until the time of death.[34]

So what *exactly* is this *'propulsive force' (vāsanā)* that 'throws the living being into *saṃsāra?'* How can it function in this store of

33 Observed object.

34 Sparham, 54.

consciousness, when according to Buddhism, there is no 'self' or 'other' that can do this propelling?

If it *(vāsanā)* is conceived of as the *momentum of consciousness* that is likened to a stream ever flowing, then this will not throw 'the living being into *saṃsāra'*. How can such a stream *cause itself* to alter its course to produce the *phenomenal appearance* of a personal-I (especially if there is 'no objective support')? To do so it must manifest as an individuality. Such individuality could then direct the momentum and course of the general current of the stream. What about the countless little swirls contained within it?[35] (We must consider such, as they account for the various *bījas* embodying the many particularised attributes of consciousness.) If each of these little swirls are also individualities, responsible somewhat for their own forms of activity, then properly planned concretions or sedimentation, the seeding of a personal-I, is possible, utilising the necessary grouping of *bījas* to do so. Such swirls are seeds that 'produce appearances of form in the *ālaya-vijñāna'*. When it is said that it is the 'force of the meditation on formless absorption *(samāpatti)* that incapacitates' them then the author is referring to the nature of formless meditation within itself. The seeds are only 'incapacitated' upon the path of yogic transformation of *saṃskāras* that produces enlightenment. Other than this the seeds remain, but one rises above them in the *arūpa* meditation. Such formless meditation may transcend the expression of individuality, but it also allows visualisation of the way individuality manifests in the processes of becoming what it is to be. One must see the *bījas* from above in order to comprehend the overview and to direct the awakening *maṇḍala*.

The momentum of consciousness in terms of evolutionary progression should also be observed, as is explained here. One can then ask the question 'why does it evolve, and where to?' The quick answer is *śūnyatā*, but why would such a consciousness-stream work towards its

35 Suzuki states, quoting scripture: 'The doctrine of the Vijñānas is described in this wise: "As the waves of the ocean depending on the wind are stirred up and roll on dancing without interruption (99); "So the Ālaya-flood constantly stirred up by the wind of individuation *(vishaya)* rolls on dancing with the waves of the various Vijñānas'. *Studies in the Lankavatara Sutra,* 171. Such symbolic waves (relating to an individual mind in this quote) would stir up the above-mentioned swirls of the consciousness-stream, but still need to be directed by something to individuate into forms.

own annihilation? The answer is that *it doesn't* (noting that the concept of annihilation is anathema to Buddhists). But then why would it flow naturally into a void? In reality it cannot. The only solution here is that the consciousness-stream becomes transformed in some way by an (extraneous) agent, one that also incorporates the stream. Such an agent is accounted for in Buddhism by the technical attributes of the *tathāgatagarbha.* A void can then appear as consciousness-attributes are transmogrified into the *dharmakāya.* This process constitutes the path of the Dharmakāya Way.

Others may postulate that the 'propulsive force' is the force of *karma.* But can *karma* precipitate such a form of its own volition? The question is in fact 'Can *karma* selectively assemble together all of the component elements from out of the *ālaya,* predetermining the complete characteristics needed for a particular incarnation of a personal-I?' This concerns the functioning of an individuality, however, the will that predetermines individuality is a functioning of an individualised consciousness, not of a universal law. As previously stated, *karma* would have to decide *which* components are needed out of the billions of possibilities, in relation to the entire constituency of all of the billions of humans presently in incarnation, and the unaccountable billions out of incarnation. Many of these may indeed be incarnate and have some type of interrelation with the person to be in the extent of its life time. One must look also to the far-distant future of the possible ramifications of all such interrelations as well as to the incarnations of those who are to manifest later in that life. I deem nay, and assert this is definitely not possible. It is asking far too much from a relatively simple law of rectifying reaction in response to an action done. The gullibility factor of the wildest optimist would have to be stretched to the limit to consider this a possibility.

Is it some *extraneous force,* presently unknown to Buddhism, but which would have to be discovered or contrived in some way to account for the phenomena? If this is the case, then we have to ask why none of the enlightened *yogins* have discovered such a force over the millennia of their activity. Perhaps such a force doesn't exist for them to discover, or if such discovery *was made,* it remained esoteric, ear whispered, and/or purposely veiled because of its incompatibility with the way the religion is formulated.

Is it some Buddha existing in *śūnyatā*, taking it upon himself to ensure that such human incarnations are possible, and as a consequence will be responsible for uncountable trillions of karmic interactions simultaneously? Again I assert not, because though Buddhists like to think that a Buddha is omnipotent and omniscient (like the 'God' of any Theistic religion is), the immense number of petty calculations upon continuous karmic volitions that are needed to be determined for each of the billions of individual human beings and their interrelationships is well beyond the purpose of such a 'thus gone' one. It necessitates continuous involvement with thought constructions, and the laws of being, needed for assessing proper energy interrelations on all levels of perception. It allows no time whatsoever for *samādhi upon any subject other than* upon the petty karmic interactions of countless individual life streams upon our earth, long into the far distant future.

The sheer complexity of dealing with such a staggering amount of personal *karma* is an overwhelming impossibility for any single individual, no matter how astoundingly enlightened or liberated he/she may be. However, if we posit an entire Hierarchical structure of a vast number of entities working upon the problem of karmic adjudication, then we enter into the domain of possibilities.

Taking all this into account, we see that the only obvious option here is the existence of subtle soul-forms, the Sambhogakāya Flowers *(tathāgatagarbhas)* existing as part of the *ālayavijñāna*. Each of these is responsible for continuous meditation upon the personal-I's that they seed to reap the crop of fragrances, as the personalities develop along the upward way. Individually and collectively they can manifest the 'propulsive force' stated to be integral to the *ālayavijñāna*. They can also direct interrelated group *karma* to produce the evolving forms they are unitedly concerned with. Continuously we come to the realisation that such subtle soul-forms *must exist* in the realms of consciousness, despite the millennial old Buddhist denial, aversion, and outright contempt of such a consideration. A contempt, it may be added, that was definitely not part of the Buddha's own itinerary for the education of the many.

The Phoenix of Mind and the bird of time

Hear the silent sounds of its wings
from the deep well of my Lord's keep.
Your *karma* it comes to sow and to reap.
Each feather spiralling the return of an interlocking plethora of
every little earthling's happenings
into major epochs of this world's lore.
Over the field of fervent emotions,
battlefield scarred screaming more,
this bird forewarns mighty changes as it sweeps
soaring outwards from the deep.
Reaping waves of what in the mind transpires,
a profiled insight into those who weep.
Many cycles of returning forebode the power of its seeing.
With Harpies and Furies this bird makes the peace.
One to bemoan everyone's troublesome past,
seeding the conscience with thoughts of the homicide,
parricide, matricide, genocide,
many loathsome, malicious and avaricious tides
of all deeds most vilely done.
Repent, repent, the Fury pierces your mind as it sings.
The other will snap the cord
if the Fury one does not heed.
And the Phoenix reaps this troublesome lot,
to take each to their appointed plot
at the end of the cycle of their deeds.
Famines, wars, and devastation
with the Phoenix proceeds.
Those ashes at its pyre it leaves
for you to contemplate what in the end of this life
all you've grappled with and what's left that you've got.

Its ‘500 years’ is what the mind doth cycle,
to reappear with the bird
bringing the myrrh of your hopes and aspirations
to purpose, that one cycle higher.
For you to enlightenment it soars to bring.

The bird of time flies and looks not behind.
It sees not, nor seeks that which is lost
or cannot be possessed, but wings on
over towering mountains
and boundless seas
to distant lands and galaxies.
On....on it flies,
into horizons vaster that the
widest imaginative mind,
where time no longer is,
and the present past is future forgot.
Fly dear one, fly to that horizon
and be mine.

11

The Examination of Time in the *Mūlamadhyamakakārikā* of Nāgārjuna

The exposition of the verses

For this exposé I shall utilise David J. Kalupahana's translation of the *Mūlamadhyamakakārikā* of Nāgārjuna. The first verse is given as:

> If the present and the future exist contingent upon the past, then the present and the future would be in the past time.[1]

This verse informs us that if the three times exist, then the existence of the present-future is contingent upon the past action. There cannot be a past without the action of consciousness of some type. This presupposes the enactment of *karma,* where all processes associated with the appearance of the three times reaps the past actions. This *kārikā* therefore begins with considerations from the realm of mind. If the present and future are contingent upon past time, then they are effectively in that past time because the experience of the related *karma* was seeded in the past. The future development is contained in the seed.

Prevision is a fundamental characteristic of the mind. Once it has recorded the need to act, then it automatically projects images of that action towards future eventuation. It instantaneously examines the future potential of that course of action, then acts. Hence the past immediately becomes the present future. An example is the lifting of

1 David J. Kalupahana, *Mūlamadhyamakakārikā of Nāgārjuna,* (Motilal Banarsidass, Delhi, 1999), 275.

a glass of water to drink. Bodily stimuli has projected to the mind the sensation of thirst, the mind then instantly makes the calculations as to the mode of quenching that thirst. Therefore, an image of a glass and filling it with water appears before the future act is consummated. (If the mind has chosen water to quench thirst.) In this way also 'the present and the future would be in the past time'.

Verse 19:2 states:

> Again, if the present and the future were not to exist therein [i.e., in the past], how could the present and the future be contingent upon that?[2]

The straightforward assumption is that this verse informs us that *karma* would not be possible if it was not seeded in the past. We can also look to a condition wherein the past and the future do not exist (therein), which brings us to conceptions of *śūnyatā*. The question that follows is 'how could the present and the future be contingent upon that?' The answer is that the present and the future are not contingent upon *śūnyatā*, except in the way that *śūnyatā* can be considered to eternally abide in the NOW. The flow of events from the past to the future also contains a method whereby karmic action can be reaped, so that all action can eventually be equilibrated, made void. When there is no consciousness to consider, then there is no involvement with time. However, is it possible to perceive the sum of the flow of events from 'above' or beyond, if one is not conditioned by that flow? Thus, even though one who is in the Void is not conditioned by *karma* (the past, present, and future), the contingencies of past-future can be visualised as they really exist in *saṃsāra, from the saṃsāra-śūnyatā* nexus.

In relation to these two verses, Kalupahana states:

> Analysing time as a separate entity, the metaphysicians assumed that if there were to be any mutual relationship between the present and the future on one hand and the past on the other, then, since they are distinct entities, the present and the future will have to be inherent in the past. In other words, the past produces the present and future from within itself. This is the identity version of causation *(svatotpatti)*. A further implication of this is that if one knows the past, one also knows

2 Ibid.

with absolute certainty what the present and the future would be. These, indeed, represent some of the basic speculations of the Sarvāstivādins.[3]

With respect to these Sarvāstivādin arguments, we can say that if one knows the past then one does not know with absolute certainty what the future is to be for humanity, because of the factor of human free will. People can modify the appearing *saṃskāras* any way they wish and thus change the way the future was to go. Therefore, the *saṃskāras* of the past can appear in the future when the corresponding cycle to when they were created appears. (They can only appear when events and psychic situations similar to when they were created have manifested.) However, they can then be immediately changed according to the wilful volitions of the person in the present.

It therefore means that nobody, not even a Buddha, can predict with unfailing accuracy what a person will do in the future (from the perspective of what is stored in the past alone). Nevertheless, certain assumptions or projections can be made that such and such will almost certainly happen, based upon an understanding of human psychology and the nature of the manifesting *saṃskāras*. Their general weight along a certain direction will tilt the balance of the scales overwhelmingly along a certain course. The more refined and consciously developed an individual, the more certain of the outcome in the future, that his behaviour will proceed along well established and therefore predictable lines. Also, the more coarse, sensual, and avaricious an individual, so also his behaviour can be reasonably well predicted.

A much surer method of predicting future tendencies lies in the Sambhogakāya Flower. It determines which of the myriads of possibilities stored in the past is to be experienced by the personal-I, and directs the *saṃskāras* in accordance with its plan for the successive incarnations of the personal-I. When an enlightened being looks to the Sambhoghakāya Flower for information, he can therefore predict with reasonable certainty what future lies in store for a personal-I or for his future incarnations. He/she will also be able see with a glance the possible variations of that probable future, because always there are

3 Ibid., 275-276.

favoured, expected outcomes, but with contingency plans pre-established in the consciousness of the Flower for any possible (temporary) deviant outcome. The contingency plans show how to rectify the possibilities, so that what is desired will manifest in time.

Verse 19:3 states:

> Moreover, non-contingent upon the past, their [i.e., of the present and future] establishment is not evident. Therefore, neither a present nor a future time is evident.[4]

This verse continues in the above vein, indicating that the future and present could not exist if there was no past action ('non-contingent upon the past'). To establish something requires a firm foundation, or base, upon which it can be made to exist and to persist. There is no such lasting base in *saṃsāra,* only relatively temporary ones exist, such as what the earth provides for our incarnations.

Consciousness, on the other hand, can be considered 'established' to see through the appearance and disappearance of the various bases existing corporeally. Like the earth, with respect to our phenomenal appearances, consciousness acts as a base for our incessant thoughts, whereby time is reckoned. But consciousness is above time, as it is only conditioned by it when directly appreciating phenomenological changes in the formed world. When in a dream state, for instance, timelessness can be considered an expression of consciousness. However, upon careful reflection we can say that the only true 'permanent' base that can be found is *śūnyatā*, and that is no base at all.

Another way of analysing this statement is to see that time only exists as long as *saṃsāra* exists to sustain it. Remove its conditionings (the past) by entering *śūnyatā* and you remove the mechanism whereby time can exist, therefore its 'establishment is not evident'. This can also be viewed from the perspective of *saṃsāra* being illusional. Or, we can say that if you remove the karmic conditionings (the past), then the present and future will not be evident. Time is an expression of the mode of manifestation of that *karma.*

Verse 19:4 states:

---

4 Ibid., 276.

> Following the same method, the remaining two periods of [time] as well as related concepts such as the highest, the lowest and the middle, and also identity, etc. should be characterized.[5]

Once the fundamental transience of time has been established, then the same logic can be used to analyse all aspects of it, from beginning to the ending (of *karma*), as well as of all aspects of *saṃsāra* that appear 'in time'. Such concepts as 'highest', 'lowest' and 'middle' are all relative and must likewise be viewed within the context of the flow of time, contingent upon the mode of expression of the *karma* that seeded it all. What is 'highest, lowest, and middle' in the atomic world, where karmic causes and effects can be reckoned in terms of nanoseconds, differs to that of the greater universe, where aeons form the basis of our reckoning. 'Identity' refers to a self-concept that arises from temporal considerations of time, of cause and effect with respect to the emanation of *karma*. Such identity is likewise an illusion, and can be characterised in a similar manner to that of the time that caused its phenomenal appearance. It is contingent upon a past wherein it was seeded, but the present-future will see its non-appearance. Also, upon proper analysis such an 'I' cannot ultimately be found.

In considering the process of time and the emanation of *karma* with respect to identity (of a personal-I), three main stages can be analysed, each with a past, present, and future. They are here termed 'the highest, the lowest and the middle'.

We first have the lowest, referring to the possession of sensual, strongly desirous, war-like and avaricious qualities, producing the type of *karma* that perpetuates rebirths into painful situations and into hell states. This represents the past for most people.

Next we have the middle order of *karmic* formations through time, where the person is well disposed spiritually and is generally charitable. He/she thus maintains the status quo of life's rewards, of both cleansing unwanted *saṃskāras* as well as creating new ones associated with more refined consciousness traits. Generally, such a person finds pleasant rebirths into situations that profits from practicing the *dharma*. This represents the present for most people.

5 Ibid., 277.

Finally there is the highest order, where good or bad *karma* is no longer created, only what produces the transmutation of all *saṃskāras* remains so that liberation from the need to incarnate again is achieved. This is the high path of Tantric *yoga*, representing the future for most people.

Verse 19:5 states:

> A non-static time is not observed. A static time is not evident. Even if the unobserved time were to be observed, how can it be made known?[6]

With regards to this, Kalupahana states that:

> A non-static time is a temporal flux. It is what the interpreters of the Abhidharma referred to as the "flowing present" (*santati paccuppanna, DhsA* 421), where the future continues to flow into the past through the present. Any attempt to grasp it would be futile, for by the time the attempt is made the present has disappeared into the past. In order to grasp it one has to stop the flow.[7]

The 'temporal flux' is the eternal Now, and can be viewed in its duration with respect to the flow of *karma* from the time of its seeding to the period of its inevitable transmutation or ending. One does not need to stop time to observe such a flow, but simply to meditatively stand above or beyond it and observe. Effectively, a movie is watched within the meditative Mind. Time, however, cannot 'be made known' because it is a continuum, a flow of events relative to what is being observed within the frame of a vaster or more encompassing time zone. (Like a human life with respect to the life of the civilisation of which one forms a part.)

When one tries to make it known then new events have transpired that have changed the signposts, because consciousness has manifested an experiential growth with respect to the passage of time. Consequently, it views things differently. Again, it is consciousness that 'makes known', that reveals things with respect to time. Hence, any analysis of what time is, is really an analysis of the nature of evolution of consciousness. From this paradigm we can ask that if time does not exist, then has consciousness been transcended? The answer is no, because consciousness actually exists beyond time, hence we can dream and

6 Ibid., 278.

7 Ibid.

imagine things, or see vast panoramas of events happening in a moment of timelessness. Time is a toll that allows consciousness to measure things and events, and therefore gauge relativity and comprehend the nature of its own evolution, of the maturation and refinement of ideas. Therefore consciousness also incorporates time.

The statement made by Kalupahana with respect to verse 19:5, that 'Absolute time makes no sense for Nāgārjuna',[8] is not quite true. It is simply that Nāgārjuna did not directly comment upon absolute time. He simply asked a question, that 'if the unobserved time were to be observed, how can it be made known?' It is difficult to conceive of what absolute time actually is, as it represents the duration of space existing before segmentation from it of the units of a containing intelligence of a personal-I. Such units then can reckon in terms of time, i.e., in terms of cycles of limited durations of consciousness unfolding. Absolute time is therefore beyond consciousness, or rather is consciousness existing within itself when not identified with form, with *saṃsāric* activity. The question that if it is beyond consciousness, then 'how can it be made known?' can be answered by an enlightened Mind that stands above empirical considerations and can therefore directly perceive, or rather, identify with such time.

In Greek mythology the concept is represented by the symbolism of Saturn, representing the temporal time of formed space, mutilating his father Chronos, who represents absolute time of abstracted space. Absolute time can be considered to represent a measure of time of such vast proportions that the cycles involved with its form of activity are relegated as virtually meaningless by consciousness. It is literally beyond its scope of evolutionary space.

To conclude, it is important to note that there are four parts to this verse:

a. 'A non-static time is not observed'. This refers to the state of awareness associated with *śūnyatā*. Here no conception of time is possible, not even that non-static time that governs evolutionary space.
b. 'A static time is not evident'. This is the condition relating to *saṃsāra,* where the flow of time that is observed is 'non-static'.

8 Ibid.

c. 'If the unobserved time were to be observed' refers to the activity of the mind, which observes the flow of events by being caught in it. It therefore observes empirical time, but cannot raise itself above it, thus cannot know time in essence, of the way that absolute time manifests.

d. 'How can it be made known?' This refers to that aspect of consciousness (the abstract Mind) that can stand above time and observe it. Essentially therefore, the abstract Mind resides in 'absolute time'.

Verse 19:6 states:

> If it is assumed that time exists depending upon an existent, how can there be time without an existent? No existent whatsoever is found to exist. Where can time be?[9]

One can concur that it is the mind (an 'existent') that recognises time. With respect to the lesser evolved species we see that time is reckoned by means of sensory input, the registering, for instance, that there is day and night and the seasons. The species can then respond with instinctual behavioural actions.

In relation to this verse, Kalupahana states:

> In the present verse, Nāgārjuna is maintaining that two independent entities—an existent *(bhāva)* and time *(kāla)*—cannot be dependent upon one another. If they are dependent upon one another *(bhāvaṃ pratītya kālaś cet),* then there cannot be time independent of an existent. An existent as such is non-existent. Whence can there be time? This is a rejection not of temporal phenomena, but only of time *and* phenomena as well as their mutual dependence so long as they are perceived as independent entities.[10]

Kalupahana's analysis probably sums up the best of contemporary thinking about the interpretation of Nāgārjuna's exegesis on time. That 'there cannot be time independent of an existent' is true, because

---

9 Ibid.

10 Ibid., 279.

without a mind to register the factor of time, time itself could not exist. Thus a billion universes could come and go, but if there is no consciousness there to perceive the fact of such expanding spaces, then such appearances and disappearances are a factual non-entity. (One cannot even use the term 'meaningless', because such a term implies a thinking mind, whereas the reality is that nothing in fact has happened.) Because there is a mind to perceive, so the factor of time can manifest.

It should be noted, however, that each verse of this *kārikā* is written as an expression of the meditation-Mind unfolding, which is the style common to all enlightened beings. Therefore, every word patterning sequenced into sentences has many levels of meaning. Thus there is much more interwoven into the statements than what is at first obvious. Consequently, the interpreting empirical mind must be trained to think esoterically.

There are actually five parts to this verse:

1. If it is assumed that time exists.
2. If it is assumed that time exists depending upon an existent.
3. How can there be time without an existent?
4. No existent whatsoever is found to exist.
5. Where can time be?

What is presented here are the five keys, or levels of interpretation to this entire question of time. They relate to the five senses, *prāṇas,* and the derived wisdoms of the Dhyāni Buddhas.

First we have the most base level of interpretation, that relating to the phenomenological aspect of *saṃsāra.* (The Earthy consideration.) Such a consideration assumes that 'time exists' because no proper reckoning of evolutionary change could exist without time, there would be no way to measure progress, or indeed of the way that *karma* manifests itself. Therefore at this level the statement 'time exists' is correct. Even the lesser species of life are conditioned by such time considerations as day and night.

Secondly, we are presented with an additional factor concerning the assumption that time exists 'depending upon an existent'. This introduces the factor of an intelligent perceiver, an 'I', that does such assuming in relation to itself and its affairs in the temporal world. Here all *saṃskāric* patterns of emotional-mental pursuits and activities are created due to conceptions that depend upon time. (Such pursuits are essentially Watery in nature.) This sentence therefore infers a consideration of the linear perspective of time, of the three times, stretching from the past to the far distant future. Whilst there is an 'existent', time is measured in terms of that existent's life, of the way the mind has developed.

The existent (the personal-I) is transient, cyclically reincarnating (similarly with time) with respect to the appearing and receding *saṃskāras*. Here then we perceive the cyclic nature of time and of the patterns of *saṃsāra* repeating themselves throughout the three times. To perceive such patterns necessitates an enlightened Mind, which introduces the *third point*, the realm of consciousness. A direct question is thereby asked: 'How can there be time without an existent?' (The Fiery consideration.) Here we see that consciousness must grapple correctly with concepts of time if it is to be freed from *saṃsāric* constraints and gain enlightenment. The answer to this question lies in the structure of consciousness, where we see that once the 'existent' (the personal-I) is gone then the concept of time also vanishes. However, the expression of time associated with cycles persists, as the *karma* remains and must appear again in cyclic space. How all such cycles are interwoven is a thing for the enlightened Mind to comprehend. Here the two main divisions of consciousness must be considered. When the empirical mind of the personal-I, and its concept of linear time, is transcended and the 'I' no longer exists, then it is supplanted by the enlightened abstract Mind. Therein the vaster view of the overriding cycles come into view. Time then becomes the eternal Now.

Nāgārjuna's *fourth statement* introduces *śūnyatā*, and thus the Airy Element. Here 'no existent whatsoever is found to exist', hence there is no consideration of time. This is true, but it should never have been the main interpretation promulgated by the Mādhyamika philosophers. (Within the context of the doctrine of the two truths.) They should have properly understood and incorporated into their logic the various levels of interpretation of Nāgārjuna's *kārikās*.

The *fifth statement* is also posed in the form of a question: 'Where can time be?' We are now to look to the highest level of interpretation, that relating to the Aetheric Element and hence to the *dharmakāya*. What exists beyond time is *śūnyatā*, however, that which relegates 'absolute time' is the *dharmakāya*. Temporal time is but a reified reflection in *saṃsāric* fields of the form of absolute reckoning of time determined by a Mind existing in *dharmakāyic* bliss. Temporal time has its modes of consciousness reckoning with the activities of phenomenal space in such a way that reason or comprehension can be applied. Absolute time is the mode of activation of cosmic events and of the delineation of space into zones of limitation called suns, galaxies, and also of Buddha fields. With this the Dharmakāyic Mind must reckon, if it is to comprehend the nature of multidimensional cosmic space. It is in reference to this *dharmakāyic* reckoning of time with respect to space that esoterically concerns the last verse, thus Nāgārjuna asks us to seriously consider 'Where can time be?' (in the realm) where 'No existent whatsoever is found'. The term 'No existent' can here be applied to the Buddha-Mind. It is a fitting conclusion to any dissertation on time. Time certainly can BE in this absolutistic sense, because here the true cycles relegating the (multidimensional) All have their source. Here time is but the carefully formulated arenas of patterns of what is to be in a Buddha's Mind, and manifests according to the rhythms of his compassionate Thought.

The seven Ray qualities

These six verses can also be explained in terms of *the seven Ray qualities:*

The seventh Ray

First Nāgārjuna presents the concept of the past, which can only exist if *karma* has manifested. This is governed by the seventh Ray of Ritualistic Activity or Ceremonial Order, as *karma* is cyclic in the nature of its appearance, as also is time. The seventh Ray also governs the physical domain, whereto are relegated the cycles of time.

It should be noted that Nāgārjuna carefully delineates the present and the future from the past. (Signified by the phrase 'if the present and the future exist contingent upon the past'.) This is important. The past acts as a type of screen whereupon the potential of the present-future can act as the actuality of the now becoming the past. The past represents all wilful conditionings that caused and sustains *saṃsāra*, from where we get the reckoning of time. Future actions are contingent upon the past, to be enacted as *karma*. *Karma* reveals the past for the present-future. Present actions produce *saṃskāras* that will find expression in a later present-future. The past then represents an event horizon. As these *saṃskāras* appear on the event horizon they produce the now. We see that this horizon is the real. It consists of surfacing *saṃskāras* (the past) devoured by the present-future actions. Thus the cycle completes itself, and spirals into a higher zone of action.

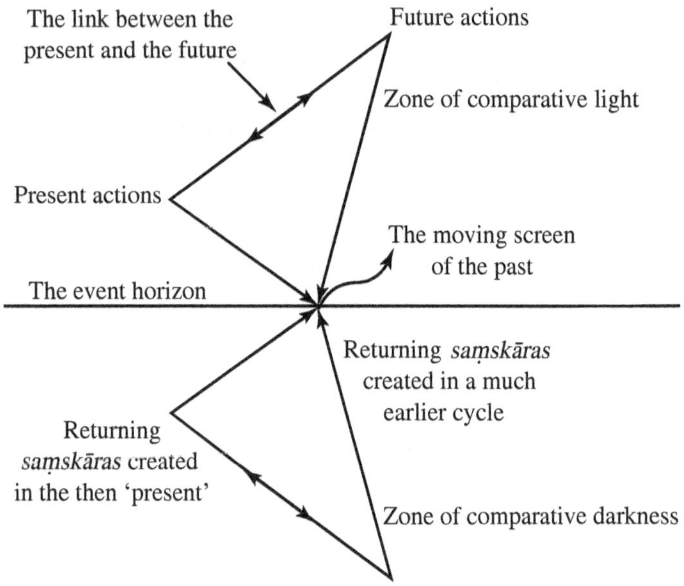

Figure 5. The Moving Screen of the Past

We see here that as the present-future meets the past *saṃskāras*, a new motion is formed as the appearing *saṃskāras* are modified by the present-future. Such modification is curved, moving one way or other, depending upon whether the present-future energy dominates in such a way as to produce consciousness-expansion, or if the *saṃskāras* are reinforced and the motion manifests further ignorance. The general thrust of the process for the great majority is toward progressive expansion, but because of the general nature of the cleansing (or non-cleansing) of the *saṃskāras* we get a snake-like (serpentine) motion:

This motion is also helical as it gradually moves into arenas of greater light. Figure 5 shows in triangular form one layer of this spiral motion and its reflection in the void of the past. It should be noted that this serpentine motion is built up of sentient and emotio-mental *saṃskāras,* and manifests a form of *kuṇḍalinī* energy (serpent power). A *nāga* (serpent) Lord is one who has mastered the process of riding his serpentine *saṃskāras* through to great light. Enlightenment is based upon transforming *saṃskāras*, by conquering the past, and by transmuting serpents—of desire, lust, greed, psychicism, etc. Figure 6 shows another way of depicting this.

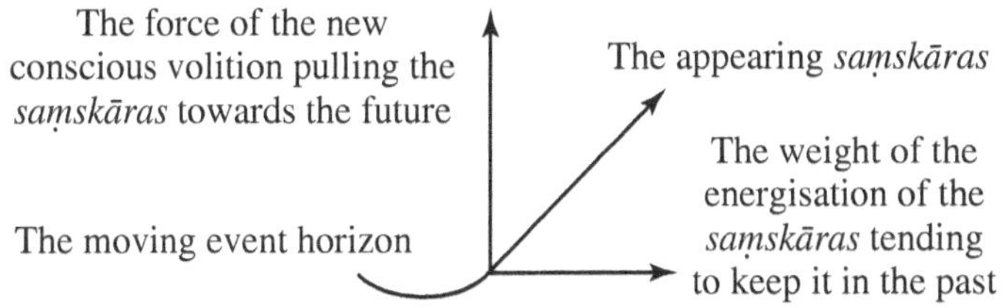

Figure 6. The Event Horizon

Consciousness is affected by the *saṃskāras* that appear. It selects what is desired and generally modifies the *saṃskāras* in a beneficent way to produce an expansive future. The remainder esoterically stay in the past and will reappear at a later time (a later present-future), influencing the new personal-I and again provide consciousness a chance to rectify the past. Consciousness will then have the added impetus of the earlier modified *saṃskāras*. The result of this tugging between the present-future and the past is a serpentine motion of the event horizon, as sometimes the tendencies to the past is victorious and at other times the movement is towards the light. Also, because the present-future's motion is the favoured outcome, the result is a general curved motion towards it. This then produces a spiral over time as the motion expands into (consciousness) space.

The sixth Ray

Nāgārjuna also introduces the three times in the same verse. The *sixth Ray of Devotion* concerns the energy that propels or impels all life or things onwards in space. In a similar manner, devotion impels the life of the spiritual being deep into an exposition of the *dharma*. The lower aspects of this devotion are the various desires and cravings that cause people to be attached to ephemeral things. This causes a lengthening of the amount of time needed for the experience of things. Therefore, we get the full flowering of the three times and the panoply of *saṃsāra* from the original karmic seed. It should be noted here that the sixth and seventh Rays generally work together, in a similar manner as the Sacral and the Base of Spine centres are a functioning pair.

The fifth Ray

The *fifth Ray of Intelligence and Scientific Reason* concerns a proper dissection and analysis of processes already established. This incorporates awakening the analytical process of the mind, and the conception of the roles of the present, and the future, and how they evolve. This is a reason why the second verse is in the form of a question, as Nāgārjuna is alluding to the necessity of cogently analysing the roles of the three times. The aspect of time is a tool whereby consciousness can measure things. The present and the future are therefore the continuous prerogative or focus of consciousness. It lives in the Now (except when purposely regurgitating images of the past, or imagining future events) and modifies appearing *saṃskāras*, but always must question 'how, why?' etc., of all the things the present-future must be contingent upon, with respect to the appearing images.

The fourth Ray

The *fourth Ray of Harmony Overcoming Strife* acts as a mirror between extremes, and therefore reflects the attributes or functions of *śūnyatā* in the realms of form. It is neither one extreme or the other. Thus it brings about a process of detachment from the cravings and desires that cause an addiction to things of the past, allowing things to be seen for what they truly are, relativistically, i.e., in relation to the two extremes. Consequently, it represents the energy that allows one to sit at the *saṃsāra-śūnyatā* nexus.

Verse 19:3 refers to this Ray quality. Here the phrase 'non-contingent upon the past' refers to the moving line of the event horizon, and therefore to the eternal Now, where neither the present or future time is evident, because time as such does not exist. It represents the middle way between the extremes of past and the present-future. In a similar manner, the fourth Ray represents the middle between the qualities of the seven Ray lines.

Upon close examination of this verse (in relation to the moving event horizon) we see that it consists of five parts, where we are indirectly presented with the motion of this event horizon from the past to the future:

a. The past.
b. That which is 'non-contingent upon the past'.
c. The non-establishment of a present-future. They are not evident.
d. A present time does not exist.
e. Nor is there a future time.

a. The past remains as is, relating to the sum of *saṃsāra* and that which can be relegated to the field of ignorance, of darkness. The event horizon moves from the zone of darkness, or relative dull light, which expresses the realm of materiality compared to that of greater light. Thus the progress of motion through time is depicted.
b. Next we have that which is 'non-contingent upon the past', which refers to the world of the emotions. Though *saṃskāras* are drawn to the surface to be experienced upon the event horizon, there is an emotional 'non-contingency' because they simply instantaneously react to what stimulates them. There is no thought there that determines past, present or the future.
c. Looking to the field of consciousness, we see that as far as the moving event horizon is concerned, there is 'non-establishment of a present-future', even though, as earlier stated, present and the future are the continuous prerogative or focus of consciousness. They may be the focus of consciousness but when consciousness considers them, then we find that the present has slid into the past and is 'non-established' whilst the future has not yet come to be, it exists only as possibilities, therefore it is also 'not established'.

Only that established in the past remains in the mind. They can be built upon to 'create' the future, but the moment this happens again we have the past. Consciousness can, however, reside in the eternal Now and view things apart from the three times.

d. When focussed upon the domain of *śūnyatā,* we see that a 'present time' does not exist. There the moving line of the event horizon no longer functions. Both consciousness and motion have been transcended. The eternal Now, however, exists and inevitably that pertaining to the future is still relevant, because the future is the revelatory expansion into the Dharmakāya Way. When that Way impinges upon consciousness via *śūnyatā* then the Now manifests.

e. Finally, we are to look to the domain of the 'thus gone' Buddhas, wherein no future time exists, because the future has been superseded by cosmos.

The third Ray

The *third Ray of Mathematically Exact Activity* concerns the complete development of the reticulation of all phenomena, therefore it produces the unveiling of all things that can be made known, which can be characterised and rectified in time. We are therefore concerned with the beginning of the sustaining activity, and the ending of the cycles of *karma.* Time is specifically exemplified in terms of large cycles and of absolute time.

The fourth verse relates to this Ray and can be divided into seven main parts:

i. The following of the same methods.
ii. The remaining two periods of time, ie., the present-future.
iii. The future aspect of these remaining two periods.
iv. The highest.
v. The lowest.
vi. The middle.
vii. Identity.

To better analyse this verse, we need to turn the listing around to reorient the ordering of the seven Ray qualities.

First the subject of identity. The focus here is not to identity with the lower form (the 'self' concept) but rather to the fundamental identity of the *tathāgatagarbha* and that which relates to it. It concerns the reason why this womb, or matrix, was seeded with Life and how the world of the personal-I transpires from its fundamental existence, its identity. We therefore look to how time and consequent *karma* evolve with respect to this Identity. Here also is veiled the mystery of the Dharmakāya Way.

Secondly, we are to analyse the middle principle of a trinity, of the first three Rays acting as a unity of Father-Son-Mother, of identity-middle-lowest. The term 'the highest' is thus concerned with the highest point of a quaternary (the four of the remaining seven). The 'middle' principle is the way of the development of Love-Wisdom, which is the essence of enlightenment. It is the middle between Identity or abstraction into the *dharmakāya* and phenomenon of all types, as bound by *karma* and the cycles of time, manifest activity, which is signified by the term 'the lowest'. This middle way is the way of the Mahāmudrā, which fuses the extremes. Here the term 'identity' relates to the qualities of a Buddha, the term 'lowest' relates to the qualities of his Consort, and the 'middle' is that which concerns the product of their union, which can be conceived of as a fusion of consciousness and bliss. The 'highest' refers to the *dharmakāya* or cosmos.

Thirdly, the term 'the lowest' therefore relates to the Mother of all things, of the plethora of the *māyā* of *saṃsāra*, and therefore of the *karma* that binds each to all. It concerns the proper functioning of the third Ray. The entire mystery of what *karma* is and is not lies hidden here.

Fourthly, the term 'the highest' relates to *śūnyatā*, which is the highest aspect that those bound to the cycles of time and of *karma* can aspire to, as it signifies liberation from all such considerations. Within *śūnyatā,* however, the Dharmakāya Way can be discovered.

Fifthly, the realm of consciousness aims to mitigate the negative influences of the past. Thus it is concerned with the future consideration of time with respect to life in *saṃsāra*, as all happenings through time in *saṃsāra* produce expansions of consciousness, of the process of growing from zones of relative darkness to realms of great light.

Sixthly, we are now brought to the mental-emotional domain, to the field of *māyā*, wherein most people reside. This is 'the present' as far as their consciousness is concerned. *Māyā* relates to the general miasma of mental-emotional currents and the *karma* created by the sum of human interaction. Most people look to the future in order to build what they consider the present. Inevitably all becomes the past.

Finally, we have the dense realm where humans are found, 'following the same methods' of karmic interaction that keep us bound cyclically to the wheel of birth and death, until we find the means of the escape from it. The method of escape (from time) can also be characterised by the correct reading of this verse in the order presented, and in relation to the information given in the other verses.

By the way that the verse is structured, we see also that there is a direct relation of 'the highest', 'the lowest', 'the middle' with 'identity'. In the context of the Mahāmudrā they represent the modes of liberation from *saṃsāra*, and can all be considered aspects of the 'identity' of a Buddha (the Real). The 'lowest' represents the expression of the *tathāgatagarbha* as a foundation of Buddhahood. The 'middle' represents the Śūnyatā Eye through which one can travel to non-conceptual bliss. The 'highest' represents the Clear Light of the abstract Mind as a springboard to *dharmakāya*. They represent the three levels of experiential life from whence the Dharmakāya Way can be trodden, away from the formed realm of mind.

The term 'etc.' in verse four indicates repetitiveness, and in the context given above, of cycle after cycle (of time) that proceeds out of the Womb of the great Mother, and into which the life process recedes again. All *saṃsāric* life is sustained within her Womb.

The second Ray

The *second Ray of Love-Wisdom* emphasises the role of consciousness. It integrates all disparate forces harmoniously through wisdom, whereby the role that consciousness plays and the way that it evolves through time can be examined in such a way that time is transcended. This is what living in the eternal Now represents. The person then views all things from the future perspective because he/she has completed the cycles of evolution, or course of action in *saṃsāra* concerning anything. Consequently, through wisdom one stands beyond the action of time. Such a flux of comprehension represents a state of mindfulness that eternally resides in the present-future. All patterns and aspects of *karma* are then seen manifesting truthfully in action as they must throughout the three times. One must also have an Eye opened to the *dharmakāya*, from whence comes another stream of revelation.

The fifth verse therefore presents us with an exposé of how time is viewed from the perspective of great wisdom. The four parts of this verse relate to the four aspects of 'the real'. With this in mind, the phrases of this verse can be further exemplified.

a. The phrase 'A non-static time is not observed' refers to the way that time is viewed from *śūnyatā*, where the temporal flux of time is not.

b. The phrase 'A static time is not evident' refers to the realm of the great Mother (which can also be labelled *ātmic* because it is the sources of all individualities found in Nature). From here the law of cycles (cyclic time) can be observed, but it certainly is not static, but rather manifests in the form of the spiral-cyclic motion described above with respect to expansion of consciousness. The sum of the *karma* of the manifestation of Nature (rather than of the life of the personal-I) proceeds and recedes from this *ātmic* realm. This *ātmic* realm relates to what I elsewhere term the third *dharmakāyic* level.

c. The phrase 'Even if the unobserved time were to be observed' refers to the next realm or dimension of being/non-being, which is beyond time, but which can view the flow and ebb of streams of sentience and consciousness in serene poise of *dhyāna* through great wisdom. This must include an instantaneous review of how all things in the *rūpa* and *arūpa* universes are interconnected throughout the course of each individualised evolutionary stream. Here is the Wisdom of the Buddhas.

d. The question 'How can it be made known?' consequently concerns those involved within the *dharmakāya,* where they are contemplating the formation of a world sphere out of compassionate grounds because of the great need for all entities to evolve in cosmos, to overcome the state termed ignorance. We can similarly ask 'How can the *tathāgatagarbha* be properly seeded so that the evolving personal-I's can rightly grow to become Buddhas?' Many are the pitfalls in *saṃsāra* that such 'I's' must experience (i.e., 'be made known') regarding the fruits of the expression of the cycles of time. Many of these pitfalls demonstrate upon the psychic realms, wherein through intensification of processes and forces of the ego, great sorcery may be possible. The person will then ensnare many into rigid bands of karmic certainty and hell zones. The sorcerer concerned will also be entrapped for many durations of lives, long after his fellow human beings have become enlightened beings. How to prevent such from happening (especially on a mass scale, and looking to available *saṃskāras* from former cycles of Logoic endeavour) is the prime concern of all meditating Buddhas that have formed world-spheres, and Bodhisattvas therein. Their compassionate concern is focussed upon those bent upon evil. This is a necessity because long, aeonic durations of time generally pass before such *karma* can be finally resolved. Thus, deep is the meditation needed (stretching through all *saṃsāric* realms to the completion of vast cycles therein) to discover the mode of helping such beings achieve release from the domains of time.

The first Ray

Finally we have *the first Ray of Will,* the destroyer Ray, pertaining to the ending of the phenomena of the causative process, hence the ending of time. This concerns the projection of the all towards *śūnyatā*. The explanation of the associated verse (six) has already been provided, thus needs no further comment.

In the above, I have presented a far deeper rendering of Nāgārjuna's verses than hitherto available. The purpose is to show that in verses written by the genuinely enlightened, there is much more veiled in the pattern of words than is generally read into them and formerly understood as the whole truth, by the general community of scholars and monks. I therefore implore all earnest students of the *dharma* to read with far greater care the sacred texts in the light of the hints given here.

12

Śūnyatā, Consciousness, and Parinirvāṇa

The driving force underlying consciousness

Śūnyatā is generally defined in terms of negatives, of what it does not contain (of what it is void of), or is not. In relation to this concept we find that everything phenomenal can be considered both true and not true (whether one is viewing from a conventional or ultimate perspective), and that anything that can be defined is not ultimately true because it is transitory. Consciousness consists of that which can be defined, and in fact does the defining. We therefore have a triplicity manifesting:

1. That which is defined or definable, and therefore ultimately 'is not'.
2. The consciousness that defines.
3. That which is non-definable and is therefore void (of characteristics). It must also be considered 'void of being void'. This is but a way of stating that what it does contain is beyond the ability of consciousness to categorise or define. However, there is an ability of consciousness to gain an apprehension, or 'taste', of the undefinable, to experience it veridically. Once experienced, it is explainable in such a way that others may be able to obtain the means to also experience, to first whiff the aroma of enlightenment and then also to taste.

The above triplicity also exists in terms of a time sequence, of things existing in relation to other things. Consciousness evolves to recognise a pattern or differentiation between such things, which allows definitions to be made. This continues until there comes a point in the evolution of consciousness where it discovers that which 'lacks character', which is not segregated or separated in terms of things, which embodies the middle way between extremes, is not dependent upon one or the other, and which remains after all that is ephemeral (and thus definable) has been eliminated. This then is the *śūnyatā* experience. It is an enigma, in that it exists out of time (as time by definition is transient) but is the result of the sequence of events (time sequences) in consciousness that leads to the fulfilment of its experience. We see, therefore, that time is an important ingredient in the production of the *saṃsāra-śūnyatā* fusion. We can say that without the progress of time, there can be no such relationship. Consciousness, however, can be said to be the mechanism of that fusion, and can therefore be said to exist in time, but is not governed by its durations. Rather, it is that which quantifies things in relation to time.

Time can also be defined in terms of the processes of the things within *saṃsāra* going through perpetual changes and transformations. The definition of time concerns the continuum of a sequence of experiential moments, as long as consciousness exists to register them. The factor of time is also cyclical and can be made redundant because of the manifestation of differing states of consciousness. This is evident whenever we take new births. The process of rebirths is sequenced through time, but there are gaps of conscious awareness through that sequence. Such gaps can be considered states of timelessness, and such states point to the illusion of time. Time is illusionary because, like all things concerning our perceptions, it is transitory. (Our thoughts are consequently illusionary.)

The Sambhogakāya Flower stands above time, above the sequences of illusion, because it can string together these 'gaps' or states of timelessness into a completed flow of unitary purpose. This then eventually engenders the enlightenment that produces the experience of *śūnyatā*.

The illusionality of time allows the appearance of the 'self' concept, whereby sequences of the continuum can be quantified in terms of minutes, hours, days, years and lifetimes of experiences. When the factor of the evolution of consciousness is added, there are groups of lifetimes to be considered, where each such grouping is particularly concerned with the development of a specific aspect of consciousness.

This introduces the concept of extended time, i.e., the cycles of events whereby the Sambhogakāya Flower reckons time, in respect to its own evolutionary progression. *Saṃskāras* are developed and then transformed during a particular sequence of lives. If there were no self-concept greater than the personal-I, what then would regulate or condition such a progress—of the organisational abilities of groups of lives, so that the right qualities are developed by the inherent consciousness that must inhabit the periodic vehicles? If there was no such thing as structured sequences of lives then it would be well nigh impossible for consciousness to evolve the beneficent *saṃskāras* pertaining to Bodhisattvahood, or *bodhicitta*, because they take many sequential progressive lifetimes of effort to develop and mature.

Bodhicitta does not spring up out of nowhere, and neither do the ten Bodhisattva stages automatically appear. *Bodhicitta* is an energy qualification of the enlightened domains which is obscured by the clothing of *saṃsāra*. That clothing must be progressively removed by an agency that can plan many life-times ahead. The Bodhisattva stages are similarly expressions from the domain of an all-presiding enlightened Mind, an Ādi Buddha, that has sequenced various Initiation testings that must be passed if Buddhahood is to be attained. The qualifications needed to become a Buddha actually change during differing world epochs, as everything is relative. The truth of this statement, and that not all Buddhas are identical, becomes self-evident to those upon the path who can review the past evolutionary history of our solar system in their meditation-Minds.

What can be said about the later stages of the development of consciousness can also be said for the stages of the patterns of lives, wherein the Sambhogakāya Flower, for instance, tries to lessen or eliminate tendencies of the personal-I to avaricious, or malicious activities. It strives to generate more open-heartedness in the personal-I. Taken as a blind law, *karma* will not do this of its own accord. It necessitates a carefully thought out, ordered sequence of lives to direct *karma,* thus to produce the right, inevitable effects along the line of gaining eventual enlightenment. Otherwise, the mode of having to 'pay back' for evil doing (or even for transforming the effects of altruistic actions that are still *saṃsāra*-clinging) would be extremely haphazard. It would not facilitate an evolutionary development that manifests in a forward-progressive manner, where wisdom and liberation are inevitable outcomes. It would rather be like a roulette wheel where blind chance rules the throws of destiny. Such things as astrological prediction and prevision would then be impossibilities.

A properly structured, ordered sequence of lives, according to the certainty of law inherent in the higher domains of the realms of consciousness, allows an enlightened being to predict with some surety the future concerning the outcome of the actions of any person, grouping of people, or even a nation. (The vagaries of human free will, however, must also be taken into account, which may impede the predicted outcome.) Similarly, highly qualified Bodhisattvas can plan their own sequence of lives so as to produce the maximal compassionate outcome upon those they have come to educate. A Bodhisattva's career would be severely hampered if there was no such sequenced structure, a planned evolutionary process to our evolving consciousness over many lifetimes of activity.

As previously stated, to answer the question of what regulates such necessary activity, one can only think in terms of an aware 'container' of consciousness that has an overview of the entire sequence of time. This involves the process starting from the inception of human intelligence (which distinguishes us from animals) to the attainment of Buddhahood. If no principle existed that could regulate things thus, directing the way *karma* interrelates with the entire process, then individual lives could not be sequenced so that consciousness could evolve anything. There would be chaotic thoughts and incarnations from one life to the next. Consequently, there could be no push to Buddhahood increasingly developed over a sequence of lives. *Vāsanā* (said to be the driving or motivating force to life's actions) might exist, in say, directing a stream's flow, but could not be a factor in directing the evolutionary expansion of consciousness in a meaningful manner over a series of lives. Wilful direction is needed, and this necessitates the existence of a directive Mind, a subtle soul-form (*tathāgatagarbha)* that can stand above the entire rebirth process of an individual human life stream. It must direct 'without moralising' in the manner previously explained, in such a way that eventually the refinement of *saṃskāras* are produced. *Nirmalā tathatā*[1] will then eventually manifest supreme, the *tathāgatagarbha* having been cleansed thereby of its covering

1 *Nirmalā tathatā,* suchness (the condition of the *tathāgatagarbha)* apart from *saṃsāric* defilements. *Samalā tathatā* on the other hand represents the (normal) condition of the *tathāgatagarbha* possessing defilements.

defilements. Through time, a quickening of the transformation processes in consciousness are speeded up, eventually producing a wise spontaneity as a response to all actions that signify the attainment of enlightenment.

This quickening process does not happen automatically, neither will consciousness develop such attributes without internal prompting. Its inherent *vāsanā* needs structured direction towards this end over many lives. A lack of a directing mechanism for *vāsanā* in relation to consciousness is thus a major flaw in the argument concerning the non-existence of a subtle 'soul' form. Without such a mechanism, Buddhists cannot account for how the major characteristics of enlightenment have evolved over many lifetimes. They have not thought out the significance of the way *vāsanā* intensifies enlightenment-producing factors over a time sequence, despite the natural intense clinging of a personal-I's desire body to objects of sensation. *Vāsanā* needs a directive will to overcome the desire-based proclivities of the mind and to cause the transference of consciousness in the rebirthing process in a progressive manner from one life to the next.

The force that drives consciousness as a whole (and not just a milliard little forces willy-nilly pushing consciousness-bits this way and that) is the consideration here. This force must be sustained and regulated so that it works with karmic law to evolve consciousness so that, inevitably, Buddhahood is gained. The billions of little forces of consciousness-bits that would ensue under the general Buddhist supposition of no-soul would be directionless and produce chaotic movements in the *ālayavijñāna*, unless regulated by the *vāsanā* of an overall Consciousness. Such chaos means that information would not be retrievable by consciousness when needed. Out of a similar necessity our societies have evolved laws, traffic police, lights, pedestrian crossings, parking spaces, and well-ordered means of traffic flows (a good road system) to properly regulate the vehicles ('consciousness-bits') in our cities (symbolising the integral organisations within our minds).

Buddhists have not cogently told us what it is that *must* direct all of these myriad streams of images in the *ālayavijñāna* so that it all becomes the highly organised and efficient system we actually observe and utilise. This is because the nature of energy and its laws have not been properly analysed. How energy directs thought, and how every image has its own energy input, its own individual *vāsanā*, needs to be clearly analysed. Such concepts need lucid definitions, and scientific concepts must be incorporated, if the philosophy is to grow enlighteningly. Buddhists must build into the general philosophy the missing blocks of comprehension, so that naïvety disappears and the fabric of enlightenment shines resplendently.

One could view the vehicle of consciousness (the I-concept) as being composed of the sum of the atoms in the body, the psyche and mind that together form the illusionality of 'self' (seen as a structural unit). In this way, Buddhists following the Abhidharma see the attributes of a personal-I in terms of atomic unities, as in the concept of *dharmas* (the 'elements' of existence). These concepts, however, become convoluted in a mass of unresolved detail. Effectively, they are trying to view things that exist too far back in time with insufficient knowledge (light) to comprehend the detail. The ignorance quotient therefore grows through regress into the darkness of incomprehension of the true nature of atomic detail. To overcome this problem, it is best to think in terms of universals and wholes, of how organisms function as a unit, which brings concepts to the present-future. The meditation of evolving unities, completed *maṇḍalas* of expression, inevitably necessitates thinking in terms of a subtle 'soul' concept.

Buddhist syllogisms and logic may have been correct in the past when dealing with Brahmanical notions about an *ātman*, because such notions were not error free. However, the old Brahmanical system is no longer the main adversary, and many new schools of Buddhist thought have arisen. Still, there are many obstinate Buddhists that have their heads in the sands of time, that find the continuous progression of enlightened revelations unwelcome. Change is inevitable for all in *saṃsāra*. If one does not change and adapt to evolving times, then one slows down one's evolution, and in the present epoch there is a universe of ideas to contend with. If aspects of the mind express stasis, being resistant to change, it produces darkened areas of consciousness. Forms of intensified light should be produced instead, which are always dynamic and mutable. Stasis is not the way intended for the *buddhadharma*, thus inevitably growing fields of strong light appearing will illumine the arenas of darkness, stimulating its change. This is the way light works via the compassionate acts of Bodhisattvas. Evolutionary progression, or force, imposes changes from the outside in. (The alternate direction from within to without concerns changes occurring because of meditative development.)

The past is but an echo of the future, and generally one visualises the distant past in small doses of limited perspective. It can be viewed in terms of the amount of light that has evolved to consume the darkness. Light becomes more expansive as one observes entire panoramas of events that march to the future. We must similarly learn to broaden our vision about all things. How consciousness increases as the years and lives progress during entire epochs, through interrelationships with other units of consciousness, must be analysed by philosophers. The past is added onto constantly by little increments of the future (by being defined by consciousness) and all the subsequent moments in between. Instead of being resistant to the consequence of time, Buddhists should think of it as an accounting process, where undefined objects become whole and definable, where the categories of the universe mix and chain to each other concepts of 'self', yet producing a synthesis, an 'All-Self' that is also a 'not-self' in the end.

The *nāḍīs* of the enlightened are inherent in the unenlightened structures, allowing the inevitable production of perfect structural thinking. The *nāḍīs* can also be conceived of as the rivulets and rivers of time containing the *saṃskāras* of evolutionary being.

Consciousness, relativity, and the *catuṣkoṭikā*

If we can talk plainly, then Buddhists will acknowledge that when using impeccable logic, one will come upon truthful answers to the age old questions and assumptions found in the original documents they possess. The commonality of mind/Mind shines clear throughout each exegetical, epistemic or eschatological query. Each truthful answer must have a logical sequence to it that is deducible by similar minds. If they reach the heights obtained by the vaster Minds that formerly perceived reality, then many will notice that they had clearly not used proper logic when previously reading the presented literature and *sūtras*. This is obvious because most Buddhists have not noticed the errors and contradictions therein. Heartily I say 'welcome to the future of humanity, rest inside the (new) curves of understanding formulated by your mind's logic, as you open your eyes to greater meanings in the *sūtras* and *śāstras* you read, and which we (Bodhisattvas) are happy to reveal'.

One should then have to apply the logic of Nāgārjuna to consciousness, and all the terms that delineate truth. Full stop. The phrase goes as follows when adapting his famous *catuṣkoṭikā,* the four categories of existence: *being, non-being, both being and non-being, neither being and non-being.* From here all lower streams of logic emanate and fall. Also, all things can be reduced to their bare essentials of the ultimate truth of being *śūnyā,* void. What can the *catuṣkoṭikā* tell us about 'enlightenment' in relation to the word 'consciousness'? (By the definition that nothing can exist without consideration of its opposite, which makes it truly defined in Nāgārjuna's literature.)

Enlightenment is the expression of a perfected consciousness and incorporates transcended states of awareness. 'Consciousness' referring to a state of awareness or conscious mental identification with things. It is the content of a mind, allowing it to delineate something in relation to a categorisation of something else. When using the *catuṣkoṭikā* of Nāgārjuna, enlightenment can be defined as follows: *Enlightenment is consciousness, yet also not-consciousness, though neither of these states are true, yet both are together.* Now, how does one reconcile these seeming contradictory, incongruent statements? If we investigate this definition under the guise of *relativity,* then Nāgārjuna's *catuṣkoṭikā* should be seen to be true from all perspectives. If not so, then Mādhyamika ontology (that incorporates the *catuṣkoṭikā)* should be redefined. The philosophy notes that there is a prime difference between being a Buddha, who can be styled 'superconscious', fully liberated, and a person who is not enlightened.

In utilising the *catuṣkoṭikā* in relation to a Buddha one would have to say that a Buddha is superconscious, is not superconscious, both is and is not superconscious, and is neither superconscious and not superconscious. Does this actually define what a Buddha is? Or, one can simply say that we can't understand him because of the seeming contradictions, and thus stop trying altogether. (Instead of the word 'superconscious' used here one can use any applicable descriptive adjective, such as 'enlightened'.)

First let us acknowledge the fact that what is indicated as superconscious above includes the state of being conscious, and also connotes a transcendence of the conscious state, or being brought to the greatest limits of being conscious.

The problem is that utilising this formula, the statement 'not superconscious' implies that a Buddha has not attained full Buddhahood. He may be conscious of normal human functions and mental forms of activity, but not of transcendental states of awareness. Clearly, this part of the formula is not true, as the Buddha has aptly demonstrated that he possessed superlative logic, and transcendent awareness. If the *catuṣkoṭikā* is erroneous here, then will other aspects of Nāgārjuna's logic be found lacking? One could also reason that there are limits to the usage of the *catuṣkoṭikā*. If the state of being Buddha is an exception to the *catuṣkoṭikā* formula, then do all enlightened beings also fall under the same categories of being exceptions?

Also by this logic, a Buddha is someone who also contains consciousness (is superconscious), so then, what is the difference between a normal person and a Buddha?

If the definition states that a Buddha is both conscious and not-conscious (both is and is not superconscious), then what is the difference between him and one who is insane? Such a person is both conscious and not conscious, or unaware, of what he is doing or saying.

If the definition states that a Buddha is neither conscious and unconscious (is neither superconscious and not superconscious), then what is the difference between him and members of the animal kingdom, who are not consciously aware, in the sense that a human being is, who has the rationality of the intellect to guide him, but neither are they unconscious, for they have sentience?

Therefore, in utilising this formula in this manner we can be lead to believe that a Buddha is: a) not human, b) human, c) insane, d) an animal. The interpretation of having attained *śūnyatā* is not a necessary deduction when used in this way. Is therefore a Buddha (or an enlightened Being) all of these at once, for the logic admits the possibility?

If the logic given above has produced a confusing result, it illustrates the fact that all things are relative and exist in differing states of relativity. This is something that Buddhists must seriously take into account in their analysis of the nature of things.

So, when talking about a Buddha and including *relativity* in our consideration, we can say that:

1. A Buddha is both conscious and unconscious in relation to what a normal human takes to be consciousness. He can choose to enter

the universe of the thought streams of normal humans, but relative to this he heralds from a far greater universe of superconsciousness. He has transcended the normal human modes of thought, thus is generally 'unconscious' to them. He is a human because he has heralded from the human kingdom and can choose to enter their mindset, and yet is not a human, because he no longer thinks or acts like them, or incarnates as such. His way of thinking and acting is alien to that manifested by unenlightened humanity. Such understanding is already established in the concept of 'non-abiding *nirvāṇa',* as explained by Makransky:

> In classical Indian Mahāyāna texts, a Buddha's nirvāṇa was unconditioned (he was personally freed from the causes of the conditioned world) and at the same time, conditioned (manifesting pervasively in the conditioned world for others). It was given the name "non abiding nirvāṇa" *(apratiṣṭhita nirvāṇa),* because it was bound neither to the causal chain of conditioned existence, nor to the isolation of a quiescent (pre-Mahāyāna type) final nirvāṇa. On one hand, it was asserted, Buddhahood is highest nirvāṇa, free from all the dichotomous conceptualization (*vikalpa*) that constructs the phenomenological worlds of suffering beings. On the other hand, Buddhahood remains an active part of saṃsāra by appearing to beings within the phenomenological worlds of *their* conceptual construction. A Buddha had, in some sense, to be both unconditioned and operative within conditions.[2]

2. Insanity is but a name for one who does not display the ability of normal human thought processes. The mind of such a one is highly erratic or deranged in its expression. Such a being can be mentally disabled, or possess other psychosomatic disorders. Such definitions can also be interpreted to refer to one who is not understood by the normally sane, as represented by the average population. From this perspective, many who present higher esoteric teachings could be interpreted thus, as many *yogins* and enlightened ones have been. A Buddha can easily fit into this category. Everything is relative to the state of awareness of the listener, of his comprehension level.

2 John J. Makransky, *Buddhahood Embodied,* (Sri Satguru, Delhi, 1998), 11-12.

3. An animal lives and acts by instinct, rather than by intelligence. Instinctual actions are automatic, below the threshold of consciousness. Animals do not have to think about things, they automatically act and react to external stimuli and life's proceedings according to instinctual habits. Humans can teach some higher animals new tricks, which is but the beginning of the onerous road to the development of intelligence. Moving from the animal kingdom to the human is a momentous step, necessitating the formation of a *tathāgatagarbha,* allowing the individuation of mind. Evolving out of the womb of our earth sphere can imply the progression of a Buddha along the road to such Individuation within a boundless cosmic landscape. A Buddha can certainly embody the attributes of a transcended form of animal in cosmos. The qualities he has developed on earth simply represent the transmuted aspects of instinct within cosmos. The processes of the mind/Mind (as we understand them) have become instinctual to him, as he has fully perfected and transmuted them. The vision here concerns the transmuted correspondences of what is known on earth. We must view qualities developed in cosmos many orders of magnitude greater than what can be found upon the earth with respect to sentience and human consciousness. The mind can stretch in leaps and bounds to accommodate such concepts, even if things have to be defined in metaphorical language. The five Jina wisdoms become instincts at this level of expression because they now function automatically. They are innately integrated into the constitution of a Buddha. Consequently, he needs no more to think of engendering them than a normal human needs to wilfully generate say the instinct to self-preservation or the sexual instinct.

The universe is a far vaster place than the earth, or our solar system. Stars have come and gone long before the appearance of our sun, and the associated humanity have also evolved to Buddhas long before those stars died. It is certainly not out of the question therefore, to think that the evolutionary progress of life on a minuscule planet such as ours can simply represent a type of nursery or rather, womb condition. From this 'womb' is born a tiny cosmic being that those on our minuscule schema consider to be fully enlightened. From a cosmic perspective, such a one would be considered akin to a baby. From another viewpoint, he can be considered to have gained entry into the evolutionary form of a less evolved status than the human represents upon the earth, thus born into the cosmic animal kingdom composed of Buddha-like animal forms from an inconceivably vast scale, or perspective. Such consideration could be from the point of view of those Great Awarenesses governing the evolutionary development of stars, constellations, and even a galaxy, composed of billions of suns such as ours. From a galactic perspective, a newly evolved Buddha therein could be represented as a cosmic unicellular being.

We see here that a relativistic concept of scale is necessary. How does one gauge the Buddha's attainment relative to that of a cosmic Logos that had entered *parinirvāṇa* aeons earlier? Buddhist eschatological and cosmological doctrines should change to accommodate such epistemic concepts.

By 'transmuted correspondence' I mean that one must first, for instance, analyse what an animal has developed and then transmute and transpose those qualities to a higher level or perspective of realisation. Thus, that a Buddha may indeed have evolved to the level of a member of the cosmic animal kingdom can be seen in the way that the Buddha automatically and spontaneously works for the salvation of all sentient beings. He does not have to think about such things at all; there is 'no-thought' in him (as in the case of animals with respect to their instincts), it has become a transcendent form of instinct to him. His accomplishment, in fact, is likened in the texts to that of an animal, to the pride of a lion, who has mastered the jungle scenario.[3] As Brown states concerning the Tathāgata:

> His alone is the authentic Lion's Roar because He alone has achieved an unqualified understanding of all natures; has become omniscient and all-seeing, unrestrained from all faults, liberated from all defilements, and possessed of infinite merit.[4]

With respect to this, Alex and Hideko Wayman state in their translation of *Śrī-Mālā Sūtra*:

3 The simile of a lion is here used because it compares the attainment of a Buddha, with respect to *saṃsāra,* to that of a lion, who is lord of the jungle.

4 Brown, *The Buddha Nature,* 16. The quotation is in reference to an analysis of the *Śrī Mālā Sūtra.*

> Having been made Lord of the Doctrine unhindered in all stages of the knowable, he rightly saw that there is no duty or stage beyond this to be left over or to be understood. Having properly entered the supreme incomparable stage which is fearless and endowed with the power of the ten powers, and having clearly seen all the knowable with unhindered knowledge, he uttered the Lion's roar with the knowing, 'There is nothing to be known beyond this.' [5]

We can quite clearly see here that when interpreting we are always viewing things as relative to something else. Thus for instance, in the above quote we see that the list of what the Buddha had attained, such as being made 'Lord of the Doctrine' to 'There is nothing to be known beyond this', are things relative to the human kingdom, wherein he has 'properly entered this supreme incomparable stage which is fearless and endowed with the power of the ten powers'. He is 'fearless' in relation to the problems that beset normal human evolution. He has nothing more to gain in relation to the succession or sequence of human rebirths. But nothing is mentioned here in relation to the new cosmic world that his *parinirvāṇa* has opened the door to, when he will leave the human world far behind, except this utterance of a 'lion's roar'. This hints at a possibility that in the immense, unfathomable, multidimensional universe he now enters, that his standing is comparable to that of a lion on our tiny, relatively insignificant world. Relatively, and that which concerns the transmuted correspondence that can be projected from one scenario to the next, is the import of what needs to be emphasised here.

People need to think of kingdoms of Nature and orders of being of far vaster magnitude and scope of awareness in the Universe's environment than anything possible by the consciousness-sphere that represents our tiny planet. What is considered 'omnipotent' or 'omniscient' to that

---

5 Alex and Hideko Wayman, *The Lion's Roar of Queen Śrī Mālā: A Buddhist Scripture on the Tathāgatagarbha Theory,* (Columbia University Press, New York, 1974), 90-91.

See also Evans-Wentz, *The Tibetan Book of the Great Liberation,* 159, where it is stated with reference to Padmasambhava 'Thus Padma really became a Buddha at Bōdh-Gayā; and from the roof of the palace there he roared like a lion. The non-Buddhists were much agitated; and he converted them; and they named him '*Guru* Seng-ge Dradog.' The accompanying footnote states: 'That is, "The Lion-roaring *Guru*", the name of one of the eight chief forms assumed by Padma'.

cosmic Humanity is relative, and manifests in a similar way that the intelligence level of an ordinary human is omnipotent and omniscient relative to the sentience of the cellular constituency of the human body. Parochial thinking must be eschewed by all thinkers and relativity used to relate such conceptions as cosmic universals to the organic structures and constituency of the biodiversity of the environment wherein humanity finds a home. Rational thinkers must be encouraged to begin to get a grip on the nature of evolution of all orders and levels of life in the realms of being/non-being, far beyond what humanity represents. The human kingdom is certainly not all there is in the universe wherein we find a home. Consequently, *parinirvāṇa* must begin to be viewed not as an ending, but as a relative beginning to a completely new journey of Life in the realms of meaning, away from the womb of time-space that our earth system represents.

The new generation of Buddhists aspiring to enlightenment should now obtain understanding that a Buddha has been born out of that womb as a 'baby' into a far greater environment than what was previously possible. The necessary lighted quotient for achievement has been raised for all aspiring Bodhisattvas in this new epoch. The ignorance levels that were permissible in the past for all aspirants to enlightenment will always be superseded as the march of time reveals broader vistas of meaning as fodder for the aspiring ones to chew upon.

The concept of time is found throughout the history of human thought and the correlating terminology should be used to comprehend relativity, for if the Buddha is said to be younger in comparison to other Buddhas from previous aeons, this is because the epoch which birthed him is closest to our present era. Therefore he is a relative youth, more 'unaware' cosmically, in proportionate comparison to their Cosmic Individuation. Thus such a Jina still retains a certain 'ignorance quotient' in respect to Them. How could it be otherwise? It is illogical, nay an absurdity, to think that all Buddhas are equal, no matter what the scriptures may say on the subject. They infer that those that entered upon the path of cosmic Individuation, maybe many aeons before our solar system was even formed (when the present Buddha will have been no more than an atomic entity, a speck of sentient matter), have not grown or evolved one iota right up to the time of the Buddha, and never will, nor will the Buddha further evolve. It implies that they have entered a cosmic swamp of utter stagnation, that they have literally nothing more to do, (other than to play consciousness-games with other beings in Buddha-fields), simply because they are no longer reincarnating upon an earth sphere in the vastness of the cosmic infinitude.

The Mahāyāna conception here is really nothing more than a version of the Hinayāna *nirvāṇa*. This is because the momentum (*vāsanā*) of the Bodhisattva ideal that had come to make a Buddha has not been thought out to conclusion as to the way that it would *still* work upon a Buddha, when dealing with orders of magnitude of Awareness far vaster than anything obtainable upon the earth before his *parinirvāṇa*. They have not properly conceived of what it is that exists out *there* in cosmos. Their parameters of thinking must therefore begin to open up to the real nature of the multidimensional vastness of the space all are in. Forms of medieval geo-centred thinking must vanish as we enter into a new, enlightened era. Consequently, people must more accurately conceptualise what it is that constitutes enlightenment.

The Buddha can be considered to be older than the present humanity, and is the Father/Guru of future Buddhas to be. This is logical, as all present, advanced Bodhisattvas were his students and had grown much under his tutelage. There is a genealogy, a family tree, where generations of Bodhisattvas are set amongst each other and which delineate their nature and the order of awareness with respect to evolutionary progress. For we must use the concept of separation of one from another as a law of life within a *maṇḍala* constituting unity, and that such interrelation is adequate and not negated by higher possibilities of the universality of the whole. Gautama was but a student of an earlier Buddha that was guru to him. The relationship persists after the Buddha's *parinirvāṇa*. So it is with those of us that loved him before his *parinirvāṇa*, we still retain *antaḥkaraṇas*[6] with him, and will long after we too enter the 'final shore'. He remains 'guru' forevermore. *Oṁ svāhā, sarva-maṇgalam,* Oṁ, excellent, auspicious goodwill, blessings to all, we say as we bow to the precious feet of this Jina. Also, as we move into the cosmic landscape, many other Jinas will be met that have similarly played a role in the evolutionary development of all life on earth. To them we similarly bow in humble gratitude and obeisance.

---

6 Normally interpreted as 'consciousness-links', but in this case one could use such a term as 'Mind-connection'.

The separations between things

We know that both separation and non-separation exist, but they do not negate each other, and in terms of the Void they don't exist. Some truths need separation in human thought to gain wisdom, and at other times we need to combine ingredients into a holistic non-separative methodology to know the higher order of enlightenment. A myriad examples can be found where Buddhists have separated through the logic of their syllogisms or rhetoric the different points of various listings of things. Sometimes things that have separated categories are placed together to show that they are aspects of each other, e.g., the wisdoms of the five Dhyāni Buddhas. We exist as separate individuals that make up one human race, and must act in accord with each other's uniqueness, and also our common humanity. Because we affect each other, for the good or bad, so it is prudent that we be loving in our actions. This epitomises a universal law for the making of enlightened Beings through the fusion of separates into unity.

Buddhas from different epochs are separated because they had evolved from different time-continuums than ours. There are differing orders of enlightenment from various *chakra* systems in cosmos, different *karma* and magnitude of purpose than any presently awakening Buddha. Yet all are part of an interdependent, interrelated whole, existing as part of a universal law of Love as a mode of (evolving) Being. All of them are thereby eliminating (or 'consuming') forms of cosmic darkness and converting it to various dynamic streams of radiatory Light. Of this a Buddha's aura is a guarantee. The reality, therefore, is that there is no separation, yet differences appear as part of the purpose of the manifesting whole. All is governed by the law of Love, which exists to bring the whole one step higher into an increasingly sublime, or intense form of Light, consubstantiated as one organism. Yet, when we think in terms of *śūnyatā* then 'no such things exist'. We see that there is a limitation also in our concept of *śūnyatā* here, that our view of this Void is from the relative perspective of our earth evolution. *Śūnyatā* is simply the base substance of a new cosmic beginning, allowing things of the earth to be left behind.

The above has been written partly as an answer to questions already posited by other Buddhist scholars, such as Griffiths:

> Clearly, the truth-conditions of these two claims cry out for some elucidation. Are all Buddhas equally (that is, maximally) great? If so, how are the relations among them to be explained? In what do they differ, and why? If they are not all equally great, how are they to be ranked and ordered?[7]

The two claims referred to are that first, Gautama was not the only being recorded in which the honorific title 'the awakened one' can be applied. Second, being 'the implicit understanding of Buddha as maximally great, maximally salvifically significant and efficacious'.[8] Griffiths then comments:

> It is not hard to see how attempts to deal with these questions, understood as attempts to deal systematically with the truth-conditions of axioms, could lead quickly to speculative system-building, culminating, among other things, in the three-body theory.[9]

Much can be revealed once one comprehends that the way Buddhas can be differentiated is through utilising the concept of transmuted correspondences. This concerns a proper sequencing of the 'relative sizes' and colourings of Buddhas from past aeons of evolutionary attainment. Such 'sizes' refers to the actual Mind-scape or extent a 'thus gone' One embodies as a salvifical space within cosmos. In direct meditative vision *(pratyakṣa)* such a One, which I term a Logos, can appear in a gigantic Buddha form, with many subservient 'thus gone' Ones administering to 'Him'. Different Logoi exist with respect to the relative vastness of their cosmic purpose. One could also look to the Ray attributes of the constellations or stars that are their new home, that indicate the fundamental energy qualification of each Buddha.

The idea of the concept of universals cannot negate speciality, identity, uniqueness, although the reality of separatism can prove unworthy in some areas of evolutionary law. (That which relates to the separative attitudes of humanity, and which forms the basis of all black magic and sorcery.) Separatism (individuation) cannot negate the law

---

7 Paul J. Griffiths, *On Being Buddha* (Sri Satguru, Delhi, 1995), 83.

8 Ibid.

9 Ibid.

of the whole, but it can intensify *māyā,* or in terms of the view of the totality of space, facilitate the higher reasoning mind and intuition. Thus, it can manifest as an example of the way things function in the now.

There are two basic extremes by which the concepts we formulate can be answered; yea and nay. Either can be considered flawless when considered rightly. Their existence, however, will not be found true in all examples and contexts. Things in their various categories can be considered as either the truth and not true, as well as neither true and not true, or both true and not-true, as most arguments can be true in many ways when taken relatively, and also possess errors. Exalted and base aspects of anything can also exist because they are not negated by the concepts of unity, or individuation.

We are not nihilists, believing in nothing, nor do we believe in everything answerable to a 'self' concept, for we know that things change in relation to each other. This means that there is then a relative scale to all things and occurrences. The relationships manifest certain predictable laws, until one discovers a more subtle, transcendent reasoning and revelation. A more comprehensive understanding of any law than what the human intellect can bring into fruition will then flower. This produces relatively greater understandings of the nature of the appearance of things, the ordering or sequencing of all evolved beings, and the role that death plays in the progress of the human spirit. There is always the next level of transcendent awareness to reach. The process is never-ending, reaching far into unimaginable vistas of cosmos, wherein Buddhas are dwarfed by the immense magnitude of its perspicacious orders of Being/Non-being.

13

Voidness and Abundance

Hearing 'face to face'

With respect to the question of Voidness, the practical consideration of how to attain it is important. Hence a *sutta (sūtra)* translated by Wayman, the *Cūḷa-suññatā-suttam,* is of value to consider in some detail. It incorporates the yogic process, that when earnestly followed step by step, is geared to produce the required goal of liberation. I shall begin with the passage below from the first verse:

> Face to face with the Bhagavat, I heard, face to face I received (these words): 'I, Ānanda, by dwelling in voidness, now dwell in abundance.' I hope revered Sir, that I well-heard, well-received it, rightly oriented my mind, rightly reflected.'[1]

The phrase 'face to face' does not just mean that Ānanda spoke directly to the Buddha, but also meant an interrelation between them in terms of what the seven facial orifices symbolise. We have a mouth, two nostrils, two ears and two eyes. They have a reference to the seven planes of perception, the seven Rays, the seven *chakras,* and the mechanism of conveying the sense-consciousnesses. In other words, there was a complete discourse between them upon all possible levels that Ānanda was capable of experiencing. Because of the importance of

1 Alex Wayman, *Untying the Knots in Buddhism,* (Motilal Barnarsidass, Delhi, 1997), 283. This quote comes from a chapter entitled 'About Voidness: Two Scriptures'.

this multileveled interrelation, the phrase 'face to face' was repeated as a hint that the perceptive reader should analyse deeper than the surface meaning. Consequently, in Wayman's rendition of this *sutta* there is a series of seven levels (sections to the text) of increasingly subtle forms of elimination of characteristics relating to the facial orifices.[2] A link, consequently, can be made between the facial orifices and the seven levels of a monk's meditation. The Buddha's discourse to Ānanda teaches how meditating monks can eventually dwell in Voidness. This is achieved through a process of 'non paying attention' to aspects of the environment and of the vicissitudes of the mind.

In the second verse, the Buddha starts his discourse concerning meditation, speaking of the necessity to develop a singleness of mind. No attention is to be paid to the 'idea of a forest', village or human beings. The Buddha concludes with the statement 'Whatever is not there, one observes to be the void of it. And whatever remains there, he knows: That being, this is. Thus, Ānanda, this becomes for him a genuine, non-deviant, utterly pure manifestation of voidness'.[3] All of the other passages, except for the last, end with this statement, which resonates the keynote of the Buddha's intent, and of the meditation for each cycle of refinement of *saṃskāras* represented by each passage.[4]

The main ideas that constitute the remaining nine verses shall now be outlined. They refer to the yoga-meditation process, whereby a monk pays no attention to the 'embrasures' associated with any of the ideas associated with the respective verse.

Concerning use of the term 'embrasure' in the text (a translation of the Pāli and Sanskrit word *daratha),* Wayman states that:

> The Monier-Williams Sanskrit-English dictionary provides for the term *daratha* the meanings 'cave' and 'taking flight' from Ujjvaladatta's commentary on the *Uṇādi-sūtras*. If we put the two senses together: the

---

2 They are statements 3 through to 10, dealing with the meditative attitude of an ideal monk. The tenth statement deals with the attainment of voidness, whilst the eleventh statement is: 'Enraptured, the venerable Ānanda rejoiced in the Bhagavat's words'. (Ibid, 287.)

3 Ibid., 283.

4 Because of its repetition, I will not repeat this passage at the ending of the quotations for the various passages. Consequently, the reader needs to include this passage in their reading of the texts provided.

> one taking flight would [be *sic*] like a kind of 'cave' to hide in: so 'cave' can be interpreted as 'making a cave'...[another sense being] widening a hole in a rampart so that the sides flare out...It is this cave which is understood to be void of this or that, and to be non-void of this or that.[5]

Thus we have the concept of a monk sitting inside the cave of his meditation Mind, able to see outside through the 'ramparts' of his mind to the external world, so that appropriate deductions can be made.

Verse three, that focusses upon 'the idea of the earth', concerns the level of activity of *the mouth,* when relating to the facial orifices. The mouth relates to the Base of Spine centre, it being the most southern of the orifices, and the Base of the Spine being the most southern of the centres. Also, the mouth articulates sound, that either empowers or reifies subtle mental impressions and ideas. In a similar manner, the Base of Spine centre deals with the expression of the Element Earth, governing dense physical activities. It supports all that must come, with respect to the awakening of the perceptions that inevitably produce liberation. Also, the mouth intones the mantras that the meditating monk uses to assist his visualisations and *dhāranīs* (mechanisms of fixing the mind in meditation).

The onus of verse four, with its base of 'infinite space', relates to the expression of the *nāḍī* system, activated by the right nostril. This nostril deals with the flow of the *piṇgalā nāḍī* stream, hence the flow of the *prāṇas* that express the experience of such spaciousness. This *nāḍī* has its basis in the desire based *prāṇas* generated by the Sacral centre.

Verse five, where 'the base of infinite perception' is focussed upon, relates to the expression of the left nostril, and hence the flow of the *iḍā nāḍī,* which channels the Fiery *manasic* energies pertaining to the Throat centre.

Verse six pertains to the functioning of the left ear, yogically associated with the hearing of the outer sounds, generally of the emotionally driven speech of humans. Here the base is that of 'nothing-at-all', which the common articulations of humans generally amounts to. The associated *chakra* is the Solar Plexus centre.

Verse seven pertains to the functioning of the right ear, which yogically concerns listening to the inner subjective sounds, conscience

5 Ibid., 279.

or intuitive perceptions. The base is 'neither-ideation-nor-non-ideation' related to the quality expressed by the Heart centre.

Verse eight pertains to the functioning of the left eye, which is the eye of perception, of intellectual discrimination. The keen perceptiveness associated with the left lobe of the Ājñā centre absorbs the *prāṇas* of the *iḍā nāḍī* directed via this eye. The base given is 'mind fixation'.

Verse nine pertains to the functioning of the right eye, which is the eye of wisdom, representing the gain of all of the activities of the various orifices of expression. The right lobe of the Ājñā centre absorbs the *prāṇas* of the *piṅgalā nāḍī* directed via this eye. Together the right and left lobes of the Ājñā centre direct *prāṇas* to the Head centre, which consequently awakens as a product of the yogic methodology provided in the text, hence the basis given is 'liberation'.

Verse ten is concerned with 'ultimate voidness' in terms of the three times. It can be related to the complete awakening of the Head lotus, and indirectly to the Sambhogakāya Flower, which produces repeated incarnations of the personal-I to achieve such an outcome.

The nine main verses of the *sūtra* examined

I shall introduce these statements with respect to the foundational idea, or base, to which they refer.

The idea of a forest (verse two).

The main part of this verse is:

> Certainly, Ānanda, you well-heard, well-received it, rightly oriented your mind and rightly reflected upon it. Formerly, Ānanda, as well as now, by dwelling in voidness, I dwell in abundance. For example, Ānanda, this palace of Migāra's mother is void of elephants, cows, horses, and mares, void of gold and silver; void of an assemblage of [lay] women and men; and there is just this non-voidness, to wit, this singleness depending on the congregation of monks. So also, you should know, Ānanda, is the monk paying no attention to the idea of a village, paying no attention to the idea of human beings, and orienting his mind to the singleness depending on the idea of a forest. His mind rejoices in, trusts in, takes the shape of and is convinced of the idea of a forest. He knows this: There are no embrasures depending on the idea of a village, there are no embrasures depending upon the idea of

> human beings. There is only this measure of embrasure: the singleness depending upon the idea of a forest. He knows: This ideation is void of the idea of human beings. And there is only this which is non-void: the singleness dependent on a forest.[6]

The village concerns the sum of human social interaction, with dwellings and sheds for the habitation of people and animals. The focus is the mental-emotional interrelation between humans, but the symbolism also concerns the animal-like nature of the (Watery) emotions, thus to the animal kingdom generally. The lives of animals are controlled by the villagers who have domesticated them. Much of the villager's time is spent in looking after animals, utilising them to plough fields, gathering plants and other edibles for their fodder, as well as consuming animals and their produce.

Monks retreated to forests in Gautama's day to meditate in solitude, to develop yogic prowess in their quest for enlightenment. The forest provides a place for abstracting oneself away from human habitation, in quiet surroundings free from distractions, that would tend to agitate the mind, preventing right contemplation. Within the seclusion of the forest, the monk can begin his inner contemplation and discover the *nāḍīs* and *chakra* system, which are plant-like, to which the forest indirectly refers.

In this statement we find the five Elements symbolised, at the elementary stages of their expression. Elephants, with their four large feet firmly planted upon the ground (related to the four petals of the Base of Spine centre), symbolise the Earthy Element. Cows, which provide milk, represent the Watery Element. Horses and mares, ridden by humans, thus directed by the mind, represent the Fiery Element. Gold and silver represent the Airy Element, as they are the symbols of the two principal *nāḍīs,* silver the *iḍā nāḍī,* and gold the *piṅgalā nāḍī.* In relation to the animals and metals, lay men and women represent the Aetheric Element.

The 'singleness depending on the congregation of monks' relates to taking aboard the attributes of meditation and following the *dharma* in all respects, with single focussed motive. The 'idea of a forest' relates to the entire *nāḍī* system upon which to meditate.

---

6 Ibid., 283.

The overall Element inferred is Water. This is signified by the various animals and average emotional humans that the listing provides.

The idea of the earth (verse three).

The third passage quoted below outlines what is further refined in the remaining seven passages. It deals subjectively with the yogic inbreathing of the *prāṇas* from the left nostril, thus the awakening of the *iḍā nāḍī* stream, where the attributes of the five sense-consciousnesses in relation to the developing intelligent mind are processed. Hence the process of 'not paying attention' is stressed.

> And besides, Ānanda, a monk, not paying attention to the idea of human beings, not paying attention to the idea of a forest, pays attention of the singleness depending on the idea of earth. For example, Ānanda, when a bull's hide is well-stretched out with a hundred spikes, its wrinkles are gone. In the same way, Ānanda, you should know, a monk, paying no attention to anything [in particular] on the earth, promontories or gullies, difficult passageways such as rivers, spots with tree stumps or thorns, uneven places like hills; [rather] pays attention to the singleness depending on the idea of earth. His mind rejoices in, trusts in, takes the shape of, and is convinced of the idea of earth. He knows this: There are no embrasures depending upon human beings; there are no embrasures depending on a forest. There is only this measure of embrasure: the singleness depending on the idea of earth. He knows: This ideation is void of the idea of human beings. This ideation is void of the ideation of a forest. And there is only this which is non-void: the singleness depending on earth.[7]

In considering all *sūtras,* it should be obvious that no symbolic expression or allegory of the Buddha is without many layers of meaning. An example as to the nature of analysis can be given in the imagery of a bull's hide: 'when a bull's hide is well-stretched out with a hundred spikes, its wrinkles are gone'. The straitening of the wrinkles refers to the cleansing (straightening) of attitudes of mind concerning any subject at hand (the elimination of aberrant thinking). The thinking process must be wizened (symbolised by the significance of the bull in Hinduism) and perfected (symbolised by the number 100, which is the number

7 Ibid., 283-284.

signifying great perfection or final accomplishment; as the number 10 is the number signifying the ending or completion of something).

We also have the statement that a monk should pay 'no attention to anything [in particular] on the earth, promontories or gullies, difficult passageways such as rivers, spots with tree stumps or thorns, uneven places like hills'. This list can be explained thus:

1. *No attention to anything [in particular].* This refers to obtaining the general overview of the situation, to review consciously all of the particulars involved and to assess how to properly tackle them. In this case, they were to be disempowered through lack of attention.
2. *Promontories* refer to the high or lofty points in one's thought life, the highlights of the way the personal-I thinks, producing memories and attitudes that may not be viable in a monk's meditative pursuits.
3. *Gullies* refer to the low points of a person's thought life, the emotional-mental depressions, worries, anxieties, etc., or else base, sensual or mundane ideas and thoughts.
4. *Difficult passageways* refers to emotions of all types. Two main categories are provided.
   a. *Rivers.* This refers to the unceasing flow of emotional thoughts and prattle, the continuous chatter of the emotional-mind. A river has rapids, it may be sluggish or turbulent, be full of rocks, etc. All such concourses are obstacles to the meditation-Mind.
   b. *Spots* (ungainly aspects to the mind), which are further subdivided into:
      i. *Tree stumps,* the obtrusive *saṃskāras* that are not really mastered and which stand out as a blot upon the monk's psyche. These stumps of meditative concern must be fully removed if he is to achieve his goal in meditation.
      ii. *Thorns,* the prickly, irritating, critical thoughts and emotions that are sharp reminders of the lack of meditative equipoise.

1. *Uneven places, i.e., hills,* which refer to the loftier, though not conclusive thoughts about any subject. For every such elevated thought there is always the problem of descent into valleys of despondency and erroneous attitudes.

To each of these five categories can be assigned the base qualities of one of the five Elements. 'No attention to anything [in particular]' is an expression of the Aetheric Element, being the overview of them all. The promontories that are 'high and lofty' refer to the Airy Element. Gullies, to the general intelligence quotient of the being (relatively low levels of thought) and thus to the Fiery Element. Difficult passageways refer to the often turbulent emotions and thus the Watery Element, and 'uneven places' to the Earthy terrain that one must trample over by means of the feet.

This verse concerns the ability of the mind to begin meditating upon all of the attributes of the physical domain. With the mind appropriately focussed, the meditator speaks not and yogically converts unwanted attributes so that liberation can be attained. The Element inferred is Earth, where physical plane attributes are focussed upon, as governed by the Base of Spine centre.

The base of infinite space (verse four).

> And further, Ānanda, a monk paying no attention to the idea of a forest, and paying no attention to the idea of earth, orients his mind to the singleness depending on the idea of the base of infinite space. His mind rejoices in, trusts in, takes the shape of and is convinced of the base of infinite space. He knows this: There are no embrasures depending on the idea of a forest; there are no embrasures depending on the idea of earth. There is only this measure of embrasure: the singleness depending on the idea of the base of infinite space. He knows: This ideation is void of the idea of forest; this ideation is void of the idea of earth. And there is only this which is not void, the singleness depending on the idea of the base of infinite space.[8]

By now the monk no longer needs to meditate upon things concerning life upon the physical plane. The nature of the entire internal psychic constitution becomes the focus, being 'the base of infinite space'. The *prāṇas* associated with the right nostril are now also fully utilised. Their focus is specifically via the *piṇgalā nāḍī,* and the control of the ramifications of the energy of desire, as governed by the Sacral

8 Ibid., 284.

centre. Once controlled, the energies released can be directed via this centre to flood the *nāḍīs,* which awaken the attributes of spaciousness. The meditation-Mind of the monk consequently becomes exhilarated, according to the degree that breath is yogically controlled. The vegetable kingdom and the Airy Element is exemplified (signifying the *prāṇas* coursing through the *chakras* in general and the *piṅgalā nāḍī* specifically).

The base of infinite perception (verse five).

> Ānanda, a monk, paying no attention to the idea of earth, and paying no attention to the idea of the base of infinite space, orients his mind to the singleness of the idea of the base of infinite perception. His mind rejoices in, trusts in, takes the shape of and is convinced of the base of infinite perception. He knows this: There are no embrasures depending on the idea of earth, there are no embrasures depending on the idea of the base of infinite space. He knows: This ideation is void of the idea of earth; this ideation is void of the idea of the base of infinite space. And there is only this, which is non-void, the singleness depending on the idea of the base of infinite perception.[9]

We can see that at each verse the focus of the earlier verse has become transcended in the meditation, has been made 'void'. So also we move up the hierarchy of the subtle body, exploring the attributes of one *chakra,* or *nāḍī* after another.

The idea of earth concerns the sum of the environment one resides in, from which one gains all forms of empirical knowledge by means of input from the sense-consciousnesses. Thus, physicality is left behind in serene contemplative reverie. We move to ever-broadening vistas: from the relatively restricting emotional imbroglio of family and village life, to that of the occupancy of the world of ideas of the intelligent mind, to the concept of internal spaciousness that a reclusive meditative retreat in a forest provides. Now the nature of the *saṃskāras* constituting the *prāṇas* that flow in the *iḍā naḍī* (via the left nostril) that awaken intellectual discrimination must be thoroughly examined. The monk thus observes the effects upon consciousness of the movement of the *prāṇas* through both the *iḍā* and *piṅgalā nāḍīs.* The energy effects of

9 Ibid.

spaciousness awaken the images pertaining to the domain of mind. Analysis of the visual impression the *prāṇas* produce, denoted here as 'infinite perception', becomes the onus of the monk's meditation. The way the mind actually functions, and the characteristics of that mind, is consequently understood. Here all of the *saṃskāras* concerning the mind must be correctly, contemplatively analysed as to their worthiness for future inclusion in the mental itinerary of the monk/*yogin.*

When cleansed of all defilements and thus properly clarified so as to be brought into the condition of its original state, the Mind becomes the base for the Discriminating Inner Wisdom of Amitābha, who embodies the gesture of meditation. Perceptions become infinite, as the vast domains of the content of mind are comprehended, especially when the domain of the abstract Mind is discovered. The Element inferred is Fire, and the *chakra* that is fully awakened here is the Throat centre (*viśuddha chakra),* allowing full experience of the nature of *manas.*

In the above description, we find thc four main Elements indicated, which govern normal concourse in the field of life.[10] They manifest in the form of the four main groups of *saṃskāras,* whose influences the *yogin* must directly mitigate, eliminate or transform if *śūnyatā* is to be attained. The transmutation of these *saṃskāras* into enlightenment-attributes is the major imperative of all meditators upon the enlightenment path. The generation of *dhyāna* eliminates the distractions of meditation and of defilements, producing a consequent clarification of consciousness and eventually the experience of Voidness.

Such achievement is gradual, wherein the monk at first principally works upon quieting the emotional and desire impulses that were gathered mainly from social intercourse and the family life from the village from which he heralded. This training primarily concerns the novitiate stage of a monk's life. Once full ordainment into the monkish community has been achieved, it is possible to retreat to the forest and meditate upon the internal psychic constitution.

The next major stage of training, and generally by far the longest, concerns the development and disciplining of the mind. All aspects of the *dharma* and the precepts of the gurus must be learnt. Here entire

---

10 Verse two the Watery, verse three the Earthy, verse four the Airy, and verse five the Fiery Elements.

belief systems are confronted. They must be methodically analysed to remove everything harmful to the quest for liberation. Fiery *saṃskāras* must therefore be cleansed of their dross and impediments so that the Void can be experienced. The monk becomes thoroughly indoctrinated to the requirements of the *dharma*. He cleanses his base *saṃskāras* so as to be naturally contemplative, and is sufficiently inspired to undergo the necessary yogic austerities that deep meditation demands, having been trained in *prāṇic* techniques. A qualified preceptor will have taught the necessary *mantras, sadhana,* and *dhāraṇīs* to accomplish the goal of liberation. Retirement away from all distractions, even from that of his fellow monks, is necessary in order to practice. The fruits of the sum of his incarnations upon the earth can then be gained.

The base of nothing-at-all (verse six).

> Ānanda, a monk, paying no attention to the idea of the base of infinite space, and paying no attention to the idea of the base of infinite perception, orients his mind to the singleness of the idea of the base of nothing-at-all. His mind rejoices in, trust in, takes the shape of, and is convinced of the idea of the base of nothing-at-all. He knows this: There are no embrasures depending upon the base of infinite space; there are no embrasures depending upon the idea of the base of infinite perception. There is only this measure of embrasure: the singleness depending upon the idea of the base of nothing-at-all. He knows: This ideation is void of the base of infinite perception. And there is only this, which is not void, the singleness depending on the idea of nothing-at-all.[11]

Residing in the domain of the mind/Mind, the *yogin*/monk now analyses the base of that which has represented the most troublesome part of his psyche—the emotions, and the way that they influence consciousness. Here the Equalising Wisdom of Ratnasambhava is developed. Ratnasmabhava's emanation is the southern direction of the *maṇḍala* of the Dhyāni Buddhas. Total control of the emotions to dry up the Watery Element is needed until nothing remains, as the illusion-forming propensity of the emotions are the deadly enemy to the meditation-Mind. They are, however, the base of the energy of

11 Ibid., 284-5.

Love and hence the evocation of *bodhicitta*. If there is nothing in the meditator's mind, then *bodhicitta* may also be lacking, and this grievous error must be rectified at this stage.

In transforming the associated *saṃskāras* into compassionate attributes, the monk sees that the emotions represent 'nothing-at-all', as they no longer exist in his serene contemplative life. The entire path of meditation is geared for this conversion process.

Having successfully mastered the formed or concrete side of his meditative mind (associated with the conditions of life upon the earth), the monk now tackles the formless (*arūpa*) aspects. The emotional, or desire generated mental illusions revealed by the abstract Mind display their baselessness. The way consciousness is structured is consequently rearranged to prevent the formation of such images. This necessitates mastering all attributes of the Solar Plexus centre (*maṇipūra chakra*) so that the energies from the Heart centre completely dominate. Here we have the basis to the expression of Ratnasambhava's Wisdom, allowing the minor *siddhis* to inevitably awaken.[12]

This meditation is necessarily five-fold because of the qualities of the five *prāṇas* that permeate all mind/Mind-space. The attributes developed from verses five to nine are but expressions of the five Jina wisdoms, which the meditating monk, consequently, is in the process of mastering. We thus enter into the Tantric aspect of yogic practice, with what in esoteric Buddhism is seen as the purifying effect of the vivifying *vajra*/dorje. The dorje grows in consciousness, to include the sum of immaculate space, which is now perceived where formerly there was 'nothing-at-all'. Vairocana occupies the central point of the *maṇḍala* of the five Dhyāni Buddhas (which governs the emanation of the other four) and has space (*ākāśa*-Aether) as his Element. He is embraced by his Prajñā (Consort) Ākāśādhātvīśvari, the 'Mother of the Space of Heaven'[13] according to *The Tibetan Book of the Dead*. Inevitably, the evocation of this Element will awaken the full 1,000 petalled lotus, the *sahasrāra padma*. Infinite space can be equated with the Voidness developed in verse ten, which is the objective of the monk's meditation.

---

12 This yogic process is detailed in Volume 5A.

13 W.Y. Evans-Wentz, *The Tibetan Book of the Dead*, (Oxford University Press, London, 1960), 106.

The four accompanying 'bases' are arranged in the order of the four directions of space in the traditional Tibetan *maṇḍala* of the Dhyāni Buddhas. The list starts at the western direction occupied by Amitābha ('infinite perception'), then Ratnasambhava in the Southern direction ('nothing-at-all'), followed by Akṣobhya ('neither-ideation-nor-non-ideation') in the eastern direction, and finally Amoghasiddhi ('mind fixation' that is signless) in the northern direction.

The base of neither ideation nor non ideation (verse seven).

> Ānanda, a monk, paying no attention to the idea of the base of infinite perception, and paying no attention to the base-of-nothing at all, orients his mind to a singleness depending on the idea of the base of neither-ideation-nor-non-ideation. His mind rejoices in, trusts in, takes the shape of, and is convinced of the idea of the base of neither-ideation-nor-non-ideation. He knows this: There are no embrasures depending upon the idea of the base of infinite perception; there are no embrasures depending upon the idea of the base of nothing-at-all. There is only this measure of embrasure: the singleness depending upon the idea of the base of neither-ideation-nor-non-ideation. He knows: This ideation is void of the idea of the base of infinite perception; this ideation is void of the idea of the base of nothing-at-all. And there is only this which is non-void, the singleness depending on the idea of the base of neither-ideation-nor-non-ideation.[14]

It is probable that the Buddha started the list of the four petals of the *maṇḍala* of the Jinas with the analysis of the mind (verse five) because, as Mipham states:

> Mind is the root of both Samsara and Nirvana:
> There is no entity of reality that has not sprung from mind.
> The frolicking and dancing of worldly and transwordly apparitions in all their multiplicity
> Comes to an end when its creator, mind as a magician, has been overpowered.
>
> Non-understanding is the mind gone astray into any of its six kinds of existences;

14 Wayman, 285.

Understanding this mind is 'pristine awareness.'
Pristine awareness is Buddhahood, and
As the quintessence of happiness it resides in one's heart.[15]

The base of 'neither-ideation-nor-non-ideation' introduces the analysis of the attributes of the Heart centre,[16] wherein such 'pristine awareness' is developed. The way of compassion *(bodhicitta)* is exemplified. It represents the Middle Way between all extremes *(mādhyamapratipad),* and is precisely where one must reside to experience Voidness, the epitome of Akṣobhya's Mirror-like Wisdom. The mirror reflects the non-ideation into the Mind in the form of spontaneous insight. From the other direction, the ideation of the mind is directed to the Heart of all things, but the process strips bare thought from its illusions, and the remainder merges into an ocean of revelatory bliss (of no thought).

The *samādhi* of mind fixation (verse eight).

> Ānanda, a monk, paying no attention to the idea of nothing-at-all; and paying no attention to the idea of neither-ideation-nor-non-ideation, orients his mind to the singleness depending on the *ceto-samādhi (samādhi* of mind fixation) that is signless *(animitta).* His mind rejoices in, trusts in, takes the shape of and is convinced of the *ceto-samādhi* that is signless. He knows this: There are no embrasures depending on the idea of the base of nothing-at-all; and no embrasures depending on the idea of the base of neither-ideation-nor-non-ideation. There is only this measure of embrasure—the six sense bases which, depending on the body *(kāya),* follow upon the condition of life *(jīva* = Skt. *āyuḥsaṃskāra).* He knows: This ideation is void of the idea of the base of nothing-at-all, and is void of the idea of the base of neither-ideation-nor-non-ideation. And there is that which is non-void, the six sense bases that, depending upon the body, follow upon the condition of life.[17]

Here is indicated the state of Mind where the meditator has eliminated all objects of thoughts. He is left in a state of 'no thought',

---

15 This is the opening verse of Mipham's song, 'Mind is the Root'. Translation from: Tarthang Tulku, ed., *The Crystal Mirror,* Vol. III, (Dharma Publishing. Emeryville, Calif., 1974), 3.

16 The attributes of this centre shall be provided in Volume 3, when commenting upon the Tantra 'Great Gate of Diamond Liberation', translated by Wayman.

17 Wayman, 285-6.

of what some texts, especially of the zen tradition, indicate as 'no mind'. (The term *'animitta'* that Wayman translates as 'signless' means 'formless, lack of the appearance of things'.) There is a sense of joyous equanimity, a vacuity of mind that is void of all concepts. This stage can also be described as the *dhyāna* accessed by the *arhat*. This state cannot however be held as permanent, because one must come out from its spell sometime in order to serve all beings; to present the fruits of one's meditative path to others, and to develop further wisdom.

This *'samādhi* of mind fixation' comes under the auspices of Amoghasiddhi's All-Accomplishing Wisdom, and the gesture of fearlessness. He steadfastly overcomes all of the obstacles that *saṃsāra* presents, every dark force that lurks in the mind, to integrate *saṃsāra* and *śūnyatā* into unity. *Saṃsāra* becomes a place of manifestation of benevolent *siddhis* for the liberation of the suffering, illusion-fettered ones. *Śūnyatā* becomes a stable abode, wherein the Dharmakāya Way is evoked to produce further links to the other shore of cosmos.

Here the function of the left lobe of the Ājñā centre (symbolised by the left eye, the eye of reason, of intellectual discursiveness and discrimination) is utilised as the organ of fixation by the Mind. With the fully functioning Eye, all aspects of the sense consciousnesses and the intellect can be thoroughly examined so that *saṃsāra* can be transformed into *śūnyatā*. The mindful *yogin* discerns every aspect of what is normally considered as 'life' *(jīva)* that may obscure the revelation of the Void. 'And whatever remains there' (upon our world-sphere), 'he knows: That being this is. Thus, Ānanda,[18] this becomes for him, a genuine, non-deviant, utterly pure, ultimate manifestation of voidness'.

The *samādhi* that is signless (verse nine).

> Ānanda, a monk, paying no attention to the idea of the base of nothing-at-all; and paying no attention to the idea of the base of neither-ideation-nor-non-ideation, orients his mind to the singleness depending on the *ceto-samādhi* that is signless. His mind rejoices in, trusts in, takes the shape of and is convinced of the *ceto-samādhi* that is signless. And he knows: This *ceto-samādhi* that is signless is instigated and motivated. He knows whatever is instigated and motivated is impermanent, has the

18 Here there is also an implied reference to the meaning of the Sanskrit term *ānanda*, 'bliss'.

> nature of cessation (*nirodhadharma*). The mind of the one who knows thus and sees thus, is freed from the flux of sense attractions (*kāmāsava*), is freed from the flux of gestation (*bhavāsava*), and is freed from the flux of nescience (*avijjāsava*). When there is liberation, there is knowledge, '[I] am liberated;' and he knows—'ended is birth, fulfilled is the career in purity; done is the duty; no more is the becoming a such.' He knows: the embrasures that in the three times [i.e. past, present, future] depend on the flux of sense attractions no longer exist. The embrasures that in the three times depend upon the flux of gestation, no longer exist. The embrasures that in the three times depend on the flux of nescience, no longer exist. And there is only this measure of embrasure, the six sense bases that, depending on the body, follow upon the condition of life.[19]

This signless *(animitta) samādhi* (where there is a lack of appearance of things) differs from 'nothing-at-all', because here the Mind is held steady in the light at the fulcrum of the balance wherein one side is ideation and the other is non-ideation. Consequently, the Mind can instantaneously go to either at need, to reside in *samādhi* or to apply its logic and wisdom to the task at hand, and for this purpose it looks to signs. The signs point the way that the meditation is to proceed. Hence the six sense bases remain (but are not indulged in) so that the monk can function in *saṃsāra*. If the balance swings to non-ideation, then the Mind stays in abeyance, ready to swing into action as an interpretative tool in response to the pure ideation that comes from the Heart of all. This is the pristine awareness that resides in one's Heart centre. If the balance swings to ideation, then the Mind is actively involved in the formulation of the ideas and images at hand. The consciousness of the Heart centre, and hence the entire *piṅgalā nāḍī* system, is here evoked and directed to the right eye, the eye of wisdom, and the right lobe of the Ājñā centre. Compassionate wisdom then determines which way 'the balance' swings.

Here is implied the ability of the meditator to hold the Mind steady in the Clear Light that is the base for the demonstration of *śūnyatā*, which is the gain of the entire life process. With both lobes of the Ājñā centre now fully functioning, the complete evocation of the powers of the 1,000 petalled lotus is possible. This happens as a consequence of the elimination of the fluxes of sense attractions, gestation, and nescience,

19 Alex Wayman, 286.

producing 'the knowledge of liberation', that only an awakened one residing in the Head centre can attain.[20]

Such *samādhi* is formless because the meditation Mind is absorbed in revelatory experience and consequently cannot be distracted. This betokens mastery of the meditation process, as embodied by the Dharmadhātu Wisdom of Vairocana. In the practice producing such liberation, the *yogin* seeks none of the signs (images) that would divert the meditation away from its fixed goal. This allows such techniques as the intonation of specific mantras or visualisations to be accomplished with certitude. The process has a beginning, must be sustained for the duration for the purpose to be accomplished, and then is terminated. Such termination can be abstraction into the Void, or else the commencement of a new meditative cycle.

There is no true elimination of gestation, as there is always a new commencement. A Bodhisattva inevitably arises that compassionately chooses subsequent rebirth. The awakened one formulates a plan to determine how best this can be achieved. Liberation of the all is the goal, and Buddhahood is obtained upon that road.

Dwelling in ultimate voidness (verse ten).

The last major statement relates to the three times, to all those that have awakened, are liberated, or will awaken the Head lotus. It acts as a summary of the teachings presented, emphasising how Ānanda, or any candidate for enlightenment, should train.

> And, Ānanda, those ascetics (Skt. *śramaṇa)* and brahmans who in past time attained and dwelled in the pure, ultimate voidness, all these did attain and dwell in precisely the pure, ultimate voidness. And, Ānanda, those ascetics and brahmans who in future time will attain and dwell in the pure, ultimate voidness, all these will attain and dwell in the pure, ultimate voidness. And, Ānanda, those ascetics and brahmans who in present time attain and dwell in the pure, ultimate voidness, all these are attaining and dwelling in precisely the pure, ultimate voidness. Consequently, Ānanda, thinking, 'Attaining, I shall dwell in the pure ultimate voidness,' this is how you should train, Ānanda.[21]

---

20 The meditations associated with verses eight and nine are nearly identical because of the fact that the Ājñā centre and the Head lotus are conjoined and function as a unity.

21 Ibid.

Though the three times are here emphasised, there is also the undercurrent of finality, that once the Voidness has been attained then the three times are one, the embrasure of the eternal Now that is timeless. Here the hint refers to the Sambhogakāya Flower, which is the custodian of the expression of the three times for the meditating monk, and is also the place of absorption of the *dhyāna* of an *arhat*. From there the 'pure ultimate voidness' can be achieved.

The final verse simply describes Ānanda's rejoicing in having been taught these yoga precepts. 'Thus spoke the Bhagavat. Enraptured the venerable Ānanda rejoiced in the Bhagavat's words.'[22]

Having described the above meditation, it should be noted that nowadays retirement into a forest is not needed to gain the Void experience. Rather, a place of solitude that prevents distractions suffices. However, the more advanced Bodhisattvas are also expected to gain this momentous achievement whilst still actively engaged in compassionate undertaking in the material domain. The entire force of prior meditations along this line from former lives has produced a proclivity for such an outcome, facilitating its eventuation whilst engaged in *saṃsāra*. *Saṃsāra* and *śūnyatā* are ridden together in one great *mahāmudrā* of expression.

Voidness and abundance

The gain of all this meditative activity is epitomised by the words of the Buddha: 'I, Ānanda, by dwelling in voidness, now dwell in abundance'. The vast Mind-spaces of the meditation Mind exist beyond the duration of time, and this the awakened Head centre experiences, yet there are cycles, encompassed by the nature of the unfoldment of its twelve main petals and all the subsidiary petals. The way of meditation is consequently patterned in accord with the awakening of the twelve main petals of the Head centre within the meditator's consciousness. The Heart's Mind (the integration of the Heart lotus with the Head lotus), whose emanation is *bodhicitta,* is the key to revelation of the All, and will be explained in some detail in this *Treatise on Mind.* Here is the union of compassion (the expression of the Void experienced in the Heart) and insight (the expression of wisdom when that experience is integrated with the expansiveness of the petals of the 1,000 petalled lotus). There we have 'abundance'.

---

22 Ibid., 287.

This phrase, which starts the Buddha's discussion, is of great significance because it indicates that the Void is not void, but rather full of 'something other', which the Buddha here calls 'abundance', and which I have also termed 'cosmos'. There is much yet to be revealed here. We also know that such a thing as cosmos persists, because the Buddha states that 'whatever remains there, he knows: That being, this is'. Once an enlightened being has transcended the state of being human, and thus has developed the state of being superhuman, he/she has begun to properly identify with what lies beyond the human condition, with whatever 'remains' after the human condition is eliminated. With this, even human consciousness has gone—then all that remains has gone to 'the other shore' (of *saṃsāra)*—that is cosmos.

The qualifying term *dharmakāya* can also be utilised for cosmos. It is my intent to provide a greater depth of meaning to the term *dharmakāya* than has hitherto been given to it. All can then begin to fathom a little of what it is to possess a Buddha-Mind, and not be left in the outer darkness, imagining that such a consideration is an impossibility until one actually becomes a Buddha. I say nay—all upon the path to enlightenment are piercing the associated veils, and a major veil they must pierce is the deceptive glamour that they cannot accommodate what a Buddha-Mind is in their conceptualisations. They may not have awakened a full Buddha-Mind, but they have made links *(antaḥkaraṇas)* thereto, via which revelations can and assuredly must come, otherwise the Buddha could not be considered all-compassionate, or all-wise. This means that as one aspires towards the Buddha-Mind by overcoming the obscurations of mind thereto, so then it allows a compliant, supremely compassionate and omnipresent Buddha to project gift-waves of revelation, of aspects of this Buddha-Mind, to the worthy one. If such revelation is considered 'all that remains', so be it. But more, ever more, remains to be experienced as one journeys to and through the vast expanse of *dharmakāya.*

Oṁ Tat Sat

Bibliography

Bailey, Alice A. *The Rays and the Initiations.* New York: Lucis Publishing Company, 1988.

Balsys, Bodo. *A Treatise on Mind, Volume 1.* Sydney: Universal Dharma Publishing, 2016.

——. *A Treatise on Mind, Volume 3.* Sydney: Universal Dharma Publishing, 2016.

——. *A Treatise on Mind, Volume 4.* Sydney: Universal Dharma Publishing, 2015.

——. *A Treatise on Mind, Volume 5a.* Sydney: Universal Dharma Publishing, 2015.

——. *A Treatise on Mind, Volume 5b.* Sydney: Universal Dharma Publishing, 2015.

——. *Karma and the Rebirth of Consciousness.* Delhi: Munshiram Manoharlal, 2006.

Bernbaum, Edwin. *The Way to Shambhala.* New York: Anchor Books, 1980.

Blavatsky, H.P. *The Voice of Silence.* Wheaton: Theosophical Publishing House, 1982.

——.*The Secret Doctrine. Vol. 1.* Adyar: Theosophical Publishing House, 1971

Brown, Brian Edward. *The Buddha Nature.* India: Motilal Banarsidass, 2004.

Conze, Edward. *The Buddha's Law Among the Birds*. Delhi: Motilal Banarsidass, 1996.

Dargyay, Eva K. "The Concept of a 'Creator God' in Tantric Buddhism", *The Journal of the International Association of Buddhist Studies, Vol. 8, No. 1*. Madison: University of Wisconsin, 1985.

Dudjom Rinpoche, *The Nyingma School of Tibetan Buddhism*. Translated by Gyurme Dorje and Matthew Kapstein. Boston: Wisdom, 1991.

Evans-Wentz, W.Y. *The Tibetan Book of the Dead*. London: Oxford University Press, 1960.

——. *The Tibetan Book of the Great Liberation*. London: Oxford University Press, 1968.

Griffiths, P.J. *On Being Buddha, The Classical Doctrine of Buddhahood*. Delhi: Sri Satguru Publications, 1995.

Hookham, S.K. *The Buddha Within: Tathagatagarbha Doctrine According to the Shentog Interpretation of the Ratnagotravibhaga*. Delhi: Sri Satguru Publications, 1992.

Kalupahana, D.J. Trans. *Mūlamadhyamakakārikā of Nāgārjuna. The Philosophy of the Middle Way*. Delhi: Motilal Banarsidass, 1999.

Lerner, Eric. *The Big Bang Never Happened*. New York: Times Books 1991.

Lopez, D.S. Jr. *A Study of Svātantrika*. New York: Snow Lion Publications, 1987.

Makransky, John. *Buddhahood Embodied, Sources of Controversy in India and Tibet*. Delhi: Sri Satguru, 1998.

Matics, Marion L. *Entering the Path of Enlightenment, The Bodhicaryāvatāra of the Buddhist Poet Śāntideva*. London: George Allen & Urwin, 1970.

Mittal, Kewal Krishan. *Perspectives on Karma and Rebirth*. Delhi: Dept. of Buddhist Studies, Delhi University, 1990.

Neumaier-Dargyay, E.K. *The Sovereign All-Creating Mind the Motherly Buddha*. Delhi: Sri Satguru, 1992.

Obermiller, E. Trans. *The Uttaratantra of Maitreya*. Delhi: Sri Satguru Publications, 1997.

Reynolds, J.M. *The Golden Letters*. Ithaca: Snow Lion, 1996.

Sparham, Gareth. *Ocean of Eloquence, Tsong-kha-pa's Commentary on the Yogācāra Doctrine of Mind.* Delhi: Sri Satguru, 1995.

Stcherbatsky, Theodore. *The Central Conception of Buddhism.* Delhi: Motilal Baranasidass, 1994.

Stede, W. Ed. and Rhys Davids, T.W. Ed. *Pali-English Dictionary.* Delhi: Motilal Baranasidass, 2015.

Suzuki, Daisetz Teitaro. *The Lankavatara Sutra.* London: Routledge & Kegan Paul Ltd, 1973.

——. *Studies in The Lankavatara Sutra.* London: Routledge & Kegan Paul Ltd, 1975.

Swati Ganguly. Trans. *Treatise in Thirty Verses on Mere-Consciousness. A critical English translation of Hsüan-tsang's Chinese version of the Vijñaptimātratātriṃśikā with notes from Dharmapāla's commentary in Chinese.* Delhi: Motilal Banarsidass, 1992.

Takasaki, Jikido. Trans. *A Study on the Ratnagotravibhāga.* Rome: Instituto Italiano per il Medio ed Estremo Oriente, 1966.

Tarthang Tulku. Ed. *The Crystal Mirror, Vol. III.* California: Dharma Publishing, 1974.

The King James Version Bible. London: Oxford University Press, 1922.

Wayman, Alex. *Untying the Knots in Buddhism, Selected Essays.* Delhi: Motilal Banarsidass, 1997.

——. *Buddhist Insight.* Delhi: Motilal Banarsidass, 1990.

Wayman, Alex and Hideko. *The Lion's Roar of Queen Śrīmālā.* Delhi: Motilal Banarsidass, 1990.

Index

A

Abdominal brain, 101
Abhidharma, 324
Absolutes, 257
Abundance, 374–375
Acupuncture, 2
Adhipati-pratyaya, 280
Adhivacana, 270
Ādi Buddha, 64, 76, 147, 170, 198, 200, 203, 210, 216, 220, 221, 285, 286, 341
Advayadharma, 58
After death state, 185–186
Aggregates and revelation, 235
Agni, 14
Ahamkāra, 103–104
Ahosti, 270
Ākāra, 301, 305
Ākāśa, 368
Ākāśādhātvīśvari, 368
Ālambana, 145, 301, 313
Ālaya, 130, 280, 286
  explained, 277
  two aspects, 278
Ālayavijñāna, 67, 77, 78, 80, 84, 90–91, 92, 103, 106, 112, 119, 127, 129, 142, 146, 151, 152, 171, 197, 204–205, 235, 248, 277, 279–289, 298, 301–316
  and arhant, 290
  and Base of Spine centre, 305
  and death process, 284
  and formless realms, 310–316
  and homogeneity, 79
  and membranes, 137
  and mental factors, 296–297
  and not moralising, 306
  and perfumes, 289, 291, 296–297
  and Sambhogakāya Flower, 147, 281, 296–297
  and saṃskāras, 159
  and seed growth, 282, 297
  and 'selves', 82
  and sense perception, 309
  and sentient beings, 79–80
  and vāsanā, 343
  and wisdom, 159
  as a basis, 304–305, 306–307
  as manas store, 282
  as tapestry, 213
  conversion of, 160
  genesis of, 107
  organisation of, 284–285
  ripple in, 212–213
  supports of, 302–303
Alexander, 285
All-Creating King, 199–201, 203, 207, 209, 220
  feminine, 201–202
Anāgata, 270

Ānanda, 357–358, 360, 362, 364, 365, 367, 369, 370, 371, 373, 374
Anātman, 48
Angelic beings, 66
Animal chakras, 184
Anima mundi, 278
Animitta, 370, 371, 372
Anivṛtāvyākṛta, 301
Aniyatā, 52
Antaḥkaraṇa/s, 234, 243, 301, 353, 375
Anubis, 17
Anupadāka defined, 172
Anvayavyāpti, 229
Apratiṣṭhita nirvāṇa, 348
Arhant/Arhat, 41
  absorption, 171
  and ālayavijñāna, 290
  dhyāna, 371
Ariadne, 24
Asaṃskṛta, 135, 144, 294
Asaṅga, 1
Ashoka, 285
Asmimāna, 4
Aspirational idealism, 118
Aspiration, explained, 238, 240
Āśrayapaṛtti, 56
Astral plane, 42
Aśūnya, 49
Atīta, 270
Ati yoga, 211
Atlantis, 20
Ātmagrāha, 77
Ātmamahāmatām, 148
Ātman, 49, 144, 344
  and consciousness, 145
  and ego, 48
  and enlightenment, 146
  and nairātmya, 146
  and 'self', 47–48, 145–146
  and tathatā, 53
  transcendental aspect, 147
Ātmic realm, 337
Atthi, 270
Aura, 2
Avarice, 267–268
Avidyā, 261
Avijjāsava, 372
Avikāra, 51
Awareness, requirements of, 273

B

Basis, meaning of, 304–305
Bhāgas, 134, 139, 144
Bhāva, 326
Bhāvanā, 40
Bhāvanāmārga, 77
Bhavāsava, 372
Bhavissati, 270
Bhūmis, ten, 61, 114, 126, 128, 129, 167, 174, 212, 244
  and aura, 74
  and skilful means, 75
Bhūtadravya, 144
Big Bang, 179
Bīja/s, 10, 51, 59, 77–80, 104, 106, 125, 141, 142, 166, 202, 206, 215, 277, 281, 290, 293, 314
  and karma, 80, 216
  and laya-centre, 193
  and maṇḍalas, 201
  and mūlavijñāna, 90
  and own fruit, 125
  and perfumes, 291
  and Sambhogakāya Flower, 87, 126–131
  and the Sacral centre, 120–126, 122–126, 132–133
  and the Solar Plexus centre, 90–92, 103
  as containers, 80
  as 'self', 79
  as 'selves', 82–83
  as 'things', 78–79
  born of perfuming, 90, 91, 109–110
  natural, 90, 91, 109–110
  of self identification, 102

of universe, 149
of Watery qualities, 131
seven characteristics, 90–91
transformation of, 127
two kinds, 90, 109
Bindu, 10, 193
Black dharma, 219
Black magic, 219, 355
and greed, 269
Black magician, 19
Bodhicitta, 10, 11, 23, 31, 45, 74, 95, 101, 115, 118, 124, 126, 131, 132, 160, 172, 181, 186, 199, 200, 211, 220, 221, 237, 281, 298, 341, 374
and bījas, 293
and compassion, 201
and devotion, 238
and eye of insight, 42
and kliṣṭamanas, 240
and Sambhogakāya Flower, 130
and śūnyatā-saṃsāra nexus, 201
and Voidness, 200
and white path, 120
development of, 222
evocation of, 368
generation of, 112, 114, 245
Bodhisattva/s, 188, 231, 269, 286, 338
and Ādi Buddha, 220
and light, 242–243
and nirvāṇa, 258
and past lives, 234–235
and śūnyatā doctrine, 171–172
and the 2nd ray, 38
compassion of, 210
goal of, 148
making of a, 74
path, 124, 134, 223, 230
reincarnation of, 192
ten stages, 41, 174, 244, 341
Boundaries of perception, 259–260
Boundless All, 262
Brahmā, 198
Buddhadharma, history, 228
Buddha-field, 62, 147, 197
Buddha-germ, 42–43, 259
Buddhahood, attainment of, 256, 287–288
Buddha-like animals, 350
Buddha-Mind, 64, 66, 67, 147, 149, 170, 201, 221, 259, 286, 288, 329
and 'God', 203
as dharmakāya, 55
awakening of, 375
creative, 197
Buddha-Mother, 201
Buddha nature, 46
Buddha/s, 36, 65, 224, 235, 337
and Ānanda, 357–358
and anupadāka, 172
and Bodhisattvas, 353
and cosmic status, 352
and Dependent Origination, 208–210
and instinct, 349
and karmic boundaries, 215
and manasic support, 286
and māyā, 259
and memory, 54–55
and Sambhogakāya Flower, 173
and tathatā, 54–55
as a child, 209
as a lion, 351–352
differences in, 147–149, 355
radiance of, 45
vacana, 76
vāsanā of, 353
versus a Logos, 350
Buddhi, 246
and tathatā, 55
explained, 255
Bull's hide, symbolism, 362

C

Caesar, 285
Caittas, 135
Candrakīrti, 246, 248, 249, 250

Catuṣkoṭikā, 81, 223
and a Buddha, 346–349
and consciousness, 346
Causes
as conditioning law, 215
Cellular wall, 215
Cetanā, 297–298, 302, 307
Ceto-samādhi, 371
Chakra
Ājñā centre, 42, 118, 186, 360, 371, 372
Anāhata. *See* Heart centre
as a 'soul', 185
Base of Spine centre, 115, 120, 122, 133, 134, 167–168, 182, 185, 305–306, 332, 359, 361, 364
Diaphragm centre, 94, 116, 176
Feet centres, 94
Gonad centres, 94, 97, 120
Hand centres, 94, 97
Head centre, 64, 94, 114, 118, 127, 130, 160–161, 167, 184, 186, 193, 206, 305, 360, 368, 373, 374
Heart centre, 9, 35, 92, 94, 95, 97, 100, 105, 106, 108, 109, 111, 114, 115, 118, 119, 126, 128, 131, 132, 133, 167, 176, 186, 360, 368
and Airy prāṇas, 99
and bodhicitta, 115
and dharmatā, 111
and eye of insight, 42
and Inner Round, 112
and Liver centre, 95, 111
and natural bījas, 110
and piṇgalā naḍī, 130
and pristine awareness, 370, 372
and Solar Plexus centre, 99
in cosmos, 209
in the Head, 131, 206, 209
non-sacred petals, 95
Knee centres, 94
Liver centre, 92, 94, 97, 100–101, 106, 113, 114
and clairaudience, 117
and Heart centre, 111
and kliṣṭamanas, 95
as piṇgalā store, 96–97
bījas of, 109–110
prāṇas of, 108–110
seeding of, 130
Maṇipūra. *See* Solar Plexus
Mūlādhāra. *See* Base of Spine centre
Sacral centre, 95, 96, 97, 114, 115, 123, 125, 126, 127, 129, 166, 167, 185, 332, 359, 364
and Base of Spine, 134
and desire, 104
and elemental lives, 119
and momentary bījas, 122
and piṇgalā nāḍī, 105
and prāṇic vitalisation, 120–121
and Sambhoghakāya Flower, 132–134
and Solar Plexus centre, 99
seeding of, 126–127
Sahasrāra padma. *See* Head centre
Solar Plexus centre, 17, 28–29, 41–42, 93, 94, 95, 97, 108, 112, 113, 114, 115, 121, 122, 125, 126, 131, 132, 133, 185, 226, 239, 359, 368
and animals, 184
and bījas, 92–93, 103–114, 110–111
and emotions, 110
and prāṇas, 93
and Sambhoghakāya Flower, 126–132
and self-identity, 105, 106, 114
and Splenic centre I, 111
and Stomach centre, 107–109
and Throat centre, 103
as abdominal brain, 101
eight-fold expression, 116–117

in the Head, 127, 206
north-south orientation, 98–99
pentads of, 100–101, 118
petals of, 92–100
seeding of, 126
Splenic centre I, 95, 106, 113, 114, 124, 131
and Airy prāṇas, 115
and health, 115
and Heart centre, 112
and Solar Plexus centre, 111
and Throat centre, 112
Splenic centre II, 17, 95, 105, 116, 123, 130, 132
and Inner Round, 119
and yogic control, 117–118
Splenic centres, 94–95, 100, 159
yogic control of, 99
Stomach centre, 92, 94–95, 97, 100–101, 110, 113, 114
and clairvoyance, 117
and cruelty, 96
and manasic bījas, 106
and personal-I, 94
and Solar Plexus centre, 95–96, 107–109
as iḍā store, 96
qualities of, 129
Svādiṣṭhāna. *See* Sacral centre
Throat centre, 28, 94, 97, 114, 119, 125, 127, 129, 167, 185, 359, 366
and ālayavijñāna, 103
and Fiery prāṇas, 115
and iḍā nāḍī, 103
and manas, 103, 108
awakening, 95
in the Head, 206
Chakras, 17, 75, 87, 89, 183–189, 240, 243
and consciousness, 165–166
and karma, 185
and naḍīs, 181–183
and perfumes, 291
and psychic phenomena, 165–166
and the Elements, 303
as eyes, 42
as flowers, 188
as laya-centres, 193
as soul-forms, 186–187
awakening of, 193
importance of, 166–167
in Nature, 202
minor, 88, 113
of the universe, 182
seven major, 2, 184, 357–358
the Inner Round, 28, 92, 93, 94, 99, 101, 102, 107, 110, 112, 114, 117, 123, 125, 127, 131, 184
Christ, 36
Chronos, 325
Citta, 125, 152, 246, 247, 250, 252, 265, 279, 285, 312
and māyā, 248
and śūnyatā, 248
as fuel, 251
definition, 277–278
knowing itself, 248–249
Cittamātra School, 200
Cittavṛtti, 248, 250
definition, 245
Clairaudience, 117
Clairvoyance, 117
Clear Light, 4, 8, 73, 74, 95, 108, 116, 119, 156, 241, 244, 245, 275, 283, 298, 304, 336, 372
and Heart centre, 167
Compassion, 202
Consciousness, 73, 90, 217, 335
and bījas, 80
and chakras, 165–166, 181–183, 184
and darkness, 254
and digestion, 141
and prāṇas, 166
and self and things, 164–165
and sentience, 157–159

and time, 324–325, 340
as river flow, 178, 180
entering, 280, 283, 284, 286
evolution of, 151–174, 168, 191–197, 212, 263–265, 272, 345
Eye of, 204, 205
laws of, 204–205, 207
layers/levels, 162, 213
limits of, 339
momentum of, 314
overriding, 192–193
signposts of, 225–237
space, 196
speed of, 194–195, 226
stream/s, 177, 314–315
Cosmic Individuation, 352
Cosmos
chakras in, 354
evolution in, 263
explained, 375
Council of Bodhisattvas, 187
Creation Theory, 141
Creative Being, 197
Creator 'God', 198–203
Crisis, 239–241
Cycles, 179, 295

D

Ḍākinīs, 66, 172, 207, 213, 216
Daratha, 358
Dark brotherhood, 17
Dark matter, 262
Darkness
as ignorance, 242–243
cosmic, 289
definition, 253
degrees of, 252–256
forms of, 244
perpetration of, 268
versus light, 261–264
Darśanabhāga, 90, 134, 136, 138, 140, 142, 143–145, 151
and Liver centre, 109
Darśanamārga, 77, 80
Defilements, 142, 199
Dependency, 139
Dependent Origination, 43, 125, 139, 210
in cosmos, 209–210
ramifications of, 207–211
two types, 161–163
Desire, 65, 239
function of, 10–11
serpents of, 113
Destiny, 89, 282
and santāna, 86
mechanism of, 84–85
Deva/s, 19, 117, 207, 216
and karma, 221
and substance, 213
kingdom, 87, 157
Devotees, 238–239
Devotion explained, 237–239
Dhāraṇīs, 359, 367
Dharmadhātu, 39
Dharmakāya, 5–6, 8, 10, 45, 51, 57, 58, 60, 64, 65, 66, 73, 146, 147, 149–150, 168, 171, 173, 192, 196, 202, 203, 215, 228, 240, 241, 244, 275, 286, 292, 298, 301, 304, 315, 335, 336, 337
and evolution, 62
and higher laws, 207
and karma, 149, 155, 157, 162
and Sambhogakāya Flower, 159–160
and saṃsāra, 62, 200
and śūnyatā, 55
and svabhāva, 249
and tathāgatagarbha, 49–50, 52, 54–55
and time, 329
as Buddha-Mind, 55
as cosmos, 375
as directing agent, 89
focus, 172
levels, 148

Dharmakāya Eye, 42, 43
Dharmakāya Flower, 160
Dharmakāya-Mind, 147, 196, 203, 236
Dharmakāya Way, 75, 76, 159, 173, 230, 259, 289, 298, 315, 334, 335, 336, 371
    and That, 208
    and Thusness, 37
Dharma/s, 41, 90–91, 91, 122, 127, 130, 144, 146, 197, 344
    72 or so, 125
    and the Sacral centre, 104
    as bīja, 122–123, 132
    definition, 60, 112
    fruits of, 118
    perfuming of, 111
    truths of, 124
Dharmatā, 90–91, 109, 110, 111, 118
Dhātu, 56, 175
Dhyāna, 62, 243, 258, 337, 366
    and chakras, 182
    levels, four, 84
Dhyāni Buddhas, 60, 147, 183, 201, 207, 298, 327, 367
    Akṣobhya, 115, 200, 369, 370
    Amitābha, 369
        paradise realm, 21, 186
    Amoghasiddhi, 11, 369, 371
    and ālayavijñāna, 159
    Ratnasambhava, 118, 368, 369
    Vairocana, 368, 373
    Wisdoms of, 37, 366, 367, 368–369, 370, 371, 373
Dibbacakkhu, 40
Difficult passageways, 363
Digestion
    and consciousness, 141
    symbolism of, 137, 141–142, 143
Dorje (viśva-vajra), 134, 368
Duḥkha, 161
Duḥkhatā, 52

E

Ear-whispered teachings, 36, 117, 172
Eightfold Path, 109, 208
Electricity as prāṇa, 192
Elemental lives, 119
Elements, 206, 361
    Aether, 92, 128, 308, 329, 361, 364
    Air, 114, 130, 131, 301, 309, 328, 361, 364, 365
    and Dhyāni Buddhas, 183
    and the senses, 301
    Earth, 95, 130, 167, 185, 301, 359, 361, 364
    Fire, 130, 133, 261, 301, 308, 361, 364, 366
    prāṇas of, 101
    two esoteric, 303
    Void, 10–11, 201
    Water, 28, 93, 115, 129, 185, 239, 301, 361, 362, 364, 367
Elephants, symbolism, 361
Embrasure, 358–359
Emotional body, 2–3
Emotional-mind
    and Solar Plexus centre, 28–29
    Crabs of, 33–34
    Dog-like, 30–31
    Monkey, 32–33
    Mouse-like, 34–35
    Racing Hounds, 29–30
    seven aspects of, 27–35
    Slugs of, 32
    Spider-like, 31–32
Emotions, 5, 7
    and love, 7, 12
    and Water, 28
    animal-like, 28–35
    dissipation of, 72
    four afflictive, 4
    versus intensity, 243
Emptiness, 73–74, 236

Energy fields, 313
Enlightenment
    and ālayavijñāna, 142–143
    and future tendencies, 223
    and the 'I', 145–146
    as relative, 173
Esoteric astrology, 210
Esoteric lore, 100
Eternal Now, 58, 223–224, 272, 324, 328, 333, 334, 336
    and Voidness, 374
Etheric vehicle, 2, 185, 303
Event horizon, 334
    and saṃskāras, 330–331
Evil
    definition, 263
    forces of, 16
    weed, 16
Evolution, 81–82, 265
    and chakras, 166–167
    progress of, 211–212
Evolutionary law, 220, 220–224
Eye
    and consciousness, 205
    as Ājñā centre, 42
    as Soul-form, 43–44
    Buddha, 40–42, 42
    divine, 40, 41, 43, 75
    five eyes, 40
    god, 41, 42
    of dharma, 40–41, 42
    of flesh, 40, 41
    of insight, 40–41, 42
    symbolism, 40–45
    third, 41
    three eyes, 40
    water, 41
Eye of reason, 371
Eye of wisdom, 41, 42, 372

F

Facial orifices, seven, 357
    left ear, 359
    left eye, 360, 371
    left nostril, 359, 362, 365
    right ear, 359–360
    right eye, 360, 372
    right nostril, 359, 364
Faith explained, 237–238
Father aspect, 11
Feeling/s, 65, 302
Fiery lake as ālayavijñāna, 287
Fiery principle, 256
Fingers
    forefinger, 101, 104
    little finger, 101, 106, 110
    middle finger, 101, 111, 112–113
    ring finger, 101, 105, 106
    thumb, 101, 107
Fire defined, 14
Fire-mist, 128
Flowers, three types, 160
Forest symbolism, 361
Formless realms, 312–313
Fourth-dimensional motion, 283
Free will, 142, 222, 237
    and karma, 227
Furies, 317
Future, 320–321
    as pure potential, 260–261
    prediction of, 321–322
Future tendencies, 218–219
    and enlightenment, 223

G

Garbha, 53
    as container, 59–60
    as process, 50
Gati, 78, 84, 89, 282
Gautama, 285
    as perpetual guru, 353
Gibb's Free Energy, 19, 213
Gift waves, 211
Glamour explained, 221
God, 8, 195–203, 237
    and higher Mind, 197

as a 'one', 263
as Fire, 262
Gorgons, 18
Gotra explained, 50
Gravity and karma, 214
Great Mother, 336, 337
Greed or avarice, 97
Gullies, symbolism, 363
Guṇas, 264
rajas, 264
Sattva, 264
tamas, 264

H

Harpies, 317
Hatred, 96
Healing, key to, 98
Hearing, 299, 307
and speech, 300
Heart's Mind, 36, 245, 374
and truth, 76
Height, concept of, 292
Herd-consciousness, 70
Hetu-pratyaya, 280
Hexagram, 120
Hierarchy of Light, 174
and bodhicitta, 31
structure, 316
Hinayāna, 73, 171, 353
Hindu gods, 198
Holy Path, 124
H.P. Blavatsky, 262
Hubble redshift, 179

I

I-consciousness, 4, 45, 57, 73, 79, 241, 304
and abstract Mind, 5
and five senses, 309
as Sambhogakāya Flower, 60
as tathāgatagarbha, 43
Identity, 73
Ignorance
as darkness, 242–243, 261–263
fostering of, 266
Ignorance quotient, 344
Imagination, 66
Incarnation into animals, 184–185
Individuality, 250, 272, 314
importance of, 227, 288
Infinite perception, 365–366
Infinite space, 364–365, 368
Initiation of Buddhas, 209
Initiation process, 126, 341
Inquisition, 219
Insanity, 348
Instinct, 65, 121, 158, 264
Intellect, 66, 304
and manas, 278
as empirical mind, 3
as pravṛttivijñāna, 152
Intensity, 242–244
and Bodhisattva path, 283
of Mind, 275
Intuition, 66, 146, 205, 228
Involutionary process, 210, 281

J

Jina/s. *See also* Dhyāni Buddhas
explained, 149
Jīva, 176, 370, 371
Jñeyāvaraṇa, 282

K

Kāla, 326
Kālī yuga, 23
Kāma, 25
Kāma-manas, 28, 103, 104, 127, 307
and kliṣṭamanas, 5
and saṃskāras, 133
Kāmāsava, 372
Karma, 18, 19, 20, 22, 42, 62, 71, 73, 78, 81, 82, 85, 87, 110, 112, 122, 143, 177–178, 181, 201, 210, 212–220, 223, 227, 234, 235, 256, 272, 281, 300, 316, 319, 320, 324, 328, 335, 336, 337, 338

and astral zones, 118
and bījas, 206
and chakras, 182, 185, 186–187
and citta, 278
and dharmakāya, 157, 162, 172
and evolution, 55, 219
and moralising, 293
and originating causes, 211–212
and perfumes, 291
and Sambhogakāya Flower, 86, 142
and sambhoghakāya, 156, 162
and signs, 231
and tathāgatagarbha, 335
and time, 322–324, 330
and transmigration, 188–189
as directing agent, 341
as Love, 263
collective, 64, 83
cosmic, 221
driving force of, 303, 315
group, 136, 177, 316
knots of, 80, 204
linits to, 214–215
Lords of, 216
of physical body, 61–62
organisation of, 286
origination of, 149
ribbons of, 304
rings of, 213
ripples of, 212–214
two streams of, 154–155, 161
Karmaphala, 78
Kāya, 60, 176
Khandha, 176
Kleśa/s, 78, 84, 87, 161
as afflictive emotions, 5
definition, 11
Kleśavaraṇa, 282
Kliṣṭamanas, 28, 92, 118, 239, 281, 289, 307
and ālayavijñāna, 279
and bodhicitta, 240
and devotion, 238
and emotions, 282
and Liver centre, 95
and love, 281
and manas, 249
and manovijñāna, 152
and neutral perfumes, 280–281
defintion, 5–6
Kośas, 1
Krishna, 36
Kṣaṇika, 90, 122
Kuṇḍalinī, 42, 99, 115, 118, 134, 331

L

Lakṣaṇa, 278
Law and causes, 212
Law of dependency, 197
Laya-centre, 193, 223
Left hand path, 120, 219
Liberation, 147, 150, 275
Life, 167
Light, 242, 242–265, 251
and a maṇḍala, 244
and consciousness, 44–45
and darkness, 261–264
and Mind, 43
and nirvāṇa, 170
as mental substance, 252
bearers of, 266
genesis of, 262
Lion, 272
Logoi, 172
Logos, 76, 170, 260–261, 263, 355
birth of, 174
Heart of, 74
Loka/s
arūpa, 84, 199, 210, 230, 243, 292, 313, 368
kāma, 199
rūpa, 84, 125, 199, 210, 230
Lords of Life, 217
Love, 12, 210–211, 245
and Sambhogakāya Flower, 309–310

evolution of, 281
law of, 263, 354
Love-Wisdom, 115

M

Mādhyamapratipad, 370
Madness, 162–163
Mahāmudrā, 211, 298, 336, 374
Mahāsiddha, 168
Mahāyāna, 171
Maitreya, 210
Maṃsacakkhu, 40
Manana, 151
Manas, 4, 131, 133, 144, 213, 248, 282, 366
and dharmakāya, 249
and kliṣṭamanas, 249
and pravṛttivijñāna, 249
and Stomach centre, 95
and svabhāva, 248
as filter, 155
definition, 152, 278–279
Manasic Fire, 263
Manasic space, 285
Manaskāra, 297–298, 306, 307
Maṇḍala/s, 193, 196, 314
and dividing lines, 180–181
and light, 244
function of, 218
Manomayakāya, 40
Manovijñāna, 5, 151–152, 153, 279
and kliṣṭamanas, 152
as manas, 278–279
Mantra/s, 367
and dharmakāya, 150
and Sambhogakāya Flower, 309
Mānuśi Buddhas, 259
Marpa, 171
Material comforts, 97
Māyā, 10, 14, 17, 58, 116, 167–171, 169, 174, 247, 335–336
and enlightenment, 257
and liberating Fire, 168
and nirvāṇa, 170
and seperatism, 356
and śūnyatā, 256
definition, 168
fabric of, 206
in cosmos, 260
relativity of, 256–258
Māyāvirūpa, 19
Māyāvirūpic zeal, 14
Meditation, formlessness, 314
Meditation Mind, 36, 359, 373, 374
Meditation process, 358
Medusa, 18
Memory, 222, 232
and Buddhahood, 54
Mental factors, five, 296–301
Mere-consciousness, 143
Milarepa, 235
mind, 65–66, 83–84, 94, 369–370
concrete, 3, 13, 23–24, 238
critical, 12, 17–18, 96
desire, 13, 25–26, 35–36
dual aspect of, 4–5
empirical, 3, 248
loving, 12, 16–17
pride of, 12–13, 21–23
will of, 12, 15–16
wrongly faceted, 13–14, 26–27
Mind, 9, 36, 170, 250, 262
abstract, 3–4, 5–6, 39, 60, 128, 206, 213, 216, 366, 368
and cittavṛtti, 248
and the 'I', 146
and time, 326, 328
and 'God', 197
clear light of, 4, 8, 206, 304, 336
cosmic, 147, 202–203
laws of, 89, 183
primordial, 38
universal, 66, 241
Mind-space, 196
Minos, 24
Minotaur, 24

Monadic expression, 67
Mother, 10–11
Mouth, 18–20, 359
Mūlaprakṛti, 81, 201
Mūlavijñāna, 77, 79, 83, 87, 128
  and bījas, 90–91
  and Solar Plexus centre, 105
  definition, 78, 105

N

Nāḍīs, 2, 185, 187, 345, 361
  and chakras, 181–183
  as a web, 31
  iḍā, 93, 95, 98–99, 103, 106, 107, 113, 115, 119, 126, 133, 160, 359, 360, 361, 362, 365
    and taste, 308–309
    generation of, 124
    genesis of, 104
    purpose of, 127
  of lesser kingdoms, 184
  piṅgalā, 93, 95, 98–99, 105, 106, 113, 114, 115, 117, 119, 126, 128, 133, 160, 181, 308, 359, 360, 361, 364–365, 365, 372
    and taste, 309
    generation of, 124
    genesis of, 97
  suśumṇā, 127, 160, 308
Nāḍī system, 15, 134, 160, 181, 188, 193, 221, 359, 361
Nāga Lord, 331
Nāgārjuna, 81, 346
  on time, 319–338
Nairātmya, 145, 146
Nāropā, 171
Nature, Lord of, 288
Nexus
  śūnyatā-saṃsāra (saṃsāra-śūnyatā), 81, 201, 248, 255, 298, 332
Nibbāna, 246
Nimittabhāga, 134, 136, 138, 140, 143–146, 151
  and bījas, 90–91
  and Liver centre, 108–109
Nirātmatā, 52
Nirmalā tathatā, 50, 56, 342
  relation to samalā-tathatā, 56–60
Nirmaṇakāya, 65, 146, 286
  definition, 60–62
Nirodhadharma, 372
Niruttipatha, 270
Nirvāṇa, 89, 169–170, 258
  and change, 168
  and māyā, 170
  as beginning, 173
  as relative, 170
  non-abiding, 348
  perception of, 258–260
Nitya, 51, 53
Noble Truths, 71, 109
  and Dependent Origination, 161–162
No mind, 371
No-self as extremism, 48
Nothing-at-all, 367–368
Numerology
  24 symbolism, 133
  50 symbolism, 93
  100 symbolism, 362–363
  500 symbolism, 93
  1000 symbolism, 93

O

Objective support, 311, 314
  and energy fields, 313
  and sense perceptors, 302
Oṁ svāhā, 353
Originating causes, 211–212

P

Padmasambhava, 171, 173
Pakṣadharma, 229
Pancreas, 97, 101, 113, 114, 130
Paññā, 40

Paññācakkhu, 40
Paramārthatas, 41
Paramātman, 148
Parikalpita-svabhāva, 301
Parinirvāṇa, 62, 209, 259, 353
  and Mind, 197
  as new beginning, 352
Past, the, 223
  time zones, 266
Pendulum effect, 188
Perception, boundaries of, 259–260
Perfumes, 290
Perfuming, 289–296
Perfuming energy, 153
Personal-I
  composition of, 1–4
  seeding of, 314
Phoenix, 317
Photons, 192, 261
Plasma cosmology, 179
Prabandha, 278
Prajñā, 10
Prajñā-cakṣus, 40
Prajñāpāramitā, 78, 172
Pramāṇas, 247
Prāṇa/s, 2, 16, 19, 28, 366
  Aetheric, 306
  Airy, 106, 306
  and consciousness, 166
  and etheric vehicle, 303
  and healing, 98
  as perfumes, 291, 295
  Earthy, 97, 103, 122, 182, 305
  Fiery, 107, 306
  fifty types, 93
  five, 183
  iḍā naḍī, 94
  manasic, 107, 128
  of Sacral centre, 120
  piṇgalā naḍī, 99, 108
  Watery, 103, 106, 107, 108, 122, 306
Prāṇic flow, 18, 176
Pratyakṣa, 355
Pravṛtti, 278, 279, 283
Pravṛttivijñāna, 151, 152, 153, 158, 181, 248, 249, 255, 279
Prayoga, 229
Primordial Buddha, 288–289
Primordial Mind, 221
Promontories, symbolism, 363
Propulsive force, 313–314
Psychic continuum and animals, 274
Psychic history, 219
Psychic powers, 219
Psychic protectors, 220
Psychometry, 119
Puccuppanna, 270

R

Ray aspects/qualities, 308
  1st ray, 38, 338
  2nd ray, 38, 131, 336–338
  3rd ray, 38, 334–336
  4th ray, 38–39, 332–334
  5th ray, 39, 332
  6th ray, 28, 39, 332
  7th ray, 39–40, 329–331
  seven of Mind, 11–27
  seven rays, 37–40, 131, 329–338, 357
rDzogs chen, 9
Real entities, 128, 129, 130
Rebirth
  and 'subtle-soul', 287
  into animals, 102, 188, 274
  mechanism of, 87
  process, 303
Relativity, importance, 346–351
Residual impression, 303–304
Rigpa, 9–10, 11
River
  definition, 176–177
  simile, 175–188
  symbolism, 363

Roman empire, 269
Rūpa, 14

S

Sacrifice, 241
Sadhana, 367
Sādhya, 229
Sahaja, 77
Śakti/s, 93, 134
Samādhi, 41, 59, 312, 373
 and all-seeing eye, 42
 and divine eye, 40
 of mind fixation, 370
 signless, 372
Samalā tathatā, 342
 and defilements, 57
 and Sambhogakāya Flower, 87
 definition, 50, 55–56
 relation to nirmalā tathatā, 55–60
Samanantara, 4
Samanantara-pratyaya, 4
Samantabhadra. *See* Ādi Buddha
Samantabhadrā, 202
Samāpatti, 310, 312, 313, 314
Samaya, 14
Sambhogakāya, 146
 and karma, 156, 162
 definition, 46, 61, 63–65, 67
 evolution of, 62
 form, 244, 251, 313
 of Buddhas, 37
Sambhogakāya Flower, 44, 45, 63–64, 65, 76, 80, 89, 109, 110, 142, 160, 181, 182, 186, 192, 204, 205–206, 207, 216, 218, 220, 221, 230, 233–235, 240, 250, 263, 284, 300, 301, 306, 310, 340–341, 360, 374
 and abstracted thoughts, 82–83
 and ālayavijñāna, 108, 281, 290–291, 296, 305
 and arhat, 171
 and Ātman, 146
 and bījas, 107–108
 and bodhicitta, 294
 and destiny, 86–87, 285
 and dharmakāya, 159–160, 202
 and driving force, 316
 and five senses, 298–300
 and karma, 154–155, 316
 and memories, 222
 and mental factors, 296–298
 and moralising, 293–294
 and past life images, 234
 and perfuming, 294–295
 and Sacral centre, 132–134
 and santāna, 84
 and seeding, 297
 and Solar Plexus centre, 126–132
 and śūnyatā, 147
 and Śūnyatā Eye, 150
 and the Bodhisattva, 243–244
 and the future, 321–322
 and Vijñānavādins, 89–90
 as a chakra, 187–188, 189
 as I-consciousness, 60
 fragrance of, 282–283
 Knowledge--Knowledge petal, 129–130, 132
 Knowledge--Love-Wisdom petal, 128–129, 132–133
 Knowledge--Sacrifice petal, 127–128
 Love-Wisdom--Knowledge petal, 130
 Love-Wisdom--Love-Wisdom petal, 130–131
 petals of, 126–131, 298, 313
 Sacrifice--Knowledge petal, 134
Saṁjñā, 297–298, 302, 308
Saṃprayukta, 301
Saṃsāra, 199, 202
 and siddhis, 371
 and śūnyatā, 5–6, 81–82, 223, 256
 definition, 5

Saṃskāras, 10–11, 14, 28, 35, 62, 65, 79, 89, 94, 95, 100, 114, 123, 129, 141, 180–181, 187, 191, 192, 217, 222, 225, 228, 244, 264, 284, 366, 367
 and ālayavijñāna, 159
 and enlightenment, 331
 and event horizon, 330–331
 and Eye, 44
 and light, 45
 and Sambhogakāya Flower, 87
 and serpentine motion, 331
 and tathāgatagarbha, 60–61
 of Liver centre, 96
 strands of, 218
 transmutation of, 72–73, 324
Saṃskāric impetus, 222–223
Saṃskāric roots, 240
Saṃskṛta, 135, 144
Saṃskṛta-dharmas, 112
Saṃvittibhāga, 151
Saṃvṛtitas, 41
Samyaksambodhi, 160
Santāna, 83–88, 286
Śāntideva, 246, 255, 256, 257
Sapakṣa, 229
Sarva-maṇgalam, 353
Sarvāstivādins, 321
Sāsrava, 78, 84, 87
Sat, 147
Satkāyadṛṣṭi, 4
Saturn, 325
Scorpion, symbolism, 18
Sedimentation, 88–89, 314
Seed formation, 289
Self, 8, 74, 77, 251
 and consciousness, 89, 135–137
 and homogeneity, 79
 and 'not-self', 70–74
 and 'things', 211
 and time, 340–341
 as thought process, 250
 higher, 135
Self-identification, 8
Self Paramita, 47
Self-will, 92
Selves, 82–83
Sense-perceptions, 302
Senses and Elements, 301
Sentience, 156–158, 274
 and chakras, 184
 animal vs human thought, 274
Separation, lines of, 178–180
Separativeness, 96
Serenity, 224
Series, homogeneous, 77–78
Serpent, 17–18
Serpentine motion, 331
Seven layers of mind/Mind, 249
Sex-yoga, 219
Shambhala, 286
Shambhalic Lords of Life, 20
Siddha/s, 98, 183
Siddhis, 93, 101, 121, 164, 186, 188, 197, 243, 254, 267, 371
 and chakras, 2, 187–189
 and personal will, 120
 awakening of, 99
 minor, 115–120, 116, 368
 supramundane, 116, 150
Sight, 242, 299, 307
Signless samādhi, 371–372
Signs, 225–227, 229–232, 372
 and devotion, 238–240
 and faith, 238
 and Sambhogakāya Flower, 233–235
 as seeds, 241
 necessity of, 230–231
Sīla, 40
Six Realms, 87, 88, 126
 and gods, 198
Skandhas, 246, 264
Skilful means, 74–76
Smell/s, 119, 299, 308, 310
 strong or bland, 292–293

Son, aspects of, 10–11
Sorcerers, 219, 338
Sorcery, 355
Soul form, 46, 58–59, 192, 244, 306, 316
  and 'God', 197–198
  and tathāgatagarbha, 47, 67
  and vāsanā, 343
  definition, 46–47
  non-eternal, 286
  subtle, 218, 293
Space
  and emptiness, 9
  and Heart centre, 9
  and mind/Mind, 9, 285
Sparśa, 122, 296–298, 302, 307
Spiral-cyclic motion, 88
Spiritual age, 147
Spots, symbolism, 363
Śramaṇa, 373
Stagnation, 138, 142
Stellar fields, 209
Subtle 'self' and śūnyatā, 81
Suchness as tathatā, 58
Śuddhātma, 148
Śūnya, 49
Śūnyatā, 8, 39, 53, 65, 78, 80, 119, 147, 148, 154, 156–157, 161, 171, 173, 178, 179, 186, 196, 197, 205, 208, 230, 236, 241, 244, 258, 259, 273, 287, 320, 325, 335, 340, 354, 371
  and causes, 211
  and citta, 248
  and consciousness, 192, 314, 339–356
  and dharmakāya, 55
  and individuality, 81
  and karmic boundary, 213
  and māyā, 256
  and present time, 334
  and Sambhogakāya Flower, 296
  and saṃsāra, 223, 256
  and 'self', 81
  and substance, 312
  and tathatā, 58
  and the first Ray, 338
  and time, 275, 322, 328–329, 337
  as mirror, 5, 146–147, 150, 207
  as veil, 150
  bījas of, 106
  containment of, 64, 73
  seed, 196
Śūnyatā Eye, 42, 45, 51, 149, 150, 171–172, 236, 240, 286, 313, 336
Svabhāva, 10, 81, 201, 248, 301, 306
Svabhāvikakāya, 65
Svasaṁvitti, 246, 247, 249
Svasaṃvittibhāga, 145, 151
Svatotpatti, 320
Swastika, 134
Symbols of life, 244

T

Tantric doctrines, 187
Taste, 119, 299
  five aspects of, 308
Tat, 147
Tathāgata, 59
Tathāgata-embryo, 49, 56
Tathāgatagarbha, 10, 42–43, 48, 49–51, 55, 57, 58, 64, 66, 76, 147, 149, 187, 206, 211, 259, 282, 336, 349
  and change, 53
  and consciousness-stream, 315
  and defilements, 57
  and dharmakāya, 49–50, 52, 54–55, 150
  and evolution, 54
  and karma, 285
  and Life, 335
  and saṃskāras, 45
  and soul, 47
  and Śūnyatā Eye, 42
  and tathatā, 57

as container, 44
as directive Mind, 342
as I-consciousness, 43
as 'subtle self', 75
domain of, 204
evolution of, 59
flowering of, 11
seeding of, 337
three renderings, 51–52
Tathatā, 50, 64, 105, 128, 130, 148, 197, 207, 247
and ātman, 53
and bījas, 90–91
and eternal Now, 58
and Heart centre, 106, 133
and śūnyatā, 58
and unchangeability, 52–55
as flux, 52
defilement of, 56
definition, 51–52, 55
Telepathy, 250
Television and clairvoyance, 267
Temporal flux, 324
That, 208
Theseus, 24
Things, appearance of, 113
Thorns, 363
Thought/s
and phenomena, 216
as a thing, 35–36
as signposts, 254
bubbles, 248, 249, 250
commingling, 285
flow of, 193
originating, 271
substance of, 251
watery, 28
Threefold Nature, 202
Three times, 374
Tila, 280
Time, 269–275, 319–338, 327–329
absolute, 325, 326, 329
and consciousness, 271–272, 324–325
and śūnyatā, 340
and wisdom, 337
as an existent, 326–327
cycles of, 328, 336, 337
definition, 194, 340
evolutionary, 55
flow of, 264, 324
illusion of, 275
reckoning of, 322–323
speed of, 194–195, 264, 270–272
temporal, 329
Timeless state, 269
Touch, 119, 300, 307
Transcendent awareness, 356
Transmigration, 28–29, 188
reason against, 274
Transmutation, 140
Tree stumps, symbolism, 363
Trikāya, 60–67
Trirūpa, 229
Truth
definition, 76
finding, 76
search for, 1
Tum mo, 118

U

Ultimate Reality, 48, 168–169
relative, 258
Ultimate Truth, 258, 259
Uneven places, 363
Unity, 138–139
Universal Heart, 272
Upādhi, 43
Upāya, 247

V

Vajra, 368
Vajrasattva, 198–200, 203, 207
and Akṣobhya, 200
and bodhicitta, 200
Vajrayāna, 171, 182, 211

Vāsanā, 77–78, 81, 82, 105, 109, 151, 152, 154, 301, 313–314, 342–343
  and Sambhogakāya Flowers, 83–84
  definition, 153, 303
  of a Buddha, 353
Vasubandhu, 1
Vedanā, 296–298, 307
Veil/s
  and bīja/s, 141
  and śūnyatā, 150
  in texts, 100
  obscuring, 8
Victorious Ones, 148, 149
Vijñāna, 4, 48, 105, 279
  definition, 277–278
  doctrine, 314
Vijñānavāda, 246
Vijñānavādin/s
  concepts of self, 77–78, 80–81
  doctrine, 89, 251
  logic, 84
Vijñaptimātratā, 135
Vikalpa, 144, 145, 151, 348
Vikalpita, 77, 80
Village, symbolism, 361
Vinaya, 171
Viññāṇa, 175–176
Vipakṣa, 230
Vishaya, 314
Vision, 9
Voice of silence, 12, 17
Void, 147, 205, 258, 262, 309, 367, 371
  Elements, 10–11, 201
  illumination of, 244–245
  not void, 375
Voidness, 199
  and abundance, 374–375
  and bodhicitta, 200
  attainment of, 357–375
  ultimate, 360, 373
Vyatirekavyāpti, 229
Vyavahara, 58

W

White dharma, 220
Will-of-love, 132
Wisdom, mirror-like, 39
Wolves, 17
Words as signposts, 228
World Soul, 278
World-sphere, birthing of, 202

Y

Yab-yum, 120
Ye-shes, 9
Yidam, 39
Yogācāra doctrine, 311–312
  and the five eyes, 40–41
  reasoning, 154
Yogācāra school, 1, 215
Yogācāra-Vijñānavāda philosophy, 1, 77, 143, 277
Yoga-meditation, 101
Yogipratyakṣa, 229

About the Author

BODO BALSYS is the founder of The School of Esoteric Sciences. He is an author of many books on subjects centred on Buddhism and the Esoteric Sciences, a meditation teacher, poet, artist, spiritual scientist and healer. He has studied extensively across multiple traditions including Esoteric Science, Buddhism, Christianity, Esoteric Healing, Western Science, Art, Politics and History. His advanced esoteric insights, gained through decades of meditative contemplation, enable him to provide a rich understanding of the spiritual pathway toward enlightenment, healing and service.

Bodo's teachings can be accessed via the School of Esoteric Science's website:
http://universaldharma.com

For any other enquiries, please email
sangha@universaldharma.com

About Universal Dharma Publishing

Universal Dharma Publishing is a not for profit publisher. Our aim is make innovative, original and esoteric spiritual teachings accessible to all who genuinely aspire to awaken and serve humanity. The books published aim in part to provide an esoteric interpretation of the meaning of Buddhist *dharma* with view of reformation of the way people perceive the meaning of the related teachings. Hopefully then Buddhism can more effectively serve its principal function as a vehicle for enlightenment, and further prosper into the future. A further aim is to provide the next level of exposition of the esoteric doctrines to be revealed to humanity following on the wisdom tradition pioneered by H.P. Blavatsky and A.A. Bailey.

Cover Design by
Angie O'Sullivan & Kylie Smith

www.ingramcontent.com/pod-product-compliance
Lightning Source LLC
Chambersburg PA
CBHW021814300426
44114CB00009BA/177
9780992356811